Homelessness
Comes to School

For Linny von Holste

—Joseph Murphy

For Jantice and Adriana . . . and Stephen, of course

—Kerri Tobin

Homelessness
Comes to School

Joseph Murphy
Kerri Tobin

CORWIN
A SAGE Company

CORWIN
A SAGE Company

FOR INFORMATION:

Corwin
A SAGE Company
2455 Teller Road
Thousand Oaks, California 91320
(800) 233-9936
Fax: (800) 417-2466
www.corwin.com

SAGE Ltd.
1 Oliver's Yard
55 City Road
London EC1Y 1SP
United Kingdom

SAGE India Pvt. Ltd.
B 1/I 1 Mohan Cooperative Industrial Area
Mathura Road, New Delhi 110 044
India

SAGE Asia-Pacific Pte. Ltd.
33 Pekin Street #02-01
Far East Square
Singapore 048763

Acquisitions Editor: Hudson Perigo
Associate Editor: Allison Scott
Editorial Assistant: Lisa Whitney
Production Editor: Melanie Birdsall
Copy Editor: Tina Hardy
Typesetter: C&M Digitals (P) Ltd.
Proofreader: Cheryl Rivard
Indexer: Sheila Bodell
Cover Designer: Michael Dubowe
Permissions Editor: Adele Hutchinson

Printed in the United States of America

Library of Congress
Cataloging-in-Publication Data

Murphy, Joseph, 1949-

Homelessness comes to school / Joseph Murphy, Kerri Tobin.

p. cm.
Includes bibliographical references and index.

ISBN 978-1-4129-8054-8 (pbk.)

1. Homeless students—Services for—United States. 2. Homeless children—Education—United States. 3. School management and organization—United States. I. Tobin, Kerri. II. Title.

LC5144.2.M87 2011
371.826'942—dc22
2010045950

This book is printed on acid-free paper.

11 12 13 14 15 10 9 8 7 6 5 4 3 2 1

Contents

About the Authors

**Joseph Murphy** is the Frank W. Mayborn Chair and associate dean at Vanderbilt's Peabody College of Education. He has also been a faculty member at the University of Illinois and The Ohio State University, where he was the William Ray Flesher Professor of Education.

In the public schools, he has served as an administrator at the school, district, and state levels, including an appointment as the executive assistant to the chief deputy superintendent of public instruction in California. His most recent appointment was as the founding president of the Ohio Principals Leadership Academy. At the university level, he has served as department chair and associate dean.

He is past vice president of the American Educational Research Association (AERA) and was the founding chair of the Interstate School Leaders Licensure Consortium (ISLLC). He is coeditor of the AERA *Handbook on Educational Administration* (1999) and editor of the National Society for the Study of Education (NSSE) yearbook, *The Educational Leadership Challenge* (2002).

His work is in the area of school improvement, with special emphasis on leadership and policy. He has authored or coauthored 18 books in this area and edited another 12. His most recent authored volumes include the following: *Understanding and Assessing the Charter School Movement* (2002), *Leadership for Literacy: Research-Based Practice, PreK–3,* (2003), *Connecting Teacher Leadership and School Improvement* (2005), *Preparing School Leaders: Defining a Research and Action Agenda* (2006), *Turning Around Failing Schools: Leadership Lessons From the Organizational Sciences* (2008), and *The Educator's Handbook for Understanding and Closing Achievement Gaps* (2010).

Kerri Tobin is a PhD student at Vanderbilt University's Peabody College. She has worked with underserved students in many contexts, including teaching in public and charter schools in the South Bronx and Philadelphia. Her research focuses on the social contexts of education, with particular attention to issues of equity and social justice. She has written on civic education, how out-of-school behaviors impact educational outcomes, and how teacher attitudes shape classroom experiences.

THE PROBLEM

♦ Homelessness among children is a national problem of substantial proportions. (Alker, 1992, p. 186)

♦ School age children in homeless families and independent homeless youth represent the fastest-growing population of homeless individuals in the United States. (Ritter & Gottfried, 2002, p. 41)

THE MEANING

♦ It is virtually impossible to reclaim the life of a child who has spent his childhood without a home. (National Center on Family Homelessness, 2009, p. ii)

ATTENTION

♦ Children define our future and therefore, lay claim to our nation's consciences, but little attention has been given to the tragic plight of more than 1.5 million children without homes. (National Center on Family Homelessness, 2009, p. 5)

♦ During the past three decades, the problem of runaway and homeless youth has emerged as a serious and significant social challenge to policy makers, human services providers, and communities. (Kurtz, Lindsey, Jarvis, & Nackerud, 2000, p. 382)

ACTION

♦ Given the multiple risks these children and youth face, evaluating the scope of the problem and developing interventions continue to be a priority for providers and policy makers. (Kidd & Scrimenti, 2004, p. 331)

♦ Ending child homelessness is within our reach, but we must act now before it becomes a permanent feature of the American landscape. (National Center on Family Homelessness, 2009, p. i)

PART I

Portraying Homelessness

1

Understanding the Concept of Homelessness

*Images and observations of contemporary homelessness
abound but they cannot substitute for a thoroughgoing
review of the subject. (Hopper & Hamberg, 1984, p. 7)*

I n this introductory chapter, we complete a number of stocktaking assignments. Our goal is to explore the idea of homelessness from a variety of perspectives so that the reader develops a well-grounded understanding of the concept of homelessness in the United States.[1] We reveal that the idea is a good deal more complex than is often assumed and we explain why this is the case. We present a collection of typologies that have been used to study and portray homelessness and we highlight well-accepted definitions of the phenomenon. We also introduce various "frames" that can be used to describe homelessness at the start of the 21st century. In the second chapter of Part I (Chapter 2), we provide an historical analysis of homelessness in the United States. In the third chapter of Part I (Chapter 3), we explore the demographics of homelessness and populate categories of homelessness with data from an assortment of research studies.

❖ HOMELESSNESS AS A COMPLEX CONCEPT

*Homelessness is an immensely complex and multidimensional
social problem. (Stronge, 1992a, p. 3)*

*Definitional quandaries have long plagued discussions
of American homelessness. (Hopper, 2003, p. 15)*

As we discuss throughout this volume, homelessness and poverty are intricately linked. So too are homelessness and mobility (Peroff, 1987). Thus, in many ways homelessness is complex because it is not a distinct idea but rather a segment of the larger mosaic of the underclass (Hopper & Hamberg, 1984; Swick, 2004). It is an added risk factor in the equation of failure for individuals, families, and children, "a condition which compounds the issues faced by families in poverty" (Schmitz, Wagner, & Menke, 2001, p. 69). Relatedly, it is a point on a housed continuum that shares many features with close neighbors such as prehomelessness and being precariously housed (Hopper & Hamberg, 1984; Shlay & Rossi, 1992) and with situations confronted by foster care youngsters and children from migrant families (Swick, 2004). As such, at times "the line between being homeless and being domiciled is a fuzzy boundary" (Kusmer, 2002; Shlay & Rossi, 1992, p. 133).

Beyond this, a number of factors add to the "complexity, subjectivity, and ambiguity of homelessness" (James & Lopez, 2003, p. 129). The issue of definition merits special attention here (Hallett, 2007; Jencks, 1994; Johnson, 1988; Mihaly, 1991; Shane, 1996). According to scholars in this area, while the construct may appear rather simple, "the social interactions and constructions related to the concept are complex" (Jahiel, 1992d, p. 4) and "defining homelessness is an illusive task" (Stronge, 1992a, p. 7): "The definition of who is homeless has been as much a subject of debate as the question of how many homeless there are" (Peroff, 1987, p. 37). To be sure, while "defining who is homeless may seem fairly straightforward, the issues are as complex as they are in defining . . . other important constructs in clinical psychology" (Toro, 1998, p. 121). According to Hopper and Baumohl (1996), for example,

> homelessness is a term that covers a big territory. Indeed, as we reviewed the record of the past, we were struck by the disparate phenomena indexed by the term at one time or another. It seems that homelessness is at best an odd-job word, pressed into service to impose order on a hodgepodge of social dislocation, extreme poverty, seasonal or itinerant work, and unconventional ways of life. (p. 3)

Not surprisingly, then, "because research [has] offered little consensus on definitions of homeless experiences" (Ringwalt, Greene, Robertson, & McPheeters, 1998, p. 1326), "definitions of what is meant by homelessness vary from study to study" (Stefl, 1987, p. 47): "There is no standard or uniform definition of homelessness that has been agreed on by researchers or policy makers" (Mawhinney-Rhoads & Stahler, 2006, p. 289; Mihaly, 1991); definitions "differ widely" (Burt, 2001, p. 4). As Johnson (1988) cautions, "operationalizing the concept of homelessness, i.e., providing a standard definition to measure the phenomenon, has not been accomplished in more than 80 years of research" (p. 32).

Complexity issues are amplified when we turn our analytic lenses on definitions of youth homelessness. To begin with, as Whitbeck and Hoyt (1999) conclude, "defining homelessness among young people is even more difficult than for adults" (p. 3): "There is no consensus on a definition of homelessness for youth" (Russell, 1998, p. 7).

> Many unhoused young people have homes they can return to—if not the home they left, then that of a relative or family of a friend. Many drift in and out of settings that may or may not include adult caretakers, changing environments frequently with little adult monitoring. A significant proportion cannot return home and literally have no family that will take them in. Even these children may have institutional options for housing from which they have run or become disenchanted by rules, multiple moves, or a "revolving door" of caseworkers and foster parents. Homelessness for young people is a continuum that ranges from living at home with parents and running away for a night to independently making one's way on the streets. In between, there are stays with friends, stays with relatives, foster care, group homes, juvenile detention, and a range of shelter options, both supervised and unsupervised. The duration of being unhoused may be as short as a single night. (Whitbeck & Hoyt, 1999, pp. 3–4)

Indeed, the term "homeless children" is ambiguous (Burt, Aron, Lee, & Valente, 2001, p. 139). In a technical and legal sense, "youth homelessness" is impossible (Caton, 1986) for, as Russell (1998) correctly observes, minors are either in the custody of their parents/guardians "or the state via the child welfare system" (pp. 9–10).

There is no agreed-upon framework for capturing the key components of unaccompanied youth, either runaways or throwaways (Rotheram-Borus, 1991). Even basic definitions such as determining whether a homeless youth is a runaway or a throwaway "frequently depend entirely on whether the information [is] gathered from the youth . . . or the caretakers" (Hammer, Finkelhor, & Sedlak, 2002, p. 2; Levine, Metzendorf, & VanBoskirk, 1986). Studies employ different definitions and often fail to provide specific operational criteria (Brennan, Huizinga, & Elliott, 1978;

Ensign & Bell, 2004). Not surprisingly, therefore, many of the categories used in the youth homelessness literature are not mutually exclusive (Aviles & Helfrich, 1991; Hallett, 2007; Moore, 2007); "there are several overlapping subgroups" (Rotheram-Borus, 1991, p. 24). Thus, distinctions are often arbitrary (Rotheram-Borus, 1991; Russell, 1998) and fluid (Tierney, Gupton, & Hallett, 2008). For example, Hammer and colleagues (2002) conclude "that the distinction between runaway and throwaway [is] less than clear cut. Many youth have both runaway and throwaway elements" (p. 2).

Of particular interest on the definitional front is "how tightly or loosely the definitional boundaries are drawn" (Peroff, 1987, p. 34). Burt and colleagues (2001) refer to this as

> balancing two horns of a dilemma. If the definitions are too inclusive, they become useless; the phenomenon becomes too diffuse, ultimately covering too many people. With homelessness, this tendency is manifested by definitions that threaten to include the entire population in poverty, or everyone who is poorly housed. But if the definitions are too specific, they focus too exclusively on the homelessness of the moment. They can lead to policies and practices that are ameliorative but not preventive, that fail to address the larger question of desperate poverty and the pool of people at high risk for periodic bouts of literal homelessness. (p. 6)

In the research, we find that "definitions range from ones that follow a strict interpretation to ones that encompass a much broader perspective" (Stronge, 1992a, p. 7). As a consequence, "'homelessness' can have several different connotations. It can simply refer to a lack of one's own stable residence where one can sleep and receive mail. A broader sociological definition of homelessness may include a recognition of the quality of interactions and of material and social supports a person has" (Jackson, 2000; Ropers, 1988, p. 175; Wright, Capsi, Moffitt, & Silva, 1998). We see that even in "contemporary definitions of homelessness [that] are more directly linked to the housing situation of persons . . . there is [still] much disagreement on detail" (Shlay & Rossi, 1992, p. 132). For example, as we report later, the U.S. Department of Education employs a broader definition of homelessness, one that includes persons "doubled up" with friends or relatives, than does the U.S. Department of Housing and Urban Development (HUD).[2] In some definitions, foster children in temporary placements are counted and in others they are not (Iowa Department of Education, 2004b). The same is true of citizens in jails and hospitals (Emerson & Lovitt, 2003; Jahiel, 1992d).

Also contributing to definitional complexity is the fact that definitions have changed over time. As "social values concerning what constitutes adequate housing situations" (Shlay & Rossi, 1992, p. 132) have evolved, what might be labeled as "homelessness" today might have been considered merely "marginally housed" in the past (Peroff, 1987).[3] For example, the key idea in homelessness of having a home and living with a family that held sway through the first 75 years of the 20th century—and the idea of "homelessness defined in terms of personal ties and relationships to the broader society" (Shlay & Rossi, 1992, p. 132)—has given way today to the idea of having a fixed address (Jencks, 1994). So too definitions have been adjusted to attend to the massive arrival of homeless families beginning in the 1980s (Hopper & Hamberg, 1984; Jozefowicz-Simbeni & Israel, 2006; Kozol, 1988; Mawhinney-Rhoads & Stahler, 2006).

Complexity in the construct of homelessness can also be traced to the variety of professions that study displaced persons and to the array of different lenses used to examine and describe the phenomenon and its prevention and/or management. While this multifaceted approach is often enriching, because agents from different traditions, backgrounds, and areas of study use different lenses, lenses that influence what is seen, and often have different goals, it also produces some confusion and leads to a variety of inconsistencies; it complexifies homelessness. That is, while using multiple frames is almost always a desirable strategy to understand constructs such as homelessness, doing so can also create pieces of understanding that do not fit well together. In this area, we learn that professionals from all the following domains have contributed to the creation of the complex mosaic known as homelessness: mental health specialists, criminologists and law enforcement personnel, social service agents, educators, medical practitioners (nurses and doctors), religious actors, community organizers, lawyers, and politicians.[4] On the discipline side of the ledger, theoretical insights from political science, anthropology, psychology, sociology, social psychology, biology, economics, and history, among other areas of study, are employed in illuminating the construct of homelessness. We find on occasion that unique insights from these diverse professions and disciplines make it difficult to form a coherent narrative. Ideas at times conflict. As we see later, this is true across the homelessness landscape—in definitions of the problem, in unpacking causes, in examining impact, and in designing solution strategies.

Homelessness is also complex because of the simple fact that the population here is heterogeneous (Boesky, Toro, & Bukowski, 1997; Hartman, 1986; Kipke, Palmer, La France, & O'Connor, 1997). While 50 years ago Levinson (1963) documented that "the situation today in the field of homelessness [was] somewhat similar to what was found to be true in psychiatric studies years ago when all mentally ill patients were thrown into one category called 'insane' and treated accordingly" (p. 592), we know now that the "homeless are not one undifferentiated mass" (Stronge, 2000, p. 7). The population is heterogeneous in nature on the one hand because it is made up of discernable subgroups such as "battered and abandoned women, single mothers, evicted families, single unemployed and older women, deinstitutionalized mental patients, illegal immigrants, street youth, drug addicts, alcoholics, and those living on skid row" (Karabanow,

2004, p. 20). It is also heterogeneous because there are "striking differences among homeless individuals and their circumstances" (Snow & Anderson, 1993, p. 7): "People's experiences of homelessness vary considerably" (Burt et al., 2001, p. 161) and "each experience of being homeless is different" (Douglass, 1996, p. 745). Burt and associates (2001) capture this second understanding of homelessness when they explain that

> for virtually every characteristic, other than extreme poverty, the common denominator of homelessness, it is rare for half, or even one-third of homeless clients to have the characteristic in common. Even factors thought to be strongly associated with the probability of homelessness, such as childhood abuse or neglect and out-of-home placement, characterize only about one-quarter of homeless people. Clearly this level of diversity, and widely varying point of vulnerability to homelessness, given extreme poverty, belie the idea of a "homeless population." (p. 93)

And as we explore in detail in the last chapters of the book, considerable variety in demographics, causes, and impacts also means significant diversity in solutions to the problems of homelessness (James & Lopez, 2003).

Finally, as we demonstrate in the second half of this chapter, measurement issues and "the type of data used in calculations" (Burt et al., 2001, p. 4) complexify understanding of homelessness (Aron & Fitchen, 1996; Rafferty, 1995; Ringwalt, Greene, Robertson, & McPheeters, 1998).

❖ TOWARD A DEFINITION

Definitions are necessary, though, from several perspectives. (Burt et al., 2001, p. 6)

The various definitions of homelessness fall into two groups: some of them try to incorporate a concept of the social meaning or causes of homelessness, thus associating the definition with theories of homelessness; others propose criteria of place to be used in designating people as homeless. (Jahiel, 1992d, p. 1)

Americans have used the word "homeless" in something like its modern sense for roughly 150 years. Most often, its meaning is literal and prosaic: the absence of a domicile. (Hopper & Baumohl, 1996, p. 3)

A simple, commonsensical definition of homelessness is the absence of a home or lack of a stable, dependable, source of housing. (Johnson, 1988, p. 33)

⌁⌁⌁

We have already reported that "there is no single, generally accepted definition of homelessness" (Hombs, 2001, p. 6), either in general or for youth in particular (Whitbeck & Hoyt, 1999). We confirmed that the definitional issue is complex and contested (Jencks, 1994). Nonetheless, as Burt and colleagues (2001) assert, the definition of homelessness is important for a variety of reasons:

> From the perspective of immediate action, definitions identify who is eligible to receive whatever assistance is available specifically for homeless people. From a research perspective, definitions identify who should be counted and described. And from a policy perspective, definitions identify who should be planned for and what policies will be most relevant to the type of assistance needed. (p. 6)

Perhaps the best place to begin is with official definitions provided by the government as these provide frameworks for addressing the problems of homeless adults and young people. According to HUD, the term "homeless" or "homeless individual or homeless person" includes the following:

1. An individual who lacks a fixed, regular, and adequate nighttime residence; and

2. An individual who has a primary nighttime residence that is

   A. a supervised publicly or privately operated shelter designed to provide temporary living accommodations (including welfare hotels, congregate shelters, and transitional housing for the mentally ill);

   B. an institution that provides a temporary residence for individuals intended to be institutionalized; or

   C. a public or private place not designed for, or ordinarily used as, a regular sleeping accommodation for human beings.

According to the McKinney-Vento Homeless Assistance Act (Title X, Part C, of the No Child Left Behind Act), homelessness for children and youths

   A. means individuals who lack a fixed, regular, and adequate nighttime residence (within the meaning of section 103(a)(1)); and

   B. includes—

      (i) children and youths who are sharing the housing of other persons due to loss of housing, economic hardship, or a similar reason; are living in motels, hotels, trailer parks, or camping grounds due to the lack of alternative adequate accommodations; are living in emergency or transitional shelters; are abandoned in hospitals; or are awaiting foster care placement;

(ii) children and youths who have a primary nighttime residence that is a public or private place not designed for or ordinarily used as a regular sleeping accommodation for human beings (within the meaning of section 103(a)(2)(C));

(iii) children and youths who are living in cars, parks, public spaces, abandoned buildings, substandard housing, bus or train stations, or similar settings; and

(iv) migratory children (as such term is defined in section 1309 of the Elementary and Secondary Education Act of 1965) who qualify as homeless for the purposes of this subtitle because the children are living in circumstances described in clauses (i) through (iii).

While Karabanow (2004) and Burt and colleagues (2001) remind us that analysts have uncovered "three elements separately or in combination [that] characterize homelessness . . . the transience or instability of *place*, the instability or absence of connections to *family*, and the instability of *housing*" (Burt et al., 2001, p. 2), it is abundantly clear that the official treatment of homelessness attends exclusively to the housing aspect of homelessness (Jackson, 2000). Thus, in general, "the term 'homeless' is actually a catchword that focuses our attention on only one aspect of the individual's plight: lack of residence" (Karabanow, 2004, p. 20). Embedded in the "homeless" aspect of homelessness is an understanding of "a home as a residence to which one is entitled; for which one has responsibility; over which one exerts control, including the right to decide whom to admit; and which has a certain degree of permanency" (Jahiel, 1992d, p. 3).

Half of the homeless portrait highlights what homeless persons are missing, that is, the idea that "homelessness is a lack of permanent housing" (Duffield, Heybach, & Julianelle, 2007, p. 3; Jackson, 2004, p. 2). These individuals "lack what society defines as a normal place to live" (Hartman, 1986, p. 71). The other half of the picture spotlights where the homeless stay. Here we see that "homeless populations are identified by their need for nighttime shelter" (Caton, 1986, p. 64) and by where they sleep. Or, more precisely, "homelessness is based on a person's sleeping arrangements" (Burt et al., 2001, p. 6). Thus, in general, "homelessness is defined as including anyone whose night residence is either in a shelter, on the street or in another public place" (Eddowes & Hranitz, 1989, p. 197). Using this definition, Roth, Toomey, and First (1992) hold that homeless people can be further "categorized by the degree to which they appear exposed to the elements" (p. 204).

A key element in homeless definitions, official and otherwise, returns us to our earlier discussion of definitional complexity and to the distinction between the narrowness or expansiveness of efforts to corral homelessness. Of particular importance here is the fact that the HUD definition presented earlier "is limited to persons who are living on the streets or who are staying in shelters" (Duffield et al., 2007, p. 8). On the other hand, "the broader McKinney-Vento Act definition of homeless includes those living doubled up with friends and families" (National Center for Homeless Education, 2006a, p. 5). Whether one attends only to the "literal homeless" (Toro, 1998, p. 121), "conventionally defined as people living on the street or in shelters" (Aron & Fitchen, 1996, p. 81), or uses the "more inclusive" (Dworsky, 2008, p. 16) definition in McKinney-Vento is consequential: "People who double up with other households because they have nowhere else to go constitute a larger group than all of the McKinney Act categories taken together" (Jahiel, 1992d, p. 2). Therefore, by including doubled-up individuals and families we significantly expand the homeless population, both exacerbating the social ill of homelessness and intensifying demands for preventing and/or treating the problem.

In this volume, we appropriate the broader definition of homelessness found in the McKinney-Vento legislation. While we acknowledge the dangers of overcounting associated with this decision (see Jencks, 1994; Stronge, 1992a) and the accompanying assessment problem of distinguishing the homeless from the marginally housed, we follow this pathway for two reasons. First, on the ideological front, it is consistent with the demands for social justice for children and youth. Second, on the practical front, it is the definition that educational agencies are required to employ. Thus, for the purposes of this volume,

> persons/families are homeless when they do not have their own home. This broad definition encompasses doubling up with friends or family, living in a temporary hotel room that one cannot develop into one's own home, living in a shelter, or spending the nights in one's car, a park, the streets, or public buildings. Homelessness is life without one's own home. (Jahiel, 1987, p. 99)

❖ FRAMEWORKS FOR UNDERSTANDING

The process by which members of some empirical domain are categorized and ordered in terms of their similarities and differences is called typologizing. The resulting classificatory scheme directs the observer's attention to certain aspects of the phenomenon under study. (Snow & Anderson, 1993, pp. 36–37)

*In response to diversity, various attempts to classify or categorize
homeless persons have been developed. (Stefl, 1987, p. 50)*

Over the last quarter century, a number of theoretical and grounded
frameworks for understanding homelessness have been created, some of
which have already been introduced. For example, many analysts have
suggested that for single adults, families, and unaccompanied youth "on
any given night, the homeless can be divided into two groups: those who
sleep in free shelters (the 'shelter homeless') and those who sleep in places
not intended for human habitation, such as bus stations, subway trains,
automobiles, doorways, and abandoned buildings. Those who sleep
outside shelters are generally known as the 'street homeless'" (Jencks,
1994, p. 4). This is the on-and-off-the-street categorical divide (Hagan &
McCarthy, 1997). We have also touched upon the two-part framework
featuring "literal homelessness," which includes both shelter-housed and
street-based homeless persons (Ensign & Bell, 2004), and "hidden
homeless," which captures those living doubled up with relatives or
friends. Snow and Anderson (1993), in turn, have forged a design
underscoring three aspects of homelessness: "a residential dimension; a
familial-support dimension; and a role-based dignity and moral-worth
dimension" (p. 7). Hartman (1986) explores six dimensions of homelessness:
"age, household composition, cause of homelessness, duration of
homelessness, disability, [and] future prospects" (p. 71). Mallett, Rosenthal,
Myers, Milburn, and Rotheram-Borus (2004) frame homelessness based on
mode of leaving, personal characteristics, and subculture. Stronge (2000)
highlights nighttime location and duration. Stefl (1987) maintains that
homelessness can be understood by examining the following categories:
sleeping accommodations, time on the street, causes of homelessness,
severity of the problem, personal characteristics, and life history. Based on
the last two dimensions, Fischer and Breakey (cited in Stefl, 1987) designate
four groups of homeless individuals: "the chronically mentally ill, chronic
alcoholics, street people, and the situationally distressed" (p. 52). Based on
the "severity" dimension, Jahiel (1987) concludes that we can distinguish
between benign and malignant homeless conditions:

> Benign homelessness means that the state of homelessness causes
> relatively little hardship, lasts for a relatively short time, and does
> not recur soon, and it is relatively easy to gain back a home and a
> stable tenure of that home. Malignant homelessness means that the
> state of homelessness is associated with considerable hardship or
> even permanent damage to the person who is homeless, it lasts for
> a relatively long time or recurs at short intervals, extraordinary
> efforts must be expended to gain back a home with stable tenure,
> and these efforts are often unsuccessful. (p. 100)

Snow and Anderson (1993) array a host of elements of homelessness under three subcultural dimensions: lifestyle dimensions, cognitive dimensions, and a temporal dimension (p. 41). Rotheram-Borus (1991) suggests that a framework for unaccompanied youth can be forged using material from five sources: "the intended length of stay away from home; personal and social characteristics that include behavioral and attitudinal factors; cognitive structure and belief system; whether youth leave on their own accord or are pushed out; and whether there is escalation to criminal offenses" (p. 31).

Building on the work of these and other scholars, we argue that homelessness can best be understood using the four broad constructs (and assorted subelements) that anchor this volume: demographics, causes, impacts, and solution strategies. Later and in Chapter 3, we examine homelessness via demographics. Here we introduce some of the central demographic concepts—household composition, residency, and severity—while in Chapter 3 we populate these categories and others (e.g., age, race) using data from across the homeless literature. In Chapter 4, we delve into the impacts of homelessness. And in the final chapters, we turn to an analysis of schooling-based strategies designed to prevent and/or alleviate the consequences of homelessness.

Household Composition

The most well-established framework divides individuals experiencing homelessness into three groups: single adults, families with children (i.e., accompanied children), and unaccompanied youth (The National Center on Family Homelessness [NCFH], 2009; Toro, 1998). Single adults, in turn, are often clustered into subcategories. For example, Anderson (cited in Bahr, 1973) describes five types of homeless: the seasonal worker, the occasional worker, the wandering tramp, the bum, and the home guard (p. 110).

Homeless Families and Children

Homeless children and youth are found in the second and third groups, those attached to a homeless family (accompanied homeless children) and those away from home and on their own (unaccompanied youth). *Homeless families* are defined "as one or more adults with one or more children in their charge" (Shinn & Weitzman, 1996, p. 109). Thus, *homeless children*[5] are usually those "from birth to age 18 who are accompanied by one or more parents or caregivers" (Bassuk, Rubin, & Lauriat, 1986; Iowa Department of Education, 2004a; NCFH, 2009, p. 5). And, as Shane (1996) documents,

> the *familial* homeless, or homeless families with children, are of all kinds: one adult (mother, father, grandparent, other); two adults

(with biological, step-, adopted, or common-law parents, unrelated partner, or other relationship); three generations (grandparent, parent, and child[ren]). They stay in every conceivable place—tents, cars, trucks, abandoned buildings, handmade shacks, shelters, and so on. The children, although predominantly younger, are of all ages—neonates through teenagers. There can be one child or many children in the family. (p. 4)

Unaccompanied Youth

The phrase *unaccompanied youth* is, as Moore (2007) clarifies, an umbrella term for a large assortment of young people (Julianelle, 2007; Rotheram-Borus, Mahler, Koopman, & Langabeer, 1996). It is a "generic term to refer to minors who are outside a family or an institutional setting and who are unaccompanied by a parent or legal guardian" (Robertson, 1992, p. 288). It includes youngsters living on the street, in shelters, in group homes, and those doubled up with friends or relatives.

Runaways

While a variety of typologies, often with common dimensions, are used to capture the phenomenon of youth homelessness, nearly all analysts describe three categories of the unaccompanied homeless: runaway homeless, throwaway homeless, and system homeless (Barry, Ensign, & Lippek, 2002). McCaskill, Toro, and Wolfe (1998) define *runaways* as those young people "who [leave] home for at least 24 hours without their parents' permission and whose parents [do] not know their whereabouts" (p. 308). Based on criteria "such as degree of school success, existence of peer influences and/or supports, the degree of criminal behavior involved, and the extent to which the individual is committed to street life" (Rothman, 1991, p. 106), a number of conceptual and empirical efforts have been undertaken to describe homeless runaways. Brennan (cited in Whitbeck & Hoyt, 1999, and in Rotheram-Borus, 1991) has built a typology featuring six different portraits of runaway homeless based on behavioral and attitudinal factors: self-confident and unrestrained runaway youth; well-adjusted runaway youth; youth who have failed at home and in school and who are involved in delinquent behavior; youth who are fleeing excessive parent control; young, highly regulated and negatively influenced youth; and young and unrestrained youth. Brennan et al. (1978) also use motivation to craft a typology of six types of runaways:

Victims are beset by assaultive, abusing parents. They feel undefended and endangered. *Exiles* experience high levels of nonviolent parent rejection. The third of these types, the *rebels*, is described as being involved in long-standing authority struggles, while at the same time being still psychologically tied to the parents. All three of these runaway types might well be subsumed by Homer's "running from" concept. The *fugitive* appears to be escaping from some negative consequence of his or her own behavior, e.g., arrest, punishment, fear of facing parents, and so forth. The implication is that the child has placed himself/herself in serious trouble, perhaps through deviant behavior, and is attempting to escape the expected consequences. The *refugee* is simply the young person who does not have a family and who is escaping some institution or foster home in which he or she has been placed. The *immigrant* is the young person who has grown up, who is psychologically independent from his/her parents, and who is ready to live the life of an emancipated adult. (p. 253)

Whitbeck and Hoyt (1999) highlight a number of typologies that appeared in the early literature on runaways:

Berger and Schmidt (1958) dichotomize runaways into "spontaneous and reactive runaways." The spontaneous group[s] were adventurers; the reactive groups were running from problems. Homer (1973) also suggested that there were essentially two types of runaways: those running to something and those running from something. The "running to" group[s] were viewed as adventurers or pleasure seekers. Other typologies innocently downplayed the seriousness of most runaways. Haupt and Offord (1972) distinguished between "gesture runaways," who were making a cry for help and "real runaways," who intended to escape a particular situation. Similarly, Shellow and colleagues (Shellow, Schamp, Liebow, & Unger, 1967) categorized runaways into those who were "pathological" and those who were "normal." The "pathological" young person was on the run for personal or family troubles and was a chronic runner. The "normal" runaway left home only one or two times, did not evidence high levels of family troubles, and showed little delinquent behavior. The Scientific Analysis Corporation (1974; cited in Brennan, 1980) identified three types of runaways: the "sick," the "bad," and the "free." The "sick" referred to those with identifiable psychopathology, the "bad" were those who engaged in delinquent behaviors, and the "free" were those who were engaged in pleasure-seeking, adventure, or exploration. (pp. 5–6)

In an empirically grounded typology "based on where and with whom they congregated and slept during the day and night and how they spent most of their time" (Mallett et al., 2004, p. 337), Mallett and associates (2004) used cluster analysis to deduce four groups of runaways (and other homeless youth): partnered, socially engaged, service connected–harm avoidant, and transgressive (p. 337).

Throwaways

Throwaway youth, on the other hand, "are young persons who have been told to leave home by a parent or guardian and are away overnight and prevented from returning home" (Hallett, 2007, p. 3; Powers & Jaklitsch, 1993). A special category of throwaways is "intervention seekers" (Boeskey et al., 1997, p. 22), those youngsters "whose parents asked them to leave home temporarily with the understanding that the adolescent would return home after a short period of time" (McCaskill et al., 1998, pp. 308–309).

System Youth

Homeless "adolescents who have been in and out of government systems such as juvenile justice and foster care are referred to as system youth" (Hallett, 2007, p. 3), although as we noted previously, youngsters in long-term foster care are not considered homeless. System youth, as MacLean, Embry, and Cauce (1999) inform us, "are those from family environments that were deemed dangerous enough to necessitate removal from the home and whose subsequent residential placements were unsuccessful" (p. 2). That is, "system kids become homeless when their social service placements are problematic" (Rotheram-Borus, 1991, p. 24).

Within these three classifications—runaway, throwaway, and system youth—special conditions are highlighted at times. For example, in the "throwaway" category, Hammer and associates (2002) single out "permanently abandoned" (p. 5) youth, those youngsters whose families have dissolved around them. Across all three classifications, reviewers describe "street kids" (Pearce, 1995, p. 16), a characterization that refers to youths "who spend all of their time in various public places" (Baron, Kennedy, & Forde, 2001, p. 767): "Most of these youth are underemployed/unemployed, often lack a permanent residence, and spend significant amounts of time without shelter" (Baron & Hartnagel, 1998, p. 166). In addition, as we demonstrate throughout this volume, homeless youth are often defined by the same categories used to examine homelessness more generally, for example, causes and experiences on the street.

Residency

Given the centrality of housing in the homeless narrative, where persons reside (or place-based understandings of displacement [Jahiel, 1992d; Johnson, 1988]) is a critical dimension of homelessness—for individuals, families, and unaccompanied youth. Indeed, "the residential dimension" (Snow & Anderson, 1993, p. 7) is generally the primary basis for conceptualizing homelessness.

Analysts typically divide homeless persons into various categories based on where they sleep at night (Hombs, 2001; Stefl, 1987), "their customary sleeping arrangements" (Snow & Anderson, 1993, p. 42), or places where they seek refuge (Tierney et al., 2008). In Chapter 2, we provide data on where the various groups of homeless reside, with the caveat that people move fluidly through various sleeping arrangements (e.g., in a transient hotel at some times, doubled up with friends or relatives at another time, and perhaps on the street at still a third point in time). Here we introduce the categories used in our residency analysis.

One category incorporates what scholars call the "sheltered homeless" (Ropers, 1988, p. 68). This includes individuals and families using shelter space, both emergency and transitional and temporary hotel space made available by service providers. A second category of sleeping arrangements captures what Stefl (1987) refers to as "resource people" (p. 51). These include persons doubling up with families or friends, couch surfing through different homes, or staying in cheap hotels/motels without public assistance—those without kitchen facilities and often with public bathrooms (Tierney et al., 2008), hotels that "most observers agree do not provide the kind of 'adequate shelter' or community ties that constitute a home" (Ropers, 1988, p. 67; Stefl, 1987; Wright et al., 1998). The final category is "street people," those homeless persons who "sleep rough" (Snow & Anderson, 1993, p. 42), that is, in public spaces not intended as dwellings, such as under bridges, in parks, in abandoned buildings, in cars, and so forth (Hagan & McCarthy, 1997; Julianelle, 2007).

Researchers and reformers sometimes stretch these groupings across a continuum "ranging from a complete absence of shelter to living arrangements approximating home-like conditions" (National Law Center on Homelessness and Poverty, 2004a; Stefl, 1987, p. 50). Stefl (1987) illustrates this idea using a study of homelessness in Ohio:

1. Limited or no shelter. This would include people who sleep on park benches, under bridges, or in cardboard boxes.

2. Use of cars, abandoned buildings, or public facilities.

3. Shelters or missions designed specifically to house homeless persons.

4. Flophouses or cheap hotels with limited stay and minimal fee.

5. Cheap hotels with longer-term rates. However, residence would be limited to less than one month. (p. 50)

Johnson (1988) provides a similar "residency" continuum, but one that incorporates a sixth category, that is, marginally housed (e.g., living in public housing). As we discussed earlier, the demarcation line between poor people who are inadequately housed and the homeless on the end of the continuum with some home-like conditions is blurry and shifting

(Jahiel, 1992b), especially for families: "Homeless families are in many ways very similar to other poor families who do not become homeless" (National Alliance to End Homelessness [NAEH], 2007, p. 1) and "a homeless person looks similar to a low-income housing tenant or other poor person" (U.S. Department of Housing and Urban Development, 2009, p. 24).

Severity of Homelessness

Four concepts allow us to develop a sense of the depth of homelessness among those on the wrong side of the housing divide. The first we illustrated earlier in the discussion of "residency." Specifically, we observed that some sleeping arrangements (e.g., doubling up) have more "home-like" elements than do others (e.g., sleeping in one's car). Accordingly, most analysts assert that "homeless persons finding refuge on the street or in public places are the most severely deprived" (Johnson, 1988, p. 40) of all homeless individuals.[6]

Because "a central question in studying homelessness is whether being homeless is a temporary, transitional, or episodic condition lasting a relatively short period of time or whether it is a permanent and chronic problem" (Shlay & Rossi, 1992, p. 141), length of time homeless (duration) and number of incidents of homelessness are the second and third elements in the homelessness severity equation (Burt et al., 2001), recognizing that "duration . . . is confounded by the seeming intermittent character of the experience" (Shlay & Rossi, 1992, p. 141) and that, as we see later, these two elements are often combined.

To begin with, scholars, policy makers, and social service providers often partition the homeless based on the amount of time they have been displaced. Shane (1996), for example, divides homeless youth into five groups: short term, midterm, long term, sporadic, and chronic. Other analysts use three categories: long term or chronic, episodic, and transitional (Johnson, 1988; NAEH, 2003; Ropers, 1988). According to the U.S. Conference of Mayors (2008), chronic homeless are those individuals "who have been living on the streets or in shelter[s] either continuously for the last two years or intermittently for the last five years" (p. 20). Most analysts put the demarcation line for chronic homelessness at one year (Pires & Silber, 1991; Rollinson & Pardeck, 2006). In either case,

> the category of chronic homelessness is reserved for people who have relied on shelters or lived on the streets for many months or years, and usually have multiple barriers to securing stable employment and housing. They may have only a few distinct spells of homelessness, but each lasts a very long time. (Burt et al., 2001, p. 164)

Episodic homeless individuals, in turn, "are those who frequently experience periods of being homed and then homeless" (Rollinson &

Pardeck, 2006, p. 7), "a tendency to cycle into and out of homelessness repeatedly, and for varying lengths of time" (Burt et al., 2001, p. 164; Mawhinney-Rhoads & Stahler, 2006; Russell, 1998). Transitional homeless persons "include individuals or families who are homeless only once or twice and usually for a relatively short time (Burt, 2001, p. 164); they have no history of homelessness (Ropers, 1988).

Earlier, we reported that sleeping rough or street homelessness is considered more severe than sheltered homelessness. Here we add that severity is likely to increase with each episode of homelessness: "In other words, each time a person becomes homeless, he/she will have fewer and fewer resources that can decrease the severity of the homeless condition" (Johnson, 1988, p. 39). Johnson (1988) goes on to argue that

> putting these two dimensions together, the shorter the experience of homelessness and the farther away the experience is from literal homelessness, the less severe it will be. Inversely, the longer the experience of homelessness and the closer the experience is to literal homelessness, the more severe it will be. (pp. 37–38)

We also know from the literature that length is consequential (Shane, 1996), that "the duration of homelessness is an important factor that influences the intensity of the effect on an individual's physical and mental health" (Ropers, 1988, p. 179). Also, there are important consequences in terms of need for services; and, as we report in the last part of the book, needs of individuals in the various duration groups often differ in important ways (United Way of New York City, 2002; U.S. Department of Housing and Urban Development, 2009).

The fourth and final piece in the "severity" narrative focuses on the nature of the experiences homeless individuals have in shelters and on the streets. For some, homelessness offers many more difficult challenges than it does for others. We turn to this dimension of homelessness in Part III when we drill down to examine the impact of homelessness on single adults, families with children, and homeless youth.

❖ UNDERSTANDING THE COUNTING PROCESS

Counting persons who are homeless is a notoriously difficult task fraught with definitional and technical challenges. (NAEH, 2003, p. 4)

Determining how many homeless people there are is quite complex. (Burt et al., 2001, p. 28)

Homeless youth are difficult to track.
(Ennett, Bailey, & Federman, 1999, p. 76)

To develop a full understanding of homeless persons, it is instructive to understand the scope and nature of the phenomenon. As we demonstrate here, however, this turns out to be a less-than-straightforward assignment, one fraught with a variety of difficulties. In the balance of the chapter, we attend to some theoretical and practical issues in the counting and arraying of America's homeless. This analysis is designed to inform interpretation in Chapter 2, where we present counting and arraying information across an assortment of demographic categories.

We begin with an overarching caution. Regardless of where the numbers take us, there is consensus in the literature about one critical point. As Mihaly (1991) states it: "What is indisputable is that there are too many homeless families, the numbers are large and growing, and there is a homelessness problem greater than at any time in recent history" (p. 4); "there is no disputing the dramatic proliferation" (Snow & Anderson, 1993, p. 233) of homeless persons in the country. Kozol (1988) offers a variation on this caution when he warns against forgetting what the numbers mean:

> We would be wise, however, to avoid the numbers game. Any search for the "right number" carries the assumption that we may at last arrive at an acceptable number. There is no acceptable number. Whether the number is 1 million or 4 million or the administration's estimate of less than a million, there are too many homeless people in America. (pp. 12–13)

Starting with this caveat, we hold with Peroff (1987) that

> it is still useful to have some idea of the size and composition of the homeless population from a policy perspective. Such information is needed to improve our understanding about this group in our society and to tailor more effectively both public and private responses to meet the needs of the homeless population. (p. 33)

An Overview

Perhaps no other population in the United States is as difficult to count as the homeless, making "collection of definitive data in this area extremely difficult" (Shane, 1996, p. 13). As Hope and Young (1986) conclude, "the problems in counting the homeless are legion" (p. 19): "Finding the homeless is not easy" (Peroff, 1987, p. 40) and, as a consequence, "estimating the number of homeless children and youth poses problems" (Penuel & Davey, 1998, p. 4).

Counting the homeless and thus developing accurate demographic portraits "depends entirely on where the homeless are counted, how representative the study is, and who is considered homeless" (Johnson, 1988, p. 49). Different studies address these issues in different ways. Thus, because of "different definitions of who the homeless are, the time intervals in counting, and the variations in geographic coverage" (Rollinson & Pardeck, 2006, p. 8), differences across research reports are often quite large. Variations that we report in Chapter 3 can also be traced to the use of different methodological approaches employed in research studies (Greene, Ringwalt, & Iachan, 1997), such as difference in "the definition of the population under study, varied and limited methods for producing population estimates, and lack of a mechanism for centralized reporting" (Russell, 1998, p. 7).

Turning specifically to the demographics of children and unaccompanied youth, Ringwalt, Greene, Robertson, and McPheeters (1998); Moore (2007); and Whitman, Accardo, Boyert, and Kendagor (1990) expose the challenges in crafting an accurate narrative for these populations:

> Obtaining reliable data on homeless children is hampered by factors such as the transiency of the population, the intermittence of the homeless status, erratic availability and use of existing support services, and the crisis conditions that affect observation and testing in any sample shelter population. (Whitman et al., 1990, p. 516)

"Contradictory definitions of what constitutes homelessness, an absence of standardized methodology for sampling homeless youths, and an over reliance on data from shelters and agencies" (Ringwalt, Greene, Robertson, & McPheeters, 1998, p. 1325) all complicate the documentation work. So too does "youth's inability to consent for participation in studies and a lack of comparison groups" (Moore, 2007, p. 6).

Counting Concerns

Difficulties Associated With Definitions

Earlier we discussed "the definitional problem" (Hombs, 2001, p. 8) in the homeless literature. What should be clear from that analysis is that the size of the homeless population has a good deal to do with the definition employed (Myers & Popp, 2003; U.S. Department of Education, 2000); size "will be larger or smaller depending on one's definition of homelessness" (Burt et al., 2001, p. 7). More specifically, "variations in the definition of 'homeless' contribute to wide fluctuations in population estimates" (Russell, 1998, p. 8). For example, some studies define homelessness in ways that pull in a good number of marginally housed persons, thus ratcheting up estimates. Other reports exclude individuals and families that are doubled up with relatives or friends, thus significantly depressing calculations of the homeless population.

Difficulties Finding Homeless Persons

Analysts from across the ideological spectrum highlight a central difficulty in counting the homeless: "Homeless people are, of course, impossible to count" (Kozol, 1988, p. 13) because "finding them is not easy" (Peroff, 1987, p. 40), and "the affected population is by nature difficult to track" (National Law Center on Homelessness and Poverty, 2004b, p. 6): Going to doors "to count people doesn't work with families that have no doors" (Mihaly, 1991, p. 2); "they have no address beyond a shelter bed, room number, tent, or cave" (Kozol, 1988, p. 13). And, as Hopper and Hamberg (1984) remind us, "homeless people cannot be tagged like geese and their patterns of migration charted" (p. 7). The consequence is "that a substantial percentage of the homeless population is simply not accessible to researchers" (Stefl, 1987, p. 47) and, therefore, many are uncounted. In summary, the "finding" problem arises from the fact that "the majority of homeless persons are invisible, they are unseen" (Medcalf, 2008, p. 8).

The Unseen by Choice

In many cases, homeless persons are unseen because they do not wish to be seen (Cunningham, 2003; Hombs & Snyder, 1982; Raleigh-DuRoff, 2004). According to analysts, "many homeless people work very hard to obscure their homelessness" (Hombs, 2001, p. 8), "either because being homeless is stigmatizing or because they fear the imposition of unwanted social control" (Link, Phelan, Bresnahan, Stueve, Moore, & Susser, 1995, p. 348). Mihaly (1991) contends, for example, that "many families hesitate to identify themselves as homeless because they are embarrassed, or because parents are afraid that they will be labeled neglectful and their children will be taken from them and placed in foster care" (p. 37). In a similar vein, many unaccompanied youth "deliberately avoid shelters and social agencies" (Taylor, Lydon, Bougie, & Johannsen, 2004, p. 1) where they could be seen because of "mistrust of persons in authority" (Aviles & Helfrich, 1991, p. 332) and for fear of being reunited with abusive families (Auerswald & Eyre, 2002; Moore, 2007; Ringwalt, Greene, Robertson, & McPheeters, 1998). In addition, "confidentiality regarding the illegality/criminality of lifestyle and coping activities may play a significant part in [the] homeless choosing to 'remain hidden'" (Kidd & Scrimenti, 2004, p. 338). Other homeless persons choose invisibility to "conceal the places where they sleep because they fear being harassed or victimized" (Peroff, 1987, p. 39). And, as Medcalf (2008) observes, "the people who do not wish to be counted among the homeless become very skilled at remaining hidden" (p. 10).

The Unseen by Lifestyle

Many other homeless individuals remain unseen because they are in residency arrangements that make it difficult for them to be found (Rollinson

& Pardeck, 2006; Vissing, 2004; Ziesemer, Marcoux, & Marwell, 1994). There is ample evidence, for example, that it is easier to count the sheltered homeless than the street homeless. Thus, many individuals sleeping rough, those "in unstable housing arrangements and those living in vehicles and makeshift housing are excluded" (National Law Center on Homelessness and Poverty, 2004a, p. 7). Counts often "miss the so-called 'hidden' homeless who sleep in automobiles, on the roofs of tenements, in campgrounds, or in other places that researchers cannot effectively search. Since they focus on literal homelessness, surveys also miss people who double up with kin or other network members rather than stay in shelters or on the streets" (Link et al., 1995, p. 347). We know also that "others achieve invisibility by sleeping in abandoned buildings, in cars parked behind shopping malls, or in tents in the woods. As revealed by the definitional problem, the homelessness of many others is hidden by precarious housing arrangements with friends or families" (Hombs, 2001, p. 8).

Relatedly, because homelessness is often considered to be an urban problem, there is considerable agreement in the literature that rural homelessness remains cloaked (Aron & Fitchen, 1996; Link, Phelan, Stueve, Moore, Bresnahan, & Struening, 1996; Rollinson & Pardeck, 2006). Finally, some analysts contend that homeless youth may remain uncounted because of the legal requirement of parental consent, or, more accurately, the inability of researchers to garner consent on a regular basis (Moore, 2007).

The Unseen by Movement

Counting homeless persons is also made difficult by the fact that homelessness is fluid (Burt et al., 2001; Hombs, 2001), "people move in and out of homelessness over time" (Rollinson & Pardeck, 2006, p. 9), and "estimating the size of this mobile and changing population is difficult" (Ringwalt, Greene, Robertson, & McPheeters, 1998, p. 1325), a task that Baron and associates (2001) label as "impossible" (p. 767). "Transient lifestyles" (Raleigh-DuRoff, 2004, p. 561) of many homeless compound the problem of fluidity, making counting even more problematic (Moore, 2007). All of this means, as we will see shortly, that when snapshot methods are used to count the homeless, underestimations result.

Difficulties Associated With the Counters

How many homeless persons one sees also depends at times on who is doing the looking. That is, a political thread runs through the census-taking work (Johnson, 1988), or, as Shlay and Rossi (1992) report, "counting the homeless is especially political" (p. 132), and Shinn and Weitzman (1996) acknowledge "estimates . . . of the homeless are shaped by social policy" (p. 109). In the domain of the homeless, Jencks (1994) observes that we would do well to "distinguish between scientific and political numbers" (p. 3). The former, he explains, are "accompanied by enough documentation so you can tell who counted what, whereas political numbers are not" (p. 3). Following this line, and as we document in Chapter 2, we find that at times, government agencies have delivered what are considered low estimates of the homeless population, while advocates for the homeless at times stand accused of overcounting homeless persons (Link et al., 1995), sometimes dramatically, in attempts to "secure better services for their clients" (Kidd & Scriminti, 2004, p. 132).

Counting is linked inexorably with the research designs employed to study homelessness. While it is beyond the scope or purpose of this volume to provide a critique of homeless research, it is important to note here that some of the variation in homeless estimates is attributable to the less-than-robust designs found across studies of homelessness (Brennan et al., 1978; Burt et al., 2001; McCaskill et al., 1998). Sampling problems and instrumentation weaknesses in particular have characterized the field (Johnson, 1988; Koegel, Burnam, & Baumohl, 1996; Russell, 1998), leading to diverse answers about the number of homeless persons and the diverse set of experiences these displaced individuals confront.

Difficulties Associated With the Timing of Counts

The homeless literature is ribboned with analyses of and cautions about timing issues in reaching accurate counts of housing displaced persons (Burt et al., 2001; Hombs, 2001). At the most base level, there are important fluctuations in homelessness by time of year (season) (Greene, Ennett, & Ringwalt, 1999). A census completed in the winter months may underestimate the number of homeless persons while counts taken in warmer months may overdocument the homeless population.

The major issue in "the controversy surrounding enumeration of the homeless revolves around whether or not a count is a point-in-time measurement (a point prevalence estimate) or a count of the number of persons experiencing homelessness during the course of one year (annual incidence estimate)" (Johnson, 1988, p. 50). Not surprisingly, given the fluid and transient nature of homelessness, "the second number is almost always a much larger figure. For example, in a particular locality, there may be 100 persons homeless on an average night; the number of those who are homeless at some point in time during the month could be 300; and the annual total could be in the thousands" (Peroff, 1987, p. 35).

Burt and associates (2001) reveal that because "it is very difficult to find most homeless people if you give yourself one day to do it" (p. 25) (i.e., "point-in-time count[ing] has inherent limits" ([Hombs, 2001, p. 8]), "data reflecting a longer period—for example, one year—capture many of the people experiencing short-term crises who leave homelessness as well as the additional people entering short-term homelessness" (Burt, 2001, p. 4). The consensus is that while "point-in-time data are the best way to understand the magnitude of homelessness on a daily basis" (NAEH, 2003, p. 4), they are inadequate in portraying the full scope of the homeless problem; that to "discover the dimensions of the problem it is important to count homeless people over an extended period of time in a community, rather than to undertake a count on a one-day or one-night basis" (Hombs, 2001, p. 6): "Period prevalence estimates are particularly important for planning purposes because they include individuals who experience short-term episodes of homelessness" (Ringwalt, Greene, Robertson, & McPheeters, 1998, p. 1326). Shinn and Weitzman (1996) provide a nice encapsulation of the issue as follows:

> Homelessness is more like a river than a lake. Most people do not stay homeless forever: on any given day, some find housing and others become homeless. Thus, far more people are homeless over an extended period of time than on any given night. To estimate the numbers of people homeless over a period of time, we must examine both the capacity of the river and its speed of flow. (p. 110)

What We Know About the Numbers

Before we review the demographic data in Chapter 3, given the analysis just provided, we can cull out several themes associated with counting homeless people in the United States—caveats for our voyage if you will. First, findings (i.e., numbers) are often controversial (Alker, 1992): "There has been enormous controversy over the numbers since homelessness began to burgeon in the early 1980s" (Hombs, 2001, p. 7); "findings are often contradictory and it is difficult to acquire a realistic picture of homelessness" (Moore, 2007, p. 6). Debates about numbers rage (Mihaly, 1991; Snow & Anderson, 1993): "Estimation of the prevalence of homelessness is fraught with problems and, no matter which method is used, it is likely to be criticized by someone" (Toro, 1998, p. 120). Or, as Rollinson and Pardeck (2006) describe the estimation landscape, the difficulties we outlined earlier "leave nearly all attempts at counting open to criticism" (p. 8).

Second, existing estimates need to be consumed guardedly (Brennan et al., 1978; Shlay & Rossi, 1992; Whitbeck & Hoyt, 1999):

> With invisibility established as a necessary protective cover, and an infinite number of places to hide at night, the only reasonable and honest answer to the question of how many homeless people there are in the United States is this: there is no one who knows for sure and only a handful can venture an intelligent estimate. (Hombs & Snyder, 1982, p. 9)

"Since the numbers provided by various researchers and agencies that have investigated this question are as varied as the purposes and methodologies employed in their quests" (Stronge, 1992a, p. 9), it is "fair to say that substantial uncertainty persists over the numbers" (Rollinson & Pardeck, 2006, p. 8). Thus, it is extremely difficult to interpret the available data (Kidd & Scrimenti, 2004, p. 331).

Third, given variations in definitions, measurement strategies, census takers, homeless groups, and so forth, in the body of available studies, it is very difficult to aggregate results across research reports (Greene et al., 1997; Johnson, 1988).

Finally, there is a consensus that given the extensive use of point-in-time methods, the temporary and episodically homeless are undercounted and those who remain homeless for a long time are overrepresented in homeless counts (Moore, 2007; Ringwalt, Greene, Robertson, & McPheeters, 1998; Shinn & Weitzman, 1996). Or more concretely, "the proportion of those who have been homeless for a long time [is] exaggerated" (Burt et al., 2001, p. 163). This is the case "simply because point-in-time snap-shots cannot adequately represent the large number of persons who are homeless for only short periods" (Burt et al., 2001, p. 162).

A Note on Heterogeneity

There are two generalizations in the scholarship about individuals on the wrong side of the housing divide. First, almost all of them are poor. Second, the homeless are not a single entity but rather a "highly heteroge-neous group" (Bassuk, 1984; Jahiel, 1992d; Johnson, 1988, p. 55). We exam-ine the poverty issue in Chapter 2. Here we drive home lesson number two: "If there is one point of agreement about the homeless, it is that they do not constitute a homogeneous population" (Snow & Anderson, 1993, p. 36)[7]: "Perhaps the most important findings of this research are that homelessness is a multifaceted issue, that homeless people have a variety of problems and needs, and that the homeless population contains sub-types that need to be distinguished so that the phenomenon of homeless-ness can be understood more fully" (Roth et al., 1992, p. 210). Research reviewed in Chapter 2 shows that "variations exist in the homeless popu-lation on such basic dimensions as sex, race, and age" (Roth et al., 1992, p. 199). The homeless population is "heterogeneous with respect to the duration of homelessness, marital history, ethnicity, education, previous occupation, socioeconomic status, welfare experience, geographic mobil-ity, current means of subsistence, health status, alcohol or drug use, mental disorder, and history of criminal actions or victimization. About the only common feature is extreme poverty" (Jahiel, 1992c, p. 12).

Equally important, there is considerable diversity within the various disaggregated homeless subgroups (Kipke et al., 1997); that is, "even within subgroups, characteristics may differ considerably" (Burt et al., 2001, p. 63). As an example, we know that street youth are quite varied on many dimensions (Auerswald & Eyre, 2002; Hammer et al., 2002). Youngsters on the street make up a "population [that] is heterogeneous in nature and comprised of different subcultural groups" (Kipke et al., 1997, p. 658), "youth who have diverse life experiences and reasons for living or spending time on the street" (Kipke et al., 1997, p. 657).

❖ CONCLUSION

In this introductory chapter, we unpacked the concept of homelessness as a prelude to examining the history of homelessness in Chapter 2. We reported that what appears oftentimes as a rather simple and straightforward idea is actually quite complex and nuanced. We explored the place of definitional problems in the complexity narrative. We also observed that the variety of lenses used to understand and prevent homelessness helps complexify the concept. We revealed how the diverse nature of the homeless population makes understanding more difficult to secure. Next we developed an initial definition of homelessness, employing both the general literature and official government documents on homelessness. In the third part of the chapter, we presented the framework that we use in this volume to portray homelessness and the strategies to cushion its effects or to prevent it altogether. We broke off three concepts for analysis: household composition, residency, and severity. We turn to the other components of the framework (causes, impacts, and solutions) in later parts of the book. We closed with an extensive discussion on the enumeration of the homeless, documenting that counting homeless persons is an incredibly uneven process. In Chapter 3, we review the demographics in the homeless chronicle, keeping in mind definitions, insights, and cautions presented in this chapter. Before we do so, however, we provide a brief history of homelessness in the United States.

❖ NOTES

1. While we acknowledge that homelessness is an international problem (Brickner, 1985; Farrow, Deisher, Brown, Kulig, & Kipke, 1992; Glasser, 1994; Spence, Stephens, & Parks, 2004), our focus herein is on the United States.

2. Jencks (1994) argues that we should be attentive to separating voluntarily and involuntarily doubled-up individuals and families in counts of homelessness.

3. We examine the history of homelessness in Chapter 2.

4. Roth et al. (1992) remind us, however, that "the major analysis of the homeless issue has been developed in the mental health field" (p. 200).

5. In this book, we use the word "children" for accompanied homeless minors and the word "youth" for unaccompanied homeless minors.

6. This is not always as clear as it appears, however. For example, a number of studies confirm that some homeless persons find shelters and cheap hotels to be more dangerous (i.e., less home-like) than sleeping in public spaces (Jencks, 1994; Stefl, 1987).

7. Shlay and Rossi (1992) acknowledge, however, that when contrasted with the general population, the homeless do appear as a more homogeneous population.

2

A Brief History of Homelessness

There have always been people who were homeless. The problem may have been called by a different name or may have been dealt with in different ways, but the fact is that homelessness has existed through the centuries. (Tower & White, 1989, p. 9)

The homeless man has been a social and psychological enigma from time immemorial. (Levinson, 1963, p. 590)

The homeless have been a part of American civilization almost since the founding of the first English colonies four hundred years ago. (Kusmer, 2002, p. 13)

It is beyond our charge to provide an extensive analysis of the history of homelessness in the United States.[1] At the same time, since we know that the use of historical lenses offers important insights into our understanding of social phenomena, especially those as complex as homelessness, we spend a bit of time examining the history of displaced persons in America. We look at homelessness across time and examine, in an introductory way, homelessness today. First, we cull important themes that ribbon homelessness in America over the last 300 years. Next, we offer

29

a period analysis of homelessness from the birth of the country through the late 1970s. Last, we discuss the new homelessness, which began around 1980.

❖ THEMES

Karabanow (2004) provides the backdrop for our narrative with these two insightful remarks:

> Homelessness is not a new phenomenon. Throughout history, the image of homelessness has been variously portrayed, usually reflecting the values of the dominant culture of the historical period in which they are in use. (p. 10)

> While homelessness has worn assorted masks at different times, it has been a steady facet of North American culture with a very long history. (p. 11)

Stability

To begin with, it is instructive to review the stability side of the homeless ledger book, the acknowledgment that "homelessness in one form or another has existed throughout much of human history" (Snow & Anderson, 1993, p. 7). Homelessness in America is not a new condition (Stronge, 1992a); "it has been present in one form or another since at least the second quarter of the 18th century" (Johnson, 1988, p. 8). Or as Shlay and Rossi (1992) observe, "social researchers today can look back to a long and rich history" (p. 130) of homelessness. And what holds for homelessness in general is true for homeless youth in particular (Wells & Sandhu, 1986). As scholars in this domain remind us, "in the United States, running away from home is not a new phenomenon (Farrow et al., 1992, p. 718), and "homelessness of children . . . has existed since the beginning of civilization" (Shane, 1996, p. 7).

Change

When we redirect our gaze to the evolutionary side of the ledger book on homelessness, historians help us see that the meaning of homelessness and "the meaning of the homeless problem [have] changed many times since the early years of the colonial settlement" (Hoch, 1987, p. 16). More specifically, during each historical period, the definition, recognition, incidence, and severity of homelessness within society have varied, sometimes significantly. We learn, for example, that well-accepted images of homelessness and homeless people have shifted throughout history, for example, from the bum who is responsible for his own troubles to that of the victim who was forced into homelessness, perhaps from economic hard times or spousal abuse, and back again. Looking at these changes in the area of unaccompanied adolescents, for example, we discover that

> the stereotypes responsible for shaping Euro-American ideas of homeless youth are similar to those that have informed our ideas of homelessness in general, in that they too have a history of image transformations. For instance, early nineteenth-century labeling referred to street youth as "petty thieves," "street sinners," "street urchins," and "begging impostors," while in the early twentieth century street youth were commonly branded as "young barbarians" and "street wandering children." By the 1950s, popular perceptions of this same population were influenced by notions of psychological deviance; street youth were thought to be mentally disturbed. Just twenty years later in the 1970s, we renamed street youth yet again, calling them this time "enfants perdus," which is to say, our lost children. The present day image of street youth is that of the sexually and/or physically abused runaway. (Karabanow, 2004, pp. 18–19)

We also learn that "different definitions [of homelessness] have emerged and taken root at different times" (Hoch, 1987, p. 16). For example, as we observed in Chapter 1, at times men were "called homeless because they lived outside normal family life. Having a place to live with family made a house into a home. Without a place and a family to live with, a man was homeless" (Shlay & Rossi, 1992, p. 131). At other times, "the term homeless, once generically used to describe the vagrant classes as a whole, became specifically applied to the single unattached workers who lived on skid row between jobs" (Wallace, 1965, p. 18). During the period after World War II, homelessness was not defined primarily in terms of residency but in terms of affiliation, or more accurately, disaffiliation (Hoch, 1987). Today, the family dimension of homelessness is less salient, whereas a fixed residency is highlighted.

The homeless population has changed over time as well. To begin with, the size of the population has ebbed and flowed (Stronge, 1992a), generally "in response to swings in national and regional economic development" (Hoch, 1987, p. 16) and in lockstep with "national business cycles" (Hoch, 1987, p. 20). Historians have documented that homeless populations "increased during the economic depressions of 1873, 1885, [and] 1930–1938" (Ropers, 1988, p. 91). We also discover that the homeless population in the United States rises dramatically in response to "social upheavals such as war" (p. 91), or more precisely, the termination of wars and the winding down of military activity,[2] massive immigration, and fundamental changes in the economy. For example, in the 1950s and 1960s, estimates of the homeless population were relatively low—in the 100,000-person range (Wallace, 1965, p. 24). Estimates from the Depression era and the modern era (today) are considerably larger.

The composition of the homeless population has taken on different forms at various points in time, with patterns visible in earlier epochs sometimes returning in later periods.[3] For example, much has been made in the current literature about the "age" pattern in the modern homeless mosaic, with analysts consistently documenting that the homeless as a group are becoming younger, younger than ever before, it is sometimes suggested. The first part of the claim is correct. However, the second is not. What some scholars fail to acknowledge is that in earlier periods, the homeless population was equally young (Kusmer, 2002). In fact, it is more accurate to conclude that it is the older-age phenomenon of the 1950–1980 period rather than the youthfulness of today's homeless that is the outlier in the shifts in the age variable across time.

This same ebb and flow is discernable in the patterns of other variables as well. In earlier periods (1865–1930), for example, veterans comprised about one-fourth of the homeless population (Wallace, 1965). In the 1950–1980 era, there were relatively few veterans among the homeless. Today, the percentage of homeless veterans has crept back up to the one-quarter level. A similar ebb and flow can be seen with homeless women. "Prior to the 1870s, women made up a significant fraction of the homeless population of urban America. By the end of the nineteenth century, however, the world of the homeless had become an overwhelmingly masculine realm" (Kusmer, 2002, p. 10). And while that condition held for much of the 20th century, after 1980 we witnessed a dramatic increase in the number of homeless women, both as single adults and as heads of homeless families.

The visibility of homeless persons has also morphed across the last 150 years. The subtheme of a much-enhanced visibility of individuals is a dominant motif in the text on modern homelessness. But as Kusmer (2002) and others confirm, while homelessness during the 1950–1980 era was more confined and thus seen less by the average citizen, it was never more visible than in America's industrial age and during the depression of the 1930s.

> The homeless were more visible, and far more assertive, during the industrial era than at any other time in American history. Prior to World War II, tramps and beggars could scarcely be avoided. Most Americans regularly encountered people begging for a handout, either at their back door or on street corners, and stories about the homeless were common in magazines and daily newspapers. (Kusmer, 2002, p. 7)

Over the last 200 years, the rationale for homelessness that has held the high ground in society has moved about a good deal as well. And, as we explore later, this has meant parallel shifts in society's judgments about and responses to homelessness. For example, the image of a life choice freely selected has been dominant at times. So too has the image of the lazy and self-destructive person unworthy of assistance. During the Depression, however, homeless persons were much more likely to be seen as victims of forces beyond their control and worthy of a more sympathetic response (Kusmer, 2002; Levinson, 1963; Wallace, 1965). The victim perspective has returned to favor in the modern epoch of homelessness as well (Karabanow, 2004).

Finally, as we presaged earlier, societal responses to homelessness have mirrored changes in assessment of causes. Thus, we see an ebb and flow between more humane and harsher treatments of the homeless population in general and adolescent youth in particular over the epochs outlined later.

❖ PERIOD ANALYSIS

In order to help in the understanding process, historians sometimes categorize homelessness into distinct periods. Wells and Sandhu (1986), for example, portray historical phases of homelessness among unaccompanied youth from colonial America into the 1980s. Hoch (1987) divides general "homelessness into four historical periods based on major changes in the classification and care of the homeless performed by their caretakers. Each period is marked by the label for the homeless problem that predominated during that time" (p. 16)—vagrancy, tramping, deviant, and victim. Johnson (1988), in her review, depicts five historical epochs of homelessness: Vagrants: Colonial Period, 1725–1864; Tramps: Post–Civil War Period, 1865–1900; Deviants: Progressive Era, 1900–1929; Victims: Depression Era, 1929–1944; and Deviants: Recent Skid Row Era, 1950–1979. We employ this framework here.

Colonial Period, 1725–1864

Wallace (1965) maintains that the initial homeless problem in the United States was "literally thrust upon us with the arrival in the early 1600s of the first boatload of England's homeless, dependent children" (p. 4). He argues that "it was in fact England's policy of forcibly deporting her vagrants to the Colonies which forced us to come face to face with the issue of homelessness—and to do something about it" (p. 10). Nonetheless, homelessness remained "relatively insignificant prior to the 1730s but increased substantially in the late eighteenth century and again in the 1820s" (Kusmer, 2002, p. 5), acknowledging that records that can provide reliable estimates are sketchy at best. Shane (1996) reports that "in 1854 an estimated 10,000 orphans or homeless children lived on the streets, in back alleys, and abandoned buildings of New York City" (p. 9). Karabanow (2004) documented that around 1860, New York State had more than 30,000 street youth (p. 17). According to Johnson (1988), the homeless in the Colonial Period were generally the worthy poor, those who were displaced through no fault of their own. The most common solution to the problem was for individuals "to provide rooms for the poor in private homes" (Johnson, 1988, p. 12); "families in return received a small fee from the town overseers" (Hoch, 1987, p. 17).

Kusmer (2002) concluded that after 1820, however, "accelerating economic change forced many more individuals into the ranks of vagrants and beggars, prompting the first concerted attempt by private charities to deal with this problem" (p. 13). In the two decades before the Civil War, "towns were setting aside rooms in police stations for overnight lodging of the destitute, and organized charities began to grapple with the problem of the homeless for the first time" (p. 3). "Institutional care" (Johnson, 1988, p. 13) made its first appearance on the homeless landscape.

Post–Civil War Period, 1865–1900

According to Snow and Anderson (1993), "during the pre-Civil War years the American economy suffered several minor economic depressions that swelled the ranks of the homeless, but it was after the Civil War that homelessness rose most dramatically" (p. 13). That is, "homelessness emerged as a national issue in the 1870s. During that decade, the homeless population increased dramatically in size and assumed a distinctive form" (Kusmer, 2002, p. 3). At least four major factors combined to cause homelessness to mushroom in the 35 years after the Civil War.

The Civil War itself was a major factor (Johnson, 1988). As Ropers (1988) describes it, "massive homelessness was first documented as a result of the Civil War" (p. 89). According to Bahr (1973), the Civil War "created homelessness on a vast scale, and many of those uprooted by the war—the orphaned, the impoverished, the widowed, and the discharged soldiers—were drawn to the nation's cities" (p. 35).

> The Civil War brought about extensive social dislocation and movement of populations. Thousands of civilians were displaced from their homes, and in many cases, traditional patterns of social interaction were destroyed. After the war, many Union and Confederate soldiers had to forage their way home on their own resources. Some of these veterans, finding no jobs available for them in the postwar economy, continued their homeless nomadic existence. The term "hobo" probably is derived from "*homeward bound*," the answer given by soldiers after the Civil War when asked where they were going. (Ropers, 1988, p. 89)

> The Civil War had turned thousands of boys into disciplined foragers, resilient, hardened, able to find food and shelter in all conditions, proficient in the use of the railroad. After the war, many of these men, uprooted and inured to years of wandering and fighting for survival, found peace an unsettled time. Many had no homes or ties—or had forgotten them. Few jobs awaited. Now, with the days of troop movements and army camp life and dodging hostile forces behind, many continued their wandering—picking up odd jobs, sleeping outdoors under any available cover, begging meals, a new kind of adventure for which they were well trained. They followed wagon roads and trails. But mostly they hit the tracks. (Bruns, 1980, p. 7)

Homelessness during this period has also been linked to alterations in the American economy. According to Snow and Anderson (1993), "the industrial and agricultural state of the nation demanded large numbers of mobile workers" (p. 13; Hoch, 1987). Homelessness thus served the "economic and social functions" (Ropers, 1988, p. 91) of the nation in general and the urban industrial society that took form in the last half of the 19th century in particular (Kusmer, 2002; Miller, 1982). "Battalions of workers marched to the pulse of on-again, off-again employment" (Bruns, 1980, p. 14).

> In this swelling cadre of wandering, homeless men were those that were to comprise an important labor force. The drive of American industry westward opened new kinds of jobs—at the railroad construction sites, in the mines, in the timberlands, on the sheep and cattle ranches, in the grain belt, in the orchards. The call was for a special kind of labor, a labor remote from family and community life. The jobs were irregular, in scattered and often isolated areas. The itinerant miners, loggers, bridge snakes, skinners, muckers, tunnel workers, and ice harvesters who answered the call were mobile and adaptable. (Bruns, 1980, p. 8)

> During the last quarter of the century hundreds of thousands of such transient workers, called *tramps,* traveled across the United States, especially the western states. They mined, lumbered, herded, harvested, built, and otherwise labored to provide a crucial but overlooked economic contribution to national development. (Hoch, 1987, p. 19)

Relatedly, the 1865–1900 period was rocked by a series of severe economic contractions that threw multitudes of former employees into the ranks of the homeless (Bruns, 1980; Kusmer, 2002; Ropers, 1988). The depressions of 1873 and 1893 had a particularly strong influence on the expanding size of the homeless population (Johnson, 1988). Wallace (1965) depicts the linkage between the first depression and homelessness as follows:

> Then, in 1873, panic ushered in by Black September, hit the Nation. Mercantile failures soared and unemployment rose to encompass between thirty and forty percent of the population. Again, there were bread lines, soup kitchens, shelters, and other means of emergency relief. Homelessness had turned into something just short of a national way of life. (p. 15)

Finally, there is abundant evidence that immigration was a contributing cause to the increase in homelessness in the 1865–1900 period. In the last half of the 19th century

> economic and political disruption in Europe and the promise of opportunity in America brought hundreds of thousands of immigrants to America's shores. Unable to find jobs in the settled industrial East, many of the immigrants also became workers of the road. (Ropers, 1988, p. 90)

> As each successive wave of emigres added its share to the numbers of those made homeless by the Civil War, vagrancy in the United States reached heights previously unknown. (Wallace, 1965, pp. 14–15)

According to Riis (cited in Ropers, 1988), in 1890 the total homeless population was 5,200,000. These individuals were characterized by two distinct patterns of residency: Some tramped throughout the country, living on the road; the balance gravitated to the nation's cities (Kusmer, 2002). It was also during this era that "skid rows" in the nation's urban centers took form (Wallace, 1965) and reached their maturity (Bahr, 1973). Bogue (1963) describes a skid row area as follows:

> The term "Skid Row" has come to denote a district in the city where there is a concentration of substandard hotels and rooming houses charging very low rates and catering primarily to men with low incomes. These hotels are intermingled with numerous taverns, employment agencies offering jobs as unskilled laborers, restaurants serving low-cost meals, pawnshops and secondhand stores, and missions that daily provide a free meal after the service. . . . Most are frequently located near the Business District and also near a factory district or major heavy transportation facilities such as a waterfront, freight yards, or a trucking and storage depot. (p. 1)

In his review of the skid row in America, Ropers (1988) explains that

> the expression "skid row" is derived from "Skid Road," which originally referred to Yessler Way in downtown Seattle. In the latter

part of the nineteenth century, the Northwestern loggers would utilize various streets by freezing them over, by laying logs across them, or by actually greasing them to facilitate the movement of lumber down to waterways. The term "skid row" later came to connote not only the downward movement of timber, but also the apparent downward social mobility of skid row's inhabitants. (pp. 90–91; see also Bahr, 1973; Bogue, 1963; Miller, 1982)

It was also during this era that earlier societal assessments of homelessness as benign and the homeless as casualties of larger economic and social forces lost dominance. Homelessness began to be seen through the prism of "personal deficiencies and faults of moral character" (Hoch, 1987, p. 21) and the homeless as a burlesque parade of the marginal and untrustworthy. Treatment took on increasingly harsh overtones (Hoch, 1987).

Progressive Era, 1900–1929

The Progressive Era witnessed a decline in homelessness through 1920, or at least a halt to previous growth patterns (Stronge, 1992a) as structural shifts in the economy during this era no longer pushed people into the streets but rather pulled them into the workforce (Hoch, 1987). As a result, "the number of transient homeless dwindled" (p. 24). "By the mid-1920s, the hobo era died" (Snow & Anderson, 1993, p. 14):

Mechanization of agriculture had depleted the job market for seasonal farm workers. The western frontier had largely been settled. The American economy became strong enough to support large numbers of Americans in more stable jobs. Finally, the railroad, the matrix of the hobo life, had gradually been replaced by automobiles as the major mode of transportation, and those remaining switched from steam to diesel locomotion, a change that made it more difficult to ride the rails. (Snow & Anderson, 1993, p. 14)

Concomitantly, the vitality of the skid row areas in America's core cities declined (Hoch, 1987). "Wartime manpower needs and prosperity were soon to drain the country's skid rows of the major portion of their population" (Wallace, 1965, p. 20). And while the end of World War I helped to reestablish the skid row (Wallace, 1965), it did not return to the level of prominence it enjoyed at the end of the 19th century.

The best portrait we have of homelessness in the Progressive Era comes from a 1911 Chicago-based study by Solenberger (cited in Johnson, 1988). According to this early scholar of homelessness, "the average man was white, less than forty, single, physically defected, and native born.

Nearly 5% were blind, 5% mentally ill, 4% too senile to work, and 33% physically disabled" (Johnson, 1988, p. 17). The homelessness that did exist came to be viewed as a consequence of unemployment (Hoch, 1987) and homeless persons as "unwelcome by-products of the industrial system" (Johnson, 1988, p. 17): "A growing class of professional social workers began to tie the problem of the homeless to the experience of social conditions rather than defects of moral character" (Hoch, 1987, p. 23). Rescue missions and municipal lodging houses began to appear in skid row areas for the first time (Hoch, 1987).

Depression Era, 1929–1944

It should come as no surprise to hear that the "depression resulted in a dramatic increase in the ranks of the homeless" (Stronge, 1992a, p. 5). According to documents from that period, "all previous records [about homelessness] were broken in the decade after 1929" (Wallace, 1965, p. 21). Nels Anderson, the leading scholar on homelessness of this era, suggests that a minimum of 1.5 million persons were displaced (cited in Wallace, 1965, pp. 21–22). Others provided much higher counts, often in the 5 million range. Official government surveys estimated homelessness at 1% of the population or 1.2 million people in mid-January 1933 (Burt et al., 2001, p. 3). Calculations for homeless youth ranged from 100,000 (Johnson, 1988) to 200,000 in a U.S. Children's Bureau study in 1932 (Snow & Anderson, 1993). In a reverse of the situation in the Progressive Era, however, toward the end of the Depression Era the number of homeless dropped precipitously as displaced persons "were recruited into the armed services and into the war industry" (Snow & Anderson, 1993, p. 15). Indeed, "during WW II the skid row population almost disappeared" (Snow & Anderson, 1993, p. 15).

Historians also reveal that the cultural geography of homelessness changed during the early Depression years, the years before war and war-related industries reversed the profound homelessness in the nation. A "new form of homelessness appeared" (Johnson, 1988, p.18). There were more homeless families than in any pervious era (Tower & White, 1989). And there were more homeless minors, both accompanied and unaccompanied (Snow & Anderson, 1993). Homeless men in the 1930s bore little resemblance to their peers from earlier times:

> Evidence from a study of the files of 16,720 homeless men from among the more than 100,000 who had used the Chicago transient shelters between 1931 and 1934 revealed that less than half fit the profile of the main stem homeless, with only 5% bums, 20% casual workers, and 20% migrant workers. The remaining residents included 33% unskilled workers, 15% skilled workers, and 7% white-collar workers. (Hoch, 1987, p. 25)

Causes for the plight of displacement were to be found less in the foibles and defects of individuals themselves and more in the catastrophic shifts in the economy, to "profound economic dislocation" (Hoch, 1987, p. 25). Responses fit more readily into the "helping, not blaming" category. Assistance was less punitive in form: "An emerging framework of entitlement" (Hoch, 1987, p. 25) consistent with the New Deal of President Roosevelt began to take root.

Recent Skid Row Era, 1950–1979

The period from 1950 to 1979 was a relatively quiet time in the homelessness chronicle. The population decreased. Homeless persons became more centralized in the decaying skid row areas of the nation's central cities. They were less visible than at any time in our history. All in all, "as both social fact and cultural icon, the homeless receded from public consciousness after WW II; they would remain largely forgotten until the late 1970s" (Kusmer, 2002, p. 12).

From the end of WW II until the onset of the modern homeless period, the number of homeless persons steadily declined (Bahr, 1973; Hoch, 1987). Skid rows, in turn, began to shrink (Shlay & Rossi, 1992), even as the row became the almost exclusive residency of the displaced (Hopper & Hamberg, 1984). The long-term ebb-and-flow pattern hit bottom and "homelessness reached its lowest levels since the mid-eighteenth century" (Kusmer, 2002, p. 6). Bogue (1963) estimated the yearly homeless population in 1950 at only 100,000. Indeed, "during the three decades following WW II it appeared that the homeless population was disappearing" (Stronge, 1992a, p. 6).

Two reasons for the dramatic decline in homelessness in the Recent Skid Row Era stand out. To begin with, the U.S. economy after World War II was literally on fire, pulling into the workforce nearly everyone who wanted a job (Johnson, 1988): "Postwar economic prosperity reduced economic hardship and with it the incidence of homelessness. Between 1950 and 1970 the median family income nearly doubled, even when controlling for inflation" (Hoch, 1987, p. 27). At the same time, the traditional postwar spike in homelessness that was evidenced at the conclusion of the Civil War and World War I failed to materialize.

> The veterans returned from the war, and their transition to civilian status was eased by a variety of imaginative federal programs. In contrast to the aftermath of previous wars, relatively few of them became permanent residents of skid row. (Bahr, 1973, p. 36)

> Heretofore returning veterans had contributed heavily to the ranks of the homeless. Traditionally, wars had first drained skid row areas and then re-filled them to overflowing with veterans. The GI Bill of Rights, the Veterans Administration, and a series of social

welfare benefits ranging from education to psychiatric treatment enabled most veterans of World War II to return to civilian society. Very few found their way to skid row. (Wallace, 1965, pp. 22–23)

Scholars also provide data on the complexion of homelessness in the 1950–1979 era. "The skid row alcoholic was the stereotype of homelessness" (Johnson, 1988, p. 22). Between 1950 and 1970, "the composition of the homeless narrowed from a wide range of households and people displaced by the massive unemployment of the depression to include mainly older, single males surviving on pensions and marginal employment in the deteriorating hotels and flophouses of skid row" (Hoch, 1987, p. 27). Bahr (1973) and Hopper and Hamberg (1984) provide the following snapshots of the Recent Skid Row Era, the first in period time, the second in retrospect:

Skid row men are most unique in their marital histories: only about half have married and most of these marriages were short-lived and stressful. Nevertheless, the skid row men maintain some kinship ties, and perhaps one-third of them see a relative at least annually. They are extremely poor, their dominant ties to outside society are apt to be short-term, low-status jobs, and at a given time, as many as half of them may be unemployed. Disability or chronic illness characterize a majority of the men, and at least one-third are problem drinkers; they are old and seem older, are mostly white and native born, and are not particularly disadvantaged educationally. At least half are native to that section of the country where their skid row is located, and most are long-term residents of their city and often of skid row itself. (Bahr, 1973, p. 110)

The homeless were almost exclusively men, usually older white men, many of whom had long resided at the margins of polite society and a good proportion of whom suffered from chronic ailments (especially alcoholism). Depending upon local economic conditions, between one-third and one-half of skid row men worked, typically at menial jobs. The rest relied on charity, missions, public agencies, or pensions. With rare exception, and whether describing the geography of an urban niche or the ethnography of a culture, the studies of this period found not community but exile—a listless, aimless world, void of ambition or bonds, populated by casualties of poverty, pathology, old age, character deficiencies, or alcohol dependency. Victims rather than veterans of a chosen way of life, theirs was a world whose watchword could be found in the title of Tom Kromer's Depression-era memoir of life on the skids: *Waiting for Nothing* (1935). (Hopper & Hamberg, 1984, p. 18)

The homeless in this period "were mostly older males, inhabiting cheap hotels and flophouses in downtown urban areas" (Johnson, 1988, p. 21);

"by the mid-1950s the skid row population of the nation was dominated by retired, disabled, elderly white men on welfare" (Ropers, 1988, p. 92). Using real-time data, Bahr (1973) notes that

> in census tracts containing skid rows one person in nine is 65 or older; on the rows themselves, the proportion is much higher. There are no children, few young men, and many middle-aged and old men. The median age generally falls between 50 and 54. The proportion of men under 35 ranges from 5 to 15 per cent; there are from two to seven times as many men over 65. Institutions for the aged have higher proportions of old people, but there are few "open" communities with age distributions so highly skewed. (p. 109)

Most skid row men of the time were white. Across various studies and reviews from the Recent Skid Row period, blacks ranged from 3% to 40%, with most estimates bundled at the lower end of the continuum (Bahr, 1973, p. 105; Hopper & Milburn, 1996, p. 124). About half of the homeless men studied during the 1950s, 1960s, and 1970s had never been married, while another 30% to 40% were divorced or separated and 10% were widowers (Bahr, 1973, p. 89). Most were native born and most ended up in skid rows in the cities in which they had been housed; that is, they were not highly mobile. The transiency of earlier generations of homeless persons had given way to a rootedness in skid row (Bahr, 1973); the homeless "became confined" (Kusmer, 2002, p. 4). "First and foremost skid rows were centers for disaffiliates drawn from a local and regional hinterland" (Bahr, 1973, p. 107). Homelessness in the 1950–1979 time frame was "strictly an urban problem" (Kusmer, 2002, p. 4). Studies conducted at the time regularly showed that "between one-third and one-half of the homeless skid row men were gainfully employed" (Bahr, 1973, p. 95). And while the nature of employment varied from locale to locale, it "tended to be low-status and poorly-paid" (p. 95).

❖ THE CHANGING FACE OF HOMELESSNESS: A FORESHADOWING

> *The homeless once again became an important social problem in the early 1980s when the worst economic recession since the 1930s hit at the same time that a newly elected president initiated unprecedented cutbacks in federally funded public assistance programs. (Hoch, 1987, p. 27)*

⸲◠⸱◠⸲

> *Homelessness has undergone a transformation of scope and complexity not seen since the worst days of the great depression. (Hopper & Hamberg, 1984, p. 9)*

⸲◠⸱◠⸲

Over the last 25 years in the United States the makeup of the homeless population has changed significantly. (Swick, 2004, p. 116)

⟨ᴏ⟩⟨ᴏ⟩

Homeless scholars document that the narrative on displaced persons is being rewritten in important ways, a rewriting that began around 1980. Most generally, "during the 1980s throughout North America homelessness re-emerged" (Karabanow, 2004, p. 10). And as Ropers (1988) observes, "the rise of a new homeless population is occurring" (p. 29). While we return to each of the themes we introduce here in Chapter 3 when we unpack homelessness and provide estimates for homelessness on various demographic categories, our goal here is more modest: to spotlight the central facets of the shifting story line in the modern (post-1980) era of homelessness. To begin with, the problem, in terms of numbers, has exploded (Hombs, 2001; National Law Center on Homelessness and Poverty, 2004b; Ropers, 1988; United Way of New York City, 2002). Even scholars whose counts of the homeless tend to be on the lower end of the estimation continuum acknowledge that the problem is much more severe today than during the 1950–1979 period (Jencks, 1994).

Homelessness is also a much more visible phenomenon today than it was in the middle of the 20th century, more "noticeable" (Karabanow, 2004; Kusmer, 2002, p. 239; Shlay & Rossi, 1992). "Skid row areas have not only survived but are overflowing. Homeless people can be seen in all parts of our cities, not only on skid row, but also in the middle-class and even upper-class residential neighborhoods" (Ropers, 1988, p. 93). We also see that "the demography of homelessness has shifted dramatically" (Rescorla, Parker, & Stolley, 1991, p. 210). While in the most recent era (1950–1979) the archetype homeless person was a single man, a large percentage of today's homeless are women and the bulk of these are accompanied by children (Johnson, 1988; Shlay & Rossi, 1992). Thus, there are many more homeless families today than in the recent past and many more children and young people as well (Jozefowicz-Simbeni & Israel, 2006; Medcalf, 2008; Rescorla et al., 1991). Analysis also reveals that "the new homeless of the post-1975 period tend to be much younger than their skid-row predecessors" (Kusmer, 2002, p. 241). Concomitantly, more and more minorities are being pushed into literal homelessness (Hopper & Milburn, 1996; Kusmer, 2002), altering the ratio of minority to white representation in shelters and on the streets. There are also more employed homeless persons, more of the working poor (Biggar, 2001). All in all, "the new homeless are characterized by greater diversity" (Morse, 1992; Stefl, 1987, p. 47): "The 'old homeless' were fairly homogeneous; the contemporary homeless [are] a diverse group" (Shlay & Rossi, 1992, p. 133). Or more prosaically, "the population of the streets has been democratized" (Hombs,

2001, p. 10). So too has the suffering that accompanies homelessness (National Law Center on Homelessness and Poverty, 2004a).

In terms of residency, "the homeless of past decades were essentially a sheltered population" (Ropers, 1988, p. 66). Today, a growing majority of the homeless are living on the streets (Kusmer, 2002)—"many in some subpopulations of the homeless do not even have elementary shelter" (Ropers, 1988, p. 66). And an increasing number are living doubled up with friends or relatives.

As we discussed earlier, homelessness for much of the post-Depression era was associated with the urban centers of the nation and often confined to well-defined skid row areas within those core cities. Today that portrait is less accurate. To begin with, "skid row [is] no longer a geographically well-demarcated section of the inner city" (Hopper & Hamberg, 1984, p. 38); the displaced are much more dispersed throughout the city (Bassuk, 1984; Hopper & Hamberg, 1984). Second, homelessness has also become a rural and suburban problem (Kusmer, 2002). In addition, the narrative on homelessness is being rewritten as episodic and sporadic incidents of poverty comprise a much larger percentage of the population than was the case in the past (NAEH, 2003).

Equally important, the causes of displacement are shifting in the modern era. Homelessness in the Recent Skid Row Era was largely attributed to flaws in the character of the men who occupied the low-cost hotels and flophouses in the nation's skid rows. The homeless man of the era was considered culpable for his condition and therefore "blameworthy for whatever poverty, misery, or suffering accompanied [this] voluntarily chosen lifestyle" (Hombs, 2001, p. 10). Much of the problem was attributed to substance (alcohol) abuse (Kling, Dunn, & Oakley, 1996; Shane, 1996; Stefl, 1987). Today, personal conditions in general and moral failings in particular remain in the portfolio of causes for homelessness. However, much more attention is given to the role of the larger economic environment, to trends in housing, and to government policy in explaining homelessness in the United States (Hopper & Hamberg, 1984; Kusmer, 2002). Family conditions are also illuminated much more brightly than they were in the past (Hombs, 2001; McChesney, 1990).

❖ CONCLUSION

In this second chapter of our introduction to homelessness, we added historical material to deepen our understanding of the people who occupy shelter beds and/or sleep on our streets. We saw that homelessness can be defined with reference to key features, such as demographics and attributions of causes. We reported how our understanding and assessment of these key features have shifted since the birth of the nation. We also revealed how homelessness is being recast in the post-1980 era.

❖ NOTES

1. For a deeper examination of the history of homelessness, see Bahr (1973), Bogue (1963), Bruns (1980), Hoch (1987), Johnson (1988), Miller (1982), Wallace (1965), and Wells and Sandhu (1986).

2. Largely because of proactive efforts on the part of the federal government, such as the GI Bill of Rights, the period after World War II was an exception to the rule (Bahr, 1973; Wallace, 1965).

3. This point is often lost on analysts who compare modern homelessness to conditions prevalent only from 1950 to 1980. They sometimes end up making claims that fail to hold up under longer historical review.

3

Demographics of Homelessness

Understanding who the homeless are and where they come from must be the first step in proposing strategies to help. (Ropers, 1988, p. 65)

Developing an accurate understanding of the size and characteristics of the population of homeless children and youth is critically important for increasing public awareness, generating funding, planning interventions and programs, and evaluating the effectiveness of interventions. (Kidd & Scrimenti, 2004, p. 327)

To plan programs and interventions for these young people, public health professionals and social workers need accurate information on the size and characteristics of the population of homeless youths. (Ringwalt, Greene, Robertson, & McPheeters, 1998, p. 1325)

In this chapter, we examine characteristics of the homeless population. We begin with the aggregated story line. We then turn our attention to the subgroups of special interest in this volume, families with children (accompanied minors) and youth on their own (unaccompanied minors).

The questions that shape each subsection are these: How many homeless are there? What are they like? And how do they live? As we proceed, it is instructive to recall the caveats about counting and estimating that were presented in Chapter 1.

❖ CHARACTERISTICS OF THE HOMELESS: THE GENERAL STORY LINE

> *A useful tactic for making sense of those who are the homeless would be to identify categories of homeless. (Stronge, 1992a, p. 8)*

Number of Homeless

> *Currently, several national estimates of homelessness are available. (Rollinson & Pardeck, 2006, p. 9)*

> *The results indicate that millions of Americans experience homelessness at some time in their lives, whether it is narrowly defined as literal homelessness or broadly defined to include doubling up. (Link et al., 1995, p. 353)*

Point-in-Time Estimates

As we explained in Chapter 1, data on the homeless are collected in a number of ways. There are also amazingly large fluctuations in estimates of displaced persons in the United States. The most common measure is homelessness on a specific night (say, March 4, 2009). Researchers refer to this as a point-in-time or point prevalence measure. The first defensible national point-in-time estimates began to appear in the late 1980s and estimates over the last 20 years are marked by considerable variation. A 1988 study by the National Association for the Education of Homeless Children and Youth (cited in Johnson, 1988) estimated the "number of homeless persons on any given night at 735,000" (Johnson, 1988, p. 50). Jencks (1994), at this same time period (March 1987), compiled available data and concluded that the homeless population was approximately 350,000, although he also reported that the population had quadrupled during the 1980s (p. 16). HUD on a given night in the winter of 1983–1984 concluded that between 250,000 and 350,000 individuals were homeless (Hope & Young, 1986, p. 17). The Bureau of the Census pegged the homeless population in the 200,000 to 600,000 range, while suggesting that 250,000 to 350,000 was probably the most reliable band (Peroff, 1987, p. 41). The first nationwide data collection project by the Urban Institute in 1987 provided a homeless estimate in the 500,000 to 600,000 range (Burt et al., 2001, p. 34). Also during this time frame (mid-1980s), the Community for Creative Non-Violence claimed that 2.2 million individuals were homeless on any given night (Stefl, 1987, p. 48). A November 1983 document by the Department of Health and Human Services put the number at 2 million.

At the turn of the century, the U.S. Census Bureau reported that there were in the neighborhood of 230,000 homeless, 178,638 sheltered individuals, and another 50,000 persons on the street (Rollinson & Pardeck, 2006, p. 9). In the 1990s, Burt (2001) claimed that there were four times that number: "On any given day, at least 800,000 people are homeless in the United States, including about 200,000 children in homeless families" (p. 1). Bruden (cited in Biggar, 2001) arrived at a similar number—760,000 homeless persons on a single night (Biggar, 2001, p. 942). So too did the Report of the Bipartisan Millennial Housing Commission in 2002, with an estimate of 800,000.

More recently, data from the U.S. Conference of Mayors (2008), zeroing in on larger cities, suggest that between 0.15% and 1.74% of the total population is "homeless and living on the streets, in emergency shelters, or in transitional housing on an average night" (p. 16). In 2004, the National Law Center found that about 840,000 persons were "literally homeless— on the street or in temporary housing—on any given day across the United States" (National Law Center on Homelessness and Poverty, 2004a, p. i). On a single night in January 2008, HUD (2009, p. 8) counted 664,414 sheltered and street homeless persons.

Homelessness During a Given Year

Calculations of homelessness over the course of a year, not surprisingly, are both higher and less firm than point-in-time counts. During the 1980s, Jencks (1994, p. 16) estimated the yearly number of sheltered and street homeless at 400,000, Alker (1992, p. 179) and Jahiel (1992a, p. 155) at 2 million, Kozol (1988, p. 13) at between 2 and 3 million, and the NAEH at up to 2.3 million (Stronge, 1992a, p. 10). The National Coalition for the Homeless suggested that the yearly homeless population was at least 3 million (Stronge, 1992a, p. 10). So too did Hope and Young (1986).

More recent counts mirror earlier ones. Biggar (2001) writes that in 1996, 1.2 to 2.0 million individuals experienced homelessness (p. 942). Burt (2001) argued that at the turn of the century, the number of homeless exceeded 1% of the total population in the country: "Calculations from different sources show that in the late 1990s at least 2.3 million, and perhaps as many as 3.5 million people experienced homelessness at some time during an average year" (p. 1). The National Law Center on Homelessness and Poverty (2004a) reported that over a given year, the homeless population stood between 2.5 and 3.5 million (p. iii). And the National Association for the Education of Homeless Children and Youth arrived at the 3.5 million figure as well (Tierney et al., 2008, p. 3).

Lifetime

Estimates of homelessness over longer periods of time, even without considering the invisible homeless (i.e., the doubled up), are quite large. For example, Hombs (2001) documents that "the number of adults experiencing homelessness was between 4 and 8 million at some point in the latter half of the 1980s" (p. 63). The National Law Center on Homelessness and Poverty (2004a) put the same five-year estimate at 7 million (p. i). In New York during this five-year period, 3% of the population found themselves homeless at least once (Hombs, 2001, p. 62), a figure similar to the one (3.3%) reported by Culhane and colleagues (cited in Link et al., 1995, p. 353). The number increases to 5% when the nine-year period of 1987 to 1995 is used.

While there are only a few lifetime measures of homelessness, the ones we have are sobering. Based on data compiled by Link and associates (1995), it is suggested that 14% of the U.S. population experiences homelessness at some point in their lives: "When the definition [is] restricted to the literal homeless, lifetime prevalence is 7.4 percent (13 million nationwide)" (p. 349), a number close to the 12 million one provided a decade later by the National Law Center on Homelessness and Poverty (2004a, p. 4) and a percentage consistent with the one (7%–8%) provided by Toro (1998, p. 120) at the turn of the century.

Household Composition

Homelessness now describes a more recent version of very poor people, one that involves single adults, families with children, and homeless youth.
(Hombs, 2001, p. 5)

~⌒⌥⌒~

In later sections of this chapter, we delve deeply into the available data on homeless children and families. Here we simply provide a synopsis of the family composition narrative. We start with data from the 1980s, the initial phase of the modern era of homelessness. According to the Urban Institute Study of 1987, which examined homelessness in cities with populations of more than 100,000, 74% of homeless persons were alone, 18% were families with children, and 8% were childless couples (Jencks, 1994, p. 11). During this same time period, Ropers (1988, p. 29) and Rescorla et al. (1991, p. 210) reported that one-third of the homeless population consisted of families (see also Stefl, 1987). HUD noted that while the majority of homeless persons were still single men (Shlay & Rossi, 1992), 16% of the homeless were now women. Burt (2001), who led the 1987 Urban Institute Study, provides this snapshot of household composition: single men (60.7%), single women (14.9%), adults with children (14.5%), and other men and women (9.9%). Looking specifically at "men," 89% were single, 3% were with children, and 8% were other. Turning to "women," 47% were single, 38% were with children, and 15% were other (Burt, 2001, p. 60).

Slightly more recent data reveal some shifts in household composition. Based on a survey sponsored by the federal government, the National Law Center on Homelessness and Poverty (2004a) suggests that single men now comprise 41% of the homeless population, families with children 40%, single women 14%, and unaccompanied minors 5% (p. 8). Similar numbers were unveiled in the recent HUD (2009) report: About 60% of the homeless population on a specific night in January 2008 were single and 40% were homeless as members of a family (p. 8). The NCFH (2009) recorded single adults at 49% of the total homeless population (p. 2) and the National Coalition for the Homeless (2008) estimates that 51% of the homeless are single men, 30% are families with children, 17% are single women, and 2% are unaccompanied youth (p. 3).

Gender, Age, Race, and Veteran and Marital Status

Not too long ago, a women obviously living on the streets was a rare phenomenon. (Stefl, 1987, p. 56)

Unfortunately, there is an ethnic and racial as well as an economic and emotional aspect to homelessness. . . . In all available data, black families and black youth are overrepresented among the homeless. (Shane, 1996, p. 16)

Researchers who document the gender of homeless individuals affirm that at least in the recent past, the percentage of females in the homeless population was small, 5% or less (Ropers, 1988). During the modern era, however, the homeless population of women has skyrocketed. Indeed, by the mid-1980s, women comprised about 20% of the homeless population (Bassuk, 1984; Kusmer, 2002; Roth et al., 1992). Today, that number is even higher; roughly 30% of the homeless population are women (Toro, 1998).

Analysts also find that homeless persons in shelters and on the streets are younger than they were in the past (Shane, 1996; Shlay & Rossi, 1992). Hope and Young (1986) document a 20-year age change from the 1950s to the 1980s, from the mid-50s to the mid-30s (p. 23; Kusmer, 2002; Roth et al., 1992; Snow & Anderson, 1993), with 65% of the homeless in their late 20s to mid-30s (Ropers, 1988, p. 38).[1]

While there have always been persons of color in shelters and on the streets, today they represent a much more significant segment of the homeless population (Roth et al., 1992; Toro, 1998). More accurately, they are "overrepresented" (Hope & Young, 1986, p. 23): "Both Hispanics and African Americans are disproportionately represented in the overall homeless population" (HUD, 2009, p. 38). Blacks, in particular, are overrepresented—comprising

40% of the homeless population while making up only 11% of the general population (Rollinson & Pardeck, 2006, p. 11). And this "disproportionate representation of Blacks seems to be especially prominent among younger homeless persons" (Hopper & Milburn, 1996, p. 123) and in homeless families (Hopper & Milburn, 1996). Minorities are also, HUD (2009) confirms, "heavy users" (p. 38) of homeless service systems and homeless shelters (Hope & Young, 1986; Hopper & Milburn, 1996).

Snow and Anderson (1993), in their comparative studies, report that in the mid-1980s, minority persons made up 25% of the homeless population (12% black, 12% Hispanic, and 1% other). Bassuk (1984) presents parallel findings, with minorities comprising 23% of the homeless population, up from 10% in the 1950s and 1960s (Ropers, 1988, p. 38). By the mid-2000s, that number had exploded, more than doubling from the mid-1980s and expanding sixfold from the skid row era of the 1950s and 1960s. Burt and colleagues (2001), in their 2001 report, also estimated that minorities made up 60% of the homeless population (p. 58; see also Kusmer, 2002). In an even more recent report, the National Law Center on Homelessness and Poverty (2004b) estimates that only 35% of the homeless population today is white, while African Americans comprise 49%, Hispanics 13%, Native Americans 2%, and Asians 1% (p. 8; also Gargiulo, 2006, p. 358).

Studies of the homeless sometimes furnish data on demographic characteristics such as veteran status and marital status. On the first issue, there is sufficient documentation to conclude that veterans represent an important segment of the homeless population, although there is some variability in the estimates. For example, Hombs (2001) reports that "homeless veterans are widely reported to make up about 30% of the homeless population" (p. 68). Ropers (1988) suggests that approximately half the men in many cities are veterans of U.S. military service (p. 29). In another study, Roth and colleagues (1992) found that one-third of their respondents claimed veteran status (p. 204). And Scolaro and Esbach (2002) peg the veteran homeless population at 25% (p. 2), a figure supported by the work of Toro (1998), who argues that around 25%–30% of the total adult homeless population has military experience (p. 125). Indeed, among homeless men, up to one-half are veterans (Ropers, 1988, p. 39).

Using data from the mid-1980s, Snow and Anderson (1993) showed that only 8% of the homeless population was married; the remaining individuals were single or divorced. During this same era, Bassuk (1992) and Burt and associates (2001) exposed very similar pictures. However, we do learn that "homeless women are more likely to be married or to have been married than homeless men" (Stefl, 1987, pp. 55–56).

Employment, Education, and Income

Although stereotypes of the homeless as bums and hobos still abound, the
available evidence suggests that many homeless persons are unemployed but

actively looking for work. Some of them, the working homeless, are employed full time or part time. (Ropers, 1988, p. 39)

It is no surprise that the homeless in these studies are extremely poor. (Shlay & Rossi, 1992, p. 136)

Counter to prevailing stereotypes, researchers document that some of the homeless population have regular jobs. Coming at the issue from the other side, Medcalf (2008) reminds us that "for many hard work provides no escape" from homelessness (p. 8). Shlay and Rossi (1992), in their review of 60 studies from the 1980s, computed an employment rate of 19% (p. 136; see also Ropers, 1988). Data from the turn of the century show that lawfully employed persons comprised a quarter or more of the homeless population (Scolaro & Esbach, 2002). Newer reports suggest that employment among the homeless may be around 45% (Gargiulo, 2006, p. 358). We should be clear, however, that these numbers do not gainsay the fact that the majority of the homeless are unemployed, many chronically so, and most of the individuals who do have jobs are underemployed or work on the bottom rungs of the labor market ladder.

Studies that investigate the education backgrounds of the homeless conclude that more than half of the population has a high school degree (Gargiulo, 2006; Roth et al., 1992). Up to a third more have some education beyond high school (Ropers, 1988). As expected, older homeless persons are overrepresented in the limited education group, that is, those with less than a high school degree (Ropers, 1988; Roth et al., 1992). So too are homeless women (Roth et al., 1992).

While up to two-thirds of homeless individuals have some source of legitimate income (Roth et al., 1992, p. 206), among almost all these persons, amounts are extremely low. Shlay and Rossi (1992) document annual average income between $1,236 and $2,088 for homeless families (pp. 136–137). Burt (2001), a decade later, reported that "half of all homeless adults receive[d] less than $300 per month in income, putting them at about 30 to 40 percent of the federal poverty level" (p. 3) at the time (see also Burt et al., 2001, pp. 75–77). Data about sources of income reveal that public support is limited for homeless persons (National Law Center on Homelessness and Poverty, 2004b) and that "welfare [is] the most common source of income; earnings are second" (Roth et al., 1992, p. 206).

Time, Location, and Residency Patterns

One of the most interesting findings in many studies, to date, concerns the average length of homelessness. Many, perhaps most, of the homeless are so only for a limited period of time, or they are homeless on an occasional or episodic basis. The situation for homeless is often fluid as they move from shelters to the streets, spend time in SRO hotels or with family and friends. (Peroff, 1987, p. 44)

Homelessness is prevalent in urban, suburban, and rural areas.
(Julianelle, 2007, p. 13)

Time

Over the years, researchers have demonstrated a keen interest in the duration of homeless experiences. Two elements from the "severity" index introduced in Chapter 1 are linked here: the number of incidents of homelessness and the length of time for each homeless experience. Data on both expose "the fluid" (Peroff, 1987, p. 44) and "cyclical nature of homelessness for many" (NAEH, 2003, p. 6). Using point-in-time data, we learn that on any given night, about half of the population will have been homeless for more than a year (Bassuk, Rubin, & Lauriat, 1984, p. 1547; Jencks, 1994, p. 13)—16% between 13 and 24 months, 10% between 25 and 60 months, and 20% more than 5 years (Burt et al., 2001, p. 64). Employing homeless population data across a given year shows that a much smaller percentage of the homeless remain displaced for more than a year, around 12%. Average length of homelessness for shelter and street people (the literal homeless) is estimated to be less than six months (Shlay & Rossi, 1992, p. 141) and probably less than three months (Link et al., 1995, p. 352; Roth et al., 1992; Stefl, 1987), although the average is somewhat higher for stays in shelters (U.S. Conference of Mayors, 2007).

Point-in-time data also reveal that about half of the literal homeless on a given night are experiencing their first episode of homelessness and another one-third have been homeless three or more times (Hombs, 2001, pp. 57–58). Overall, then, the homelessness mosaic reveals a pattern with a hard core group of homeless individuals and a large number of persons who cycle in and out of homelessness for short periods of time (Ropers, 1988).

Location

Scholars also track the location of the homeless: the prevalence of homelessness in different areas such as cities and rural counties, the concentration of the homeless in specific areas of the country, and the stability (or movement) of homeless persons. On the initial issue, researchers offer up two insights. First, to a large extent homelessness remains an urban phenomenon; that is, "the majority of individuals and families experiencing homelessness are located in urban areas" (U.S. Conference of Mayors, 2007, p. 11). An often-cited survey conducted in 1996 found that 71% of the homeless were in central cities, 21% in the suburbs or on the urban fringe, and 9% in rural areas (Rollinson & Pardeck, 2006, p. 13), while "for poor people in general in the United States those figures are 31, 46, and 23 percent, respectively" (Hombs, 2001, p. 57). A more recent survey reported that 75% of the sheltered homeless resided in central cities (U.S. Conference of Mayors, 2007, p. 11), largely because of the presence of a greater range of services for the homeless (Stefl, 1987). We also learn "that the rate of homelessness is higher in larger cities than in smaller cities. Metropolitan areas with 250,000 or more population had a homelessness ratio of around 13 persons for every 10,000 population; in small metropolitan areas (defined as those with populations of 50,000 to 250,000), the ratio dropped by one-half (to 6.5 persons per 10,000)" (Peroff, 1987, p. 42).

Second, while primarily urban, rural homelessness is not an insignificant problem (Kusmer, 2002; Roth et al., 1992). Homeless individuals "are present outside urban areas" (Stefl, 1987, p. 58), although, as we reported earlier, they are often less visible and, therefore, more difficult to find.

> Several types of rural areas generate higher-than-average levels of homelessness. Among these are regions that are primarily agricultural, regions with economies that center on declining extractive industries (such as mining or timber) and that are located in long-standing pockets of poverty, and areas experiencing economic growth. In regions with persistent poverty (such as Appalachia), the young and able-bodied often leave to relocate in urban areas in search of employment. If after several years they return home because they have no work, they may find themselves homeless. Residents in impoverished or primarily agricultural areas may lose their livelihood as a result of changing economic conditions—a lower demand for farm labor because of mechanized and corporate farming, or a shrinking service sector because of declining populations. Finally, many communities alongside major transportation routes receive homeless people literally "off the interstate"—people on the road looking for work, or simply on the move, who have run out of resources. (Aron & Fitchen, 1996, pp. 82–83)

We also discover that the homeless experience is somewhat different in rural areas (Stefl, 1987). Homeless rural persons are "more likely to be married, and less likely to be residing in their county of birth. Persons interviewed in rural counties reported being homeless for a shorter length of time (median of 36.5 days), compared to homeless persons in mixed and urban counties (medians of 65 and 60 days, respectively)" (Stefl, 1987, p. 58). Rural homeless persons are also "more likely to be female and white than [are persons in] the urban homeless group. The rural homeless group also include[s] more young people" (Roth et al., 1992, p. 204).

While there is not an abundance of research on the issue, available studies indicate that "homeless populations vary geographically" (Whitbeck, Hoyt, & Ackley, 1997, p. 389). For example, while popular belief holds that the homeless live primarily in the Northeast and Midwest, "they are actually more concentrated in the West. Almost one-third of all homeless people are found in the West even though only 19% of the country's population lives there" (Peroff, 1987, p. 42).

Those interested in the concentration question also investigate the extent to which homeless persons cluster in defined areas, especially the limited geographical urban area historically known as skid row (Bahr, 1973; Miller, 1982). The answer seems to be that the homeless are becoming less clustered, more dispersed (Brickner, 1985; Jahiel, 1992a; Ropers, 1988): "Since the late 1960s . . . homeless people have become less confined to specific areas" (Bassuk et al., 1984, p. 1546). Thus, according to Ropers (1988), skid row is best defined "as a condition and not a place" (p. 30): "the 'skid row' way of life no longer appears to be confined to a particular geographical area: it is overflowing, and has become a way of life throughout our cities' streets" (p. 35).

Investigators also spend time exploring the stability (mobility) of homeless persons, the extent to which they stay close to their former homes or gravitate to new locales. The best evidence from the modern era of homelessness (post-1980) suggests that the majority of homeless persons are stayers, remaining close to their prehomelessness residence and living in the same area for over a year (Hope & Young, 1986; Stefl, 1987): "Homeless people typically are perceived as highly mobile, but this study does not support that contention. Overall, 40% of our sample had been born in the county in which they were interviewed. Another 24% of the sample had lived in the county of interview for more than 1 year. Only about one-third of those interviewed had moved recently to the county of interview" (Roth et al., 1992, p. 206).

Residency

Finally, a massive amount of attention has been devoted to the residency question: Where do persons without homes reside, or more precisely, where do they sleep at night? The initial cut here is usually made between the literal homeless who reside in shelters and on the streets and the invisible homeless who live doubled up with others or pay to live in cheap hotels and flophouses. Given the studies available to date, three points can be drawn with some accuracy about the doubled-up dimension of the invisible homeless population. First, "it is unclear how many people live in doubled-up housing" (Wright et al., 1998, p. 93). For a variety of reasons, doubled-up individuals are especially difficult to count. Second, not surprisingly, therefore, estimates of doubled-up persons cover a good deal of ground. Shinn and Weitzman (1996) put the number in 1987 at around 3 million, which represented "an increase from 1980 to 1987 of 98% in households with related subfamilies and an increase of 57% in households with unrelated subfamilies (p. 116). Jahiel (1992c), "on the basis of very soft data" (p. 12), suggested that about 7.5 million persons were living doubled up on any given day in 1990 (p. 12). Third, there is a consensus that "there are [at least] as many, if not substantially more, doubled up persons" (Wright et al., 1998, p. 93) as there are literal homeless individuals.[2]

As we reported in Chapter 1, scholars traditionally place those persons who are literal homeless into one of two groups: those living in shelters and those living on the streets, acknowledging a good deal of movement between the two groups, and between these two conditions and being doubled up as well. Roth and associates (1992) reported that at the end of 1980, of the total homeless population, 14% were street people and 57% were shelter people. At the turn of the century, Hombs (2001), examining the "literal homeless" issue, concluded that 31% of this group slept on the streets or in other nonstable venues, while 66% slept in shelters of one kind or another (p. 57). In a 2009 report using point-in-time data from January 2008, HUD estimated that of a total literal homeless population of 664,414, 58.2% were staying in shelters (386,361), while 41.8% were unsheltered (278,053; p. 8), with persons in families being much more likely (72.8%) to be in shelters than individuals (49.3; p. 8).

Scholars further divide sheltered persons by type of shelter. For example, HUD (2009) reported that 77.1% of all sheltered persons in the one-year period from October 2007 through September 2008 stayed in "emergency" shelters only. Another 17.6% stayed in "transitional housing" only. Still another 5.3% stayed in both types of shelters that year (p. D–2). Using point-in-time data, the U.S. Conference of Mayors (2008) estimated that 48% of the homeless were in emergency shelters and another one-third were in transitional housing (p. 16). Again, as we see consistently in this chapter, variability in estimates is a norm in the homeless literature.

❖ FAMILIES WITH CHILDREN AND UNACCOMPANIED YOUTH

For a large number of families in America, there is no such place as home. These are the nation's newest and fastest growing homeless. (Edna McConnell Clark Foundation, 1990, p. 6)

～◠❖◠～

During the 1980s, family homelessness emerged as a major social problem of a magnitude not seen since the Great Depression. (Polakow, 2003, p. 91)

～◠❖◠～

> *The escalating visibility of single mothers with preschool and school-age children living on the streets, in welfare hotels, and in emergency shelters is perhaps the most distinguishing attribute of contemporary homelessness.*
> *(Quint, 1994, p. 11)*

In this section, we delve deeply into homelessness among America's children. This carries us into three overlapping bodies of work: the story of families with children (Group A), the story of unaccompanied youth (Group B), and the story of all homeless minors (Group C; see Figure 3.1).

Figure 3.1   Populations of Interest in Exploring Homelessness of Children and Youth

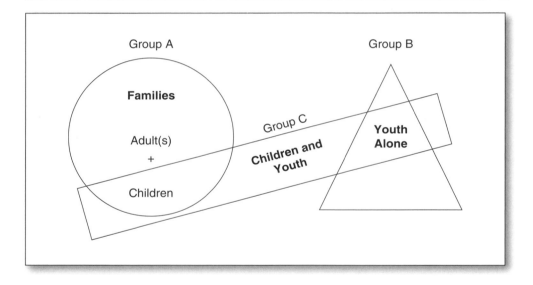

Families With Children

Estimates

According to almost everyone who studies homelessness, families with children represent the fastest-growing category of the homeless (Anooshian, 2005; Merves, 1992; NCFH, 2008, 2009; Popp, 2004; Rubin, Erickson, San Agustin, Clearly, Allen, & Cohen, 1996; Van Ry, 1992): "If asked to describe a 'typical' homeless person, few people would think of a child living with a parent in a shelter for the homeless. Yet perhaps the most alarming change in the homeless population has been the dramatic rise in the number of homeless families with children" (Solarz, 1992, p. 275). While families with children were only a small percentage of the homeless population during the last homeless era (1950–1979; but, as we saw earlier, not during the depression period of the 1930s and 1940s), they are a major story line in the modern homeless narrative. While estimates exhibit some fluctuation, an aggregation of results yields the following approximate trend line: Homeless families grew from almost nothing in the 1950s and 1960s to about 25% of the total homeless population by the 1980s, to about 33% in the 1990s, and to about 40% in the 2000s, with perhaps as much as 50% in the nation's major urban centers (see Better Homes Fund, 1999; Burt et al., 2001; Hicks-Coolick, Burnside-Eaton, & Peters, 2003; NAEH, 2007; Williams, 2003).

We also can discern something about the scope of the family homeless situation by examining requests for services. Kusmer (2002), for example, reports that in a survey of cities in 1993, "43 percent of persons seeking shelter and food at homeless facilities were women and children" (p. 241). Hombs (2001) notes that a decade earlier, "members of homeless families [made] up 34 percent of users" (p. 10). More recent reports arrive at similar numbers, with scholars documenting that families represent between one-third and one-half of persons seeking shelter (Anooshian, 2005; Hallett, 2007; HUD, 2009).

On the numbers front, we again see a good deal of variability. At the end of the 1980s, Nunez (1994a) estimated that there were "600,000 homeless families with roughly 1 million children" (p. 29), with point-in-time estimates between 61,500 and 500,000 (Shane, 1996, p. 15). A decade later, Burt (2001) confirmed that "during a typical year between 900,000 and 1.4 million children are homeless with their families" (p. 1).

Demographics: Adults (Mothers)

The most common demographic features of sheltered family members are that adults are women, children are young, the family identifies itself as belonging to a minority group, and the family has 2 or 3 members. (HUD, 2009, p. 31)

∽◠◦◡∼

Collectively, studies that explore the composition of homeless families with children illuminate three domains: overall composition, the characteristics of the women who nearly universally head these families, and demographics on the children in these families—what Hicks-Coolick and colleagues (2003) call "familial homeless children" (p. 198). Scholars such as Shinn and Weitzman (1996) help us see that "homeless families are more similar to their [poor] housed counterparts than to homeless people outside of family units" (p. 112); that is, "families that are homeless are distinct from individuals who are homeless" (Swick, 2004, p. 117). Analysts also remind us that while a particular demographic footprint is visible here, "homeless families are not all alike" (McChesney, 1992, p. 246).

In terms of structure, homeless families are of three varieties: men alone with children, women alone with children, and couples with children. There is also some information for this last category (i.e., couples) about who heads the family. The first two clusters comprise the "single parent" group. Data on these structural issues show that the average number of adults in a homeless family is 1.2 (Park, Metraux, Broadbar, & Culhane, 2004, p. 428). That is, the dominant form of family homelessness is a single adult with one or more children (Polakow, 2003; Sullivan & Damrosch, 1987). We also know that "family constellations of homeless children consistently show higher percentages of one-parent families . . . than in the general population" (Shane, 1996, p. 17). And studies consistently conclude that the overwhelming majority of single adult homeless families are headed by women; there is a much "greater tendency of women to stay connected and maintain responsibility for children" (Burt et al., 2001, p. 61).

Another way to think about structure is to examine household size. According to the most recent HUD report (2009), size for homeless families breaks out as follows: 2 persons (25.1%), 3 persons (29.5%), 4 persons (21.8%), and 5 or more persons (23.6%; p. 32). The average homeless family is 2.5 persons, an adult and 1.5 children (p. 31; Kidd & Scrimenti, 2004, p. 325). "Homeless families have smaller household sizes than the poverty population in general" (HUD, 2009, p. 32); only 7.7% of poor families have 2 people and 44.9% have more than 5 people (p. 32).

It is also instructive to examine the issue of children in homeless families who do not live with the family. For a variety of reasons (e.g., shelter regulations about age and gender), it is not unusual for only some of the family's children to be with the parent (National Law Center on Homelessness and Poverty, 2004b; Shinn & Weitzman, 1996; U.S. Conference of Mayors, 2004): "Homeless families are not just those where a child is clearly present; about half of all homeless women with children have at least one minor child living away from them. Therefore, from a policy perspective, one must think of homeless families as those where some, or perhaps all, of the children are *not* immediately present with their homeless mother" (Burt et al., 2001, p. 149). Those who are not with the mother most often reside with the other parent (65%), with relatives (21%), in foster care (6%), or some other situation (8%; p. 144). We also know that "children of homeless mothers are much more likely to stay with their homeless parent (54 percent) than are children of homeless fathers (7 percent). Children of homeless fathers typically live with their mothers outside of homelessness" (Burt, 2001, p. 3).

Returning to the gender issue, researchers inform us that 80% or more of homeless families are headed by women (Bassuk, 1992; Better Homes Fund, 1999; Lumsden & Coffey, 2001; Shinn & Weitzman, 1996), 84% according to a recent report from the NCFH (2008, p. 3). HUD (2009, p. 31) reports that 81% of all adults in homeless families (both single adult and dual adult) are women and "the overwhelming majority of homeless parents are single female heads of households" (Hart-Shegos & Associates, 1999, p. 4), "many of whom were homeless themselves as children" (Hart-Shegos & Associates, 1999, p. 2). Finally, we know that the percentage of single female-headed homeless families is considerably higher than the percentage of all poor families headed by single females (Nunez, 1994a).

In general, the women (and men) heading homeless families are young and becoming younger each year (Bassuk, 1992; Mihaly, 1991; Shinn & Weitzman, 1996). Studies show that the average homeless woman with children is in her 20s (Anooshian, 2005; Nunez, 1994a), with an increasing number of children (teens) heading homeless families (Institute for Children and Poverty, 2003). Indeed, "more than ever before, homeless heads-of-household are coming directly from childhood to parenthood on the streets" (Nunez, 1994b, p. 31). In a 2009 report, HUD reported that 54% of adults in homeless families were between the ages of 18 and 30, "a considerably larger number than the 42% of adults in poor families that are young" (p. 32).

The single women who head homeless families also come disproportionately from minority groups (Shinn & Weitzman, 1996; Sullivan & Damrosch, 1987). According to recent data assembled by the National Center on Family Homelessness (2008), 62% of homeless families are "families of color," 43% African American, 15% Hispanic, and 3% Native American (p. 3). These data are consistent with those provided in an earlier document by Burt (2001)—40% to 41% African American, 11% to 12% Hispanic, and 6% to 8% Native American (p. 3)—and Daniels (1995). Researchers also ascertain that "although people of color are disproportionately represented among both poor families and homeless adults, homeless families are even more likely to be from minority groups" (Shinn & Weitzman, 1996, p. 112).

> Many persons in families are minorities, especially African Americans and Hispanics. Less than one-quarter of sheltered persons in families were white and not Hispanic (24 percent). A much higher percentage of sheltered homeless families were African American than of families in the poverty population (51 versus 26 percent), while a lower percentage of sheltered homeless family members were Hispanic or Latino compared to the poverty population (25 versus 31 percent). (HUD, 2009, p. 31)

These young single women who head families tend to be undereducated (Jozefowicz-Simbeni & Israel, 2006; Masten, Sesma, Si-Asar, Lawrence, Miliotis, & Dionne, 1997), but not more so than housed poor peers (Shinn & Weitzman, 1996). In his analysis, Nunez (1994b) documents that nearly two-thirds of these women lacked a high school diploma—53% in the NCFH (2008) study (p. 3). According to Nunez and Collignon (1997), the average single-parent homeless mother "reads at or below the sixth-grade level and [leaves] school by the tenth grade" (p. 57).

Shinn and Weitzman (1996) also document that homeless women have weak job histories. Nunez (1994b) found, for instance, that only "40 percent of all family heads had even six months of employment" (p. 31). The NCFH (2008), in turn, reports that about 30% of adults (women and men) in homeless families are currently working (p. 3).

Demographics: Children

Given the young age of homeless mothers, we should not be surprised to learn that homeless children are very young (HUD, 2009; Kling et al., 1996; Mihaly, 1991). According to the NCFH (2008), "42 percent of children in homeless families are under age six" (p. 3; see also Burt et al., 2001). Infants and toddlers are the norm (Toro, 1998). A recent HUD (2009) report provides the following age breakdown for familial homeless children in shelters and transitional housing, almost all of the literal homeless among families: 51% under age 6, 34% age 6–12, and 15% age 13–17 (p. 32). Kidd and Scrimenti (2004) provide a more detailed partition of children in the lower age brackets: 20% age 0–2, 22% age 3–5, and 20% age 6–8 (p. 330).

Children in homeless families are also disproportionately from minority groups (Mawhinney-Rhoads & Stahler, 2006), again hardly surprising given the data presented earlier on their mothers: 47% are black, non-Hispanic; 13% are Hispanic; and 2% are Native Americans (NCFH, 2009, p. 8). Boys and girls are represented equally among homeless children (Burt, 2001; Hombs, 2001). Also in line with data outlined earlier, there is a disproportionate representation from the lower socioeconomic strata for homeless children from families.

Time, Location, and Residency Patterns

While the data here are less than robust, some information about duration and residency patterns among homeless families is available. We know, for example, that families in general are homeless for shorter periods of time than are single homeless individuals (Burt et al., 2001; Swick, 2004), although they stay longer in shelters than single homeless adults and unaccompanied youth (U.S. Conference of Mayors, 2007). Length of time in shelters is on the rise, from 2–3 months in the 1980s (Bassuk et al., 1986) to 5–6 months today (U.S. Conference of Mayors, 2007), although because of time limits, many families end up shelter-hopping (Kling et al., 1996).

On the residency front, homelessness is often the last stop in a pattern of high mobility for poor families. Bassuk and colleagues (1986) document, for example, that in the mid-1980s, "families had moved an average of 6.6 times (range 2 to 24) in the five years prior to the current homelessness episode, and 3.6 times (range one to 11) in the year before becoming homeless" (p. 1099). Homeless families are also much less likely to be on the street than single homeless individuals (Burt et al., 2001). That is, they are much more likely to be in shelters. And they are "more likely to be living doubled up with another family than staying in a shelter" (Dworsky, 2008, p. 6). They also tend to be more "local" than homeless individuals (Hombs, 2001). At the same time, movement is the norm. Hart-Shegos & Associates (1999) reports, for example, that "the average homeless child moves as many as three times in a year" (p. 7). As was the case with single homeless persons, homeless families are distributed across the country (NAEH, 2007; U.S. Conference of Mayors, 2007) but disproportionately concentrated in the nation's central cities (Burt et al., 2001).

Accompanied Children and Unaccompanied Youth

The numbers provided thus far, regardless of method, indicate that there are extremely large numbers of youth and children who are homeless, and those numbers seem to be increasing. (Kidd & Scrimenti, 2004, p. 331)

The American homeless population is composed of more children than ever before and the numbers are growing. (Stronge & Hudson, 1999, p. 8)

The problem of child homelessness is growing. (NCFH, 2009, p. i)

When we draw all homeless children and youth (both accompanied with parents and unaccompanied) into a single group, a number of points stand out. First of all, we discover that, as was the case with homelessness in general, estimating the number of young persons is not an easy assignment (Better Homes Fund, 1999; Shane, 1996). Second, as a consequence, we are often left with "informed" estimates (Stronge, 2000). Third, even with less than perfect enumerations, it is clear that we face a significant problem— and an expanding one (Cauce et al., 2000; Funkhouser, Riley, Suh, & Lennon, 2002; Markward & Biros, 2001). That is, "the number of homeless children and youth . . . is a large and apparently growing population" (Stronge, 2000, p. 3). Or, as Shane (1996) captures it, "homelessness among children appears epidemic in the United States" (p. 14). Fourth, "homelessness of children and youth is particularly tragic" (Swick, 2004, p. 117).

Data help illuminate the depth of the problem here. According to various studies, children and youth collectively comprise somewhere between 15% and 39% of the total homeless population—15% according to Hombs (2001, p. 63), 20% according to Stronge (1992a, p. 16; also Korinek, Walther-Thomas, & Laycock, 1992, p. 136), 25% according to Cauce and colleagues (2000, p. 230) and the National Law Center on Homelessness and Poverty (1990, p. 1), 27% according to Markward and Biros (2001, p. 183), 26% to

33% according to Tucker (1999, p. 90), and 39% according to Hicks-Coolick and colleagues (2003, p. 197). Employing a different metric, analysts claim that approximately 2% to 3% of American children and youth are homeless in a given year (NCFH, 2009, p. 15; Rouse & Fantuzzo, 2009, p. 10). Alternatively, every year about 1 in every 50 children experiences homelessness (NCFH, 2009, p. i).

Number estimates of homeless children and youth also dot the research landscape. Point-in-time estimates range from 100,000 (James, Smith, & Mann, 1991; Tucker, 1999, p. 90), to 200,000 (NCFH, 2009, p. i), to 273,000 (Quint, 1994, p. 11), to 500,000 (Kozol, 1988, p. 3), to 615,000 (Lumsden & Coffey, 2001, p. 16), to 750,000 (Markward & Biros, 2001, p. 183), to 1 million (Gargiulo, 2006, p. 337), to 1.2 million (Better Homes Fund, 1999, p. 31).

Estimates across time pepper the homeless narrative for minors as well. In 1990, the National Coalition for the Homeless estimated that there were 500,000 to 750,000 homeless children and youth in the United States (cited in Kling et al., 1996, p. 3). The National Law Center on Homelessness and Poverty (1990) put the number at 450,000 (p. 1; see also Rabideau & Toro, 1997; Tierney et al., 2008). Bassuk, Weinreb, Dawson, Perloff, and Buckner (1997) suggested 500,000 (p. 92). For 1997, Nunez and Collignon (1997) pegged children and youth homelessness at more than 1 million (p. 56). In 1995, the U.S. Department of Education reported about 750,000 homeless school-age minors (Tucker, 1999, p. 90). Cauce and colleagues (2000) provide a yearly estimate of between 1 million and 1.3 million (p. 230), and Mawhinney-Rhoads and Stahler (2006, p. 291) and Popp (2004, p. 5) concur, offering estimates between 900,000 and 1.5 million. The Urban Institute Study of 1987 put the yearly figure at 1.35 million homeless minors (Bowman & Barksdale, 2004, p. 2; Medcalf, 2008, p. 10). The most recent report from the NCFH (2009) contends that "more than 1.5 million of our nation's children go to sleep without a home each year" (p. i). Mihaly (1991) chimes in, arguing that "every year perhaps 2 million children live the pain of homelessness" (p. 2).

The Better Homes Fund reports that over half of the 1.2 million homeless on any given night are under the age of 6, and 42% are under the age of 5 (Duffield et al., 2007, p. 7). Kling and colleagues (1996) provide a larger number, concluding from their analysis "that children under five comprise one-half to two-thirds of the population" (p. 3) of homeless minors. Funkhouser and associates (2002) set the 0-to-6 age group at 65% of homeless children and youth (p. 13).

Other accounts reveal that homeless minors are highly concentrated. Fully 75% of homeless children reside in just 11 states (NCFH, 2009, p. 15). We also learn that over 60% of homeless children and youth are from minority groups, with 43% of African American descent (Shane, 1996; Williams, 2003, p. 14).

Residency data are available for homeless minors enrolled in school. For the 2003–2004 academic year, 50.3% of these children and youth were living doubled up, 25.3% were living in shelters, and the remaining 24.4% "were spread among emergency foster care, substandard housing, abandoned buildings and vehicles, motels, the streets, and unknown areas" (National Coalition for the Homeless, 2008, p. 1).

Finally, we know that there are conditions that place children and youth at risk of homelessness. We introduce these factors here, leaving a more in-depth analysis to the second part of the book. First and most important is living in a low-income family (Burt et al., 2001; Toro, 1998). Second is a history of high unemployment in the family (Hagan & McCarthy, 1997). Third is spending time in foster care (Burt et al., 2001). Fourth is living in a household with a history of homelessness (Hart-Shegos & Associates, 1999). Fifth is coming from a household with eight or more individuals (Terrell, 1997). Sixth is being gay or lesbian (Terrell, 1997; Tierney et al., 2008).

Unaccompanied Youth

No matter what estimates are used, it is accepted that homelessness among youth is substantial and widespread throughout the nation. (Moore, 2005b, p. 5)

Findings suggest that youth homelessness is a national phenomenon that is much more common than is generally thought. (Ringwalt, Greene, Robertson, & McPheeters, 1998, p. 1328)

Increasing numbers of homeless youth have become a serious social challenge to policy makers, human service providers, and communities. (Lindsey, Kurtz, Jarvis, Williams, & Nackerud, 2000, p. 116)

General Insights

The study of nonaccompanied youth is a slim but important chapter in the larger volume on homelessness—and given the focus of this volume more critical than its length would suggest. Before we move deeply into the phenomenon, however, we offer some important general insights on adolescent homelessness. First of all, there is a consensus that the problem is becoming more severe (Duffield & Lovell, 2008; Hammer et al., 2002; Rothman, 1991). "The severity of the problem seems striking" (Rothman, 1991, p. 3) and youth homelessness is both significant and increasing in scope (Reganick, 1997; Ringwalt, Greene,

Robertson, & McPheeters, 1998; Rotheram-Borus, Parra, Cantwell, Gwadz, & Murphy, 1996; Russell, 1998): "Although homelessness among adolescents is not a new social problem, over the past several decades it has increased in volume, scope, and visibility" (Powers & Jaklitsch, 1992, p. 117).

Second, we do not know nearly enough about homeless youth (Taylor et al., 2004). This group "remains the most understudied segment of the homeless population" (Whitbeck et al., 1997, p. 375): "Homeless adolescents living on their own comprise a subgroup on which the least research is available" (Moore, 2005b, p. 5). Some of the explanation traces to the fact that unaccompanied adolescents are only a small part of the overall homeless population.

Lack of attention can also be attributed to our third general insight: There is a lack of agreement about the definition of this group of homeless, that is, about who counts. For instance, a variety of perspectives about the appropriate age range for unaccompanied youth are found in the homeless literature (Hagan & McCarthy, 1997; Russell, 1998).

Explanations for lack of a robust knowledge base can also be found in the reality that, even more so than adults, homeless youths are difficult to count and portray (Farrow et al., 1992): "It is very difficult to get a realistic picture of everyday life of an unaccompanied . . . youth" (Moore, 2005b, p. 18); "identifying homeless youth . . . poses special challenges" (Funkhouser et al., 2002, p. 8). Homelessness is even more fluid in this group than among adults (Powers & Jaklitsch, 1993). Because of their small overall number, they are often difficult to locate (McCaskill et al., 1998).

This leads to a fifth general insight: Data on homeless youth are often imprecise (Greene et al., 1997; Powers & Jaklitsch, 1992). "Reliable estimates of homeless youth are scarce" (Whitbeck & Hoyt, 1999, p. 4) and the numbers fluctuate considerably. For example, Wells and Sandhu (1986) maintain the following:

> The definition of "juvenile runaway" can be constructed to render conservative incidence statistics which warrant concern, or liberal ones which warrant alarm. During the mid 1970's, a conservative definition rendered an incidence estimate of 733,000 runaways, while a liberal definition estimated a total of 3,000,000. Such variations aggravate the difficult task of assessing the problem of juvenile flight and the problem of comparing one era to another. (p. 147; see also Chapter 1)

Sixth, given available data, it is reasonable to conclude that, as with homeless adults, the demographics of homeless youth are quite heterogeneous; they represent "a varied and diverse population" (Kipke et al., 1997, p. 415).

Estimates

One way to better understand the size of the homeless youth problem is to nest adolescents in the larger data set on homelessness. A second is to review the estimates of unaccompanied adolescents that have been unearthed over the last quarter century. On the first issue (percentages), a key question is this: "What percentage of the overall homeless population does this subgroup represent?" According to Burt and colleagues (2001), "if one considers a homeless youth to be someone 17 and younger, then they comprise less than 1 percent of the NSHAPC homeless sub-sample. However, if one extends the age range of youth up to 24, as do many service programs targeted toward youth, then 12 percent of the NSHAPC homeless sample falls in this age range" (p. 139). The U.S. Conference of Mayors in 1996 held that "3% of the homeless population was comprised of unaccompanied minors" (Lindsey et al., 2000, p. 116). In their 2002 report, the mayors estimated that homeless youth accounted for 2% of all homeless people (Moore, 2005b, p. 5). By the time of their 2005 report, the number was back to 3% (Tierney et al., 2008, p. 3). Ringwalt, Greene, Robertson, and McPheeters (1998) put the estimate at 5% (p. 1327).

Another approach to the size and scope issue is to consider what percentage of the total youth population is homeless. Early studies from the 1970s provided answers in the 1.7% to 1.9% range (Brennan et al., 1978, p. 14). Sullivan and Knutson (2000), citing data from the late 1990s, found that 2% of the U.S. population under 18 were running away from home each year (p. 1275). According to Klein, Woods, Wilson, Prospero, Greene, and Ringwalt (2000), "in a representative household sample of 6496 adolescents surveyed in 1992 and 1993, 7.6% of youth reported spending at least one night in a youth or adult shelter, a public place, outside or in an abandoned building, underground, or with a stranger, regardless of sociodemographic or geographic factors" (p. 332). Moore (2005b) provides the highest estimate, contending that one in seven or eight youth "under the age of 18 will leave home and become a street person" (p. 9).

Still a third way to discern the scope of the problem is to review the percentage of households that have been touched by adolescent homelessness. An influential study from the 1970s suggested an answer of around 3% (Moore, 2005b, p. 5). A decade later, Janus and associates (1987) provided a similar answer.

When we turn to the second pathway of understanding counts of unaccompanied youth, we find that the seriousness of the problem is confirmed. This approach also underscores the variety of answers to the numbers question provided by researchers over the last 35 years. Information from the Opinion Research Corporation collected in 1976—and discussed by Caton and by Brennan and colleagues—set "the annual incidence of overnight runaway behavior" (Caton, 1986, p. 65) as follows: "502,000 to 613,600 families experienced an overnight runaway episode by one of their children" (Brennan et al., 1978, p. 5). In 1980, the 96th Congress estimated the population of homeless youth between 100,000 and 400,000 (Tower & White, 1989, p. 21), while a Senate subcommittee reported that there were 500,000 homeless youth in the same time period (Janus, McCormack, Burgess, & Hartman, 1987, p. 10). Still another congressional report, this time in 1982, suggested that there were between 250,000 and 500,000 homeless adolescents in the United States (Brickner, 1985, p. 8). The FBI estimated that there were about 1 million juvenile runaways in 1980 (Wells & Sandhu, 1986, p. 147). A 1984 report from the U.S. Department of Health and Human Services (HHS) put the runaway estimate from 730,000 to 1.3 million (Kipke et al., 1997, p. 415; Whitbeck et al., 1997, p. 375) and maintained "that 500,000 of these youth were for all purposes, homeless" (Janus et al., 1987, p. 12). At this same time, Janus and colleagues (1987) provided a larger estimate, arguing that runaways and homeless youth exceeded 2 million annually (p. 12), while the National Network of Runaway and Youth Services, Inc., put the number at 1 million. A 1983 report from Region X of HHS "estimated 1,155,284 runaway and homeless youth annually" (Rothman, 1991, p. 19), while Hersch (1988) reported 1.2 million (p. 31) and Sullivan and Damrosch (1987) estimated 1.2 to 1.3 million (p. 93). Others argued that counts of homeless youth in the mid-1980s might be much higher than these estimates (Powers & Jaklitsch, 1992), perhaps as high as 4 million (Sullivan & Damrosch, 1987, p. 93).

Research from the late 1980s through the early 1990s provides texture to the estimates of youth homelessness. A 1988 study by the U.S. Department of Juvenile Justice "estimated that between three-quarters and one million adolescents were living on the street at any one time" (Lindsey et al., 2000, p. 116). Feitel and colleagues (1992) found that during this time period, between 1 million and 1.3 million unaccompanied youth were living in emergency shelters or on the streets (p. 155). A 1994 HUD report put the number of homeless young people at between 1.3 and 1.6 million (Kurtz et al., 2000, p. 382). Goodman and Berecochea (cited in Pearce, 1995) argued that the homeless fell between 500,000 and 2 million (Pearce, 1995, p. 16), and Hagan and McCarthy (1997, p. 8) and Rotheram-Borus, Parra, et al. (1996, p. 390) put the number at 1.5 million. The National Network of Runaway and Youth Services found that 1.1 million minors ran away in 1992, of whom 300,000 were homeless (Whitbeck & Hoyt, 1999, p. 5), with Robertson and Greenblatt (1992) providing an estimate of homeless youth between 250,000 and 1 million annually (p. 288). Greene and colleagues (1997) suggested a range from 450,000 to 2.8 million (p. 550) in the early 1990s.

More recent reports from the end of the 1990s through the mid-2000s (Hagan & McCarthy, 1997; Julianelle, 2007; Ringwalt, Greene, Robertson, & McPheeters, 1998; Rotheram-Borus, Parra, et al., 1996) are generally in line with suggestions of a homeless youth population in the 1.5 million range, although there is variation in the estimates. Robertson and Toro (cited in Moore, 2005b) set the number at 1.6 million per year (Moore,

2005b, p. 5), a figure in line with the 1.3 million number provided by the National Runaway Switchboard (p. 5). Hammer and colleagues (2002) figure the 1999 youth homeless population at 1,682,900 (p. 5). Perhaps the most accurate position is that across any given year, 1.5 to 2.0 million unaccompanied adolescents are homeless in the United States (Moore, 2007, p. 4).

Demographics

Over the years, a variety of studies have gathered data on the characteristics of unaccompanied youth. In terms of *gender,* Hammer and colleagues (2002) conclude that the adolescent homeless mirror the population of youngsters between the ages of 7 and 17; that is, about half of the homeless adolescents are female (p. 6; see also Caton, 1986). Other studies, however, often find that there are more homeless girls than boys (Moore, 2005b; Pires & Silber, 1991; Rotheram-Borus, 1991)—57% to 43% for Shane (1996) 70% to 30% for McCaskill et al. (1998), 61% to 39% for Greene and colleagues (1999), 54% to 45% for Russell (1998), and 68% to 32% for Boesky and colleagues (1997).

Research also finds that somewhere in the neighborhood of 2% to 5% of homeless girls have children with them (Reeg, Grisham, & Shepard, 2002, p. 4; Shane, 1996, p. 15). Studies also reveal a strong association between gender and residence. More boys than girls are on the street (Hagan & McCarthy, 1997; Moore, 2005b; Whitbeck & Hoyt, 1999) and more girls than boys sleep in shelters (Farrow et al., 1992; Moore, 2007; Russell, 1998). For example, Shane (1996) found that 65% of the homeless adolescents in shelters were female (p. 15). Greene and team (1999) reported a 61% female shelter rate (p. 1408). Whitbeck and Hoyt (1999), in turn, found that "males were about 1.5 times more likely than females to spend time on the streets" (p. 41). Hagan and McCarthy (1997) documented the same pattern, finding that about two-thirds of the homeless street population in their study were male (p. 23; see also Greene et al., 1999, p. 1408).

According to Pearce (1995), the bulk of homeless youth range in *age* from 14–17 (p. 16): "The median age of runaway youth is between 14 and 16 years" (Farrow et al., 1992, p. 719) and youth from 15 to 17 make up over two-thirds of homeless adolescents (Hammer et al., 2002; Rothman, 1991). In their study, Whitbeck and Hoyt (1999) found that "the young people on average first ran at age 13.5 years for both adolescent males and females. Very few ran prior to age 10 years. The majority (80%) had run by 16 years" (p. 39).

Looking at shelter use among homeless youth, Shane (1996) provides the following age portrait: 14 or younger (38%), 15–17 (54%), 18–19 (6%), over 20 (3%). Russell (1998), looking at the same issue, provides the following breakdown by age: 0–9 (0.1%), 10–11 (0.4%), 12–13 (8.7%), 14–15

(39.2%), 16–17 (51.0%), and 18-plus (0.6%; p. 107). Using both shelter and street residence as the basis for classification, Hammer and colleagues (2002) put 4% of the homeless population in the 7–11 age range, 28% in the 12–14 group, and 68% in the 15–17 age bracket (p. 6), conclusions that parallel findings from Boesky et al. (1997).

There is some evidence that sheltered homeless adolescents (16.1) are younger than street-based peers (18.1; Greene et al., 1999, p. 1408). We also know that throwaway youth tend to be older than runaways (Moore, 2007); that is, "the curve for throwaway youth is weighted in the direction of those who are older" (Levine et al., 1986, p. 99). Finally, looking historically, we discover that "homeless youth today are both older and younger" (Pires & Silber, 1991, p. 26) than they were in the premodern era of homelessness (Raleigh-DuRoff, 2004).

When we turn the spotlight on *racial status*, we discover, as was the case with adults, that the percentage of minority homeless adolescents is growing (Biggar, 2001; Pires & Silber, 1991; Zieman & Benson, 1980). In particular, "African-Americans appear to be overrepresented in the adolescent homeless population" (Boesky et al., 1997, p. 29). We also learn that the portraits of homeless youth mirror to some extent the population of the communities in which they are found. Thus, we find considerable variation in ethnicity depending on where studies are conducted (Rotheram-Borus, Parra, et al., 1996; Russell, 1998). National counts from cities suggest that whites comprise about one-third of the unaccompanied young people (Pearce, 1995, p. 16). Finally, there is some evidence that among sheltered youth, African American youngsters are further overrepresented.

Gay, lesbian, and/or bisexual (GLB) adolescents also occupy distinct space in the homeless picture (Gwadz et al., 2009; Pearce, 1995; Woronoff, Estrada, & Sommer, 2006). Julianelle (2007) reports that 3% to 5% of the overall population is GLB (p. 7). Studies of homeless youth, on the other hand, document that about 15% to 25% of homeless adolescents fall into this category (Farrow et al., 1992; Julianelle, 2007; Woronoff et al., 2006). As we show in Chapter 4, part of this condition can be attributed to the fact that these youngsters are "ejected from their homes in response to sexual minority status" (Gwadz et al., 2009, p. 375).

The data on the *socioeconomic status* (SES) of unaccompanied youngsters are less substantial than we would like. Some studies suggest a rough equivalence of youngsters from white-collar and blue-collar homes (Rothman, 1991) and conclude that the prevalence of youth homelessness does "not vary by family poverty [or] family structure" (Ringwalt, Greene, Robertson, & McPheeters, 1998, p. 1328). Other studies turn up different conclusions (Boesky et al., 1997). For example, McCaskill and associates (1998), in a carefully designed study, found that most "homeless adolescents (79.7%) came from neighborhoods with median family incomes under $40,000 and from lower to middle-class families in which parental figures held unskilled or blue-collar jobs (68.8%). Only a small number of the parents had professional backgrounds (3.7%). The majority of home-less adolescents had parents who had completed high school (81.7%), and the parents of many (44.4%) had some college experience" (p. 311). While these data seem to fit with those on minority status presented earlier, clearly more information on the SES issue would be helpful.

Time Homeless and Residency

Data on duration and frequency of homelessness among America's youth are exceptionally thin and often unhelpful. As Ringwalt, Greene, Robertson, and McPheeters (1998) note, additional research in this area is much needed. In one study with a very small sample, Russell (1998) computed the mean of days homeless at 440, noting that 61.7% of youth studied had a lifetime homeless pattern of less than one year, while 38.3% were homeless for more than one year (p. 174). In addition, "current homeless episodes had lasted between 31 and 364 days" (p. 152) at the time of the study. In another investigation, Ensign and Bell (2004) concluded that "the average length of homelessness for clinic-based youth was 4 months (range 1 to 9 months) [while] the average length of homelessness for the street-based youth was 3 years (range 1 month to 8 years)" (p. 1244). That is, homeless youth on the street are more likely to remain homeless. In their study of street youth, Hagan and McCarthy (1997) reported that more than half (56%) of these youngsters had been living away from home for a year or longer and less than 15% had been on the street for less than a month (p. 37).

Hammer and associates (2002) provide startlingly different results. They found that only 7% of runaways were homeless for more than one month and that fully 77% were away from home for less than one week (p. 6), a figure close to the one-week estimate of 66% provided by the Boesky team (1997, p. 30). Equally incongruent data are available about the number of homeless youth who return home, only one-third according to Rotheram-Borus (1991, p. 25) but nearly 100% according to the Hammer team (2002, p. 6).

Research also offers insights into the residency of unaccompanied minors. The weight of the evidence suggests that these homeless persons are not highly mobile (Kipke et al., 1997), generally "staying within a rela-tively short distance of their place of origin" (Auerswald & Eyre, 2002, p. 1508). In his work, for example, Rothman (1991) found that "73 percent [of homeless adolescents] are locals, 11 percent are from out of the county, and 16 percent are from out of the state" (p. 19), figures that match the 75% local number offered by Farrow and colleagues (1992, p. 722). Using better metrics, Levine et al. (1986) document that 63% of youngsters ran away to an area within five miles of their home and 54% remained within their cur-rent school district (p. 100). Hammer and colleagues (2002), in turn, report that 38% of runaways remain in a 10-mile radius and fully 69% stay within 50 miles of their former home (p. 7).

Not much is reported in the literature on the geography of homeless adolescents. Most studies have been completed in urban areas; not surprisingly, therefore, "youth homelessness is most visible in major cities" (Moore, 2005b, p. 7) and "we know very little about homeless adolescents in smaller urban areas" (Whitbeck et al., 1997, p. 376) and in rural areas of the country. Perhaps the most accurate point we can draw at this time is that while youth homelessness is "considered a 'big city' problem" (Myers & Popp, 2003, p. 4), unaccompanied youngsters are to be found across the geographical landscape of the nation. It "is not simply an urban problem" (Ringwalt, Greene, Robertson, & McPheeters, 1998, p. 1325) and we should respond accordingly.

Finally, we examine data on where homeless youth spend their nights. The invisible homeless are doubled up or in temporary care provided by the child welfare system (Julianelle, 2007). The literal homeless, as is the case with adults, are found both in shelters and on the streets (Ennett et al., 1999; Hagan & McCarthy, 1997): "These youth end up in a variety of temporary situations such as an emergency shelter or transitional living programs, living in a car or campground, or staying in a park, abandoned building, train or bus station, under a bridge, or in another public place" (Julianelle, 2007, p. 1). More seem to sleep rough than in shelters (Ringwalt, Greene, Robertson, & McPheeters, 1998): "Abandoned buildings were the sleeping locations of choice when respondents could not afford to pay for a place; the street and emergency shelters were ranked as second and third choices, respectively" (Russell, 1997, p. 152). Older homeless youngsters, males, those homeless for longer periods of time, and those with more psychological problems are most likely to be on the street (Boesky et al., 1997; Ensign & Bell, 2004). Homeless adolescents often demonstrate what Hagan and McCarthy (1997) refer to as a "nomadic roaming pattern" (p. 40):

> Typically, youth arrive on the street, stay outside for a few days—perhaps in parks, all-night restaurants or walking the streets—find shelter with friends in someone's apartment or a squat, move to a hostel, migrate to another hostel, and then begin the sequence again. This was the case for over half (51 percent) of our respondents, who reported that they had used at least three different types of shelter since arriving on the street. (pp. 40–41)

❖ CONCLUSION

In this chapter, we explored the demographics of displaced individuals—both adults and unaccompanied youths—and families. We focused on three issues: the number of homeless, the characteristics of the homeless population, and the duration and residency patterns of the housing displaced.

❖ NOTES

1. Roth and associates (1992) remind us that "age makes a great deal of difference in the characteristics of homeless people and in the types of problems they have" (pp. 210–211).

2. Remember that being doubled up is often a precursor to life on the streets or in shelters (Wright et al., 1998).

PART II

The Effects of Homelessness

4

Impact of Homelessness on Children and Youth

A well-established body of research on childhood homelessness reveals a profound and accumulative negative effect on the development of children. (Hart-Shegos & Associates, 1999, p. 4)

Homelessness has profound long-term consequences for children. (Solarz, 1992, p. 284)

Homelessness is clearly a terrible hazard to children and creates potentially irreversible effects. (Jahiel, 1992a, p. 150)

In this chapter, we address the impacts of homelessness on children (and their families) and youth. In the first part of the chapter, we provide an introduction to the issue of effects. We then turn to the living conditions of the homeless that provide the caldron for many of the damages that befall homeless children and youth. In Part III, we review the states of risk that accompany the living arrangements of the homeless. In the final parts of the chapter, we delve into the physical, emotional, social, and educational impacts of homelessness on America's young people.

❖ A SYNOPSIS OF THE STORY LINE

Homeless toddlers are at risk for environmental hazards, environmentally induced illness, and delays and deviations in development of cognition, language, socialization, and emotions. (Biggar, 2001, p. 947)

Homeless children are not simply at risk; most suffer specific physical, psychological, and emotional damage due to the circumstances that accompany episodes of homelessness. (Hart-Shegos & Associates, 1999, p. 2)

Homeless youth are at risk socially, educationally, physically, and mentally. (Shane, 1996, pp. 223–224)

Starting at the End

We begin by acknowledging that "there are high costs to homelessness" (Polakow, 2003, p. 103), that there are few events that have the power to impact life in negative directions more than homelessness. As Ropers (1988) notes, "of all the possible events that could happen to an individual as a result of social disruption, short of death, homelessness is perhaps the most devastating form of personal and social disorganization" (pp. 88–89). That is, while there are a variety of non-residency-based risk factors (e.g., poverty) that often exercise a negative gravitational pull and undermine success, few are more robust than homelessness. Shane and Shinn and Weitzman describe this reality as follows:

> To be a poor child is one thing, but to be poor and homeless is a thing apart. (Shane, 1996, p. 53)

> Poor children are at greater risk than children who are not poor, and homeless children are at greater risk than other poor children. (Shinn & Weitzman, 1996, p. 119)

We also find that "homelessness is a complex social problem with economic, social, and psychological implications" (Woronoff et al., 2006, p. 36) for individuals and for society more generally. Thus,

> the phrase "situation of homelessness" may have two meanings. It may mean that situation as it is experienced by homeless persons (i.e., what happens to a person who is homeless?) or the situation of homelessness in our society (i.e., what is the significance of homelessness in our social order?). (Jahiel, 1987, p. 99)

Or as Shane (1996) captures it, "homelessness of children and families is destructive to individuals, families, and society" (p. 222).

Third, we confirm that while "there is virtually no aspect of homeless existence that does not aid in the destruction of a person's well being, whatever age, race, or gender" (Shane, 1996, p. 53), it is especially harmful for children (and their mothers) and unaccompanied youth (Hightower, Nathanson, & Wimberly, 1997; Mihaly, 1991; United Way of New York City, 2002)—"Homeless children are in a state of crisis" (Whitman et al., 1990, p. 516):

- As destructive as homelessness [is] to the adult, it [is] found to be even more serious for children. (Van Ry, 1992, p. 63)
- Homelessness is a social problem that is often devastating to families but is especially detrimental to young children. (Gargiulo, 2006, p. 357)
- Of all homeless people, homeless children are the most vulnerable. (Burt et al., 2001, p. 137)
- Experiencing homelessness is traumatic even for adults. These traumatic effects are magnified when they occur during a developmental period when young people may still expect and need caretaking adults. (Whitbeck & Hoyt, 1999, p. 107)

❖ THE LOGIC MODEL

The chronicle of the deleterious effects of homelessness runs as follows (see Figure 4.1). Homelessness (Point 1) opens the door to conditions that often amplify problems already in play in the lives of children and youth (e.g., abuse at the hands of parents/guardians, struggles in school). More expansively, homelessness leads to living conditions (Point 2) that fuel existing problems and power up new ones. Homeless minors generally enter a world of enhanced risks (Point 3). At the same time, they often find themselves enveloped in environments marked by violence that encourage the formation of dysfunctional social relationships. The result is often severe physical and social-emotional problems and failure in school (Point 4). The future for many of these youngsters is bleak, or as Hagan and McCarthy (1997) report, homelessness, especially in its most virulent forms, "does not suggest a promising future" (p. 234) for many of these young persons.

Contextual Notes

How homeless youth experience residential instability often varies.
(Tierney et al., 2008, p. 5)

Figure 4.1 The Homelessness Impact Model

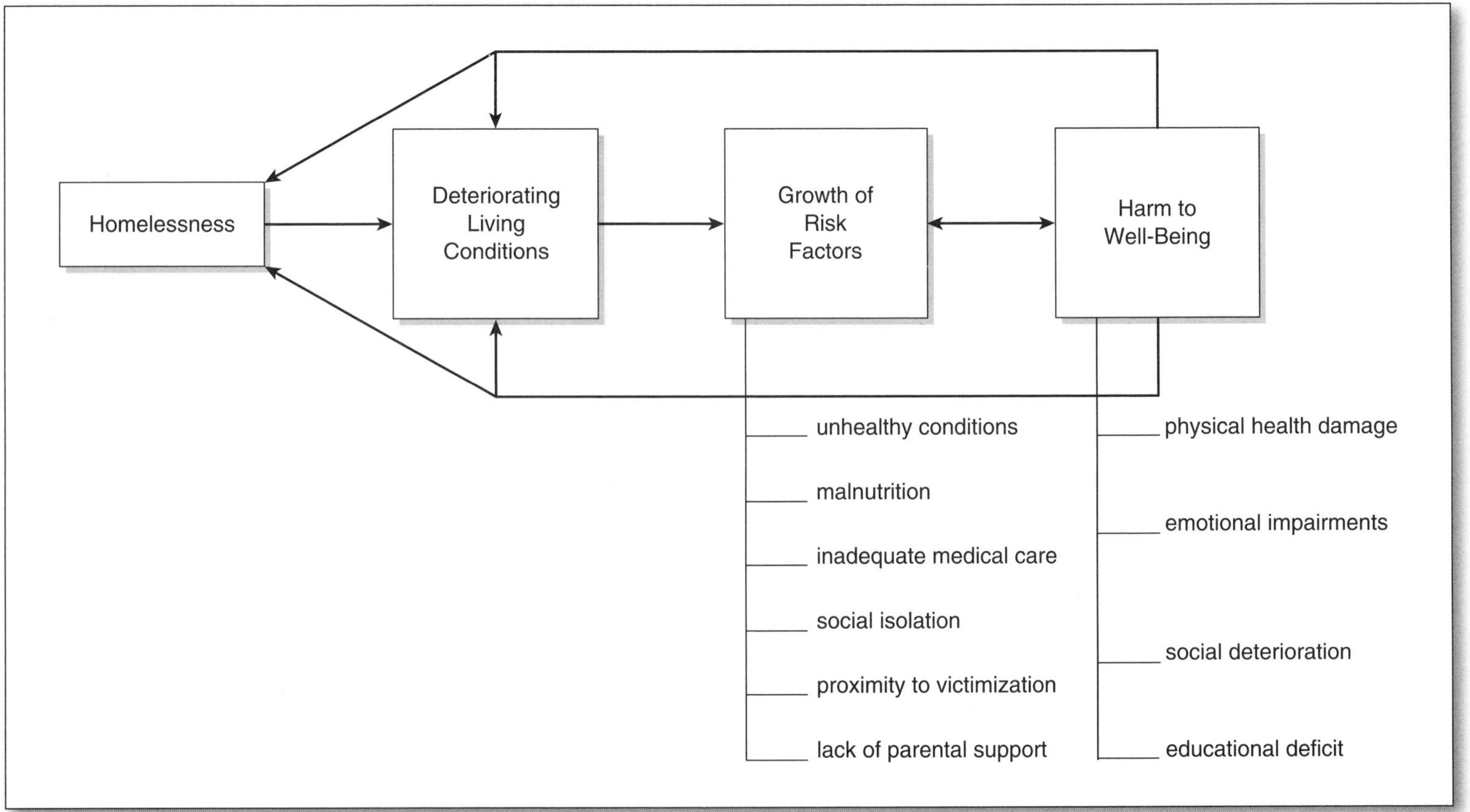

Runaway/throwaway episodes can vary a great deal in their seriousness and dangerousness. (Hammer et al., 2002, p. 3)

～⌒∿⌒～

It is important to anchor our discussion of the impact of homelessness in an acknowledgment of variability, to reinforce the point that homelessness "is a complex, multifaceted phenomenon" (Rothman, 1991, p. 106). We discussed this heterogeneity in detail in Chapters 1 and 3 when we examined the demographics of homelessness. We underscore this key understanding here again, confirming that there is variability in the "impact" of homelessness as well (Jahiel, 1992b).

While homelessness is generally a devastating life event, this is not inevitably the case (Hammer et al., 2002; Shane, 1996): "Homelessness may be benign or malignant. In benign homelessness, homeless individuals incur relatively little hardship. In malignant homelessness, homeless persons incur considerable hardship and damage to the person" (Jahiel, 1992d, p. 6). For example, later in the chapter we describe the normal impact of residential displacement on the educational success of homeless youngsters. We will see that it is a depressing narrative. However, "it is important to note that not all pupils who are homeless manifest academic weaknesses. . . . Many children who are homeless are academically successful" (Gargiulo, 2006, p. 358). Other scholars report that "a percentage of homeless children are not delayed or otherwise especially needy" (Ziesemer & Marcoux, 1992, p. 70). Ziesemer and team (1994), for example, found that about 30% of the homeless students in their study "were perceived by teachers to be functioning within normal range" (p. 663). Relatedly, while most homeless youth are nested in harmful environments, "not all runaway/throwaway youth are at such peril" (Hammer et al., 2002, p. 3). Indeed, some analysts remind us that in the disheartening story of homelessness, we should not lose sight of the strengths of individuals (Jozefowicz-Simbeni & Israel, 2006).

Context has been examined, or at least acknowledged, around a series of homelessness issues. One line of work, for example, holds that the problems of homeless adolescents are different in some important ways from those of homeless adults (Robertson, M. J., 1992; Robertson, J., 1990) and from those of homeless children in families (McCaskill et al., 1998). Other scholars urge caution in developing generalizations, explaining that there are differences even within specific dimensions of homelessness (e.g., youth). For example, Kipke and colleagues (1997) reveal that the homeless adolescent category is comprised of an assortment of different subgroups (e.g., druggies, loners) and that group affiliation shapes the effect of homelessness to some extent. Impact is also influenced by family context, especially past relationships and behaviors. For example, adolescents from abusive family environments are more likely than those from nonabusive families to (1) associate with deviant peers (Bao, Whitbeck, & Hoyt, 2000; Penuel & Davey, 2000; Whitbeck & Hoyt, 1999), (2) spend time living on the street (Whitbeck & Hoyt, 1999), (3) be victimized on the street (Terrell, 1997; Whitbeck et al., 1997), and (4) engage in deviant survival strategies (Penuel & Davey, 2000; Whitbeck & Hoyt, 1999).

Other analysts document variations in the effects of homelessness based on the following:

1. The length of time and frequency of incidences of homelessness (Moore, 2007), for example,

   The longer youths [have] been without a fixed address the greater their involvement in robbery and total violent crime in general. (Baron & Hartnagel, 1998, p. 179)

2. The percentage of time homeless that is unsupervised (Whitbeck et al., 1997), for example,

   The longer the adolescent is unsupervised . . . the greater the likelihood of serious victimization. (p. 386)

3. The age at the onset of homelessness (Whitbeck & Hoyt, 1999), for example,

   Research describing the impact on school-aged children has shown that the effect of housing status increases with age. (Bassuk, Weinreb, et al., 1997, p. 100)

4. The geographical region (Auerswald & Eyre, 2002).

5. Sexual orientation (NCFH, 2009), for example,

   Unaccompanied GLBTQ12-S youth are seven times more likely to be victims of a violent crime. (p. 2)

6. Past victimization (Whitbeck et al., 1997).

7. Gender (Janus et al., 1987).

8. Age, for example,

   Older homeless adolescents reported a higher rate of drug abuse/dependency. (Boesky et al., 1997, p. 31)

9. Resources at the disposal of the homeless person (Whitbeck et al., 1997).

10. "Residency" (Jahiel, 1992b), for example,

    Persons least likely to sleep in emergency shelters have the worst mental health, abuse drugs and alcohol the most, and are the most involved in criminal activities. (Johnson, 1988, p. 40)

    More people staying on the streets or in shelters reported health problems than did those in hotels, in motels, or doubled up; those who had spent the previous night in the street reported more chronic conditions than did those who had slept in shelters. (Jahiel, 1992a, p. 145)

11. Historical period, for example,

Compared to homeless youth in 1975, today's homeless youth experience more problems. (Rotheram-Borus, 1991, p. 25)

Two other issues regularly receive attention in the homelessness literature. One of these is the topic of cause versus impact of homelessness (Levinson, 1963). For example, does substance abuse lead to homelessness, or is it an outcome? "To what extent [do] these conditions and high-risk behaviors predict the onset of homelessness or [are] they developed and continue to escalate with the course of homelessness?" (Kipke et al., 1997, p. 424). We have explored this issue elsewhere in this volume and will not repeat that analysis here, except to say that it is an exceptionally difficult question to untangle and often the answer is yes to both.

A second question has to do with the extent to which homelessness does or does not add to the negative effects that occur because of deep poverty and high mobility (Rouse & Fantuzzo, 2009), "whether results are related to homelessness or poverty in general": (Douglass, 1996, p. 744)—to what extent is the "homeless experience in adolescence [and childhood] an important risk factor in its own right" (McCaskill et al., 1998, p. 316). Part of the difficulty in addressing the question is that "few studies have examined the difference between economically disadvantaged, housed children and children who have experienced homelessness" (Toro, 1998; Ziesemer et al., 1994, p. 659). Given this limitation, here is what we know. The consensus is that the shared space between poverty and homelessness is considerable. Poor young people, especially highly mobile ones, suffer from many of the problems that characterize homeless children and youth (Rescorla et al., 1991; Toro, 1998). There is also a growing sense that homelessness contributes unique power to the negative impact algorithm, beyond that attributable to poverty (Masten et al., 1997). That is, "homelessness relates to problems above and beyond those of poverty" (Biggar, 2001, p. 943) or "the experience of homelessness exacerbates the experience of poverty" (Hicks-Coolick et al., 2003, p. 199):

While the impact of homelessness cannot be separated from poverty, homelessness is a life event having traumatic effects beyond poverty. (Schmitz et al., 2001, p. 69)

Rates of most current and childhood problems are significantly higher for people who are or have been homeless than for people who have not, but still are poor enough to need programs such as soup kitchens. (Burt et al., 2001, p. 95)

The effect of chronic poverty on homeless children is even more devastating than poverty alone, because the effects of multiple simultaneous stresses have a stronger negative effect than the sum of individual stresses. (Ziesemer et al., 1994, p. 659)

❖ LIVING CONDITIONS AS MEDIATORS OF RISK

A homeless existence is characterized by demeaning environments.
(Morse, 1992, p. 4)

⤳〇⸙〇⤝

The homeless environment is generally brutal, demoralizing, and stigmatizing. (Jahiel, 1992d, p. 7)

⤳〇⸙〇⤝

Unstable living situations increase the likelihood of experiencing physical and emotional health problems as well as learning difficulties.
(National Center for Homeless Education, 2006a, p. 1)

⤳〇⸙〇⤝

Unstable living situations contribute enormously to the developmental delays and psychological problems often noted among homeless children.
(United Way of New York City, 2002, p. 17)

⤳〇⸙〇⤝

So far in this chapter, we have provided a general conclusion, the fact that homelessness is often toxic to the physical, emotional, social, and educational well-being of children and youth, as well as some cautions about interpreting this conclusion. Two sections hence we begin examining the final impacts of homelessness in considerable detail (Point 4 in the impact model in Figure 4.1). Before we do, however, we turn the analytic spotlight on the living conditions that accompany homelessness (Point 2), conditions that are both an impact of residential displacement and mediators of additional risks (Point 3). We note that these hazards often mirror those found in families on the cusp of homelessness (Hyde, 2005); that is, risks are amplified by homelessness (Cauce et al., 2000).

The first half of the living condition narrative argues that housing "is essential to people's well-being and sense of self because without shelter people face physiological and psychological harm" (Leavitt, 1992, p. 20). Housing, it is held, is essential "to the success of other facets of life such as employment, schooling, nutrition, and health" (Crowley, 2003, p. 23; see also Jahiel, 1992d).

The second half of the living condition story is that "homeless people lack the protective functioning of a home" (Jahiel, 1992a, p. 148). This fact generally means envelopment in living "environments rife with violence and unhygienic conditions" (Jahiel, 1992d, p. 6), what Kurtz and team

(2000) refer to as "high risk situations" (p. 383) in which children and youth "have few stable social supports, experience non-normative life events, and face multiple problems" (p. 383): "The physical and social environment [they experience] is harmful to homeless people" (Jahiel, 1992a, p. 159); it includes "agents" (p. 151; infectious agents, toxins) that result in a host of negative consequences. Indeed, the literature is quite clear on the mediating effects of living conditions: Many of the problems "exhibited by homeless and runaway youth [and accompanied children] are associated with the environments in which they must live" (Feitel et al., 1992, p. 159) and the risks that are found in those environments. As we see later in some detail, analysts find that homeless shelters often provide living arrangements that negatively impact homeless children and youth (Julianelle, 2007; Ziesemer & Marcoux, 1992). The streets generally provide even more demeaning and damaging living conditions. There we see that exposure to the elements leads to a plethora of negative effects for children and youth. As Janus and team (1987) dramatically conclude, "Today, the children and adolescents who attempt to find sanctuary on the streets are tomorrow's statistics on death, mental illness, or criminal behavior" (p. 121).

The loss of residence, in turn, leads to overarching conditions such as stress (Bassuk, Weinreb, et al., 1997; Nichols & Gault, 2003; Reganick, 1997; Rotheram-Borus, Parra, Cantwell, Gwadz, & Murphy, 1996), instability (Aviles & Helfrich, 1991; Lumsden & Coffey, 2001; Shinn & Weitzman, 1996), and uncertainty (Better Homes Fund, 1999; Bowman & Barksdale, 2004; Kling et al., 1996), conditions that act as catalysts for physical, emotional, social, and educational problems to develop (Hope & Young, 1986; Rotheram-Borus, 1991):

> The instability and chaotic nature of homelessness can have profound effects on a child's physical health, psychological development, and academic achievement. (Moore, 2005a, p. 5)

> Without a stable living environment children are subject to many forms of stress that can impair their mental and emotional health. (United Way of New York City, 2002, p. 16)

The next chapter in our story on living arrangements—after the chapters on loss of residential protections and the resulting stress—features the loss of the following: (1) personal space (Eddowes & Butcher, 2000) and privacy (Tower, 1992)—and resulting "placelessness" (Penuel & Davey, 1998, p. 6); (2) established relationships (Eddowes & Butcher, 2000), what Jahiel (1992a) calls "diminished formal and informal support networks" (p. 156); (3) health care (Bassuk, 1984; Korinek et al., 1992); (4) educational opportunities (Hope & Young, 1986); (5) personal possessions (Kling et al., 1996); (6) adequate food (Jahiel, 1987; Korinek et al., 1992); (7) "safe space necessary for physical play and motor development" (Eddowes & Butcher, 2000, p. 26); and (8) sleep (Jahiel, 1987). And in our causal chronicle of the spiraling and overlapping effects of homelessness, we argue that it is this "environmental deprivation" (Reganick, 1997, p. 133) that exposes children and youth to states of risk (Point 3 in the impact model in Figure 4.1): "Virtually all risk conditions known to have negative effects on children appear to be present during homelessness" (Anooshian, 2005, p. 140). These risk conditions, in turn, foster the critical problems that accompany homelessness, such as poor health and educational failure (Point 4 in the impact model) that we discuss in the final sections of this chapter.

❖ STATES OF RISK AS PRECURSORS TO FINAL IMPACTS

The bad physical environment in which they are sheltered often further compromises homeless children and their parents. (Mihaly, 1991, p. 4)

The physical conditions . . . render homeless vulnerable to a number of significant and chronic health problems. (Rollinson & Pardeck, 2006, p. 12)

Homelessness represents a serious at-risk condition for youth. (Rew, 1996, p. 351)

Homelessness puts them directly in the path of disease. (Hersch, 1988, p. 35)

Continuing through the storyboard, we find that the oftentimes toxic living conditions that result from homelessness create, in turn, states of risk for homeless children and youth. These states of risk then lead directly to the negative impacts we examine in the final parts of the chapter. Here the focus is on the third point in the model, the states of risk that flow from the living conditions (Point 2) and that act as precursors to the negative outcomes of homelessness (Point 4). We discuss six risk factors: unhealthy conditions, hunger and poor nutrition (malnutrition), inadequate medical care, social isolation, proximity to victimization, and lack of parental support.

Unhealthy Conditions

Several features of the homeless environment and of the life of homeless persons contribute to a greater frequency of certain medical conditions among homeless persons than among the general population. (Jahiel, 1987, p. 109)

Homelessness also exposes infants to environmental factors that can endanger their health. (Hart-Shegos & Associates, 1999, p. 2)

Probably most hazardous for homeless youth, and the homeless in general, are unstable and often unsanitary living conditions. (Shane, 1996, p. 41)

Living circumstances of the homeless often result in a variety of unhealthy conditions. According to analysts, homeless children and youth in shelters and on the street face a barrage of situations that, in turn, can impact health. Chief among these are "unhygienic living situations" (Gargiulo, 2006, p. 358) in general (Hagan & McCarthy, 1997; Molnar et al., 1990) or "an overall unhealthy lifestyle" (Karabanow, 2004, p. 64). More specifically, reviewers highlight conditions such as the following: exposure to the elements (Jahiel, 1992a; Shinn & Weitzman, 1996); "exposure to smoke and other environmental allergens" (Better Homes Fund, 1999, p. 4); "inadequate sanitary facilities" (Shinn & Weitzman, 1996, p. 119) that "increase risk of disease and make it nearly impossible to follow prescribed medical regiments" (Solarz, 1992, p. 279); "exposure to extremes of heat and cold" (Brickner, 1985, p. 3; Jahiel, 1987); "unsuitable" (Rafferty, 1995, p. 55) and "inadequate sleeping arrangements" (Johnson, 1992, p. 155), including "the inability to find a place to rest lying down" (Jahiel, 1987, p. 109), that aggravate "peripheral circulation" (Greenblatt, 1992, p. 51); exposure to health hazards such as lead (Jackson, 2004); untreated metabolic conditions (Jahiel, 1992a); lack of security (Jahiel, 1987); a heightened propensity for accidents (Jahiel, 1992d); the presence of rodents (Biggar, 2001); and "shared living and bathing quarters" (Johnson, 1992, p. 155).

Hunger and Poor Nutrition (Malnutrition)

Homelessness and hunger are inextricably interwoven. (NCFH, 2009, p. 17)

Homeless children typically experience hunger and poor nutrition. (Biggar, 2001, p. 950)

Malnutrition is another curse of the homeless child. (Tower & White, 1989, p. 19)

Related to the general category of "unhealthy conditions" but meriting special attention is the risk factor of malnutrition—hunger coupled with inadequate nutrients. We begin with a return to the impact model of homelessness in Figure 4.1. Earlier, we reported that hunger and poverty are closely linked. Here, we see that hunger also results from living conditions in which the homeless find themselves. For example, in certain types of shelters, especially motels and hotels, food is simply unavailable (Better Homes Fund, 1999). In these environments, "the homeless lack access to cooking facilities" (Hightower et al., 1997, p. 19) and there is no legal way to prepare meals (Johnson, 1992). As a consequence, "families are forced to cook on illegal hot plates, eat at fast-food restaurants, and/or subsist on junk food" (Molnar et al., 1990, pp. 110–111). Shelters that do serve food have their own problems; for example, most serve only a limited number of meals each day (Johnson, 1992). In addition, "the rigid content and schedule of meals in most shelters and soup kitchens" (Mihaly, 1991, p. 5) mean that "food is usually served at strictly scheduled times that can easily be missed when a mother is searching for housing or employment" (Better Homes Fund, 1999, p. 7). Under these circumstances, the special dietary needs of children often cannot be met. On the streets, homeless families face similar if not more bleak conditions.

For all homeless people, even when they secure food, "unbalanced diet may be a problem" (Jahiel, 1987, p. 111); that is, "they eat poorly when they do [eat]" (Shlay & Rossi, 1992, p. 139). For example, the nutritional limitations of relying on fast-food restaurants are well documented (Molnar et al., 1990). At the same time, soup kitchens, shelters, and other types of "feeding stations offer what food they receive. The food is often high in salt (detrimental to persons with hypertensions or heart failure), high in carbohydrates (contraindicated for diabetics), or low in proteins, iron, and vitamins (suboptimal for pregnant women, infants, persons with anemia, or undernourished persons" (Jahiel, 1987, p. 111).

We also want to reintroduce a point made in the introduction to this chapter (see *Contextual Notes*). That is, as is the case with most of the risk factors we examine, hunger and poor nutrition are conditions that define homeless families with children and unaccompanied youth more than poor but housed children and adolescents (Burt et al., 2001; Solarz, 1992):

> For food insecurity and hunger, we are able to compare homeless people in NSHAPC to all households in the United States in 1995 with incomes below the federal poverty level. The comparison shows that homeless people in every subgroup are very much more likely to experience hunger and food insecurity. (Burt et al., 2001, p. 80)

Many analysts review the story of malnutrition among America's homeless children (and their families) and youth. They confirm that in the face of all available supports (e.g., food stamps, meal programs at school), "many homeless children do not get the nutritional balance necessary for healthy growth" (Eddowes & Butcher, 2000, p. 24); they have "inadequate food sources" (Russell, 1998, p. 17). These homeless children and youth are hungry and malnourished (Bassuk et al., 1986; MacLean et al., 1999;

NCFH, 2009). "They often go without food" (Shlay & Rossi, 1992, p. 139) and are, therefore, at risk of physical, social, emotional, and educational harm (Hart-Shegos & Associates, 1999). More fine-grained analyses are threaded throughout the research. Various reviews of scholarship and original investigations report "that the average homeless person [eats] less than two meals per day and frequently [does] not eat for entire days" (Shlay & Rossi, 1992, p. 139). Link and colleagues (1995), studying the literal homeless, found that "60.9% reported not having enough food when they were homeless" (p. 352). The National Law Center on Homelessness and Poverty (2004a) documents that "40% of homeless clients had gone a full day without eating within the last 30 days" (p. 10).

The data on this "leading problem among homeless children" (Hightower et al., 1997, p. 19) parallel those for the general homeless population. For example, Burt and team (2001) reveal that 40% of homeless women with children reported that they "had gone at least one day without eating because they did not have the money to obtain food" (p. 84). The NCFH (2009) documents that "children without homes are twice as likely to experience hunger as other children. Two-thirds worry they won't have enough to eat. More than one-third of homeless children report being forced to skip meals" (p. i). And Wood (cited in Mihaly, 1991) provides the following data on children's hunger:

> When asked about their children's nutrition, 23 percent of the homeless parents interviewed by Wood in Los Angeles responded that there were often times when their children were hungry but there was not enough food to give them. This compared with 4 percent of the housed poor parents. In addition, 21 percent of the homeless mothers and 7 percent of the other poor mothers responded that there had been at least four days in the previous month when their children did not get enough to eat because the family simply did not have enough money. (p. 5)

Statistics on the malnutrition risk factor for homeless youth simply deepen the narrative of food insecurity, hunger, and poor nutrition. Russell (1998) documents that 57% of the adolescents in her study "reported that they had experienced one or more days with nothing to eat" (p. 113) in the past 30 days (see also Rotheram-Borus, Parra, Cantwell, Gwadz, & Murphy, 1996; Whitbeck & Hoyt, 1999). Half also noted that food was usually or sometimes difficult to obtain since becoming homeless. In a review on homeless adolescents, Rotheram-Borus (1991) reported that 8% of youth had not eaten in the last 24 hours (p. 25). And Hagan and McCarthy (1997), in their study on adolescents on the street, document that "notwithstanding the provisions available in hostels and foodbanks, finding food is a recurrent problem. Most of the youth (76 percent) indicated that on at least one occasion they had gone an entire day without eating; moreover, more than half of the youth (55 percent) said they frequently went hungry" (p. 49).

Returning to the impact model of homelessness in Figure 4.1, we remind ourselves that malnutrition is an intermediate effect. It is a risk factor that helps grow the physical, emotional, social, and educational problems that befall children (and their families) and youth (Molnar et al., 1990). Or as Shane (1996) so nicely puts it, "nutritional deficiencies set the stage for future trouble" (p. 45): "Poor nutrition may interfere with growth, while hunger may distract the child from efforts to learn" (Jahiel, 1987, p. 111). We take up these issues in the last sections of the chapter.

Inadequate Medical Care

Lack of a permanent place to live makes access to regular health care difficult. (Molnar et al., 1990, p. 113)

Homeless families often have little access to health care. (Hart-Shegos & Associates, 1999, p. 2)

Children growing up homeless today tend to suffer from more than just a lack of housing. Inadequate health care is one of the most obvious problems. (Nunez, 1994b, p. 33)

Another major hazard for unaccompanied youth is the lack or unavailability of health care. . . . Being homeless, particularly as an unaccompanied child, means one is essentially outside the health care system. (Shane, 1996, p. 42)

"Inadequate medical care" (Hightower et al., 1997, p. 18) is another risk factor related to "unhealthy conditions" that merits special attention. According to those who investigate this topic, "inconsistent or inadequate health care" (Reed-Victor, Popp, & Myers, 2003, p. 1) is a significant "risk associated with experiencing homelessness" (Reed-Victor et al., 2003, p. 1) in general. They also show that "insufficient access to health services" (Jahiel, 1992a, p. 139) is a major risk condition for the subgroups of interest in this volume: homeless families (mothers) with children and youth.

On the family front, Shane (1996) contends that "homeless children are among the most vulnerable populations in society" (p. 41) and that "lack of health care increases [that] vulnerability" (p. 41). "Homeless children have poor access to both medical and dental care" (NCFH, 2009, p. 19) and this "inadequate medical care is among the most serious problems facing homeless children" (Hightower et al., 1997, p. 18). The Better Homes Fund (1999) reports that "almost one-quarter of homeless mothers can't get timely medical care for their children because no services are available or because they are unable to take advantage of services that are available" (p. 7).

Turning to adolescents, analysts conclude that "homeless youth are [also] characterized as having inadequate access to primary health care" (Barry et al., 2002, p. 146; Bass, 1995; Duffield et al., 2007), that "significant numbers of homeless youth do not have a regular source of health care" (Klein et al., 2000, p. 331). Whitbeck and Hoyt (1999) put this issue in its starkest form when they exclaim that "access to health care essentially ends while adolescents are on the street" (p. 78). Two notes are of importance here. First, not all youth are at risk on the health care variable (Klein et al., 2000). Second, the type of living arrangement makes a difference. Sheltered youth have more access to care than do adolescents on the street (Ensign & Bell, 2004; Whitbeck & Hoyt, 1999).

Scholars also do a thorough job in exposing the barriers to health care for children (and their families) and unaccompanied minors. Central to the story at this point is the absence of the key to the medical services portal, health insurance. While the numbers bounce around somewhat across studies, the trend line on the health insurance issue is easy to grasp. The 1996 National Survey of Homeless Assistance Providers and Clients (cited in Rollinson & Pardeck, 2006) reveals that 55% of the homeless population at the time had no health insurance (p. 13). Ropers (1988), in turn, reports that 78% of the homeless in his study indicated that they lacked health insurance (p. 51). Jahiel (1992a) pegs the percentage of uninsured homeless at 74 (p. 152).

Turning to families, Mihaly (1991) reviews a Chicago study in which 27% (p. 4) lacked insurance. Solarz (1992) cites a Washington State study that found 35% of homeless children without insurance (p. 279). Russell (1998) reports that 66% of homeless adolescents were without health insurance (p. 182).

Other "formidable barriers to comprehensive health care" (Farrow et al., 1992, p. 722), or explanations for inadequate health care, can, according to Jahiel (1987, 1992a), be divided into internal and external factors. He maintains that

> external barriers include unavailability of transportation to health facilities, refusal by facilities to accept homeless persons who are not covered by Medicaid or other source of payment, time consuming referrals to facilities of last resort, and inability of staff to communicate effectively with homeless patients. (1987, p. 110)

while

> internal barriers include reluctance of homeless persons to expose themselves to inspection by others, fears that their possessions will

be stolen when they are in the hospital, distrust of medical personnel, or a desire to die. (1987, p. 110)

Shining the spotlight directly on homeless adolescents, scholars offer the following explanations for their poor access to health care services:

Homeless youth have greater problems with access to care than do their nonhomeless peers, including a more profound lack of insurance/payment source, greater anxiety over the confidentiality, and more confusion over their ability to consent for care. (Ensign & Bell, 2004, p. 240)

Youths' distrust of authority, along with issues of confidentiality, cost, and their status as minors, may dissuade them from accessing medical care. Transportation is often a problem, but once they get there, the majority of those under 18 say the major obstacle is being hassled about their ability to consent for care. Many others refuse treatment for fear their parents or social services will be contacted. In addition, even though a large majority are in or near their hometowns, most are not familiar with local health care resources. (Moore, 2005b, p. 12)

Several research accounts reveal that street youth are regularly "turned away" from doctors' offices and emergency hospital units because they lack identification (especially health cards) and a permanent address. Other barriers to access to health services for street youth include: extensive waiting times; the requirement of advanced booking; the fear that parental permission will be necessary (especially for minors); a sense that care facilities do not address their medical needs; a lack of familiarity with local health care resources; mistrust of adults/professionals due to past negative experiences; reluctance to use services outside core street youth area; and, a perceived lack of sensitivity and respect, prejudice and discrimination from health care professionals for being a "street kid." (Karabanow, 2004, p. 72)

Inadequate health care means that homeless young persons do not receive the medical care they require to stay healthy: "Primary and preventive care, which keep children [and youth] healthy, are largely absent" (NCFH, 2009, p. 20). Two dimensions of this absence of care blanket the literature on homeless children: lack of prenatal care for mothers and immunizations for babies and young children. According to analysts such as Shane (1996), "adequate prenatal care is generally unavailable for homeless women. They also often lack adequate professional help when giving birth and within the crucial days thereafter" (p. 42): "Regular prenatal care [is] key to a healthy pregnancy but [is] very difficult for homeless women to obtain or maintain" (Mihaly, 1991, p. 4). Chaukin (cited in Mihaly, 1991) "found that 40 percent of the homeless women in New York City had received no prenatal care at all before the birth of their children, a rate three times higher than among housed but poor women, four times higher than the city as a whole, and almost 20 times higher than the national average" (p. 4). In a separate study in New York City, Nunez (1994b) pegged the number of homeless mothers not receiving prenatal care at 33% (p. 33).

On the second issue, "widespread low immunization levels among homeless children" (Jahiel, 1992a, p. 150), reviewers discover that because "immunization is apt to be almost impossible under homeless situations" (Shane, 1996, p. 43), displaced children "are underimmunized or not immunized at all" (Reganick, 1997, p. 133; see also Jahiel, 1992a; Molnar et al., 1990). For example, Mihaly (1991, citing a study by Alperstein) informs us "that homeless children in New York were three times more likely than their housed poor counterparts to be behind in their immunizations" (p. 5). Overall, research indicates that between a quarter and a third of all homeless children are missing essential immunizations (Hart-Shegos & Associates, 1999, p. 5; Ziesemer et al., 1994, p. 665).

Inadequate health care also means "much higher rates of emergency room use by homeless children than for children in general" (Solarz, 1992, p. 280). And this finding holds for homeless mothers and for unaccompanied youth as well (Barry et al., 2002; Ensign & Bell, 2004; Karabanow, 2004; NCFH, 2009).

Finally, inadequate health care, as we report in detail later, means more physical and mental health-related problems for homeless children and youth and more severe and extensive problems (Rew, 1996; Rotheram-Borus, 1991), as well as an assortment of school-related difficulties. In short, "such deprivation negatively affects children's academic, social, emotional, [and physical] well-being, as well as their long-term economic outcomes" (Kozol, cited in Medcalf, 2008, pp. 9–10).

Social Isolation

Homelessness typically involves a constellation of problems, [including] social isolation and the absence of a supportive social network. (Morse, 1992, pp. 4–5)

~◦✢◦~

Social isolation (of mothers, families, and children) [is] a particularly destructive consequence of . . . homelessness. (Anooshian, 2005, p. 137)

~◦✢◦~

Homeless children endure a lack of sustaining relationships and a sense of community. (NCFH, 2009, p. i)

~◦✢◦~

A thick line of analysis informs us that homeless persons are often pushed and pulled into a "sociological context" (Kidd & Scrimenti, 2004, p. 326) in which they are largely alone (Gibbs, 2004; Hagan & McCarthy, 1997; NCFH, 2009), isolated and with little access to the social supports that could help attenuate their risks. According to Schmitz and team (2001), a "sense of isolation arises from the [homeless] data" (p. 73). To see the homeless is to see "extreme independence from others" (Miller, 1982, p. 4) and "to talk with homeless people is to be struck by how alone most of them are" (Bassuk, 1984, p. 43). We are also beginning to understand how this particular risk factor acts as a catalyst for and often leads to more devastating impacts (e.g., mental illness, victimization), especially for children and youth. Or, as Anooshian (2000) explains, "the pervasive risk conditions for homeless children often reflect the pervasiveness of their social isolation" (p. 83).

For homeless women, social isolation grows oftentimes "from violence [and] from past histories of victimization and personal trauma" (Anooshian, 2005, p. 132). Many, but not all (Ennett et al., 1999; Moore, 2005b; Rabideau & Toro, 1997), homeless youth, in turn, "are not likely to experience healthy attachments with adults; they are likely to have tremendous difficulties attaching to anyone" (Powers & Jaklitsch, 1992, p. 122). Leaving home "causes them to feel more rather than less like motherless children" (Wells & Sandhu, 1986, p. 146).

In the homeless literature, social isolation and the absence of social support—or the inability and/or unwillingness to access that support—are generally cojoined. Focusing on the latter concept, we discover that research "consistently shows that the homeless lack strong ties to social networks" (Shlay & Rossi, 1992, p. 140). Or, as Morse (1992) tells us, "the contemporary homeless population, though diverse, tends to be distinguished from the general population by low levels of social support" (p. 4). Homelessness, scholars reveal, disrupts existing social networks (Rafferty, 1995): "Homelessness induces relational breakdowns. Support systems fray under the additional stresses" (Shane, 1996, p. 29). Homelessness, we discover, also prevents the formation of new support systems, especially healthy supports.

Scholars often illustrate the social isolation and absence of support risk narrative as well. Bassuk (1984), for example, provides the following portrait of the general homeless population:

> Some 74 percent of the shelter residents we interviewed said they had no family relationships, and 73 percent said they had no friends, even within the shelter community. Those who had been hospitalized before for psychiatric reasons (about one-third of the group) reported even less social contact: more than 90 percent of them had neither friends nor family. About 40 percent of all the guests said they had no relationship with anyone or with any social institution. (p. 43)

Looking at families, Bassuk and Rosenberg (cited in Ziesemer et al., 1994)

> found that a major difference between homeless mothers and their low-income, housed counterparts was the lack of socially supportive relationships. Among the homeless mothers, 26 percent reported no supports, and 18 percent reported one support (often a friend from the shelter, a professional contact, or in some cases a child). (p. 659)

Dial (also reviewed in Ziesemer et al., 1994) "found that many homeless mothers were severely socially isolated and reported that they did not feel they could trust anyone" (p. 659). Khanna, Singh, Nemil, Best, and Ellis (1992) also report "inadequacies in the social support networks for many of the homeless women" (p. 163) in their study. Shlay and Rossi (1992), in their comprehensive review of 60 studies, peg the percentage of homeless women with no friends at 36 and those with no contact with relatives at 31 (p. 138).

Homeless children suffer from the same social isolation and lack of social support as their mothers (Hart-Shegos & Associates, 1999; Quint, 1994; United Way of New York City, 2002): "When children become homeless, they lose more than their housing. Many also lose their friends [and] their sense of security and belonging" (Rafferty, 1995, p. 55)—"The trauma accompanying the loss of one's home is compounded by dislocation from community, neighbors, services, and friends" (Rafferty, 1995, p. 48; see also Shinn & Weitzman, 1996; United Way of New York City, 2002). Johnson (1992) apprises us that "homeless children are frequently thrust into a busy, confusing world that has little time or intent to address their needs for belonging and affiliation" (p. 164). In this environment, "homeless children (like their mothers) [often] come to view social situations as potentially dangerous—to be avoided" (Anooshian, 2005, p. 134). It is not surprising, then, that analysts routinely find that "children who are homeless have less social support" (Baggerly & Borkowski, 2004, p. 117) than their housed peers.

If anything, the absence of social support is an even more powerful risk factor for unaccompanied youth than for homeless children (Karabanow, 2004; Shaffer & Caton, 1984; Tierney et al., 2008). As we saw with homeless children, but even more deeply,

> homeless youth have learned to anticipate a lack of stability and not to trust adults. If they have experienced abuse or neglect from an early age, they may find that trust is impossible. Their experiences with parental figures have taught them not to rely on adults for support, guidance, and protection. (Powers & Jaklitsch, 1992, p. 122)

Trust is a rarity among homeless youth. Their distrust of adults makes it unlikely that they will initiate contact with service providers who could help them. This distrust is often based either on prior experiences in their families or with social service agencies that placed them in foster homes, state hospitals, or detention centers based on the available resources instead of a desire to meet their needs. Many have spent years bouncing from one placement to another and have learned that they must look out for themselves. (Moore, 2005b, p. 15)

"Residential instability negatively impacts [youngsters'] ability to form and maintain relationships" (Tierney et al., 2008, p. 25; see also Reganick, 1997; Ziesemer et al., 1994). As Reganick (1997) informs us, "homeless adolescents may not want to form friendships knowing they may be forced to leave" (p. 133). In addition, homeless adolescents often develop habits that "increase the social distance between them and conventional institutions" (Fleisher, 1995, p. 119). They often enter into a reinforcing spiral of deepening isolation (Fleisher, 1995; Hagan & McCarthy, 1997) leading to an "absence of compulsory obligations toward others" (Miller, 1982, p. 4), a deepening sense of "outsideness" (Auerswald & Eyre, 2002, p. 1501), and "an alienation from the main culture" (Pears & Noller, 1995, p. 406). Consequently, there is a "paucity of social relationships" (Ennett et al., 1999, p. 75) for homeless youth. As this "disaffiliation process becomes complete, individuals may find themselves cut off from all social, psychological, institutional, and material supports" (Ropers, 1988, p. 122).

As with the other risk factors, social isolation often results in further damage to children and youth. This separation from society "increases the vulnerability of homeless minors" (Shane, 1996, p. 19). And it has the power to "interfere with the child's [or adolescent's] ability to perform academically, form supportive relationships, and develop emotionally and behaviorally" (Schmitz et al., 2001, p. 73). Isolation and accompanying lack of support keep children and youngsters "from developing cognitive and social skills necessary for adult independence in American society" (Fleisher, 1995, p. 105). They also act as catalysts for the development of all manner of physical health problems.

Proximity to Victimization

Once on the streets, homeless youth are often faced with situations of being violated and victimized. (Moore, 2005b, p. 11)

A fifth risk factor that accompanies the living arrangements of the homeless is exposure to an array of conditions that place children and youth at "risk of being victimized or exploited" (Hagan & McCarthy, 1997, p. 48). As noted earlier, "shelters housing homeless families and children are often squalid and dangerous" (Merves, 1992; Solarz, 1992, p. 282). We know that crowded, chaotic environments create ripe conditions for conflict and potentially violent interactions (Molnar et al., 1990). The streets can be and often are more forbidding and dangerous (Hagan & McCarthy, 1997). "Homeless life is a demanding existence" (Morse, 1992, p. 13) that often unfolds in very hostile environments (Hart-Shegos & Associates, 1999): "Living in a car or on the streets is not very safe and shelters can be dangerous" (Eddowes & Hranitz, 1989, p. 198) as well. Indeed, "the ability to feel safe and secure elude[s] many victims of homelessness, most noticeably children and youth" (Johnson, 1992, p. 159). And these inadequate living conditions often prevent parents from protecting their young ones (Tower, 1992).

Particularly problematic for unaccompanied minors in the vulnerability equation is the knowledge that homeless youth often seek out dangerous parts of cities.

> If geography is destiny, runaway and homeless kids gravitate to the very locations around the country where their risk is greatest. (Hersch, 1988, p. 35)

> When leaving home, runaway and homeless youths typically gravitate toward and are tolerated in the neighborhoods where they are most likely to be introduced to delinquent life styles. (Rotheram-Borus, 1991, p. 24)

Thus, "youth are often in places where criminal activity occurs" (Moore, 2005b, p. 8). We also know that homeless families often are shepherded toward the most dangerous sections of towns and cities (Kozol, 1988; Van Ry, 1992). For example, researchers confirm that "shelters often are located in high-crime areas" (Merves, 1992, p. 240) and that "in many large cities families are sheltered in hotels . . . shared by prostitutes, drug dealers, and gang members" (Mihaly, 1991, p. 7).

> Welfare hotels, where families are housed together in one room, sometimes for a year or longer, frequently are in the worst parts of the cities, expose children to the dangers of substance abuse and crime. (Solarz, 1992, p. 282)

Scholars also document that the adolescent homeless are barred even from these noxious venues, thus being forced into even more harmful environments (Reganick, 1997).

Lack of Parental Support

Homelessness often disrupts family relations. (Williams, 2003, p. 17)

Homelessness is not only associated with child difficulties, but parent and family difficulties as well. (Jozefowicz-Simbeni & Israel, 2006, p. 39)

Homelessness is an important predictor of mother–child separation among families. (Park et al., 2004, p. 424)

It is clear that mothers are their children's last line of defense. When mothers are in trouble, their children are in trouble. (Burt et al., 2001, p. 158)

"Parent involvement" (Nunez & Collignon, 1997, p. 56) is another risk factor emanating from poor living arrangements that acts as a catalyst for the development of health and educational problems that befall homeless children and youth. Confronted with the terrifying hardships of homelessness, it is difficult at times for parents to fulfill their guardianship role. Because of (1) the actions of runaways themselves (Baron & Kennedy, 1998), (2) the rules and policies of agencies serving homeless families (Fraenkel, Hameline, & Shannon, 2009; Reganick, 1997), and (3) the stresses of homelessness itself (Nichols & Gault, 2003; Van Ry, 1992), parents are often handicapped in their ability to provide security for their children.

Two dimensions of this risk factor are underscored in the literature on homelessness: the "splintering" (Jozefowicz-Simbeni & Israel, 2006, p. 39) or "dismemberment" (Shinn & Weitzman, 1996, p. 121) of families and the inability of parents to provide needed support for their children. On the first issue, we know that "homelessness [often] drives families apart" (Tower & White, 1989, p. 13). Indeed, studies reveal that a quarter or more of homeless families have children living away from the mother (Tower & White, 1989). Shelter rules and regulations around age and gender often lay behind these divisions. The National League of Cities (2004), using data from the U.S. Conference of Mayors, finds that 60% of cities reported that families may need to break up in order to be sheltered. Looking at the shelters themselves, Rafferty (1995) cites a study by Jacobs and colleagues that found that 40% of shelters had policies that excluded adolescent boys (p. 48). In addition, "shelter regulations regarding mixed-gender housing sometimes force fathers and teenage boys to find shelter apart from the rest of the family" (Williams, 2003, p. 17). In other cases, splintering can be traced to child welfare laws. Moore (2007) explains as follows:

A family's homelessness is often considered to be neglectful and therefore cause for removing a child from his/her family. Although few states specifically mention homelessness in their definition of neglect, most state laws concerning abuse and neglect include not providing adequate shelter for children. (p. 6)

Many of these children end up in foster care (Hart-Shegos & Associates, 1999; Mihaly, 1991; NCFH, 2008; Park et al., 2004). In still other cases, divisions of families result from proactive moves on the part of parents to keep some of their children with relatives or friends: "Parents sometimes send their children to live with friends or relatives to prevent the damage homelessness could do to their children" (Mihaly, 1991, p. 6), including damages of shelter life itself (NCFH, 2008). As a consequence of all these forces, as "children get older they are more likely to be separated from their families: 9 percent infants and toddlers, 19 percent of children between 3 and 6 years old, and 34 percent of school age children" (Better Homes Fund, 1999, p. 12).

Even when children are with their parents, analysts maintain that parents are often "less able to provide support" (Ennett et al., 1999, p. 73) than in prehomelessness times (Schmitz et al., 2001). This, reviewers posit, is the result of the "tremendous strain" (Reganick, 1997, p. 133) and "incredible stress they [parents] are placed under as a result of homelessness" (Tower, 1992, p. 43). Thus, parents may be "less sensitive and responsive to their children's needs" (Reganick, 1997, p. 133) and may "not be able to care for their children as they should" (Tower, 1992, p. 52). And children, in turn, may receive "inadequate parental care" (Hart-Shegos & Associates, 1999; Hersch, 1988, p. 37; Tower, 1992).

❖ IMPACTS ON THE PHYSICAL, EMOTIONAL, SOCIAL, AND EDUCATIONAL WELL-BEING OF CHILDREN AND YOUTH[1]

For a child, there is more to being homeless than not having a specific place to call home. The further implications of being homeless can affect every aspect of a child's life. (Tower, 1992, p. 42)

~╭◦╮~

Homeless children in families experience a broad range of difficulties, including physical and mental health problems and school problems. (Solarz, 1992, p. 277)

~╭◦╮~

Homelessness has a substantial adverse affect on a student's educational, emotional and social well-being. (Tierney et al., 2008, p. 22)

~╭◦╮~

Life on the streets put[s] many of these young people at risk not only for basic health and educational deficits, but for serious emotional problems as well. (Mihaly, 1991, p. 9)

~╭◦╮~

So far in our chronicle, we have seen that homelessness (the starting point in the impact model in Figure 4.1) acts as a catalyst for a series of problems for homeless children (and their families) and unaccompanied youth. It regularly results in living conditions (Point 2 in the impact model) that open onto an assortment of further problems (i.e., risk conditions such as social isolation) that place homeless young persons in harm's way (Point 3). In this final section of the chapter, we confirm that being exposed to risk states (i.e., being put in harm's way) routinely damages these young people—physically, emotionally, socially, and educationally (Point 4 in the impact model).

Damaged Physical Health

The general impression projected by these epidemiological findings is that homeless persons are in poor health. (Ropers, 1988, p. 62)

Homeless children have an excess prevalence of acute and chronic conditions over poor children. (Jahiel, 1992a, p. 142)

Both acute and chronic homeless adolescents report much higher rates of health problems. (MacLean et al., 1999, p. 180)

Getting Started

What should be abundantly clear by this point in our chronicle is that "the rigors and stresses common to street life [and shelters]—hunger, deprivation, and social isolation—ultimately take their toll" (Stefl, 1987, p. 54) on homeless individuals (Toro, 1998), but especially on youth (Barry et al., 2002; Ensign & Bell, 2004; Rew, 1996), children (Better Homes Fund, 1999; Burt et al., 2001; NCFH, 2009), and their mothers (NCFH, 2008; Sullivan & Damrosch, 1987). Homelessness literally wears people down (Gewirtzman & Fodor, 1987) and places them "at risk for a variety of health problems" (Rabideau & Toro, 1997, p. 1). Because "factors related to homelessness endanger the health of children and youth" (Johnson, 1992, p. 155)—because the problems of homelessness "jeopardize health" (Aron & Fitchen, 1996, p. 84)—"homelessness can be considered an agent of disease" (Jahiel, 1992a, p. 150). And "physical illness abound[s] among the homeless" (Greenblatt, 1992, p. 51).

As we detail later, health risks inexorably lead to health problems for the homeless, and "nowhere are these effects more marked and more damaging than in the case of homeless children" (Jahiel, 1992a, p. 151) who "are the most vulnerable of all homeless people" (Burt et al., 2001, p. 137) and who are "many times more likely to experience health problems" (Hart-Shegos & Associates 1999, p. 6): "Homeless children have high rates of both acute and chronic health problems" (Burt et al., 2001, p. 137; Rescorla et al., 1991) and "tend to be in poorer health than their housed counterparts" (NCFH, 2009, p. 19). In short, "homelessness itself makes children sick" (Better Homes Fund, 1999, p. 3). And what is true for children is true for homeless youth as well (Farrow et al., 1992; Klein et al., 2000; Rothman, 1991).

Contextual Notes

Before we expose some of the specific health problems that characterize the homeless, a few notes are in order, some of which reinforce earlier analyses. First, the damage to physical health among the homeless varies by subgroups. While harm is evident everywhere, it is worse for children, youth, and women (Bassuk et al., 1984; Burt et al., 2001; Ropers, 1988; Sullivan & Damrosch, 1987).

Second, within each of the relevant groups in this volume (i.e., children and youth), indices of health are worse for the homeless than the housed subgroups (Jahiel, 1992a; Moore, 2005b). More telling, these indices for each subgroup are worse for the homeless than other poor but domiciled persons. On the first theme, in one important investigation, "one-third (33.4 percent) of the homeless persons interviewed rated their health as fair or poor. This is a large proportion compared with that in the Los Angeles population (22.5 percent) and with national estimates" (Ropers, 1988, p. 62). Also looking at the general homeless population, Jahiel (1992a) reveals that "in local studies from 33% to 48% of homeless respondents reported their health to be poor or fair, compared to 18% to 21% in the general population" (p. 135).[2]

Turning to children and youth, Wright and Weber (cited in Johnson, 1992) "reported incidence rates of health problems for homeless children which were substantially higher than the incidence rates for other children" (p. 155). Moore's (2005a) analyses also show that homeless children have "much higher rates of acute and chronic health problems" (p. 5) than housed peers and that health risks are significantly higher for homeless youth than their housed counterparts: "While their illnesses are not atypical of children's illnesses in general, homeless children are sick at rates many times higher than the average child" (Molnar et al., 1990, p. 112). Overall, researchers confirm that "from infancy through childhood homeless children have substantially higher levels of acute and chronic illness" (Better Homes Fund, 1999, p. 3). Miller and Linn (cited in Rescorla et al., 1991) "found the incidence of health problems to be four times higher than estimates for the general U.S. pediatric population" (p. 210). Hart-Shegos & Associates (1999) provides the following data:

> Homeless children are more likely to experience chronic health problems than are housed children. They are four times more likely to need extended health care immediately post-birth. Sixteen percent of older homeless children, versus nine percent of housed

children, have one or more chronic health problems, such as cardiac disease, peripheral vascular disease, endocrine dysfunction, or neurological disorders. (p. 6)

On the second theme, reviewers routinely conclude that on most indices, the health of homeless who are poor is worse than the health of the poor who are housed: "In general, homeless children consistently exhibit more health problems than housed poor children" (Hart-Shegos & Associates, 1999, p. 2) and have problems that are more severe (Duffield & Lovell, 2008).

Our third contextual note helps us see that health damage is not constant. It worsens as homelessness lengthens. For example, in a study of general homelessness, Ropers (1988) discovered that health had deteriorated for 45.7% of the study population since they had become homeless (p. 46). Rafferty and Rollins (cited in Johnson, 1992) report that "30% of the parents in shelters in NYC indicated that their children's health had gotten worse since becoming homeless" (pp. 155–156). And in his review, Van Ry (1992) documents that "new health problems after becoming homeless were reported by 50% of homeless families. Families with existing health problems reported that they worsened after becoming homeless" (p. 67). Looking specifically at homeless adolescents, Farrow and team (1992) write that "the health of youth worsen after they become homeless" (p. 720). Russell (1998) found that the health of 22.2% of homeless youth deteriorated since becoming homeless (p. 153).

Fourth, there is a relationship between type of residency and amount and severity of physical damage. In general, homelessness is more harmful for people in shelters than for those living doubled up. And it is worse for people on the street than for sheltered homeless (Klein et al., 2000).

Fifth, types of physical maladies are not distributed equally across all subpopulations of the homeless. While some problems are similar, "some [are] particular to subsets of the homeless population" (Shane, 1996, p. 41).

Finally, to some extent gender and age matter. While "the association of some diagnoses with homelessness is more important than age" (Jahiel, 1992a, p. 143), in other cases age is relevant. Jahiel's (1992a) data confirm "increased prevalence with age for arthritis, hypertension, heart failure, cerebrovascular accidents, COPD, chronic liver disease, and neoplasms. Furthermore, in most of these instances the increase with age is independent of the effects of other variables" (p. 143). A similar pattern is seen in the gender category. While overall levels of damage do not appear to differ (Jahiel, 1992a), there is evidence that certain maladies befall homeless men more than homeless women and vice versa (Burt, 2001).

Incidence

It is helpful at this point in our narrative to illustrate some of the specific physical maladies that characterize homeless children and youth, although we are handicapped by inconsistencies in how various studies characterize maladies and an absence of an agreed-upon classification system beyond the broad architecture of acute and chronic health problems. Dishearteningly, we learn that "homeless children enter the world at serious health risk" (Molnar et al., 1990, p. 110)—"poor health for homeless children begins at birth" (NCFH, 2009, p. 19; Shinn & Weitzman, 1996). Babies delivered "to homeless mothers are often of low birth weight" (Gargiulo, 2006, p. 358). "They have lower birth weights compared with housed children" (NCFH, 2009, p. 19). According to Biggar (2001), 16% of infants born to homeless women are low birth weight babies. The comparable numbers for mothers in public housing and for women in general are 11% and 7% (p. 946). The risks associated with low birth weight translate into high rates of infant mortality. For example, Chaukin and team (referenced in Molnar et al., 1990), in their investigation of infant mortality, "documented an alarmingly high rate of 24.9 per 1000 among their homeless sample; this was half again as large as the rate of 16.6 in the public housing group, and double the rate of 12.0 for all other babies born in New York City during the study period" (p. 110). Hart-Shegos & Associates (1999) informs us that low birth weight infants whose mothers did not receive prenatal care—two health conditions common among the homeless population—are "nine times more likely to die in the first 12 months of life" (p. 4).

According to Hart-Shegos & Associates (1999), "homeless children are also more apt to test positive for lead poisoning, with more severe symptoms" (p. 7) than housed children (Kozol, 1988; Rescorla et al., 1991; Shinn & Weitzman, 1996; Solarz, 1992). As Mihaly (1991) confirms, "homeless children also have been found to be twice as likely as their housed poor counterparts to have elevated blood lead levels, a condition associated with developmental and psychological delays" (p. 5). And Hart-Shegos & Associates (1999) reminds us that lead poisoning can result in "abdominal pain, constipation, fatigue, anemia, nerve damage and altered brain functions" (p. 7). They also explain that "lead poisoning's effect on the brain can cause seizures, coma, and even death in severe cases, and long term exposure can lead to kidney, brain, and reproductive organ damage" (p. 7).

"Thermoregulatory disorders such as heat stroke, heat exhaustion, hypothermia, and frostbite are much more common among homeless people than in the general population" (Jahiel, 1992a, p. 148; National Law Center on Homelessness and Poverty, 2004b; Ropers, 1988). In particular, because "homeless youth are vulnerable to exposure to the elements" (Shane, 1996, p. 46), "to exposure to ambient cold [and] heat" (Jahiel, 1987, p. 109), they are at risk for such disorders (Shane, 1996).

There is also evidence that "injuries occur with very high frequency among homeless" (Jahiel, 1992a, p. 138) persons and that children and adolescents shoulder a disproportionate share of that trauma—a not surprising finding given our earlier discussion of their exposure to violence and victimization. Males, 16 to 18, are especially marked by traumatic injuries (Shane, 1996). Compared to housed peers, homeless youth have significantly higher rates of trauma (Jahiel, 1992a). Self-inflicted injuries also have been documented as a theme in the trauma narrative for homeless youth (Pears & Noller, 1995).

Mihaly (1991) and other analysts who review research in the health domain ascertain that asthma is a problem that often bedevils homeless youth (Barry et al., 2002; Karabanow, 2004; Williams, 2003), that "the profile of children who suffer from asthma is magnified for homeless children" (NCFH, 2009, p. 22). The NCFH (2009), for example, reports that "almost one in nine homeless children are reported to have one or more asthma-related health conditions" (p. 8). Wood (cited in Mihaly, 1991) puts this finding in perspective when noting that "homeless children suffer from asthma at rates two to three times higher than other poor children" (p. 53)—and four times higher than the general population of children (NCFH, 2008, p. 5). And Hart-Shegos & Associates (1999) teaches us that "when homeless children with asthma get sick with other ailments, their symptoms generally are more pronounced than those in housed children, and they are hospitalized for symptoms at three times the rate of the average asthma patient" (p. 7).

Significant dermatological problems have also been recorded among homeless minors. Common disorders include lice and scabies (Karabanow, 2004; Shane, 1996). Here too, as we have seen with other health problems, researchers conclude that "homeless children experience dermatological disorders at more than double the rate of other low-income children" (Nunez, 1994b, p. 33).

Homeless children and youth also suffer from iron deficiency and anemia more than youngsters in general and low-income peers specifically. Comparisons with children in general reveal that "homeless children are seven times more likely to experience iron deficiencies leading to anemia" (Hart-Shegos & Associates, 1999, p. 7). In comparisons to low-income children specifically, Molnar and team (1990; referencing the work of Acker and colleagues) report that "homeless children aged 6 months to 2 years have been found to be at significantly greater risk for iron-deficiency than a low-income housed comparison group" (p. 111). And Hart-Shegos & Associates (1999) informs us that "when found to be anemic, homeless children's iron deficiency is 50 percent worse than anemia among housed poor children" (p. 7).

Homeless children and youth suffer from an assortment of other health problems as well. According to the NCFH (2008), in addition to being "sick four times more often than other children, they have four times as many respiratory infections, twice as many ear infections, and five times more gastrointestinal problems" (p. 4; see also Better Homes Fund, 1999; Shinn & Weitzman, 1996). Childhood homelessness is also associated with unusually high rates of dental problems (Duffield, 2000) and tooth decay (NCFH, 2009), at least 10 times as high as the general population of youngsters (Jahiel, 1992a, p. 142).

Finally, researchers confirm that homeless minors are often subject to the ravages of infestations and infectious diseases (Jahiel, 1987; Ringwalt, Greene, & Robertson, 1998). "Compared with their domiciled peers, homeless youth are at significantly greater risk for . . . human immunodeficiency virus (HIV) infection and other sexually transmitted and infectious diseases" (Ringwalt, Greene, Robertson, & McPheeters, 1998, p. 1325) and "tuberculosis infection" (Toro, 1998, p. 125). Beginning with children, Medcalf (2008) finds that "in many homeless shelters infectious diseases like tuberculosis and whooping cough run rampant among youngsters who have not been properly inoculated" (p. 11; see also earlier analyses on immunizations). "As compared with housed children, homeless children suffer from five times the rate of diarrheal infections as housed children. . . . Homeless children suffer from many respiratory infections at twice the rate of housed children, and they are twice as likely to have a positive skin test showing exposure to tuberculosis" (Hart-Shegos & Associates, 1999, p. 6). In a similar vein, Shane (1996) documents that "inadequate shelter of homeless children and families exposes them to rodent bites and insect and rodent-borne disease" (p. 46).

Turning to homeless youth, we learn that adolescents contract sexually transmitted diseases at extremely high rates (Russell, 1998; Whitbeck & Hoyt, 1999; Woronoff et al., 2006), with estimates "as high as 50–71% infection rate among street youth" (Whitbeck & Hoyt, 1999, p. 101): "Sexually transmitted diseases appear common among homeless youth; they are found in 78% of females and 51% of males" (Rotheram-Borus, 1991, p. 26). Scholars also remind us that homeless youth "are significantly more likely than non-homeless youth to be diagnosed with a sexually-transmitted disease" (Farrow et al., 1992, p. 720). That is, "living on the street places youth at high risk for contracting sexually transmitted diseases" (Karabanow, 2004, p. 44).

HIV infection, in particular, is an especially serious problem (Ensign & Bell, 2004; Hersch, 1988; Lindsey & Williams, 2002; Rew, 1996). "Given the high prevalence of sexual assault, prostitution, and unprotected sexual activities, homeless youth are at increased risk for exposure to HIV compared to the housed adolescent population" (Booth, Zhang, & Kwiatkowski, 1999; Russell, 1998, p. 314). It is estimated that "four to six percent of the homeless . . . youth population in the United States [are] HIV infected" (Russell, 1998, pp. 313–314; also Farrow et al., 1992) and that these adolescents "are infected . . . at a rate two to ten times higher than among other groups of adolescents" (Rotheram-Borus, 1991, p. 26)—up to 15 times higher according to Booth and colleagues (1999, p. 1296).

Compounded Damage

This crush of physical damage and health problems "is profound" (NCFH, 2009, p. 19). It extends to all other domains of life for homeless children and youth and has "lasting effects" (Mihaly, 1991, p. 4). As Shane

(1996) notes, poor "health affects the conditions of their lives and their ability to deal with life demands" (p. 40). Health maladies "often result in missed school days, reduced classroom attention spans, and delayed language development" (Hightower et al., 1997, p. 4). Poor health "can result in cognitive impairments" (Backer & Howard, 2007, p. 386) and "stunted cognitive development" (Kozol, 1988, p. 103), and have "profound effects on their development and ability to learn" (NCFH, 2008, p. 4).

According to Kozol (1988), these physically harmed children and youth "will grow into the certainty of unemployable adulthood" (pp. 112–113). For others, a move into adulthood, with employment or otherwise, will never be a possibility. That is, "homelessness is associated with increased mortality" (Jahiel, 1992b, p. 294). Some, as we reported earlier, will die as babies (Eddowes, 1992; Kozol, 1988; Nunez, 1994b)—and at much higher rates than do infants in general: "Higher rates of . . . infant mortality are reported for homeless persons than for domiciled people, even those below poverty level" (Jahiel, 1992a, p. 150). Indeed, "stable, affordable housing [is] found to be the most important factor in explaining differences in rates of infant mortality among children born to extremely poor mothers" (Crowley, 2003, p. 23). Others will die as young adolescents on the street (Rotheram-Borus, 1991). "From related data, it can be extrapolated that . . . among unaccompanied homeless youth the death rate is much higher than for the corresponding age level in the general population" (Shane, 1996, p. 44).

Psychological and Emotional Impairments

Homeless preschoolers have emotional difficulties at greater rates than their housed counterparts. (Bassuk, Weinreb, et al., 1997, p. 92)

When income is held constant, homeless children exhibit significantly more mental health problems than do poor children with stable housing. (Biggar, 2001, p. 943)

Acute and chronic mental health problems are common among homeless youth. (Shane, 1996, p. 49)

The General Story Line

In the last section, we documented the physical damage that accompanies homelessness. Here we show that "compromised outcomes for homeless children go beyond the threat to physical health" (Kelly, Buehlman, & Caldwell, 2000, p. 175), that "the constant barrage of stressful and traumatic experiences [also] has profound effects on the emotional development of homeless children" (Better Homes Fund, 1999, p. 12): "Homeless children are also more likely to suffer from emotional problems" (Hart-Shegos & Associates, 1999, p. 2); "in addition to the many physical problems adolescents encounter in being homeless, many experience serious psychosocial and mental health problems" (Rew, 1996, p. 352). For children and youth, homelessness contributes in important ways to the following: "psychological morbidity" (Ropers, 1988, p. 164); "acute psychosocial problems" (Hicks-Coolick et al., 2003, p. 198); "impressive rates of psychosocial pathology" (Fischer, 1992, p. 57); "high rates of psychological symptoms" (Moore, 2005b, p. 10); "emotional distress" (Mihaly, 1991, p. 6), "psychiatric distress" (Mallett et al., 2004, p. 338), and "psychological distress" (McCaskill et al., 1998, p. 316); and "high incidence of mental disorders" (Kidd & Scrimenti, 2004, p. 326).

According to the research in this area, not only are homeless children and youth "emotionally vulnerable" (Schmitz et al., 2001, p. 73) and "at elevated risk for mental health problems" (Julianelle, 2007, p. 16) and "an increased risk for a range of disorders" (McCaskill et al., 1998, p. 307), but "a large majority of [homeless] young people are beset by [these] severe emotional problems" (Hersch, 1988, p. 31)—their actual "emotional health is compromised" (Rafferty, 1995, p. 55). Shelter life and "street experiences have profound mental health effects on young people" (Whitbeck & Hoyt, 1999, p. 126). In particular, "staying on the street exacts a considerable emotional and psychological toll" (Hagan & McCarthy, 1997, p. 42); the "vulnerability, stress, and actual trauma experienced by homeless adolescents when they are on their own takes a psychological toll" (Whitbeck & Hoyt, 1999, p. 134).

We learn that of all displaced persons, "homeless children [and youth] are the most vulnerable of all to mental health problems" (NCFH, 2009, p. 25): "If homelessness may be expected to be traumatic for adults, it is more so for these 'too-early adults' who have neither adult emotional resources nor adult support systems to buffer the experience" (Whitbeck & Hoyt, 1999, pp. 157–158). We discover that homeless youth and children suffer from "a wide range of mental health problems" (Fraenkel et al., 2009, p. 327), from a "myriad of psychosocial problems" (Rew, Taylor-Seehafer, Thomas, & Yockey, 2001, p. 35). We also find that the emotional impairments that do surface are more severe for homeless children and youth than for other young people.

On the comparison front, scholars document that homeless children and youth often display higher levels of emotional disorders than the general population" (Jozefowicz-Simbeni & Israel, 2006, p. 38; Herrington et al., 2006). Researchers also confirm "that homeless youngsters as a group have more internal problems than those who have homes" (Feitel et al., 1992, p. 155; Rescorla et al., 1991; Shinn & Weitzman, 1996; Whitbeck & Hoyt, 1999),[3] that "street kids are less psychologically well than other groups of young people" (Taylor et al., 2004, p. 14), and "that homeless adolescents have a higher prevalence of all mental health indicators compared to nonhomeless adolescents" (Farrow et al., 1992, p. 721). Hart-Shegos & Associates (1999) reports that "children between the ages of six and 17 have very high rates of mental disorders compared to their peers" (p. 8). Rew (1996), in turn, reveals that "mental health problems are three times more prevalent among homeless adolescents than among adolescents living in homes" (p. 349; see also Better Homes Fund, 1999; NCFH, 2008). Rotheram-Borus (1991) reaches a similar conclusion, looking specifically at the runaway population: "Emotional distress and psychiatric problems are three times more common among runaways than among nonrunaways" (p. 27). In another study (reviewed in Duffield and Lovell, 2008), researchers "found that homeless children were twice as likely as their peers to have clinical or borderline clinical mental health problems" (Duffield & Lovell, 2008, p. 8). Wright (cited in Shane, 1996) documents four times more mental health problems for homeless youth than housed adolescents.

Analysts also reveal the extent of psychological and emotional impairments among the nation's children and youth.[4] In their review, Hart-Shegos & Associates (1999) reports that "one-third of homeless children have at least one major mental disorder that interferes with daily activity" (p. 8), as "compared to 19 percent of other school-age children" (Better Homes Fund, 1999, p. 13). Cauce and team (2000) found that two-thirds of the homeless children in their study "had mental health problems that met the criteria for a disorder" (p. 237). Russell (1998) reports that "over three quarters of the sample [in her study] met caseness criteria for at least one indicator of lifetime psychological distress" (p. 155). Shaffer and Caton (1984) argue, based on their data, "that mental health problems are present in between 70% and 90% of [homeless] youth" (p. 66). Wilder, Obiakor, and Algozzine (2003) and the NCFH (2009) provide data that fall in the middle of the numbers in these reports. Wilder and colleagues note that 50% of "homeless students demonstrate emotional difficulties" (p. 9). The NCFH (2009), in turn, reports that "about half of all school-age children experiencing homelessness have problems with anxiety and deep depression" (p. 2; see also Gewirtzman & Fodor, 1987, p. 241).

As we have illustrated throughout this volume, incidence of effects are not uniform across the homeless population. In particular, "age and gender influence the psychosocial functioning of the homeless experience" (Cauce et al., 2000, p. 231). For example, older homeless youth have more emotional impairment than children (Boesky et al., 1997). And girls have higher rates on "internalizing" emotional factors such as depression and withdrawal than boys (Cauce et al., 2000; Rescorla et al., 1991).

The literature also illuminates certain conditions that "amplify existing mental problems" (Whitbeck & Hoyt, 1999, p. 10) for homeless children and youth. One is "multiple episodes of homelessness" (McCaskill et al., 1998, p. 315). A second is a history of emotional problems (Whitbeck & Hoyt, 1999). As Ropers (1988) captures it, while "the lack of proper reasonably safe shelter contributes to the psychological deterioration of relatively normal individuals [it] exacerbates the mental disorder in those with a history of psychiatric disturbances" (p. 167). Homelessness here "augments the assault" (Shane, 1996, p. 49) on young people. That is, existing emotional health symptoms "will be amplified by the trauma of homelessness" (Bao et al., 2000, p. 410). A third amplifying condition is the presence of mental health problems in one's family (Hicks-Coolick et al., 2003; Kelly et al., 2000; Solarz, 1992). Specifically, emotional "problems [of homeless youngsters] are compounded by family . . . mental health issues" (Jozefowicz-Simbeni & Israel, 2006). A fourth factor is previous exposure to abuse (Bao et al., 2000). As Janus and colleagues (1987) conclude, "victims of abuse are more likely to report symptomatology indicative of poor psychological function" (p. 52).

> Abusive family background [has] a direct effect on adolescent depressive symptoms, even after controlling for gender and race and the effects of early independence and social support networks among homeless and runaway adolescents. (Bao et al., 2000, p. 415)

Analysts also provide three other insights about homelessness and emotional impairments. First, psychological problems do not disappear after housing is secured; they can persist long after such housing is located (National Law Center on Homelessness and Poverty, 2004a). For example, Shinn and Weitzman (1996) reveal that "in one study, a sixth of formerly homeless parents reported that their children's emotional problems engendered by homelessness persisted after a move to permanent housing" (p. 199). Second, the barriers to treatment in the mental health domain are "overwhelming" (NCFH, 2009, p. 26), even more so than in the area of physical health. Access to care is limited at best (Julianelle, 2007), with homeless children receiving fewer services than their housed counterparts (Hart-Shegos & Associates, 1999). Not surprisingly, then, researchers confirm that "the myriad of psychological problems afflicting homeless children generally remain untreated" (Biggar, 2001, p. 950). Third, "psychosocial problems are related to the school setting" (Tower, 1992, p. 53). These mental impairments "severely limit" (Julianelle, 2007, p. 16) the ability of children to function effectively (Biggar, 2001) and "succeed in school" (Duffield et al., 2007, p. 49). They undermine the formation of healthy social relationships. They "lead to academic problems" (Jozefowicz-Simbeni & Israel, 2006, p. 39) and "impede academic achievement" (Mawhinney-Rhoads & Stahler, 2006, p. 293).

The Specific Story Line: Indices

Developmental Delays

> *Developmental problems often strike children whose families become homeless. (Nunez, 1994b, p. 62)*

～◦◦◦～

There is a high prevalence of developmental delays among homeless children.
(Kidd & Scrimenti, 2004, p. 325)

⌒◠⋆◠⌒

The list of emotional symptoms that often characterize homeless children and youth is extensive. Close to the top of that enumeration is the fact that "children without permanent homes are less able to negotiate the developmental tasks of early childhood than children whose housing is less precarious" (Kling et al., 1996, p. 5). That is, homeless children and youth are often "developmentally delayed" (Rubin et al., 1996, p. 289) in one or more areas; they "experience significant developmental delays" (Powers & Jaklitsch, 1992, p. 121). As a consequence of these "severe lags in developmental milestones" (Hope & Young, 1986, p. 24), they are "often less than ideally prepared for the next stage of development" (Biggar, 2001, p. 946).

Types of developmental delays, according to Shinn and Weitzman (1996), include "delays in language, in reading for school-age children, in personal and social development, and in motor development" (p. 119), or in the three buckets of motor, language, and interpersonal skills, according to Nunez (1994b); the three categories of intellectual, social, and emotional functioning, according to Kidd and Scrimenti (2004); and the three dimensions of "gross and fine motor skills, language development, and personal-social growth," according to Eddowes (1992, p. 104). Woods (1997), in a review article, outlines significant delays for homeless children "in gross-motor development (particularly problems in movement through space and spatial relationships), speech and language development (particularly restrictions in expressive language and vocabulary development), and cognitive development (particularly with tasks requiring sequencing and organization)" (p. 303).

Analysts also expose the extensiveness of these developmental delays for homeless children (primarily) and youth. According to the Better Homes Fund (1999) analysis, "proper growth and development occurs too slowly for 18 percent of homeless children" (p. 23). Bassuk et al.'s study (1986) found that 47% of children ages 0–5 "had at least one developmental lag and 33 percent had two or more lags" (p. 1099). Hart-Shegos & Associates (1999) provides even more disturbing data: "Most homeless children (75 percent) under age five have at least one major developmental delay or deviation, primarily in the areas of impulsivity or speech. Even more alarming, nearly half of homeless children (44 percent) have two or more major developmental delays" (p. 5).

These and other researchers also document disparities in delays between homeless young persons and others. They confirm "delays relative to test norms for general population samples" (Shinn & Weitzman, 1996, p. 120). More specifically, Medcalf (2008) records that "homeless children experience delays . . . at four times the rate of other children" (p. 18)—three times the rate according to Bassuk and colleagues (Bassuk, 1992; Bassuk et al., 1986). They are also "much more likely to be identified as having developmental delays than children with stable housing" (Reed-Victor et al., 2003, pp. 1–2) and low-income housed children (Bassuk et al., 1986). Developmental patterns of homeless children and youth mirror those "found in abused and neglected populations" (Douglass, 1996, p. 743).

These developmental delays mean that "homeless children face monumental obstacles in pursuit of education" (Nunez & Collignon, 1997, p. 56; Whitbeck & Hoyt, 1999). They also influence the emergence of the other emotional and psychological problems we review here (Hart-Shegos & Associates, 1999).

Disorientation

The experience of being homeless may cause young people to feel confused and out of control of their lives. (Powers & Jaklitsch, 1992, p. 121)

An assortment of analysts helps us see that homelessness can create a sense of being lost among young persons (Pears & Noller, 1995; Reganick, 1997). The analysts confirm that the "confusion under which they are forced to labor" (Tower, 1992, p. 45) and the "uncertainty of their lives" (Hightower et al., 1997, p. 20) form a type of psychological disorientation for homeless youths, an impairment in itself but one that opens the door to further emotional problems as well (National Center for Homeless Education, 2006a; Reganick, 1997; Rotheram-Borus, 1991), including "the inability to trust and commit to any social relationships" (Anooshian, 2000, p. 83) and anxiety and depression (National Center for Homeless Education, 2006a). Scholars describe this disorientation most often as a sense of being out of control over one's life (Hagan & McCarthy, 1997; Tower & White, 1989; Ziesemer & Marcoux, 1992).

Low Self-Esteem

One of the most common and serious problems of youth homelessness is low self esteem. (Moore, 2005b, p. 11)

Studies consistently affirm that homeless children and youth are likely to experience an "erosion of self-esteem" (Powers & Jaklitsch, 1992, p. 122) and lower self-esteem overall when contrasted to their housed peers (Rothman, 1991). This mental state that Snow and Anderson (1993) refer to as "the brutalization of the self" (p. 208), like "disorientation," leads to additional emotional and psychological difficulties (Baron, 2003; Biggar, 2001; Shane, 1996). These displaced children and youth "feel worse about themselves than do [children and] adolescents living at home" (Rotheram-Borus, 1991, p. 27). And the negative impact in this area is cumulative

(Powers & Jaklitsch, 1992): "As each new assault [from homelessness] on these small individuals happens, children feel less and less positive about themselves" (Tower & White, 1989, p. 31).

Guilt and Shame

The homeless child's feelings about being unable to control life have further implications and manifestations. Children often demonstrate a great deal of shame over the plight in which their family has found itself. (Tower, 1992, p. 47)

Relatedly, analysts reveal that homeless children suffer from considerable shame (Anooshian, 2005; Shane, 1996; Tower, 1992) and guilt (Feitel et al., 1992; Powers & Jaklitsch, 1992; Russell, 1998), conditions that hold for their mothers as well (Fraenkel et al., 2009; Powers & Jaklitsch, 1992).

Some homeless children feel different than and inferior to others. They believe they can't fit in with those who are not in their position. Shame and/or embarrassment develop as a result of homelessness. They fear being "look[ed] down on," which inhibits relationships with nonhomeless children and adults. (Shane, 1996, p. 31)

Once they arrive at school, this sense of shame is often fueled by negative interactions with housed peers (Anooshian, 2005; see Chapter 7 of this volume). Shame and guilt, in turn, often lead to further erosion of self-concept.

The erosion of self-esteem frequently occurs among homeless adolescents and is often associated with depression. It is common for these young people to engage in behaviors that reinforce a poor self-image, particularly in a school setting. They may blame themselves for their situation, and this continuing distortion of reality further contributes to the lowering of self-esteem to the point of immobilization. (Powers & Jaklitsch, 1992, p. 122)

Hopelessness and Futility

Homeless youth are at risk for a sense of hopelessness and despair.
(Rew, 1996, p. 353)

Given everything described earlier, it is almost inevitable that homeless children and youth would be weighed down with a sense of helplessness and see effort, energy, and commitment as futile (Gwadz et al., 2009; Polakow, 2003)—conditions well documented among homeless adults as well (Bahr, 1973; Flynn, 1985; Ropers, 1988). "The challenges noted by street youth . . . signal the high level of despair and hopelessness facing homeless youth populations in general" (Karabanow, 2004, p. 45).

Alienation, Insecurity, and Withdrawal

Homeless youth report higher levels of loneliness than do their in-school peers. (Rew et al., 2001, p. 34)

If it is true that nothing so economizes effort and energy as the knowledge that nothing can be done, then disengagement seems like a reasonable response of youth and children to the reality of homelessness. These young persons often become alienated from those around them (Helge, 1992), either directly (Rew et al., 2001) or as members of families (Anooshian, 2000). Alienation, in turn, deepens the grooves in the pathway toward isolation (Anooshian, 2000; Baron, 2003) and loneliness (Rew et al., 2001), which fosters further "mental health deterioration" (Karabanow, 2004, p. 45). In particular, scholars confirm that given low self-concept and feelings of helplessness, many homeless young people withdraw into themselves (Molnar et al., 1990; Rabideau & Toro, 1997; Van Ry, 1992), a response that is often mediated by insecurity (Anooshian, 2005; Kling et al., 1996; Tower, 1992). They become listless and apathetic (Jahiel, 1987; Korinek et al., 1992; Penuel & Davey, 1998) and unnaturally shy (Bassuk et al., 1986; Mihaly, 1991; Van Ry, 1992). For older homeless youth, "without anyone or anything to believe in their lives become aimless" (Taylor et al., 2004, p. 15). In some cases, these children escape into a world of fantasy (Tower, 1992). In other cases, it leads to regressive behaviors (Eddowes, 1992; Solarz, 1992). And in still other cases, it leads to unnatural fears and phobias (Shane, 1996). Here children internalize worries (Tower, 1992). Looking specifically at children and youth, Shane (1996) reports the following:

> Homeless children tend to be frightened. The security of stable and secure family and residence needed for positive development has been either taken away or never experienced. Fright is also an emotionally and developmentally inhibiting element. A frightened person is unwilling to tackle new experiences and trust unknown people and places. A frightened person tends to view life and other people with distrust and hostility. (p. 31)

Distrust

Our hypothesis was that street kids would be distrustful of authority, but find reliable relationships among their friends. The results paint a bleaker picture in terms of street kids. Compared to the two control groups, street kids trust neither authorities nor friends. (Taylor et al., 2004, p. 10)

Ravaged by homelessness and its accompanying dangers, homeless youth and children often fail to develop the ability to trust that is at the heart of all meaningful social relations (Biggar, 2001; Pearce, 1995; Taylor et al., 2004). Conversely, they learn to distrust the world and the people who populate it (Anooshian, 2000). For children, Tower (1992) argues that

> their new life-styles may have left them feeling betrayed and suspicious of any adults. Adults are supposed to nurture and protect children, and yet this has not necessarily been their experience. For children, adults represent faith in an ordered, consistent world. The destruction of this faith leaves them not only unable to trust others but also unable to trust their own perceptions of reality. (p. 51)

On the adolescent front, "street youth learn quickly that they must look out for themselves because no one else will" (Pearce, 1995, p. 18); they are "notoriously suspicious" (Taylor et al., 2004, p. 3) of adults in general and of friends and social service agency personnel in particular (Rew, 1996): "The experience of repeated failures, rejection, exploitation, or being hurt in a variety of ways may lead to . . . extreme suspiciousness" (Jahiel, 1987, p. 105).

Anxiety

The condition of homelessness is psychologically alarming. It results in aheightened sense of anxiety. (Whitbeck & Hoyt, 1999, p. 107)

In the bundle of emotional problems that beset homeless children and youth, anxiety is often placed near the top of the package (Bassuk et al., 1986; Caton, 1986; NCFH, 2009; Tower & White, 1989). That is, homeless young people "experience high levels of anxiety" (Penuel & Davey, 1998, p. 5). Research also confirms that this impairment disproportionately touches homeless children vis-à-vis their housed peers (Hart-Shegos & Associates, 1999; Taylor et al., 2004):

> Emotionally, children who are homeless tend to experience more depression and anxiety than children who are housed. Approximately 47% of children who were homeless were found to have clinically significant internalizing problems, such as depression and anxiety, compared to only 21% of children who were housed (Buckner et al.). Menke and Wagner (1997) also found depression and anxiety were significantly higher in children who were homeless compared to children who were never homeless. (Baggerly & Borkowski, 2004, p. 117)

In comparisons between the homeless and domiciled children on the standardized test, the only significant difference occurred in anxiety. Children homeless at the time of the interview exhibited (p < .05) higher anxiety levels (M = 55.06) than domiciled children (M = 51.37). (Schmitz et al., 2001, p. 72)

So too for youth: "Homeless adolescents [are] more likely to report anxiety . . . as compared to teens living at home" (McCaskill et al., 1998, p. 315).

Depression

Homeless children are particularly prone to suffer depression.
(Eddowes, 1992, p. 104)

Depression is one of the most common psychological effects of adolescent homelessness. (Powers & Jaklitsch, 1992, p. 122)

Depression forms the central pattern in the "psychological effects" (Pears & Noller, 1995, p. 406) mosaic of homelessness. It is the cardinal impairment in the host of psychological problems that confound homeless children and youth (Kidd & Scrimenti, 2004). "Depressive behaviors in children are environmentally and situationally induced by the experience of homelessness" (Ziesemer & Marcoux, 1992, p. 83)—and are accompanied by depression in their mothers (NCFH, 2008; Shane, 1996). Alternatively, "the psychological effects of homelessness include depression" (Pears & Noller, 1995, p. 406).

Depression is featured in every investigation and review of the damage caused by homelessness. Analysts note that youth and children are at "particular risk" (Bao et al., 2000, p. 410) "for depressive symptoms" (Whitbeck & Hoyt, 1999, p. 119). And they confirm that risk generally leads to the presence of the impairment, recording a high rate of depression among homeless youth (Ferguson & Xie, 2008; McCaskill et al., 1998; Whitbeck & Hoyt, 1999) and children (Boesky et al., 1997; NCFH, 2009; Tower & White, 1989) and their families (Van Ry, 1992).

The extent of depression's grip on young homeless persons varies across studies. On the lower end of the continuum, Russell (1998) and McCaskill and colleagues (1998) report rates in the 20% range. Cauce and team (2000; 33%), Whitbeck and Hoyt (1999; 23% males, 39% females), Smart and team (cited in Russell, 1998; 33%), Shaffer and Caton (1994; 30%), Bassuk and Rosenberg (cited in Johnson, 1992; 31%), and the NCFH (2009; 33%) document slightly higher rates of homeless children and youth who display depressive symptoms. At the high end of the extent continuum, quite startling rates of depression have been uncovered by Feitel and associates (1992; 75%) and Farrow and colleagues (1992; 85%).

There is consensus among analysts that rates of depression for homeless children and youth are higher than for their housed peers (Cause et al., 2000; Farrow et al., 1992; Shane, 1996). There is also evidence that depression is often deeper for homeless children and youth compared to housed young people (Taylor et al., 2004).

Suicide

Suffering from depression and without hope for the future, homeless adolescents may not want to continue living. Several studies have reported high rates of suicidal behavior among unaccompanied homeless youth.
(Powers & Jaklitsch, 1992, p. 123)

Suicidal thoughts and behaviors often accompany adolescent homelessness (Farrow et al., 1992; Rotheram-Borus, 1991; Rothman, 1991). The data here are alarming and worse (Karabanow, 2004). For example, Bassuk (1992), in an investigation of homeless school-age children, found that "almost all the children tested stated that they had thought of suicide" (p. 261). Rotheram-Borus, Mahler, Koopman, and Langabeer (1996) report that almost 50% of the homeless adolescents in their study had attempted suicide. Shaffer and Caton (1984) document percentages of 33 for girls and 16 for boys. Russell's (1998) work supports those findings, documenting a suicide attempt rate among homeless youth of 47%. She also found that fully two-thirds of her adolescent sample had thoughts of suicide. So too does the research of Cauce and associates (2000), who found a 45% rate of attempted suicide among homeless youth (54% for girls, 40% for boys), and Tierney and team (2008), who report that "approximately 75% of homeless youth have suicidal thoughts at some point during their adolescence" (p. 4).

Social Deterioration

A macroeffect of homelessness on children is that in essence they are cast out and lost from society. (Shane, 1996, p. 27)

Homeless children manifest a wide range of social difficulties.
(Korinek et al., 1992, p. 136)

In addition to the physical and emotional damage accompanying homelessness, displaced youth and children suffer significant social harm as well. Cut off from the protections provided by traditional social moorings, they become a vulnerable population (National Law Center on Homelessness and Poverty, 2004a; Schmitz et al., 2001). Their lives "are both unstable and hazardous" (Rothman, 1991, p. 2). Homeless adolescents in general and street youth in particular "have life courses wrought with violent experiences" (Baron, 2003, p. 22). Or, as Hagan and McCarthy (1997) teach us, "the street is a downward spiral of deviance and danger" (p. 3). The double-barreled theme of the social impact of homelessness has been nicely captured by Moore (2005b): "Homelessness destroys traditional ties and puts youth in violence prone situations" (p. 11).

In this part of the chapter, we unpack the social impact of homelessness as follows: In the first section (social isolation and a subculture of violence), we explore how homelessness can destroy normal social supports and often pulls young persons into a social milieu characterized by violence. In the second section (antisocial behavior), we examine the deviant and sometimes criminal behavior that results from the earlier two dynamics. We highlight damage to self (e.g., substance abuse) and harm to others (e.g., robbery). In the final section (victimization), we discuss how homelessness often leads to young persons becoming the victims of violence (e.g., sexual abuse).

Social Isolation and a Subculture of Violence

As just noted, homelessness often strips away the web of social supports that bind young persons to societal norms and that permit children and youth to grow into well-integrated members of society. In almost all cases, displacement stunts and generally prevents the growth of new supportive structures. Once this process is set in motion, young persons often are pushed and pulled into a parallel social environment, one in which the formation of criminal capital replaces the development of social capital and in which antisocial norms and behaviors come to dominate. As a result, homeless young persons find themselves on a downhill pathway to further social isolation and violence.

Social Isolation

> *Homelessness leads to the disintegration of social bonds and networks and a sense of isolation. (Anooshian, 2005, p. 133)*

⁓◠◟◝⁓

Researchers conclude that "the social isolation of homeless children is often pervasive" (Anooshian, 2000, p. 80). They also teach us about the meaning of social isolation. Anooshian (2005), for example, explains that "it is important to recognize that 'isolation' is not synonymous with physical distance or separation from others. The concern is with the scarcity of social attachments and high-quality social interactions experienced by homeless individuals" (p. 132).

Social isolation is defined by a "lack of stable social relationships" (Williams, 2003, p. 27). On the one front, it is defined as a "deterioration"

(Shane, 1996, p. 30) of existing relations (Janus et al., 1987). For adolescents, this means "leaving the sphere of influential adults" (Whitbeck & Hoyt, 1999, p. 80) and increasingly "tenuous ties to family" (Cauce et al., 2000, p. 233). For children, it means "difficulty in maintaining social connections" (Anooshian, 2005, p. 137), difficulty in "forg[ing] and maintain[ing] friendships" (National Center for Homeless Education, 2006a, p. 1). On a second front, social isolation is defined as a "disconnect from conventional life" (Inciardi and team, cited in Fleisher, 1995, p. 109) and "prosocial support networks" (Whitbeck & Hoyt, 1999, p. 79). That is, homelessness "weakens or reduces ties to and involvement in conventional organizations and institutions" (Hagan & McCarthy, 1997, p. 83): "Street youth are outside most social institutions that conventionally provide young people with emotional and economic rewards, security, and status: the family, stable social networks, school, and work" (Hagan & McCarthy, 1997, p. 205). On a third front, social isolation is defined in terms of the inability to form new relationships. Scholars regularly confirm that "homelessness interferes with the development of these relationships" (Biggar, 2001, p. 952), that "homeless children and youth have difficulty developing stable relationships" (Penuel & Davey, 1998, pp. 5–6) and, of central importance in this volume, these "failed relationships can be formidable barriers to educational success" (Anooshian, 2005, p. 137). They also affirm that the poor social skill development that accompanies homelessness is indicated in the inability of children and youth to forge appropriate social relationships (Rouse & Fantuzzo, 2009).

Where all this leads, oftentimes, is to a position of "social isolation" (Anooshian, 2005, p. 132) and a state of "social disaffiliation" (Merves, 1992, p. 237; Ropers, 1988, p. 147), to "the feeling of outsiderness" (Auerswald & Eyre, 2002, p. 1501) and "loneliness" (Karabanow, 2004, p. 57)—and, in the worst cases, to a sense of "alienation from society" (Farrow et al., 1992, p. 723). Homeless children and "youth often find themselves alone in a difficult, dangerous, and uncaring world" (Shane, 1996, p. 6), more socially isolated than poor housed children and youth (Anooshian, 2005).

The fact that homeless youth and children are socially isolated is consequential (Whitbeck & Hoyt, 1999). It means that these young persons receive "less social support" (Wright et al., 1998, p. 94), "fewer sources of social support than either previously homeless or never homeless children" (Anooshian, 2005, p. 137). According to Whitbeck and Hoyt (1999), for homeless youth, "conventional intergenerational sources of support and influence [are] largely interrupted" (p. 70), and "primary supportive ties to caretaker adults are weakened" (Bao et al., 2000, p. 409). In its strongest form, Swick (2005) asserts that *the most damaging facet* of being homeless is the isolation of children from needed supports and resources" (p. 195, emphasis added). "To have a home is to be anchored to some form of social network and to have a basis for establishing other social supports" (Ropers, 1988, p. 89). To be homeless means that these networks are weakened or eliminated (Anooshian, 2005; Reganick, 1997). And the absence of this social support is also meaningful. Poor support results in adjustment problems for homeless children and youth and a lack of "buffer[ing] to protect homeless children from the influence of stressful life events" (Anooshian, 2005, p. 137).

Social isolation and its impact can loosen "normal" confining webs of prosocial expectations for behavior (Hagan & McCarthy, 1997): "Adult perspectives are lost as are adult-initiated behavioral expectations and limits" (Whitbeck & Hoyt, 1999, p. 81): "Living on the margins can alter the perceptions of punishment" (Baron & Kennedy, 1998, p. 27); it can "lead to a decrease in the threats of formal sanctions for engaging in violence" (Baron, 2003, p. 33). Foreshadowing the line of analysis immediately following, we know first that isolation from conventional social relationships and organizations opens the door to the formation of less-than-productive peer networks, relationships that can fill a void for displaced children (and their families) and adolescents but are often dysfunctional to the goal of returning to mainstream society (Bao et al., 2000; Jahiel, 1992d; Snow & Anderson, 1993). Second, because "the quality and supportiveness of the relationships youth experience are source[s] of potentially risk-enhancing or risk-decreasing effects on behavior" (Ennett et al., 1999, p. 65), social isolation contributes to emotional and behavioral problems for homeless young people (Cauce et al., 2000; Ennett et al., 1999; Rotheram-Borus, Rosario, & Koopman, 1991). In particular, we see that "social isolation for homeless children . . . can be a significant risk factor for aggressive and antisocial behavior" (Anooshian, 2005, p. 133).

Specific indicators of social isolation for young persons and their families have been exposed in a variety of studies. (For information on the general homeless population, see Bahr, 1973; Bassuk, 1984; Shlay & Rossi, 1992.) For example, Ennett and associates (1999) report that about one-quarter of the homeless youth in their sample provided no name when asked about current social relationships. In research by Feitel and colleagues (1992), fully 40% of homeless youth remarked that they "had no one they could call on for help, even in a dire emergency" (p. 156). Looking at homeless mothers of accompanied children, Anooshian (2005) reports that "compared to poor housed mothers, homeless mothers report less contact with friends and relatives, fewer people they can count on for help, and social networks that are less helpful in raising children" (p. 133). And Bassuk (1992) concludes that "although most mothers had grown up in the geographical area where they were sheltered, the majority had minimal or no social supports. In response to the question, 'Who are the three people most important to you that you could depend on during difficult times?,' 26% could not think of anyone, 18% could name only one person, and 20% could name only two people. One-fourth named a child as their only support" (p. 259).

Criminal Capital and a Subculture of Violence

There are few if any prosocial options available on the street.
(Whitbeck & Hoyt, 1999, p. 171)

Social isolation (1) exposes homeless youth to "highly criminogenic" (Hagan & McCarthy, 1997, p. 70) environments, (2) promotes the accumulation of criminal capital, and (3) fosters the formation of antisocial behavior. In short, it is asserted, "being homeless puts the adolescent into contact with peers and situations that promote delinquency" (McCaskill et al., 1998, p. 315). In the next section, we explore issue number three, the antisocial behavior that is often associated with homelessness, looking at both the deviant (risky) behaviors that cause damage to the self and the criminal behaviors directed at others (also known as deviant survival strategies). Here we focus on the first two issues, the crime-infested environment and the formation of criminal capital.

Analysts routinely find that homeless youth are enmeshed in a culture that induces risk taking and criminal activities (Auerswald & Erye, 2002), what Baron and colleagues (2001) refer to as a "highly aversive environment" (p. 763). According to Baron (2003), homelessness places youth in "locations and situations in which violence is more likely" (p. 28) and, most critically, in the company of deviant and dangerous peers (Hagan & McCarthy, 1997). Thus, youth can be "swept and pushed into criminal involvements by the circumstances they encounter on the street" (Hagan & McCarthy, 1997, p. 231), a "criminal opportunity structure" (Baron & Hartnagel, 1998, p. 170) and a "supportive context" (Ennett et al., 1999, p. 74) for antisocial behavior.

We can sort these adverse elements and dynamics into three categories: place, context, and people. To begin with, researchers document that homelessness often deposits youth in unsafe "places," physical locales that "increase one's accessibility to crime in addition to increasing the likelihood of contact between oneself and potential offenders" (Tyler, Whitbeck, Hoyt, & Cauce, 2004, pp. 505–506) and other victims: "Their lifestyles and routines expose them to dangerous locations (Moore, 2005b, p. 11).

"Context" refers to the conditions of homelessness, that is, the reality of few resources and an oftentimes much reduced system of social supports. In particular, analysts are quick to acknowledge that it is extremely difficult for homeless youth to find much in the way of gainful employment (Whitbeck & Hoyt, 1999), that "economic survival on [one's] own is almost impossible" (Rothman, 1991, p. 2). They also document that "the absence of adult supervision and control" (Whitbeck & Hoyt, 1999, p. 12) in the environment "encourages adultlike behaviors such as drug and alcohol use and early sexuality" (Whitbeck & Hoyt, 1999, p. 12).

Finally, scholars examine changes in the "people" profiles for homeless adolescents. As they are pulling away—and being pushed away—from conventional connections and normal social relationships, that is, as social isolation envelopes them, homeless youth move into a world with a peer-dominated center of gravity (Bao et al., 2000; Karabanow, 2004). "As adolescents move away from adult spheres a process is set in motion that is difficult to reverse. Adult influences are replaced by the influence of 'adultlike' peers" (Whitbeck & Hoyt, 1999, p. 156), "an age-segregated, predominantly nonconventional support system made up of young people who, for the most part, are in similar circumstances" (p. 70). "They band together" (Baron, 2003, p. 30). Analysts explain that these are often deviant peer affiliations (Baron & Hartnagel, 1998), "destructive relationships" (Reed-Victor, 2000, p. 103). That is, as homeless youth become "increasingly separated from family influence, they [are] more apt to affiliate with deviant peers" (Bao et al., 2000, p. 416) "who serve as socialization agents for antisocial behaviors as well as exploitation within the group" (Terrell, 1997, p. 268). According to Baron (2003), "the end result is that homeless youth are more likely to interact with aggressive peer groups and thus acquire definitions favorable to using violence to solve problems" (p. 29).

Scholars who study homeless adolescents note that these peer-dominated social networks are not all bad, that they "may be a source of personal support" (Whitbeck & Hoyt, 1999, p. 70). Peers often teach other homeless youth "rules of survival" (Karabanow, 2004, p. 53) on the street. Such networks can "provide adolescents with protection, people to talk to about their troubles, and information about how to get by" (Whitbeck & Hoyt, 1999, p. 81).

> Adaptive to the context on the street, the peer support system becomes an important primary source of social support to a distressed runaway. It provides not only companionship but also material aid, emotional support, and teaching of survival skills on the streets, all which help the child cope with increasingly stressful situations. To survive street life, homeless adolescents band together to develop supportive networks, coping strategies, and meaningful relationships that impact their psychological development at the very time when such support networks are most needed. (Bao et al., 2000, p. 409)

On balance, however, the peer relations that dominate the homeless youth environment are found to be a serious problem for the well-being of young people (Baron et al., 2001). Almost all of the scholarship in this area links these age-segregated networks with the development and maintenance of a "subculture of violence" (Baron & Hartnagel, 1998, p. 180), one defined by "peer pressure to deviant behavior" (Bao et al., 2000, p. 409) and norms supporting antisocial and illegal behavior (Hagan & McCarthy, 1997; Whitbeck & Hoyt, 1999)—"positive attitudes toward the use of violence" (Baron, 2003, p. 30) and "a shared rejection of the mainstream culture" (Auerswald & Eyre, 2002, p. 1505). For example, "there is evidence that street youth have acquired values that are supportive of violence and that these values are linked to violent behavior" (Baron, 2003, p. 29). Peer networks foster an environment "where rules supportive of violence emerge and where these rules guide behavior" (p. 31). Because "affiliation with deviant peers [is] strongly associated with all deviant street behaviors and street victimization" (Whitbeck & Hoyt, 1999, pp. 152–153), interactions with deviant peers, in turn, "place an increased risk in the lives of homeless youth" (Bao et al., 2000, p. 410). They also go a long way toward ensuring that homeless youth remain homeless (Snow & Anderson, 1993).

> Connections into the life of the street may be just as likely in a converse way to increase the probability of unemployment and downward life trajectories once youth leave home and take to the street. For example, the criminal involvements of street peers are more likely to integrate young people into the criminal underworld than into referral networks of legal employment. And involvements in street networks are likely to further distance youth from the school and job contacts that are important in developing legitimate pathways into later life opportunities. (Hagan & McCarthy, 1997, pp. 232–233)

Finally, it is important to acknowledge that this subculture of violence that emerges from deviant peer connections exerts powerful forces that become "more and more difficult to escape as the duration of [homelessness] increases" (Whitbeck & Hoyt, 1999, p. 10). Similarly, it is instructive to note that the subculture of violence is cyclical and mutually reinforcing. Being a victim often leads homeless youth to victimize others. And victimizing, in turn, increases the odds of being a victim. "The street culture and deviant behavior" (Fleisher, 1995, p. 146) are reinforced. And aggressive behaviors, in turn, reinforce "social isolation and relationship problems" (Anooshian, 2005, p. 142).

Antisocial Behavior

The environmental realities of being homeless can contribute to behavioral problems. (Powers & Jaklitsch, 1992, p. 123)

~◠╳◠~

Homeless adolescents are more likely than their housed peers to engage in antisocial behavior. (Tierney et al., 2008, p. 4)

~◠╳◠~

So far, we have seen that homelessness negatively impacts the development of social capital while nurturing the formulation of criminal capital.

Here we examine the actual behaviors that play out in the subculture of violence that often marks homelessness for adolescents. After a few introductory remarks about the presence of behavior problems, we explore the two domains of antisocial actions: behaviors that damage the self (risky behaviors) and behaviors that harm others (criminal actions/deviant survival strategies).

The literature is replete with references to the behavior problems and "conduct disorders" (Whitbeck & Hoyt, 1999, p. 142) that accompany homelessness for children and youth (Hart-Shegos & Associates, 1999). Researchers conclude that behavior problems are not unusual among homeless children (Anooshian, 2005; Hicks-Coolick et al., 2003) and that "delinquent behaviors" (Janus et al., 1987, p. 95) or "disruptive behavior disorders also appear to be common among the homeless teen population" (McCaskill et al., 1998, p. 306).

Analysts document high levels of behavioral problems (Shane, 1996), significantly higher than for housed *youth* (Rabideau & Toro, 1997; Sullivan & Knutson, 2000; Toro, 1998), and a high level of "conduct-disordered behaviors" (Farrow et al., 1992, p. 721). According to Russell (1998), "the lifetime prevalence of conduct disorder among the general child/adolescent (i.e., under 18 years of age) population has been estimated at 2–9% for female children and 6–16% for male children" (p. 319). Studies of homeless youth, on the other hand, report considerably higher rates of conduct disorder: 59% in a study by Feitel and associates (cited in Whitbeck & Hoyt, 1999, p. 142), 64–84% in work by Russell (1998), and 93% in an investigation by Robertson (cited in McCaskill et al., 1998, p. 306).

Analysts also affirm that homeless *children* "have abnormally elevated scores on parental reports of behavior problems" (Shinn & Weitzman, 1996, p. 119). They "have three times the rate of behavioral problems compared to non-homeless children," according to the NCFH (2008, p. 5). Kelly and team (2000, referencing the work of Masten) note that "behavioral problems among homeless children were apparent at a rate three to four times than that expected in the general population, exceeding the relatively elevated rates found in a comparison sample of poor but housed children" (p. 175). According to Rabideau and Toro (1997), "children were experiencing more behavior problems as compared to community norms. Based on maternal report, six times as many children as expected were exhibiting externalizing behavior problems that indicated the need for mental health services and four times more were exhibiting internalizing behavior problems" (p. 12). Korinek and team (1992), Masten and associates (1997), Rescorla and colleagues (1991), and Toro (1998) provide parallel findings, documenting "levels of behavior problems above national norms" (Jozefowicz-Simbeni & Israel, 2006, p. 38), "significantly higher rates of behavioral symptoms [for homeless children] relative to children of similar age and background living in homes" (Rescorla et al., 1991, p. 218).

On the adolescent front, it is held that behavior problems or acts of delinquency are often "a maladaptive strategy employed to survive the hostile and abusive environment of the street" (Janus et al., 1987, p. 50). That is, homeless youth lacking networks of positive support and "confront[ing] desperate situations on a daily basis" (Hagan & McCarthy, 1997, p. 1) turn to violent behavior to meet their needs: "The adolescent behaviors labeled as deviant or problematic . . . are viewed as adaptive solutions by homeless youth" (Rew, 1996, p. 355).

In the sections that follow, we explore the antisocial behavior that has been linked to the social isolation and subculture of violence that often defines youth homelessness. We divide that analysis of antisocial behavior into two categories: risky behaviors that damage primarily the self and criminal activity against others (i.e., deviant survival strategies). We close this part of the chapter on social deterioration by documenting how homeless youth also become victims of violence. The starting point for all this analysis is that homeless youth, especially street youth, "are heavily involved in violence as offenders [and] they are extremely vulnerable to victimization" (Baron, 2003, p. 33): "Street youth are frequently both perpetrators and victims of street violence" (Karabanow, 2004, p. 42). The second point is that there is overlap among the three domains we explore later: risky behaviors, deviant subsistence strategies, and victimization. Finally, it is essential to acknowledge that these three dimensions of the violent subculture of youth homelessness are mutually reinforcing. Risky behaviors (e.g., drug abuse) often encourage deviant survival strategies (e.g., prostitution) and together they can lead to victimization (e.g., being sexually abused). Victimization, in turn, has consistently been shown to ratchet up criminal behavior, "which has the effect of increasing future victimization" (Baron et al., 2001, p. 764). And thus the loop of violence and antisocial behavior deepens and hardens for homeless adolescents.

Risky Behavior (Damage to Self)

Alcohol and drugs are woven through the life experiences of many homeless adolescents. (Whitbeck & Hoyt, 1999, p. 135)

There is a robust body of research which reveals that homeless adolescents "and their lived experiences are defined in terms of the participation in and/ or exposure to risk behaviors" (Mallett et al., 2004, p. 338), that "homeless friends may influence homeless teens to engage in risky behavior" (Penuel & Davey, 2000, p. 67). Three bundles of risky behaviors are underscored in the literature: substance abuse, survival sex, and unsafe sexual practices.

We know from the research that *substance abuse*, especially alcohol abuse, is a central theme in the general narrative on homelessness (Bahr,

1973; Fischer, 1992; Snow & Anderson, 1993; Toro, 1998): "Alcohol and drug abuse characterize a significant proportion of homeless persons" (Shlay & Rossi, 1992, p. 139), and alcoholism is the most frequently recorded disorder among homeless adults, with an abuse rate in the 50% to 70% range (Rollinson & Pardeck, 2006; Toro, 1998). More to the point here, research affirms that "alcohol and other drug abuse also appears to be a pervasive problem among homeless youth" (Farrow et al., 1992, p. 720). Especially on the street (Ennett et al., 1999; Hagan & McCarthy, 1997; Taylor et al., 2004), homeless "youth are caught up in a lifestyle that includes the heavy use of alcohol and drugs" (Baron, 2003, p. 32)—"part and parcel of the street lifestyle is the use of drugs and alcohol" (Baron & Hartnagel, 1998, p. 169).

Data on the prevalence of substance abuse among homeless youth confirm the depth of alcohol and drug use and dependency. In their report, Feitel and team (1992) describe a homeless sample in which 47% of youth consumed alcohol frequently and 46% abused alcohol. The corresponding figures for marijuana use and abuse were 42% and 20%. Overall substance abuse was calculated at 41%. Yates and team (referenced in Rotheram-Borus, Mahler, Koopman, & Langabeer, 1996) "reported that 84% of runaways seeking services at a health clinic used alcohol or drugs" (p. 391). In their study of street youth, Hagan and McCarthy (1997) uncovered very significant rates of substance abuse: "Once on the street, 80 percent of our respondents smoked marijuana, 55 percent took LSD or other chemicals, and 43 percent used cocaine" (p. 52). Cauce and associates (2000) add the following data: "Alcohol was the most commonly used substance, followed by marijuana and hard drugs. Roughly one-third of study participants (35%) drank alcohol 10 or more times in the 3 months prior to being interviewed. Twenty-seven percent of participants used marijuana 10 or more times, and approximately 10% used hard drugs as frequently" (p. 234). Ennett et al.'s study (1999) documents that "current marijuana use was reported by 61.5 percent of youth, current heavy alcohol use by 31.3 percent, and current illicit drug use by 25.9 percent" (p. 68). Gwadz and colleagues (2009) provide data consistent with these other researchers: "Approximately half of the youth interviewed (48.0%) had used alcohol in the past three months, 56.3% had used drugs, and a third (33.8%) exhibited polysubstance use. Among those using alcohol, the average number of drinks per week was 24.4. Regular (45%) and daily (33.8%) drug use were common, and marijuana was the most commonly used drug, used by 56.6% of youth" (p. 365). Russell (1998) provides data showing that almost one-half of the homeless youth in her study "met caseness criteria for alcohol abuse and/or dependence, and over one-third met caseness criteria for drug abuse and/or dependence. Among those respondents who met diagnostic criteria for drug abuse and/or dependence, criteria were most commonly met for cannabis, amphetamines, cocaine, and opiates" (p. 320). Whitbeck and Hoyt's (1999) research confirms that alcohol and marijuana are the most used and abused substances for homeless youth, reporting a marijuana use rate of about 70% for displaced adolescents.

A critical question, of course, is this: How do these numbers compare to rates of substance abuse among adolescents in general? A second and even more essential question is this: How do substance abuse patterns of homeless youth compare to rates of abuse before they became homeless? On the second issue, unfortunately, we have very little information. On the one hand, Russell (1998) reports that "most youth claimed that their substance use had not increased since becoming homeless" (p. 153). On the other hand, Hagan and McCarthy (1997) arrive at the opposite conclusion, noting that "reports of substance abuse were significantly higher than the level reported before leaving home" (p. 52). Without more data here, it is impossible to estimate how much of the substance abuse of homeless adolescents can be attributed to homelessness, to get a scientific handle on the "impact" question; that is, to test the claim that substance abuse "is a product of homelessness" (Jencks, 1994, p. 43), "an effect [rather] than a cause of homelessness" (Kusmer, 2002, p. 243).

We do have some evidence, however, to help answer the first question: How does substance abuse among homeless youth compare to such abuse among the adolescent population generally? Hagan and McCarthy (1997) document that the high rate of substance abuse found among their street population is "higher than that reported in studies of high-school students" (p. 52), and for the general youth population, according to other scholars (Pires & Silber, 1991; Taylor et al., 2004; Tierney et al., 2008). Wright (cited in Shane, 1996) "found alcohol and drug abuse rates among teenage homeless youth to be significantly higher than in the control group" (p. 45). Rotheram-Borus (1991) provides the following comparisons: "IV drug use was found in 7% of homeless youths in Houston, and 3% to 7% heroin and cocaine use was reported in New York City. . . . These compare to national rates for adolescents of less than 1% heroin use to 3.1% IV drug use in a recent national survey of high school students" (p. 26). Reviews of research that shed light on this question reveal that drug abuse for runaways is about four times the rate for nonrunaway youth (Rotheram-Borus, 1991). Homeless youth alcohol abuse rates, in turn, are six to eight times higher (Farrow et al., 1992). Russell's (1998) review offers the following comparative data:

> Studies of substance use among street-involved youth in the U.S. have revealed that these youth are almost five times as likely to be heavy drinkers and three times as likely to be daily users of marihuana, as compared to a national sample of same aged school youth.
>
> These street youth revealed rates of illicit drug use ten times higher compared with Toronto school students. A study of clinic youth yielded a diagnosis of drug abuse in 57% of the clinic's runaway clientele compared to 14% of the nonrunaways. (p. 16)

We also learn the following lessons from the research. First, "longer exposure to cumulative lifetime homelessness positively covaries with symptoms of lifetime substance abuse" (Russell, 1998, p. 157). Second, as suggested earlier, deviant peer affiliations are "the most important predictor of daily or almost daily substance abuse" (Whitbeck & Hoyt, 1999, p. 147). Third, street homelessness leads to more abuse than sheltered homelessness (Russell, 1998). And fourth, consistent with a central theme of this volume, substance abuse, in turn, often has severe negative consequences. Or, as Shane (1996) pens it, "alcohol and/or substance abuse are dangers" (p. 20), dangers that negatively impact the physical and emotional health of young people (Farrow et al., 1992; Shane, 1996; Stefl, 1987) and deepen the culture of violence in which homeless youth are often ensnarled (Baron, 2003).

"Survival sex" (Rew, 1996, p. 351), or "trading sexual favors for money, drugs, food, or shelter" (Whitbeck & Hoyt, 1999, pp. 85–86), is the second of three categories of risky, self-harming behaviors linked to youth homelessness, one that shares space with the criminal activity of prostitution that we examine in the next section. Analysts consistently underscore this high-risk behavior in their discussions of homeless youth (Farrow et al., 1992; Pearce, 1995; Pires & Silber, 1991; Raleigh-DuRoff, 2004; Tyler & Cauce, 2002; Wells & Sandhu, 1986). They also confirm that it "is one of the most damaging consequences of homelessness" (Moore, 2005b, p. 9).

The extent of this activity among homeless youth, however, is open to debate, debate compounded by definitional problems (Greene et al., 1999). According to Whitbeck and colleagues, survival sex is much less prevalent than commonly thought. In one study (Whitbeck & Hoyt, 1999), they report that while many homeless youth had thought about engaging in survival sex (12% or so), and many more claimed to have a friend who had done so (40% or so), only 6% of the homeless men (boys) and 3% of the homeless women (girls) had ever traded sex for necessities. In another study (Whitbeck et al., 1997), they found that "about 5% of young men and young women had traded sex for money or drugs. Nine percent of young men and 5% of young women said they had traded sex for food or shelter" (Whitbeck et al., 1997, p. 383).

Other investigators arrive at considerably higher empirically anchored estimates. Greene and team (1999), for example, document rates of survival sex at 28% for their street sample and 10% for their shelter sample (p. 1408), figures they suggest are "probably minimum estimates because of the likelihood that respondents underreported their participation in survival sex, a highly stigmatized behavior" (p. 1408). Similar estimates can be found in studies and reviews by Booth and colleagues (1999), Reganick (1997), Rotheram-Borus (1991), and Taylor and team (2004).

Higher estimates still have been surfaced by Stahler and associates (1997), who peg the number of homeless youth trading sex for survival at about 33%, and by Russell (1998), who also found that "nearly one-third of the sample disclosed trading sex for money, food, shelter, or drugs" (p. 153). Gwadz and team (2009) provide an even higher estimate, recording that "about one-third to one-half of homeless youth exchange sex for money, drugs, food, a place to stay, or other resources" (p. 358).

There is also evidence that survival sex is even more widespread for homeless GLB youth, especially homeless males. For example, in their review, Tyler and associates (2004) highlight two studies that throw some light on this subset of homeless youth:

> Kipke and colleagues (1997) found that homeless GLB youth were 3 times as likely to have engaged in survival sex. In terms of gender, Kruks (1991) found that 72% of homeless male youth who reported engaging in survival sex were gay or bisexual, whereas among homeless female youth, only 8% involved in survival sex were gay or bisexual. (p. 507)

Perspective on the issue of survival sex is provided by Tierney and colleagues (2008). These scholars report that in the overall youth population, "less than 4% of adolescents exchange sex for money" (p. 4), considerably less than we documented earlier for homeless youth.

As with most conditions of homelessness, context matters for survival sex. For example, trading sex for survival is more common on the street than in shelters (Greene et al., 1999). A history of sexual assault enhances the chances of engaging in survival sex (Russell, 1998). So too does a history of physical abuse by family members and others (Greene et al., 1999). "Homeless youth with a history of substance abuse have significantly higher rates of survival sex" (Auerswald & Eyre, 2002, p. 1498). Russell (1998) informs us that "lifetime cumulative homelessness of one year or greater [also] appear[s] to be a risk factor for involvement in sex work" (p. 316); that is, "there is a positive relationship between participation in survival sex and length of time away from home" (Greene et al., 1999, p. 1408).

Finally, researchers affirm that trading sex for survival often has further deleterious effects. That is, "trading sex for food and shelter provides an avenue for self-sufficiency for those who cannot support themselves in any other way but comes with great cost and risk for those involved" (Helge, 1992, p. 219). It puts homeless adolescents in "dangerous and vulnerable positions with little or no protection (Baron, 2003, p. 29). It makes homeless youth "vulnerable to sexually transmitted diseases" (Rew, 1996, p. 348) and pregnancy (Helge, 1992). Thus, according to Greene and associates (1999), "the health implications of survival sex are underscored by the strong associations between survival sex and other high-risk behaviors and characteristics: substance use, suicide attempts, STDs, pregnancy, and criminal behavior" (p. 1408). In short, survival sex fosters physical and sexual abuse, that is, victimization (Tyler et al., 2004).

Related to survival sex is a third category of self-harming behaviors documented throughout the research on homeless youth, *risky sexual activities*. Scholars consistently document that "high-risk sexual behavior is common among runaways" (Rotheram-Borus, Mahler, Koopman, & Langabeer, 1996, p. 391) and other homeless youth (Hagan & McCarthy, 1997; Rew, 1996; Tyler et al., 2004). "Unsafe sex practices" (Pires & Silber, 1991, p. 30) are the norm and "the likelihood is high for an unsafe sex life" (Shane, 1996, p. 20).

Studies reveal that homeless youth are more sexually active than the general youth population. Whitbeck and Hoyt (1999), for example, report that 84% of homeless youth were sexually experienced, compared to 53% of high school students in Grades 9 to 12 (p. 95). These displaced young persons are also more sexually precocious than the general youth population (Auerswald & Eyre, 2002; Whitbeck & Hoyt, 1999): "Each indicator points to substantial numbers of sexual risk behaviors at an early age among runaways" (Rotheram-Borus, 1991, p. 26). Booth and colleagues' (1999) work shows "that initial sexual intercourse among runaways occurs at about 12.5 years, or 2 years earlier than that of non-runaways" (p. 1296).

Unprotected sex also characterizes homeless youth (Auerswald & Eyre, 2002; Booth et al., 1999; Pearce, 1995). While 54% of "high school students used a condom at last sexual intercourse" (Whitbeck & Hoyt, 1999, p. 97), only 34% of homeless youth in the Hollywood homeless study did so (Russell, 1998, p. 183).

Finally, homeless youth often have multiple sexual partners (Booth et al., 1999; Ennett et al., 1999), more than nonhomeless youth (Klein et al., 2000; Whitbeck & Hoyt, 1999)—"multiple and high-risk sexual partners," according to Auerswald and Eyre (2002, p. 1498). In particular, "their sexual partners are more likely to be HIV positive" (Whitbeck & Hoyt, 1999, p. 101). And, of course, as we have already noted, "engaging in risky sexual behavior is linked to victimization among homeless adolescents" (Tyler et al., 2004, p. 506).

Earlier in our discussion of health, we explained that homelessness and unwanted pregnancies are linked: "Pregnancy and teenage motherhood are associated with homelessness" (Rotheram-Borus, 1991, p. 26), and "pregnancy among homeless adolescents is extremely prevalent" (Whitbeck & Hoyt, 1999, p. 103). Here we make explicit that sexual "high-risk behavior is reflected in the levels of pregnancies found among homeless youths" (Rotheram-Borus, Mahler, Koopman, & Langabeer, 1996, p. 391): "Homeless youth are more likely than their domiciled counterparts to engage in risky sexual behavior, increasing their chances of becoming pregnant" (Klein et al., 2000, p. 331). We reported earlier that homeless youth become sexually active at 12.5 years of age and often have unprotected sex. Whitbeck and Hoyt (1999) connect the dots between these risky behaviors and pregnancy: "Becoming sexually active at the age of 13 years or younger increase[s] the likelihood of pregnancy among women twofold. . . . Inconsistent condom use increase[s] the likelihood of pregnancy by 64%" (p. 104). We learn that while the teenage birth rate nationally has decreased to 5%, in the "homeless [youth] population it is on the rise" (Institute for Children and Poverty, 2003, p. 3). We also learn that "homeless females have a higher rate of teenage pregnancy than counterparts who have a stable living environment" (Tierney et al., 2008, p. 4). Overall, then, Whitbeck and Hoyt (1999) report that "the combined pregnancy rates among the runaway adolescent males and females were 3 times the rate reported for ninth-to-twelfth graders in the CDC study (22 vs. 7%)" (p. 103).

Criminal Behavior (Harm to Others)

Although street youth constitute a relatively small proportion of all adolescents, they are involved in a substantial and disproportionate amount of crime. (Hagan & McCarthy, 1997, p. 10)

Homeless youth frequently report involvement in antisocial and criminal activities such as street prostitution, drug-dealing, theft, and assault. (Farrow et al., 1992, p. 721)

We just finished exploring antisocial behavior that primarily damages the homeless young person himself, acknowledging collateral harm to others. Here we explain how youth homelessness results in criminal activity directed at others, acknowledging collateral damage to self. Our starting point has been provided by scholars such as Baron (2003), Fleisher (1995), and Hagan and McCarthy (1997): "There is a link between homelessness . . . and violent behavior" (Baron, 2003, p. 23); "criminal activity remains a prominent characteristic of the contemporary homeless population" (Fischer, 1992, p. 60). In short, "homelessness leads to crime" (Baron et al., 2001, p. 761): "Some of the most serious problems of crime in North America are found among the homeless" (Hagan & McCarthy, 1997, p. 227). In particular, we learn that homeless youth, especially street-based adolescents, "participate in violence" (Baron et al., 2001, p. 760) against others.

Considerable analysis has been devoted to the linkage between homelessness and crime. Most of it concludes "that situational problems [accompanying homelessness] of sustenance and security cause street crime" (Hagan & McCarthy, 1997, p. 101): "Situational deprivation often leads to criminal behavior as a means of survival" (Whitbeck et al., 1997, p. 378). That is, "illegal behavior is a response to conditions of being 'on the street' rather than as an original condition" (Karabanow, 2004, p. 39), and "illegal street activities are more accurately understood as coping mechanisms for difficult situations rather than as deviant or pathological vices" (Karabanow, 2004, p. 54): "Youths' participation in crime is most likely the result of the homeless experience itself" (Baron & Hartnagel, 1998, p. 167). According to this line of analysis, "criminal activity[, especially for youth,] is one of the few available means of augmenting meager resources" (Fischer, 1992, p. 61); "criminal activity grows out of necessity more than intent" (Fischer, 1992, p. 61), from "the need to survive" (Fischer, 1992, p. 61). As a consequence, "criminal behavior is a 'definitional characteristic' of a street lifestyle and subculture for those who spend considerable amounts of time on the street" (Baron & Hartnagel, 1998, p. 169). In addition, for a minority of the homeless population, "there is a direct correlation between addiction and illegal or delinquent moneymaking activities" (Karabanow, 2004, p. 41).

We explored earlier how associations with deviant peers amplify violent, antisocial activities among homeless adolescents (Bao et al., 2000). We also explained how the context of homelessness and the location of homeless youth "expose street youth to more potential victims from which they can pick and choose according to risk and desired items" (Baron & Hartnagel, 1998, p. 180). Scholars often collect this antisocial behavior into a taxonomy with the general heading of "deviant subsistence strategies" (Whitbeck & Hoyt, 1999, p. 84). These tactics, it is held, are needed to live outside the formal economy (Fleisher, 1995) in a parallel "street economy" (Gwadz et al., 2009, p. 370). Engagement in "the unofficial economy of the street" (Barry et al., 2002, p. 149) means involvement survival strategies such as prostitution, drug dealing, robbery, shoplifting, and assault (Barry et al., 2002; Gwadz et al., 2009; Hagan & McCarthy, 1997).

Prostitution occupies important space in the taxonomy of antisocial behavior of homeless youth, being cited in nearly every study of these adolescents (Boesky et al., 1997; Hagan & McCarthy, 1997; Janus et al., 1987; Levine et al., 1986; Taylor et al., 2004). At the same time, estimates of the depth of this activity vary. Whitbeck and Hoyt (1999) report an overall rate of 2.3% (p. 84). Whitbeck and Simons (cited in Hagan & McCarthy, 1997) found in another study that "9 percent of homeless youth worked in prostitution" (p. 9). Russell (1998), using a slightly broader category of prostitution and pornography, found that 11.5% of homeless youth engaged in antisocial sexual activity. Farrow and team (1992) document a prostitution rate among homeless adolescents of 19% (p. 722). Higher rates are reported in three other studies reviewed by Rotheram-Borus, Mahler, Koopman, and Langabeer (1996):

> Rotheram-Borus et al. (1992) found that 22% of boys and 7% of girls studied in New York City had engaged in prostitution at some point. In the Los Angeles area, Robertson (1990) found the percentage to be 28% of males and 31% of females, and Yates et al (1988) reported a similar rate (26%). (p. 391)

In addition, researchers reveal that some homeless youth are also "involved in the *drug trade*" (Karabanow, 2004; Kipke et al., 1997; Powers & Jaklitsch, 1992, p. 120; Tierney et al., 2008), that they "sell drugs to survive on the street" (Pires & Silber, 1991, p. 31). Gwadz and team (2009) report that 28% of homeless youth supported themselves through the drug economy in the last three months (p. 364), while fully 56% had been involved in "dealing, selling, bagging, or running drugs" (p. 364) during homelessness. In the Whitbeck and Simons study (cited in Hagan & McCarthy, 1997), fully one-third of homeless youth sold drugs (p. 9). Whitbeck and Hoyt (1999) report a similar figure (30.4%; p. 84), while Hagan and McCarthy (1997) document that 46% of the homeless street youth in their study were involved in the drug trade. We also learn that any individual homeless youth is more likely to turn to drug dealing if he or she has parents who are substance abusers (Whitbeck & Hoyt, 1999).

On the criminal behavior front, investigators also conclude that "homelessness increase[s] street youths participation in *robbery*" (Baron, 2003, p. 28). Whitbeck and Hoyt (1999), for example, found that 23% of homeless youth reported taking money or something else of value from others, while 14% reported breaking into and stealing from a store or house (p. 84). In the Gwadz and team (2009) study, 31% of homeless youth reported that they engaged in mugging or robbery (p. 364), while in the Hagan and McCarthy (1997) study, 27% said they had broken into a home or business (p. 10).

Stealing, shoplifting, purse snatching, and *petty theft* are also common illegal activities among homeless youth (Fleisher, 1995; Gwadz et al., 2009; Karabanow, 2004), with a 23% engagement rate according to Whitbeck and Hoyt (1999), 43% according to Whitbeck and Simons (cited in Hagan & McCarthy, 1997, p. 9), and a 62% rate according to Gwadz and colleagues (2009, p. 364). In total, some homeless youth come "to view theft as an occupation" (Wells & Sandhu, 1986, p. 144). Indeed, according to Hagan and McCarthy (1997), "theft appears to be the most common criminal solution to the search for necessities [among] street youth" (p. 87).

To some extent, homeless youth are "active participants in serious *assaults*" (Baron & Hartnagel, 1998, p. 167) as well (Fleisher, 1995). Homelessness for adolescents is "linked with an increase in assaults, assaults with weapons, group assaults, and nonspecific assaults" (Baron, 2003, p. 28).

Collectively, participation in crime while homeless is the norm (Hagan & McCarthy, 1997): "Crime become[s] a way of life for many youth living on the streets" (Levine et al., 1986, p. 94). We also know that "criminal involvement is not simply more prevalent among street youth but also more frequent and serious" (Hagan & McCarthy, 1997, p. 9). For example,

> data collected in an outpatient medical clinic in Los Angeles revealed that 16% of homeless adolescents and 4% of the nonhomeless adolescents reported having been arrested during the previous 12 months . . . a total of 41% of the homeless adolescents and 8% of

the nonhomeless youth were reportedly involved in illegal activities; homeless adolescents were 17 times more likely to have been arrested in the previous year and twice as likely to be involved in a gang. (Farrow et al., 1992, pp. 721–722)

We learn too that the quarter of the homeless youth population that are hard-core street kids are even more active in criminal activity than other homeless adolescents; fully 75% of these youth engage in criminal activity (Rothman, 1991, p. 19). Analysts explain that criminal activity in the home before youngsters become homeless translates into more illegal behavior on the street once homeless (Moore, 2005b). We also know that there are gender differences associated with this illegal enterprise. For example, according to Hagan and McCarthy (1997), "homeless males are more likely to steal while females are more likely to work in the sex trade" (p. 92). Finally, scholars reveal that these "high-risk behaviors associated with deviant subsistence strategies increase the exposure and risk for victimization" (Whitbeck et al., 1997, p. 388); "risky lifestyles expose actors to victimization" (Baron & Hartnagel, 1998, p. 182) and exploitation (Rothman, 1991). According to Whitbeck and Hoyt (1999), "engaging in victimizing behavior almost doubled the odds of adolescent males becoming victims themselves" (p. 113). And, as we observed earlier, victimization, in turn, reinforces criminal activity among homeless youth, thus closing the loop in a vicious cycle of violence. We turn to "victimization" next.

Victimization

Homeless adolescents are uniquely subject to victimization.
(Reganick, 1997, p. 134)

~∽∿∾~

Homeless adolescents are easy targets for victimization and exploitation.
(Powers & Jaklitsch, 1992, p. 118)

~∽∿∾~

Homeless youth experience high rates of victimization on the streets.
(Tyler et al., 2004, p. 503)

~∽∿∾~

To this point, we have explored two of the three dimensions of the social impact of homelessness on displaced youth and children—social isolation/disaffiliation and antisocial behavior directed at self and others. Here we turn our attention to the third part of the social impact narrative, victimization. There is considerable consensus in the research that homeless children and youth in general and street youth in particular are subject to becoming victims of crime (Baron, 2003; Klein et al., 2000; Lindsey & Williams, 2002; Terrell, 1997). "The street leaves these youth vulnerable to victimization" (Baron et al., 2001, p. 781): "Among the many hazards of homelessness, victimization through criminal attack is one that epitomizes the vulnerability of not having four walls and a door" (Burt et al., 2001, p. 69):

> One characteristic that all runaway youth share is the extreme risk of serious harm while they are on their own. (Whitbeck & Hoyt, 1999, p. 8)

> Youth living on the street are in significant danger as they are targets for adult sexual exploitation and assault. (Duffield et al., 2007, p. 36)

> Although many of us see such young people as predators, the kinds of experiences they had led them to see themselves as extremely vulnerable, immersed in an unrelievedly malevolent environment. (Feitel et al., 1992, p. 158)

> The risks associated with being homeless include the risk of being a victim of crime. (Ropers, 1988, p. 166)

There is also agreement that this vulnerability generally leads to actual victimization, that "runaway and throwaway children are frequent victims of street crime and exploitation" (Sullivan & Damrosch, 1987, p. 93): "Homeless children will often be victimized themselves" (Toro, 1998, p. 126). Indeed, researchers expose very high rates of victimization among homeless youth and children, as high as 81% (Moore, 2005b, p. 11).

The central theme in the victimization chronicle is that the living conditions of homelessness and the resultant social isolation, culture of violence, and antisocial (criminal) behavior all coalesce to place homeless persons in general (Bahr, 1973; Jahiel, 1987) and homeless youth in particular in a highly vulnerable position for exploitation and assault (Baron, 2003; Tyler et al., 2004; Whitbeck et al., 1997). Overall, then, "there is evidence to suggest that the social hazards of leading these risky lifestyles are reflected in greater risks of experiencing violent victimization" (Baron & Hartnagel, 1998, p. 171).

We add here the knowledge that victimization reinforces criminal behavior. That is, "victimization within this environment leads to greater violent offending behavior" (Baron & Hartnagel, 1998, p. 171) because "people are expected to legitimate more readily the use of violence because of their victimization experience" (p. 171). Street assaults often leave the homeless "with no choice but to use violence" (Hagan & McCarthy, 1997, p. 46): "Victimization seems to be a fertile breeding ground for the creation of violent offenders" (Baron & Hartnagel, 1998, p. 183). Thus, all the pieces are in place for a loop of violent activity with a reinforcement of the other negative impacts (e.g., physical health) of homelessness (Whitbeck & Hoyt, 1999).

What is especially tragic here is the mistaken idea that running away from outrages at home can help reduce the violence that befalls children and youth (Farrow et al., 1992; Whitbeck et al., 1997). In reality, investigations affirm, homeless adolescents "often are doubly victimized. In their attempts to escape often intolerable situations and victimization at home, many take to the streets where they are victimized by peers, exploitative adults, and others" (Terrell, 1997, p. 268): "Once on the street, they are doubly victimized as they are exposed to dangers that equal or exceed the home situations they sought to escape" (Moore, 2005b, p. 18).

Equally troubling is the mistaken belief that by affiliating with other homeless peers, youth can protect themselves from violence. While this remains a possibility, more frequently, peers place homeless youth at risk of assault and cause even more victimization (Terrell, 1997). Indeed, affiliation with deviant peers "dramatically increase[s] the odds of physical victimization" (Whitbeck & Hoyt, 1999, p. 113). More disheartening still is the research that concludes that it is often the peers themselves who are doing the victimizing (Baron, 2003; Shane, 1996; Tyler et al., 2004): "Many of the people with whom street people affiliate are the same persons who are victimizing them" (Tyler et al., 2004, p. 505): Indeed, "the greatest threats encountered by runaway adolescent young men and women is from peers" (Whitbeck & Hoyt, 1999, p. 111).

Sexual Assault

Children are routinely victims of sexual abuse. (NCFH, 2009, p. 24)

～◠ᵜ◠～

Sexual assault is a common life-threatening situation that many [homeless] adolescents encounter while on the street. (Terrell, 1997, p. 268)

～◠ᵜ◠～

A sizeable body of evidence confirms that displaced youth and children are often sexually abused (Helge, 1992; Shane, 1996; Tyler et al., 2004). The research informs us that there are conditions that increase the likelihood of sexual victimization. Four variables in the "sexual activity" category are of particular note. To begin with, investigators report that homeless "adolescent girls who participated in survival sex . . . were more likely to be victimized" (Whitbeck & Hoyt, 1999, p. 153). Second, "sexual abuse [is also] significantly associated with having engaged in sex work" (Rotheram-Borus, Mahler, Koopman, & Langabeer, 1996, p. 395), that is, prostitution. Third, homeless "youth with a history of sexual abuse [have had] significantly more partners" (Rotheram-Borus, Mahler, Koopman, & Langabeer, 1996): "Adolescent girls who had a higher number of sexual partners were more likely to be victimized" (Whitbeck & Hoyt, 1999, p. 153). Finally, more unprotected sex translates into more sexual assault for homeless youth (Rotheram-Borus, Mahler, Koopman, & Langabeer, 1996).

Sexual victimization also increases when homeless children and youth engage in "daily routines that expose them to dangerous people and places" (Tyler et al., 2004, p. 517), "in circumstances that make them vulnerable" (Whitbeck & Hoyt, 1999, p. 108); that is, in places where criminal activity is the norm (Hammer et al., 2002) and in the company of deviant peers. Thus, "the street life situations of homeless adolescents have significant impacts on the possibility that they will be assaulted sexually" (Terrell, 1997, p. 267). Not surprisingly, then, we learn that engaging in deviant subsistence strategies to support oneself on the street is linked to sexual assault (Terrell, 1997). So too alcohol abuse and drug abuse have been connected to more sexual assaults on homeless young persons (Hagan & McCarthy, 1997; Tyler et al., 2004). For example, Tyler and associates (2004) ascertain "that for each unit increase in different type of drug use, the odds of females being sexually victimized by a stranger increase[s] 28%" (p. 513). And Rotheram-Borus, Mahler, Koopman, and Langabeer (1996) affirm that "a history of sexual abuse [is] also related to increased use of drugs and alcohol among runaway youths" (p. 398).

Context issues are also visible in the literature on the sexual assault of homeless youth. For example, all studies uncover gender variations, documenting that homeless "females are victimized sexually at a higher rate compared to runaway males" (Baron, 2003, p. 38), although sexual assault of males is far from rare (Shane, 1996):

> The current study found that both males and females experienced sexual victimization since being on the street but that the percentage for females was twice that of males (23% versus 11%). (Tyler et al., 2004, pp. 513–515)

> Gender [is] a highly significant predictor of sexual victimization. Adolescent females [are] . . . four times more likely than males to be victimized on the streets. (Whitbeck & Hoyt, 1999, p. 111)

In a similar vein, previous abuse at home increases the odds of sexual abuse once homeless (Terrell, 1997). As Whitbeck and Hoyt (1999) argue: "Sexual scripts are being formed. Those most damaged by the families they have left are at greatest risk for revictimization" (p. 115). They reveal that "when age and gender were controlled, adolescent females who had been sexually abused at home by an adult caretaker were two times more likely to be revictimized when they were on their own" (p. 114). Frequency of running away also increases sexual assault (Tyler et al., 2004), as does better grooming (Tyler et al., 2004). Sexual orientation comes into play here as well, with GLB status being a strong predictor of increased sexual victimization (Tyler et al., 2004).

The extensiveness of sexual assault among homeless youth is fairly well documented. Jahiel (1992a) reports a rate of 13%; Kipke and team (1997) 15%; Whitbeck and colleagues (1997), Rotheram-Borus (1991), Helge (1992), Terrell (1997), and Tyler and team (2004) around 20%. Comparative data peg the rate of sexual abuse for homeless youth at "five times higher than rates in the general population" (Rotheram-Borus, Mahler, Koopman, & Langabeer, 1996, p. 390).

Physical Assault

> *Homeless adolescents are at high risk for physical abuse.*
> *(Klein et al., 2000, p. 331)*

⁓◠ᵛ◠⁓

Scholars who examine the effects of homelessness argue "that the street life situations of homeless adolescents have significant impacts on the probability that they will become assaulted aggravatedly" (Terrell, 1997, p. 267). As was the case with sexual assault, the use of deviant subsistence strategies and affiliation with deviant peers increase the odds of victimization via physical abuse (Terrell, 1997).

On the numbers front, Powers and Jaklitsch (1992) assert that a "large percentage of the homeless youth population have experienced physical abuse" (p. 121). Rotheram-Borus (1991) documents a rate of physical assault of 20% (p. 25). According to Kipke and associates (cited in Whitbeck & Hoyt, 1999), "51% of a sample of Hollywood street youth had been beaten up since being on the streets, 45% had been chased, and 26% had been shot at. Nineteen percent had been stabbed while living on the street, and 7% wounded by gunfire" (p. 108). Whitbeck and Simons (referenced in Terrell, 1997), in turn, "found that 43% of adolescent men and 39% of adolescent women had been assaulted with a weapon while living on the streets" (p. 268). Terrell (1997) reports a physical assault rate of 35% and Helge (1992) 31%. Whitbeck and associates (references in Baron, 2003) "found that more than one third of the street youth in their sample recounted being beaten up while on the street (43% young men and 30% young women)" (p. 34). In Alder's study (referenced in Baron, 2003), 65% of the homeless youth sample had been physically assaulted (p. 34).

We close here by noting a similarity and a difference with the story line on sexual abuse. On the similarity side, we find that physical abuse is much higher for homeless youth than their domiciled peers. On the difference side of the ledger, physical abuse is higher for males than for females (Terrell, 1997):

Most research suggests that male street youth are more likely than female street youth to disclose histories of physical assault whereas females are more likely to disclose histories of sexual assault than are males. Russell (1998) for example, reported that male respondents were 2.4 times more likely to disclose histories of physical assault (without sexual assault) than were females. The odds of a female respondent disclosing a history of sexual assault were 1.7 times that of a male respondent. Similarly, Molnar et al. (1998) found females were more likely to report sexual abuse (70%)

than physical abuse (35%), whereas males were more likely to report physical abuse (35%) compared with sexual abuse (24%). (Baron, 2003, pp. 24–25)

Physical assaults were more common among the young men. Adolescent males (47%) were more than twice as likely to have been threatened with a weapon than young women (21%). They were also more than twice as likely to report having been assaulted with a weapon (25% of males vs. 9% of females). (Whitbeck & Hoyt, 1999, p. 108)

Robbery

Theft is particularly common, and regardless of where they find shelter, street youth are usually at risk. (Hagan & McCarthy, 1997, p. 46)

High rates of victimization via robbery are also reported for homeless youth. In the Terrell (1997) study, nearly a quarter (23.2%) of homeless youth reported being robbed—27% of the men and 18% of the women. Rotheram-Borus (1991) and Whitbeck and Hoyt (1999) provide similar figures.

Educational Deficits

Homeless children of school age suffer educational impairments relative to housed poor children or general population samples. (Shinn & Weitzman, 1996, p. 120)

Homelessness harms children in many ways—they suffer from health problems, nutritional deficiencies, and developmental delays—but its impact on children's education is equally damaging. (National Law Center on Homelessness and Poverty, 1995, p. 1)

Even more than poverty, homelessness is profoundly destructive to the educational outcomes of children. (NCFH, 2009, p. 28)

Homeless youth are at high risk for school failure. (Shane, 1996, p. 39)

In the material presented earlier, we revealed how homelessness shapes the physical, emotional, and social well-being of children and youth. We extend that work here by exposing the ways homelessness influences the educational well-being of these youngsters. We begin with the summative observation that "homelessness [is] a significant risk factor that can have debilitating effects on the educational attainment of children and adolescents" (Duffield, 2000, p. 225). Homelessness is an added risk factor that "exacerbates whatever else interferes with a child's learning" (Shane, 1996, p. 37). From the research here, we discover that homeless students are "academically compromised" (Sullivan & Knutson, 2000, p. 1286) and "academically challenged" (Gibbs, 2004, p. 26), and they are at risk of becoming "academic casualties" (Masten et al., 1997, p. 28): "The deprivations that plunge many families into homelessness undermine the school success of their children" (Rafferty, 1995, p. 55). Or, as Stronge and Hudson (1999) capture it, "no population is more at risk of school failure . . . than homeless children" (p. 9); "the very experience of homelessness further diminishes the already meager chance for . . . academic success" (Nunez, 1994b, p. 57).

In the final chapters of the book, we explore the mechanisms between homelessness and school results, with an eye on using these strategies to improve the rather dismal outcomes associated with homelessness. Here we presage that analysis, noting that "children faced with homelessness often have serious educational problems" (Masten et al., 1997, p. 40) and that schools often compound those difficulties by building "discouraging barriers to their academic success" (Better Homes Fund, 1999, p. 23): "The educational development of children and educational systems suffer on all levels and in all time frames from homelessness. Learning is greatly impeded and made difficult for the child. Teaching is impeded and made more difficult for the educational institution and the teacher" (Shane, 1996, p. 39). "The stress of homelessness greatly diminishes children's ability to succeed in school" (Rafferty, 1995, p. 39) and the school's often-unproductive responses, in turn, exacerbate the problems (Wilder et al., 2003).

We also reinforce a point raised a number of times previously; that is, while the problems unearthed when studying homeless children and youth are often experienced by children of the poor, especially youngsters from highly mobile, poor families (Anooshian, 2000; Masten et al., 1997), homelessness adds to the difficulties brought to the table by these risk factors (Dworsky, 2008). We also remind the reader that, consistent with earlier analysis, the negative associations between homelessness and educational success vary by the form of homelessness. The strongest negative relationship is found with street homelessness and the weakest with invisible homelessness, with sheltered homelessness in the middle (Shinn & Weitzman, 1996).

We begin our review with a variable, mobility, that has a good deal of explanatory power for both the physical and emotional impacts discussed earlier and the educational impacts examined here. We then discuss an assortment of outcome factors: placement in special education, attendance (once enrolled in school), suspensions, academic success, graduation, and postschool success. We begin at the end: "Research on school performance of homeless students shows that these youth are significantly less likely to succeed than their peers with more stable housing" (Penuel & Davey, 1998, pp. 6–7).

Mobility: Lost Time in Transitions

Frequent changes of school are detrimental to the intellectual development of homeless children. (Jahiel, 1987, p. 111)

Scholars who investigate youth homelessness consistently confirm the toxic relationship between mobility and educational success (Medcalf, 2008; Nunez & Collignon, 1997). They observe that the high rates of mobility associated with homelessness "wreak havoc with attempts to obtain consistent education" (NCFH, 2009, p. 28). They document that mobility "is one of the greatest barriers to educational achievement" (Penuel & Davey, 1998, p. 9).

The starting point here is the evidence showing that high rates of mobility for homeless children are the norm (Dworsky, 2008; Mihaly, 1991; Tierney et al., 2008)—"homeless students' mobility is not a temporary phenomenon but appears to be a consistent feature of homeless students' lives" (Penuel & Davey, 1998, p. 9). Analysts also reveal that mobility is much higher for homeless children and youth than it is for other children in general or for poor housed children in particular (Biggar, 2001). They link movement to the shifting residency patterns of the homeless that we documented in Chapter 3.

More specifically, analysts illustrate the connection between homelessness and school mobility. For example, in their analysis, the Better Homes Fund (1999) reported that "within a single year 41 percent of the [homeless] students attended two different schools; 28 percent attended three or more different schools" (p. 25). Nunez (1994b) provides parallel figures, documenting that "in the 1992 school year, nearly half of all school-age children entering HFH's facilities had attended at least two different schools. Another third had attended three separate schools, while 13 percent had been to at least four" (p. 62). In a more recent study in Chicago, Dworsky (2008) found on average that homeless children across their school careers "had changed schools 3.2 times, although the number of school changes ranged from a low of 0.6 to a high of 5.3 depending on the number of years they had been enrolled" (p. 44). Dworsky (2008) notes further that "of more concern than the total number of school changes these children had experienced was the frequency with which those changes occurred during the school year, when they are likely to be especially disruptive. Overall, 60 percent of these children had changed schools at least once mid-year, and these changes accounted for more than one-third of all the changes that occurred" (p. 20).

The problem with mobility is, of course, loss of time—both the actual time when students are not in school during "residency" transitions and the adjustment time when these youngsters are trying to connect to learning in their new schools (Whitman et al., 1990), collectively described as interruptions in the educational process (Emerson & Lovitt, 2003; Whitbeck & Hoyt, 1999). On the first issue, loss of actual time, Duffield and Lovell (2008) maintain the following:

> One of the primary reasons that homeless children are likely to perform poorly in school is because homelessness is characterized by turmoil, and homeless students are at risk of bouncing from one school to another and missing several days, if not weeks or more, of school as their families attempt to meet the most basic of human needs. (p. 9)

Other analysts reinforce this point:

> These students missed classes or, on occasion, years of schooling because they were constantly on the move. The importance of school fell by the wayside as they searched for housing or personal stability. (Tierney et al., 2008, p. 23)

> When students move frequently because of involuntary housing instability, there can be major gaps in their school attendance—ranging from several days to even weeks and months. (James & Lopez, 2003, p. 131)

More concretely, Rafferty and Rollins (cited in Johnson, 1992) reported that "on average, children missed 5 days of school each time they moved into a new shelter facility" (p. 173); "20 percent missed 10 or more days with each move" (Rafferty, 1995, p. 49).

On the second issue, time to reconnect to learning, "with each change in schools it is estimated that a student is set back an average of four to six months" (National Center for Homeless Education, 2006a, p. 1).

Finally, as we noted at the beginning of this section and illustrate in considerable detail later, "the high mobility associated with homelessness has severe educational consequences" (National Coalition for the Homeless, 2008, p. 1). That is, "school transfers have a well-documented effect on academic achievement" (Duffield et al., 2007, p. 11), what James and Lopez (2003) label a "devastating impact" (p. 135). This is the case, Dworsky (2008) maintains, because "children who change schools make less academic progress than their peers, and each time they change schools, they fall farther and farther behind" (p. 2). This pattern of decelerating progress results because "residential instability influences youth's participation in education and the stability of relationships" (Tierney et al., 2008, p. 24). It is also true because "children's sense of industry is [often] disrupted by continually changing schools" (Eddowes, 1992, p. 105).

> Children who do attend school find that the developmental delays, inability to concentrate, and fears and anxieties that are part of their lives make school a difficult experience. The experience of homelessness also adds its own punctuation to the child's ability to do school work. Teachers find that these children frequently do not finish their work. Homeless children's experiences have taught them to live for today. Thus, while the immediate task may be important, if something else comes up they turn to the new stimulus. Furthermore many of these children lack the organizational skills to complete school assignments. (Tower, 1992, p. 54)

There is even evidence that "the survival skills acquired by homeless children in the hotel, shelter, or street environment may be counteradaptive in the school environment and help create behavioral problems there" (Jahiel, 1987, p. 111). Constant change "results in discontinuous instruction" (Powers & Jaklitsch, 1992, p. 121) and "creates program discontinuity, and it is difficult for students who transfer to several schools each year to acquire even the basic skills" (Gonzalez, 1992, p. 196): "The cumulative effect of many moves and of missing lessons that teach core concepts is devastating. Prerequisite learning does not take place, causing the student to fall further and further behind" (Williams, 2003, p. 12).[5]

Absence of Needed Special Education Services

The literature on the connection between homeless children and special education features two lines of analysis: the number of students requiring placements and the failure of students to receive needed services. On the first issue, there is nearly universal agreement. Given the physical, social, and emotional damages associated with homelessness, and detailed earlier, it will come as no surprise to hear that "homelessness has been characterized as a breeding ground for disabilities" (Gargiulo, 2006, p. 358). That is, "conditions associated with homelessness substantially increase the risk of a youngster requiring special education services" (Gargiulo, 2006, p. 358). For example, the Better Homes Fund (1999) discovered in their study that "14 percent of homeless children were diagnosed with learning disabilities—double the rate of other children" (p. 23). According to Jackson (2004), "45 percent of homeless students in a Los Angeles-based study were in need of special education evaluation" (p. 3; see also Newman & Beck, 1996). In the Dworsky (2008) study in Chicago, "22 percent [of the homeless youngsters] were identified as having special education needs" (p. 36), with a range from 11% to 36%, depending on grade level (p. 36). In the general population, the percentage of students "receiving special education services ranged from 7 percent to 16 percent" (p. 36). Referencing the Better Homes Fund report at the turn of the century, Gargiulo (2006) reports that "youngsters who are homeless are twice as likely to have a learning disability and three times more likely to manifest emotional problems than their classmates who are not homeless" (p. 358).

Twenty-five percent of the children in the Bassuk (1992) study were in special classes (p. 261), a "figure in stark contrast to the 10.9% of students enrolled in special education services for the entire school population" (Molnar et al., 1990, p. 117; see also Pires & Silber, 1991, p. 29). In a New York City–based investigation, Nunez (1994b) found that 24% of homeless youngsters were in special education compared to only 7% for children citywide (p. 63). Russell (1998), in turn, in a study in Los Angeles, found that "the proportion [of homeless children] that attended special education classes was exponentially higher than that of the Los Angeles Unified School District student population" (p. 323). Mihaly (1991) arrived at a less dramatic conclusion when he compared homeless children in special education (28%) to housed low-income students (24%; p. 7).

Even in the face of these data on the overrepresentation of homeless children and youth in the special education system, there is a thick line of analysis suggesting the homeless students are being underserved by the schools they attend (Better Homes Fund, 1999; Crowley, 2003; Hart-Shegos & Associates, 1999; Wilder et al., 2003). "In spite of evidence that children who are homeless are more likely to have disabilities than other students" (Jackson, 2004, p. 3) and "despite IDEA's protections, students who are homeless and have disabilities often do not receive the special education services for which they are eligible" (Duffield et al., 2007, p. 49). "Homeless students with disabilities have extensive needs—physical, social/emotional, and academic—unlike any other school population, and too often their unique needs go unnoticed and unmet" (Wilder et al., 2003, p. 9). The central position in this line of analysis is that "children and youth who are homeless experience significant difficulties accessing special education programs" (Jackson, 2004, p. 3).[6] This may be the case, it is argued, because these youngsters "do not stay in school for an extended period, [they] may not be fully evaluated and thus may be denied adequate services" (Emerson & Lovitt, 2003, p. 200). It is held that homelessness "often lengthens and/or disrupts the evaluation process" (Jackson, 2004, p. 4). Thus, according to Whitman and team (1990),

> even when children have such obvious problems that they are referred for testing, they may move before the testing is completed or the results available. Each move brings a new school, a new referral, and further delays; ultimately, the children may never be effectively identified as needing special education services. Thus, the very children who need a special education setting to maximize

their potential are doubly penalized by the inappropriateness of their school experiences. (p. 519)

Reduced School Attendance: Absenteeism

When we examine the topic of school attendance, we need to consider three factors: whether students are enrolled in school, the loss associated with high mobility, and showing up for school once enrolled. The macro-level issue here is enrollment in school. We explore this aspect of attendance in Chapter 6 where we unpack the legal structure that envelopes homeless children and youth. We just finished our discussion of the mid-level element, loss associated with mobility. Here, then, the spotlight is turned directly on absence from school once one is enrolled. Turning to this point, we learn that "enrollment in school does not protect homeless students from absences" (Biggar, 2001, p. 951). That is, homeless children and youth compared with housed children are disproportionately absent from school (Dworsky, 2008; Nunez, 1994b; Sullivan & Knutson, 2000; United Way of New York City, 2002). "School attendance is often sporadic" (Shane, 1996, p. 34)—those who are enrolled in school are often absent (Gonzalez, 1992; Penuel & Davey, 2000; Rubin et al., 1996).

In her review, Biggar (2001) examined two studies that shed light on the magnitude of the problem. One study by Zima and colleagues revealed that "16% [of homeless children] had missed more than three weeks of school in the past three months. . . . Another study by Rafferty and Shinn showed that homeless students were more likely than poor housed children to have missed more than one week of school, 42% versus 22% respectively" (p. 951). In a third study, Rafferty and Rollins (cited in Molnar et al., 1990) found that

> attendance rates declined for all students as the grade level increased. However, not only did homeless children have poorer attendance at all levels, but their attendance rate declined at a faster rate than for students in the system as a whole. Thus, attendance rates for homeless vs. all students, respectively, in the New York City system were as follows: 73.6% vs. 88.7% at the elementary level, 63.6% vs. 85.5% at the junior high school level, and 50.9% vs. 83.9% at the high school level. (p. 116)

A fourth study presents a similar story line:

> Data obtained from the New York City Public Schools (1994) indicate that the overall attendance of homeless students continues to be substantially lower than the overall citywide rates. High school students ($n = 510$) had the poorest rate of attendance during the 1991–1992 school year (55% vs. 85% citywide), followed by

junior high school (n = 603) students (70% vs. 87%) and elementary
school age (n = 2,641) children (77% vs. 91%). (Rafferty, 1995, p. 44)

And in a fifth investigation, Rouse and Fantuzzo (2009) discovered that
"homelessness increased the odds of poor attendance in the second grade
by 54 percent" (p. 8).

Shifting the analytic spotlight back to the calendar, Dworsky (2008)
calculated that the mean number of days absent for homeless youngsters
ranged from 12 to 15 (p. 39), or 6.7% to 8.3% of the school year. Rafferty
(1995), in turn, discovered "that 15% of high school students who were
homeless during February, 1991, were absent from school for more than 20
continuous days during the month. The comparison rate for high school
students citywide was 3.5%" (pp. 44–45).

We close here with two reminders. First, the children of homeless parents and homeless adolescents have a thick portfolio of reasons not to
attend school on a regular basis (e.g., poor health, the crisis mode of living
associated with homelessness; Biggar, 2001; Nunez & Collignon, 1997).
Second, "sporadic school attendance has a negative effect upon learning"
(Shane, 1996, p. 34) and "educational success" (Tierney et al., 2008, p. 24).

Increased Rates of Suspension/Expulsion

Homeless students are also suspended and expelled from school much
more frequently than their housed counterparts (Brennan et al., 1978; Shaffer
& Caton, 1984; Tierney et al., 2008). In a study in Chicago, Russell (1998)
reported that about 25% of regular students were expelled from school
compared to about 38% of homeless youth (p. 309). The Better Homes
Fund (1999) review found that 14% of homeless children had been
"suspended from school, double the rate of other children" (p. 24).

Lower Levels of Academic Success

Studies routinely confirm that homeless children and youth perform
worse than housed students on an array of important measures of academic
performance (Masten et al., 1997; Sullivan & Knutson, 2000; Yon, 1995).

The results of this controlled study suggest that homeless children
perform at a lower academic level and have a higher rate of grade
repetition compared with housed children in New York City.
(Rubin et al., 1996, p. 292)

Homelessness is associated with many problems, one of the most
urgent of which is poor academic performance. Relative to their
housed peers, homeless children consistently perform more poorly
in school; they often fail, repeat grades, or drop out of school.
(Biggar, 2001, pp. 941–942)

Grade Level

Homeless youngsters generally perform below grade level (Pawlas, 1994; Popp, 2004). The Better Homes Fund (1999) describes a study in New York City that "found 75 percent of homeless children performing below grade level in reading, 72 percent below grade level in spelling, and 54 percent below grade level in math" (p. 24). Ziesemer et al. (1994) and Ziesemer and Marcoux (1992) report parallel findings, showing about two-thirds of homeless students below grade level in reading and mathematics—and adaptive functioning (Ziesemer et al., 1994, p. 662; Ziesemer & Marcoux, 1992, p. 83). "In a review of educational performance among homeless students in San Diego on a standardized achievement test, students average approximately 1 year below their grade level in reading, spelling, and mathematics in Grades 4 through 6; students in Grades 7 and 8 averaged 1 to 3 years below in the various academic areas" (Stronge, 1992a, p. 21). The National Center for Homeless Education (cited in Tierney et al., 2008) reinforces this theme, documenting that "nearly two-thirds of homeless youth in high school are not proficient in math and English" (p. 13).

Studies that contrast homeless children and youth with their housed peers reveal that not only are homeless students behind academically but they are below grade level at much higher rates than the general student population (Better Homes Fund, 1999; Rafferty, 1995). For example, in an investigation by Rafferty and Rollins (cited in Molnar et al., 1990), we discover that

> in reading, less than half (42.3%) of the homeless students in Grades 3–10 who took the Degrees of Reading Power test scored at or above grade level, compared to 68.1% of all New York City students who took the test. In math, for students in Grades 2–8 who took the Metropolitan Achievement Test, only 28.1% of students living in temporary housing scored at or above grade level, compared to 56.7% of all New York City students who took the test. These results are consistent with Shaffer and Caton's (1984) findings that over half of their sample of homeless 10–17 year-olds were more than one standard deviation behind on their reading achievement tests. Sixteen percent of the boys and 10% of the girls read at not more than a fourth grade reading level, essentially making them functionally illiterate. (pp. 117–118)

Relatedly, Duffield and Lovell (2008) report on this condition as follows:

> Researchers from the School of Public Health at Columbia University and others found that, in comparison to their housed peers, homeless children were

- 1.5 times more likely to perform below grade level in reading;
- 1.5 times more likely to perform below grade level in spelling; and
- 2.5 times more likely to perform below grade level in math. (p. 8)

And Rubin and colleagues (1996) "found significantly more homeless children performing below grade level on the reading, spelling, and arithmetic sections of the WRAT-R compared with the housed group and many fewer homeless children performing above grade level on the WRAT-R compared with the housed group" (p. 292).

Grades

Homeless youngsters and children also have, in general, poor to average grades (Nunez, 1994a; Van Ry, 1992), scores categorized by Dworsky (2008) as "alarming" (p. 45). In a Bassuk and Rubin study (cited in Tower, 1992), we learn that half of the homeless youth were "failing or doing below average work" (p. 54). A similar finding was unearthed by Timberlake (cited in Biggar, 2001), who found 35% of the homeless sample in his study receiving failing grades (p. 945).

Retention

Homelessness is also correlated with being left behind in grade (Masten et al., 1997; Rouse & Fantuzzo, 2009; Tucker, 1999):[7] "Several studies indicate that homeless students are less likely to be promoted at the end of the school year" (Rafferty, 1995, p. 42). Robertson (cited in Pires & Silber, 1991) documents a homeless retention rate of 25% (p. 29). In her study in Chicago, Dworsky (2008) confirms an overall retention of about one-third of the homeless students and remarks that "more than one-quarter of the retained children had been left back repeatedly" (p. 44). Maza and Hall (cited in Molnar et al., 1990) provide a similar figure, 30% (p. 116)—as do Rescorla et al. (1991, p. 215), 35%, and as does the National Center on Family Homelessness (2008, p. 5), 36%. Bassuk and associates (1986) report a 43% retention rate for homeless students (p. 1099), and Shaffer and Caton (cited in Robertson, 1992) found that 55% of the boys and 47% of the girls in their study had repeated a grade (p. 292).

> Other studies without comparison groups have also found high holdover rates among homeless children: 50% of children in 53 homeless families in New York City (Dumpson & Dinkins, 1987); 32% of 50 homeless children in New York City (Fox et al., 1990); 57% of 28 children in Suffolk County, New York (Board of Cooperative Educational Services, 1992). (Rafferty, 1995, p. 43)

Investigations that employ comparisons with housed students reveal that the retained category is disproportionately populated with homeless children and adolescents (Biggar, 2001; NCFH, 2009; Rubin et al., 1996). One study, for example, informs us that the 36% retention rate for homeless minors is "twice the rate of other children" (Better Homes Fund, 1999, p. 25), comparable to the 2.8 ratio cited by Rubin and associates (1996, p. 292) but higher than the 1.2 ratio uncovered by Russell (1998). In a more refined study by Wood (cited by Mihaly, 1991), the retention rate "for homeless children" was calculated at 30%, while the rate for "housed low-income children" was 18% (p. 7), a 1.6 ratio. A particularly high ratio has been provided by Nunez (1994a), 37% of school-age sheltered children compared with 4% citywide (p. 25).

We close with a reminder about the importance of grade retention in the larger equation of school success. Specifically, we confirm that "research shows a strong connection between grade retention and dropping out of school. . . . A student who is retained once faces a 40% increase in the likelihood of dropping out. If retained twice, that likelihood increases by 90%" (Rafferty, 1995, p. 43).

Achievement Scores

Data from a series of investigations over the last quarter century "indicate persistent underachievement of homeless students" (Rafferty, 1995, p. 43); that is, "homeless children are more likely to score poorly on standardized reading and mathematics tests" (p. 42) and "have lower overall academic achievement" (Williams, 2003, p. 17). In a Chicago-based study, Dworsky (2008) found that "only a minority of [homeless] children scored at or above the national average in reading or math" (p. 27). In a 1994 study of sheltered homeless minors, Zima and team (cited in Biggar, 2001) "found that 47% scored at or below the 10th percentile in receptive vocabulary. In addition, 39% of this sample demonstrated reading skills at or below the lowest decile, performance worthy of an F letter grade" (p. 945). In turn, Ziesemer and Marcoux (1992) report that 63% of boys and 61% of girls in their study on homeless children had scores below the 13th percentile (pp. 82–83). Masten and team (1997) confirm these figures. And the NCFH reported in 2008 "that of children in Grades 3 through 12 who are homeless and participated in state assessment tests, only 48% were proficient in reading and only 43% were proficient in math" (p. 5).

Research that compares the achievement of homeless children and youth with housed students reinforces the aforementioned "homeless only" findings. For example, in a 1993 study by Rafferty (1995),

> only 13% of 157 students in sixth grade scored at or above grade level in reading ability compared with 37% of all fifth graders taking the same test. Findings for other grades were consistent (e.g., 24% of 247 fourth graders vs. 49% of all fourth graders). An analysis of mathematics scores at each grade level shows similar

results. For example, only 28% of 286 students in third grade scored at or above grade level versus 51% of all third graders. (p. 43)

Dworsky (2008), in turn, chronicles how "on the math [and reading] ISAT in Grades 3, 5, and 8 [homeless] children were consistently out-performed by their Chicago Public School (CPS) peers" (p. 33). She also found that the homeless children were "less likely to have met or exceeded standards than CPS students generally" (p. 45). Robertson (1992) reported that the "mean score for homeless youngsters on the Reading Accuracy Test of the Wide Range Achievement Test [WRAT] was 87.76, compared to a mean of 100 for the general population" (p. 292). In 2009, the NCFH revealed that homeless elementary students lagged badly behind the total student population in both reading (24.4% vs. 33.8%) and math (21.5% vs. 39.6%) proficiency. At the high school level, discrepancies were even larger, 14.6% versus 30.9% in reading and 11.4% versus 32.2% in math. Finally, Rubin and team (1996) found in their study that while half of the housed children were performing below grade level on the WRAT reading and spelling tests, fully three-quarters of the homeless youngsters were below the bar. In math, "one fifth of the housed children were performing below grade level, compared with half of the homeless group" (p. 293).

Dropouts

Perhaps nowhere is the connection between homelessness and education bleaker than in the area of high school graduation (Farrow et al., 1992; Gwadz et al., 2009; Lindsey & Williams, 2002). The NCFH (2009) reports that less than a quarter of the homeless children in the United States complete high school (p. 9; also National Center for Homeless Education, 2006a, p. 1). Nunez (1994b), in a study in New York City, found that homeless adolescents were four times more likely to drop out of school than nonhomeless youth (p. 58).

Future Success

While there is very little direct research on the issues, there is a consensus in the literature that "housing problems early in life can have detrimental long-term consequences" (Wright et al., 1998, p. 94), that there are "long-term consequences for homeless children's future capacity to function effectively as parents and productively as members of society" (Kelly et al., 2000, p. 175). There is a general sense that these young people have a hopeless future (Rotheram-Borus, 1991), a "feeling of futurelessness" (Powers & Jaklitsch, 1992, p. 122). Analysts suggest that for some homeless young people, "the damage will be permanent" (Solarz, 1992, p. 284). They maintain that "those who have not been able to navigate through the educational system are also most vulnerable to not being able to navigate through the economic and social systems of life" (Shane, 1996, p. 37) and that they will not be able to overcome the "range of significant barriers to entering and succeeding in the formal economy" (Gwadz et al., 2009, p. 368). Thus, there is a consensus that "the educational deficits that homeless youth develop are serious economic, social, and health handicaps for their reintegration into society as they become adults" (Shane, 1996, p. 32). The "poor educational outcomes [detailed earlier] can have lifetime consequences for their future livelihood and economic independence" (Mawhinney-Rhoads & Stahler, 2006, p. 289).

There is also an emerging line of reasoning that posits that "not having access to stable housing negatively influences how youth transition to adulthood" (Tierney et al., 2008, p. 4). Reviewers here assert that because homelessness provides only "the most rudimentary introduction to adult life" (Janus et al., 1987, p. 34), "chronic homeless adolescents are literally learning to become marginal adults" (Whitbeck & Hoyt, 1999, p. 171): "The trajectory into adulthood [for homeless children and youth] appears bleak" (p. 158); "most will experience profound difficulties in making the transition from adolescent to adult roles" (Hagan & McCarthy, 1997, p. 200).

Homelessness during childhood (Burt, 2001) and adolescence "increases the likelihood of an individual experiencing homelessness as an adult" (Tierney et al., 2008, p. 2): "Further, childhood homelessness and its accompanying vulnerabilities appear to translate into greater risk of homelessness as an adult, and also, most especially, as a young adult" (Burt et al., 2001, pp. 137–138).

Homeless students are also much more likely than students who never experienced homelessness to be unemployed as adults (Bass, 1995; Lindsey & Williams, 2002). Thus, "homelessness may threaten children's long-term chances for escaping poverty" (Nunez, 1994a, p. 25).

❖ CONCLUSION

In this chapter, we reviewed the pathway by which homelessness damages children and youth. We saw that homelessness leads to unhealthy living conditions, which give rise to a series of states of risk for displaced young persons. We also explained how these risks lead to physical, emotional, social, and educational harm.

❖ NOTES

1. While the focus of this section is on the impact of displacement on the physical, emotional, social, and educational well-being of homeless children and youth, it is important to acknowledge that homelessness "engenders tremendous costs for society" (Biggar, 2001, p. 941) as well, for the nation as a whole and for individual homeless persons (Barry et al., 2002): "Homelessness has deleterious effects on society as well as homeless individuals and their families" (National Law Center on Homelessness and Poverty, 2004a,

p. 11). Or, as the Edna McConnell Clark Foundation (1990) report maintains, "the long-term societal costs of fueling further cycles of homelessness are incalculable" (p. 43), especially "when one considers the resultant problems being passed from one generation to the next" (Swick, 2004, p. 117). It is generally held, therefore, that the "social costs stemming from the general waste and destruction of these young lives should be of major concern to American society" (Shane, 1996, p. 20). Such interest and attention, it is asserted, can help "save the long-term costs of illness, crime, and lost productivity" (Mihaly, 1991, p. 9).

Such concern has economic, political, and social roots (Bassuk, 1984; Molnar et al., 1990): "The costs . . . are high both socially and economically" (Shane, 1996, p. 32). On the first front, scholars expose the "damaging costs" (Biggar, 2001, p. 953) to the economy from homelessness. They argue that "the significant human and financial costs make youth homelessness an important issue" (Moore, 2005b, p. 19). They confirm that "the long-term consequences for the nation's human capital are . . . severe" (Duffield & Lovell, 2008, p. 2). And these scholars assert that "a lack of investment in homeless children at present will lead to substantial public costs in the future" (Biggar, 2001, p. 944), public costs in the areas of health care, housing, and law enforcement (Powers & Jaklitsch, 1992; Shane, 1996).

On the political front, because "homelessness results in a de facto exclusion of a significant portion of the population from participation in democratic life" (National Law Center on Homelessness and Poverty, 2004b, p. 12), critics foretell of an unraveling of the political fabric supporting the nation.

On the societal front, scholars link homelessness with the solidification of a nation of haves and have-nots and with the reinforcement of a continuous cycle of poverty (Nunez, 1994a, 1994b). Scholars and advocates such as Kozol (1988) see homelessness nurturing the development of the underclass. According to Shane (1996), "the impaired physical and mental health of youth who experience homelessness often leaves them less able or unable to contribute their talents to the society. Many of them remain dependent on the society rather than contributors to its development. Possibly worse are the dangers of passing homelessness and its sequelae on to further generations" (p. 52).

2. It is important to point out that because "homeless people often tend to underestimate the severity of their health problems" (Jahiel, 1992a, p. 134), the story line here may actually be a good deal more grim.

3. McCaskill and team (1998) offer a caution here, however, when they note "that when demographic variables associated with socioeconomic disadvantage are isolated from homelessness, there are fewer mental health discrepancies between housed and homeless adolescents" (p. 316).

4. While our focus is on homeless children and youth, analysts expose the extent of emotional and psychological impairments in the single adult population as well. They confirm "high rates of severe mental illness" (Koegel et al., 1996, p. 31), much higher rates than are reported in the general population of adults in the United States (Bahr, 1973; Brickner, 1985; Khanna et al., 1992). Unlike with children, where major mental illness is limited, somewhere in the neighborhood of 10% of homeless adults are likely to have a major mental illness such as a schizophrenic disorder (Bahr, 1973, p. 101; Toro, 1998, p. 121)—although, as Ropers (1988) reminds us, this is considerably less than commonly assumed or portrayed. Beyond this, there is considerable variation in reports about the extent of mental illness among homeless individuals, with reports running from around 20% to 80% and higher (see Bahr, 1973; Bassuk, 1984; Bassuk et al., 1984; Flynn, 1985; Shlay & Rossi, 1992; Tierney et al., 2008; Toro, 1998).

5. Scholars also confirm that high rates of mobility have negative educational consequences not only for homeless youth but for everyone in the school, those "who stay put and mobile students" (Williams, 2003, p. 6): "And it is not only the frequent movers who suffer. The stable students in a classroom afflicted with high transience experience serious educational and social disruptions" (Williams, 2003, p. 11).

6. There is an alternative perspective in the literature here as well. This point of view holds that homeless youngsters are being sent to special education classes in much larger numbers because educators lack the will and/or skills to serve them appropriately in the regular system, that they are being dumped into the special education tracks from which they are never likely to return (Lumsden & Coffey, 2001; Nunez & Collignon, 1997).

7. Rubin and colleagues (1996) provide a cautionary note here, suggesting that "grade repetition may not be a particularly sensitive measure of academic underachievement, as children may be promoted through the academic system despite poor academic results" (p. 292).

PART III

The Role of Society in Addressing Homelessness

5

Addressing Homelessness

Only through comprehensive, cross systems strategies will we be able to fully assist people to access and sustain affordable housing and achieve community integration and economic stability. (NAEH, 2003, p. 1)

The definition of the condition that is targeted . . . determines the scope and nature of the [response] . . . if the definition of homelessness is "being without a roof over one's head," the solution is shelter; if it is "being without one's own home," the solution is a home; if it is "being without resources to make a living," the solution is income or empowerment. (Jahiel, 1992d, p. 11)

A s we have seen, homelessness in the United States after World War II was a problem of adult men, and initial attempts to address the problem were generally aimed at getting these men treatment for alcohol abuse and mental illness (Bahr, 1973). Many programs by the 1950s and 1960s involved referrals to community-based programs, based on the assumption that these homeless men either did not know about or could not access these services on their own (Bahr, 1973). In the modern era of homelessness, the housing-displaced population also includes single women, families with children, and unaccompanied youth, necessitating distinct policies and programs to meet the needs of each group (NCFH, 2009). Substance abuse and mental illness are still seen as causes of homelessness, but our understanding has been broadened to include poverty and lack of available housing as well (Burt, 2001). Accordingly, solutions generally fall into one of three categories, with some overlap: addressing poverty, increasing access to low-income housing, and providing social services.

❖ ADDRESSING POVERTY

> *Obviously, lasting solutions to the problem of homelessness will necessarily address structural causes; the 'resolution [of homelessness] will require tackling the enduring roots of poverty.' (National Law Center on Homelessness and Poverty, 2004a, p. 10)*

> *Interventions oriented toward preventing homelessness have yet to be developed, though some promising approaches for preventing the closely related problem of poverty have begun to emerge. (Toro, 1998, p. 129)*

In 2008, 13.2% of Americans, about 39.1 million people, lived in poverty (Bishaw & Renwick, 2009). According to Medcalf (2008), over one-third of all people living in poverty had incomes less than half the poverty level. Researchers who view homelessness as a structural problem rather than an individual one believe that homelessness is caused by poverty and that addressing poverty is its logical solution. "The issue of poverty itself, which demoralizes and destroys people, must be dealt with" (Shane, 1996, p. 215). These researchers call for changes to structural factors such as the minimum wage and insufficient public assistance to people living in poverty.

Some authors call for policies simply to end poverty. Recognizing, however, that ending poverty altogether "would mean a major economic and social restructuring of society" (Shane, 1996, p. 215) and that "this is a long term effort" (Better Homes Fund, 1999, p. x), others promote ameliorating homelessness by taking short-term measures to lessen the effects of poverty. And many see addressing the structural roots of poverty as just one part of solving the homelessness crisis (Edna McConnell Clark Foundation, 1990; McChesney, 1992; Mihaly, 1991). For example, Flaming and Tepper (2006) recommend that Los Angeles begin to address its homelessness problem by "raising the income floor under the working poor, creating living-wage jobs, providing job training and education that will enable low-wage workers to obtain living-wage jobs" (p. 25). In this section, we examine the two most popular strategies researchers and advocates suggest to address the poverty that leads to homelessness: increasing public assistance and expanding employment opportunities.

Public Assistance

Income policies directly caused the national problem of the homeless and only other income policies will solve the problem. (Kiesler, 1991, p. 1248)

Proponents of increasing public assistance to help address homelessness work from a fairly straightforward assumption that with more assistance to pay for food and health care, individuals and families will be able to afford to pay for housing. Public assistance, also called welfare or direct income support, takes the form of money given to impoverished individuals and families and takes form through programs like Temporary Aid to Needy Families (TANF), the Supplemental Nutrition Assistance Program (SNAP, also referred to as food stamps), or other cash benefit programs. Proponents of addressing poverty in order to eliminate homelessness argue for increasing levels of support, lessening eligibility requirements, and creating special one-time assistance programs designed to help prevent homelessness.

Many authors cite the link between federal income policies and increases in homelessness as evidence that increasing income is the only way to solve the problem. When explaining the rise in homelessness in recent decades, Kiesler refers specifically to regressive tax policies and declining levels of public assistance during the Reagan presidency, while Bassuk, Weinreb, Buckner, Browne, Salomon, and Bassuk (1996) express "serious concerns about welfare reform efforts [the Clinton administration's Personal Responsibility and Work Opportunity Reconciliation Act (PRWORA)], deep cuts in human service programs, and transfer of fiscal and programmatic responsibility" to "already overburdened" states (p. 645). Pardeck (2005) points to "massive" social program cutbacks compounding an already-existing lack of adequate income supports to explain why "no other developed nation has anywhere near the numbers of homeless people and families as the United States. In the developed welfare states of Europe, homelessness is virtually non-existent" (p. 341).

These cutbacks in income support programs have happened in two ways. First, levels of assistance have failed to keep up with inflation, meaning that support levels have declined dramatically in real dollars since the 1970s (McChesney, 1992). Second, eligibility for federal assistance has become laden with requirements that often exclude the neediest people from getting help. "There is a fundamental mismatch between the categorical requirements of federally assisted income maintenance programs and the relevant characteristics of the homeless population" (Greenberg & Baumohl, 1996, p. 77). Echoing this sentiment, Flaming and Tepper (2006) call for Los Angeles to address homelessness by enrolling 33% of its homeless population in the Supplemental Security Income (SSI) program and by expanding enrollment in food stamps and Medicaid programs.

These income support programs could all help alleviate the stresses of poverty if they were expanded or their rules were relaxed to make more people eligible to receive assistance.

Recommendations that include increasing such public assistance programs as AFDC (Aid to Families with Dependent Children), TANF, Medicaid, and food stamps abound (McChesney, 1992; Mihaly, 1991; Shinn & Weitzman, 1996; Shlay & Rossi, 1992). However, not all calls for cash assistance involve major overhauls or long-term changes. Burt et al. (2001) point out that some people are homeless only once or twice and for relatively short periods; in these instances, it is possible that "only a simple form of emergency assistance that tides them through whatever crisis triggered their fall into literal homelessness" (p. 182) would suffice.

Employment Opportunities

Economic policies that foster employment at livable wages are [most] likely to end the crisis of homelessness. (Shinn & Weitzman, 1996, p. 120)

Some scholars believe the solution to homelessness will come through decreasing individual and family poverty with employment: job training, more job opportunities, and a higher minimum wage that keeps pace with inflation. Job training programs for the homeless are a very popular strategy. Two decades ago, Gore (1990) called for more job training and remedial education for people experiencing homelessness. The McKinney-Vento Law has provided funding for demonstration job training programs (Foscarinis, 1996), and some states have had success using PRWORA moneys to help people overcome barriers to employment (Burt et al., 2001).

Although Nunez (1994b) asserts that most homeless families lack employment skills, concluding that education holds the key to ameliorating homelessness, Snow, Anderson, Quist, and Cress (1996) point out that homeless people tend to be willing and able to do odd jobs and often go to great lengths just to get by, concluding the following:

> The fact that most homeless people are active agents in pursuit of subsistence suggests that a good number of them may benefit directly from programs that build on that agency—for example, by providing training that builds on existing skills and jobs that pay a living wage . . . programs that stereotypically homogenize the homeless as helpless and dysfunctional are likely to be of limited success. (p. 96)

Toro (1998) also points out that "many young homeless men have some employable skills and many women homeless with their children have good parenting abilities" (p. 130) that could be capitalized upon by job training programs.

Hardin (1996) and Rotheram-Borus (1991) argue that existing job training programs have not been successful in ameliorating homelessness because of the lack of availability of well-paying jobs, not because of inherent problems with the programs or their participants. Shinn and Weitzman (1996) would like to see job training programs with guaranteed job placement. Some communities have experimented with offering financial incentives to encourage businesses to move into low-income areas (Flynn, 1985), but creating well-paying jobs has proven difficult (Oakley & Dennis, 1996). Many see a direct role for government in increasing employment opportunities and wages: "We must urge Congress to ensure economic security by creating jobs . . . and providing job training" (Rafferty, 1995, p. 56). Johnson (1988) calls for publicly funded employment opportunities and vocational training. "Although job creation requires expenditure of public funds, it is an investment that will reduce future spending for government support services" (Biggar, 2001, p. 926). Shlay and Rossi (1992) enjoin the government to engage in "national economic planning, joint coordination of housing and welfare subsidies, and public sector intervention into the labor market" (pp. 151–152). Indeed, the unemployed homeless could be given work in the construction of low-income housing. Ropers (1988) and others argue that "the resources are available; all we need is the will" (p. 212).

Increasing the earning power of jobs is another crucial element to lessening poverty. Rafferty cites "increasing the minimum wage" specifically as a strategy to combat homelessness (1995, p. 56). And belief in the power of gainful employment to address homelessness is not unique to researchers. When the leaders of 25 major U.S. cities were asked to name the top three things needed to solve the homelessness crisis in their cities, 68% responded "better paying employment opportunities" (U.S. Conference of Mayors, 2008, p. 20). Although Hopper and Hamberg (1984) called for "measures [to be] taken to cushion the regional impact of economic restructuring at large" (p. 70) almost 30 years ago, it is important to note that as the nation has once again descended into economic recession, well-paying jobs have disappeared. "Cities were more than twice as likely to cite the need for better employment opportunities in 2008 than they were in 2007" (U.S. Conference of Mayors, 2008, p. 20).

❖ INCREASING THE STOCK OF HOUSING

Our nation's capacity to house people who are homeless increased six percent between 1996 and 2005. Despite these gains, we still fall far short of the supply needed to ensure that no one is left without a place to call home.
(NCFH, 2009, p. 35)

*The effects of a decade and a half of research to determine what works to end
homelessness are fairly conclusive about the most effective approaches. Providing
housing helps currently homeless people leave homelessness . . . without housing,
virtually nothing else works. (Burt, 2001, p. 5)*

Some researchers believe that more than decreasing poverty, the most
obvious solution to homelessness is the provision of housing. As Johnson
(1988) succinctly points out, "all homeless persons share the need for housing, despite the fact that many of them are homeless for different reasons"
(p. 134). Some advocates (see, for example, Hartman, 1986; Hopper &
Hamberg, 1984) believe in a fundamental human right to housing. In New
York City, homeless people have a constitutional right to shelter, and the
city has created a large system of emergency and supportive housing
(United Way of New York City, 2002). Support for the belief that humans
do have an inherent right to shelter can be seen in Al Gore and Daniel
Patrick Moynihan's 1986 Homeless Persons' Survival Act, forerunner to
the Stewart B. McKinney Homeless Assistance Act, which noted that
"every homeless person is entitled as a matter of right to decent overnight
shelter" (Gore, 1990, p. 962).

Although they tend to believe that housing alone is not sufficient,
many researchers focus on the provision of housing as the most crucial
step in combating homelessness. However, *housing* is a broad term
encompassing many forms: temporary shelter, welfare hotels, transitional housing, supportive housing, and permanent housing. These
components are thought to comprise a tiered system that "moves those
who are homeless through a succession of shelter programs designed to
graduate them to permanent housing and self-sufficiency" (NAEH,
2003, p. 7). Some would argue that the system rarely works in this way
(Johnson, 1988) and that an emphasis on coordinating such a "continuum of care" is crucial to combating homelessness (Burt, Hedderson,
Zweig, Ortiz, Aron-Turnham, & Johnson, 2004; Hombs, 2001; United
Way of New York City, 2002). Nevertheless, an examination of the different types of housing—emergency shelters, transitional housing,
housing first/rapid rehousing, permanent housing, and supportive
permanent housing—is crucial to understanding the potential resources
available to the homeless.

Emergency Shelters

*The provision of emergency shelter for homeless families is essential.
(McChesney, 1992, p. 253)*

Homeless policy has faltered most fundamentally because of a well-intentioned but misguided focus on emergency shelter as the primary goal . . . (Nunez, 1994b, p. 43)

Temporary housing, most often in the form of emergency shelters, is emphasized in the McKinney-Vento Act and is the "primary mechanism for providing direct services to homeless families and children" (Solarz, 1992, p. 282) and single homeless adults (McChesney, 1990). Emergency shelters are usually run by community organizations or faith-based groups and provide "a temporary haven for families to 're-group'; determine how best to address economic, educational, and health issues that have contributed to their homelessness; and move to stable, permanent housing" (NCFH, 2009, p. 35). Medcalf (2008) describes emergency shelters as places that provide "a clean environment to sleep, humane care, some meals, and referrals to other agencies" (p. 104). But not all emergency shelters are the same (Dworsky, 2008). In their 1995 report, Rog, Holupka, and McCombs-Thornton (1995) show that "emergency shelters are a heterogeneous lot, ranging greatly in capacity, staffing patterns, types of service provided, and resident restrictions . . . there are no clear categories or types of shelters" (p. 502). In addition, shelters often vary in physical structure. Many emergency shelters for individuals are simply large halls filled with beds (Ropers, 1988). Others, particularly those designed for families, consist of separate rooms or apartments. Homeless people are also sometimes placed in Single Room Occupancy (SRO) hotels, often referred to as welfare hotels (Ropers, 1998; Williams, 2003).

Unfortunately, emergency shelters are believed by many analysts to be insufficient to meet the needs of individuals and families experiencing homelessness (Kiesler, 1991). One problem with shelters is that they are often crowded, chaotic, and stress-producing, particularly for families with children (Nunez, 1994b). Personal safety is a concern for many residents (Anooshian, 2005; Karabanow, 2004; Shlay & Rossi, 1992). Many emergency shelters allow residents to spend only the night, requiring them to leave early in the morning, taking all of their possessions with them, and return in the evening for readmission. When residents are permitted to stay more than one night, there are usually limits on the number of nights they can stay (Shinn & Weitzman, 1996).

Another problem is lack of emergency shelter capacity. Despite increases in funding through the Emergency Shelter Grant Program (part of the McKinney-Vento Act) and a 200% increase in shelter capacity between 1988 and 1996 (Burt et al., 2001; Foscarinis, 1996), funding remains "woefully inadequate" (National League of Cities, 2004, p. 197), and many shelters have to turn people away. In 1997, the Child Welfare League found that one-fourth of family requests for emergency shelter were turned down due to lack of space (as cited in Markward & Biros, 2001). Burt and colleagues reported in 2001 that the average rate of availability of shelter housing was 178 units per 10,000 people in poverty nationwide (p. 276). A 2001 study of U.S. cities found that 37% of all requests for emergency shelter, and 52% of requests from families, went unmet because of lack of resources (Medcalf, 2008, p. 10). Although the federal Emergency Shelter Grant program is the source of funding for many of these facilities, and many receive private funding as well (Weinreb & Buckner, 1993), there are simply not enough beds (Bassuk, 1984). "The number of homeless greatly exceeds the number of emergency shelter and transitional housing spaces" (Medcalf, 2008, p. 10), in part because the average length of stay in one of these facilities has risen from five months to nearly one year (Medcalf, 2008).

Additionally, some researchers believe that people experiencing homelessness need to be given tools in order to achieve the goal of living independently, and emergency shelters are ill-equipped to provide the necessary skills (Swick, 2005). Originally designed to provide only shelter, food, and basic necessities (Weinreb & Buckner, 1993), these sites are increasingly finding it difficult, but necessary, to provide services in the areas of case management, mental health, and physical health. Particularly since the deinstitutionalization movement of the 1960s failed to replace mental hospitals with sufficient community-based facilities, "shelters have been saddled with the impossible task of replacing not only the almshouses of the past but also the large state mental institutions" (Bassuk, 1984, p. 40). Shlay and Rossi (1992) recommend augmenting the levels of financial support given to emergency housing facilities so they can offer more case management and other crucial services for residents.

Even if there were enough beds in emergency shelters and these sites could provide sufficient services, many scholars remind us that they are not the whole solution to the problem of homelessness. Snow and Anderson (1993) assert that the shelter system merely perpetuates homelessness by helping the homeless manage street life, rather than helping them off the streets. Karabanow (2004) describes a culture in adult shelters that serves to "legitimize and perpetuate social marginality and . . . the status quo" (p. 24) by warehousing poor people in "filthy, violent, and dehumanizing environments" (p. 24). To other researchers, emergency shelters comprise "a stopgap, band-aid response to a tragic problem" (Bassuk, 1992, p. 264; Ropers, 1988), "the implicit rationale behind [which] is that homelessness is due to temporary displacement" (McChesney, 1990). Although "emergency shelters provide a natural intervention point for disrupting the severity of homelessness" (Johnson, 1988, p. 154), placing homeless people into emergency shelters is "nothing more than warehousing poverty" (Swick, 2005, p. 198) and "putting a temporary dressing on what has become a large, festering wound in the social body" (Bassuk, 1984, p. 45), particularly when insufficient permanent housing exists: "Indeed, a massive emergency shelter system has mushroomed and threatens to persist despite the fact that, for many individuals and families, the 'emergency' has solidified into a chronic condition" (Weinreb & Buckner, 1993, p. 401). These calls have not gone unheeded: Nationwide, between 1988 and 1996, more growth occurred in transitional housing facilities than in emergency shelter capacity (Burt et al., 2001). We next turn to a close examination of transitional housing and how it differs from emergency housing.

Transitional Housing

Homelessness may not be only *a housing problem, but it is* always *a housing problem; housing is necessary, although sometimes not sufficient, to solve the problem of homelessness. (Dolbeare, 1996, p. 34)*

Transitional housing, often called "bridge" or "second-stage" housing, refers to those facilities intended to fill the gap between emergency shelters and independent permanent housing, usually allowing longer stays than shelters and providing more intensive services designed to prepare people for independent living (NCFH, 2009; Rog et al., 1995). "Transitional programs, designed to help families move from shelter to permanent housing, provide homeless families with six months to two years of residence and support services" (Weinreb & Buckner, 1993, p. 401). This type of facility became popular in the late 1980s, when "communities realized that for some, emergency shelter services were not sufficient to ensure a permanent exit from homelessness" (NCFH, 2009, p. 35). These sites may "focus on particular barriers to stable housing and provide services and supports to address issues [such as] fleeing domestic violence or struggling with addictions" (NCFH, 2009, p. 35), provide more general counseling (Ropers, 1988), or offer training in such "living skills" as "budgeting, shopping, and home management" (McChesney, 1990, p. 197). Nunez (1994b) states that "although most of the factors responsible for the shortage of affordable, quality housing are beyond their control, learning about tenant rights, resources and budgeting helps homeless families better respond to any threats to their stability" (p. 158). Indeed, studies of one transitional housing model in New York City demonstrated that only 6% of families returned to shelters from transitional housing facilities (Nunez, 1994b, p. 48).

Some researchers would prefer service-linked permanent housing in lieu of transitional facilities (Rog et al., 1995), contending that transitional facilities have been misused "to cope with the scarcity of affordable permanent housing, lack of community services, and limitations of the emergency shelter system" (Weinreb & Buckner, 1993, p. 401). Lindblom (1996) offers evidence from California that families given even low levels of financial support for one-time moving costs were able to stay in their permanent housing six months after receiving the help.

Permanent Housing

To end homelessness, society must invest in affordable housing.
(Williams, 2003, p. 27)

European discussions of the causes of homelessness, it is noteworthy, usually start from the premise that root causes are high housing cost and reduced availability. . . . (Burt et al., 2001, p. 329)

Many argue that housing efforts should focus on increasing the stock of available affordable permanent housing (Biggar, 2001; Burt et al., 2001; Ely, 1987; Gore, 1990; Leavitt, 1992; McChesney, 1990, 1992; Medcalf, 2008; Shlay & Rossi, 1992; Solarz, 1992; Stronge, 1992a; Williams, 2003). Hombs (2001) found that 38% of people surveyed said they needed housing, and 30% said they needed housing assistance. Both changing voucher programs to be more accessible and physically creating new homes—by building new structures or renovating older ones—form part of this approach. Flaming and Tepper (2006) call upon Los Angeles and neighboring cities to recognize their responsibility to use whatever resources they can to build and maintain housing for extremely low-income people. As McChesney (1990) points out, by focusing on emergency shelter, cities have for decades squandered precious resources on expensive temporary accommodations instead of using those resources to build permanent low-income housing. In this section, we review the history of permanent low-income housing initiatives and their current state. We also explore supportive permanent housing, housing first, and rapid rehousing programs.

The oldest form of federally supported permanent housing is public housing, owned and run directly by the government, which was created for low-income families and people with disabilities and presently houses approximately 1.2 million individuals and families (NCFH, 2009). However, Burt and colleagues (2001) note that government-subsidized housing comprises 20% of all housing in many European nations, a much greater proportion than it does in the United States. Additionally, the Quality Housing and Work Responsibility Act of 1998 allows public housing authorities to set admissions criteria that favor higher-income eligible people, keeping out over two-thirds of the 13 million lowest-income families (Crowley, 2003).

In the 1960s, federal initiatives shifted from building public housing developments to offering subsidies to private developers who agree to allow a certain percentage of low-income households to rent their units (Carliner, 1987). As Johnson (1988) points out, the Reagan administration specifically voiced a desire to get the federal government out of the business of providing housing, and it largely met its goal. Currently, most housing subsidies, such as Section 8 vouchers, are given directly to tenants to help them rent private units, but the current levels need to be expanded and adjusted (Better Homes Fund, 1999; Jencks, 1994; Roy, Maynard, & Weiss, 2008; Williams, 2003) so that "no low-income family is forced to spend more than 30% of its income to live in decent and stable housing" (Mihaly, 1991, p. 22). Likewise, because budgets have been dramatically reduced in the last several decades (Burt et al., 2001; Carliner, 1987), many low-income housing programs have long waiting lists. Advocates recommend giving priority to homeless families (NCFH, 2009). Unfortunately, some waiting lists are so long that they are closed. For example, "over 40% of Section 8 and 15% of public housing waiting lists are closed to new applicants" (NCFH, 2009, p. 36). Another challenge of Section 8 vouchers is that families who receive them still have to negotiate with landlords on their own, and in tight markets, landlords generally choose nonsubsidy tenants; similarly, Section 8 does not provide funding for the security deposits that most landlords require (NCFH, 2009).

"Studies have shown that families exiting homelessness with a housing subsidy . . . are 21 times more likely to remain stably housed than comparable families exiting a shelter without a subsidy" (NAEH, 2007, p. 2), but these subsidy programs cannot correct the fact that many cities have a severe shortage of low-income housing available. Many researchers (e.g., Better Homes Fund, 1999; Biggar, 2001; Duffield & Lovell, 2008; McChesney, 1990; Medcalf, 2008; Mihaly, 1991; Shane, 1996) advocate construction of new housing units, rehabilitation of existing structures, and prevention of gentrification and abandonment in both rural and urban areas. Although "supplying affordable housing sufficient for the need and demand would be very expensive," Shane (1996, p. 215) is quick to point out that it has been successful in other developed nations. This approach is popular among those who believe that homelessness is caused by lack of available housing rather than personal characteristics. "There is no reason to believe [people]'s personal characteristics—their ability to manage money or to look for new housing, for example—have changed in the last 20 years. What has changed is the low-income housing market" (McChesney, 1990, p. 198).

Ziesemer and Marcoux (1992) push for policy initiatives at local, state, and federal levels to aid in the creation of more low-income housing. Some promising approaches to creating quality, affordable low-income housing have emerged in recent years (Roy et al., 2008). Shlay and Rossi (1992) and Johnson (1988) suggest such housing solutions as nonconventional housing forms (like shared housing), alterations to zoning codes to allow for more low-income housing construction, increasing housing credit availability, and community land trusts. Similarly, housing trust funds have increased in popularity. Originally proposed in 1994 by the National Low Income Housing Coalition (Dolbeare, 1996), a National Housing Trust Fund was established by the Housing and Economic Recovery Act of 2008—the first new production program since the Section 8 program specifically targeted high-poverty households in the 1970s (NCFH, 2009). Many states, counties, and cities have developed these trust funds, which draw revenue from public sources and are used to create housing for extremely low-income families (Better Homes Fund, 1999). "State housing trust funds create long-term capacity and have significant economic impact" (NCFH, 2009, p. 38). Some more radical proposals, such as adopting the developing world's practice of allowing unemployed homeless residents to construct their own homes or allowing the homeless to squat in vacant housing, have been suggested as well (Shlay & Rossi, 1992).

Housing First and Rapid Rehousing

No matter what you provided—food, clothing, counseling, family
support—nothing really changed until the family had a permanent
place to live. (Quint, 1994, p. 53)

Evaluations of programs serving severely disabled homeless people show that
they can achieve a condition of stable housing. But first, they need the
housing, without which nothing helps. (Burt et al., 2001, p. 327)

Some programs, usually directed at dual-diagnosed single adults—those with serious mental and physical issues—are known as "housing first" because they aim to get homeless people into permanent housing immediately (Burt et al., 2004; U.S. Conference of Mayors, 2008). They can be controversial because some, known as "harm reduction" or "low demand," do not require residents to maintain total sobriety or to participate in any services (Burt et al., 2004; Oakley & Dennis, 1996). However, these programs have been shown to be successful in achieving stable housing and employment for dual-diagnosed individuals (Burt et al., 2001). They operate from the assumption that the primary need of any homeless individual is housing—"adequate permanent housing is, of course, the most important intervention in cases of homelessness" (D'Ercole & Struening, 1990, p. 149)—and that "the factors that have contributed to a household's homelessness can best be remedied once the household is housed" (NAEH, 2003, p. 9). The housing first model includes a component of choice over the location and type of housing and no time limit on the length of stay (NAEH, 2003). Oakley and Dennis (1996) explain that this approach is supported by research showing that individuals are more likely to accept treatment once their basic needs have been met, not when "they are fearful and ostracized" (p. 184).

Following the housing first example, many cities have developed rapid rehousing programs for homeless families. Research shows that not every family needs transitional housing before entering permanent housing. "Results of [evaluative studies] call into question the need for all families to take such a step" (Rog et al., 1995, p. 512). Rapid rehousing programs are "aimed at reducing the time it takes for families to move out of shelters and into permanent housing" (U.S. Conference of Mayors, 2008, p. 21), often by providing short-term rental assistance, help searching for housing, and case management to help the family prepare for the move (NAEH, 2007). The NCFH (2009) points out that "it is less expensive to pay a family's rent than to pay for their stay in a motel" (p. iii).

Most researchers agree that rapid rehousing programs are most likely to be successful if they also include follow-up services for residents. The Edna McConnell Clark Foundation (1990) recommends supportive services for resettling families because "simply providing new apartments neither guarantees a family's stability nor prevents future homelessness" (p. 43). Rog and colleagues (1995) studied six programs providing rapid rehousing and supportive services and found that they were largely successful. "These preliminary findings suggest that immediate placement in permanent housing is a workable option even for families with multiple and severe needs" (Rog et al., 1995, p. 521). Likewise, McChesney (1990) argues that permanent housing with services is better than transitional housing because it "enables families to put down roots—develop their own support networks and community ties—in a community where they expect to remain, as opposed to spending six months . . . developing friendships and ties that will end when they leave transitional housing" (p. 198).

Supportive Permanent Housing

Supportive permanent housing is generally aimed at single homeless adults suffering from serious mental illnesses, chemical dependencies, and/or physical disabilities that inhibit them from remaining stably housed independently (NCFH, 2009). These facilities have an unlimited length of stay and include services to help residents cope with their issues. Before the 1987 passage of the McKinney-Vento Homeless Assistance Act and its annual modifications, supportive housing was almost nonexistent, but by 1996, approximately 114,000 permanent supportive housing units had been established (Burt, 2001). In particular, the Supportive Housing Demonstration program increased the number of these types of facilities (Foscarinis, 1996).

❖ PROVIDING SOCIAL SERVICES

In order to break the cycle of short-term shelter stays, human services must be connected into an effective resource system. (Swick, 1997, p. 33)

Along with housing, people need an integrated array of social services. (Medcalf, 2008, p. 103)

Although some researchers and advocates believe that decreasing poverty or increasing housing could be enough to address the problem of homelessness, most analysts assert that housing is not the only answer (e.g., Baron, 2003; Hartman, 1986; Jahiel, 1992d; Jencks, 1994; Leavitt, 1992; Nunez, 1994b; Toro, 1998). These researchers maintain that the homeless "also need help with job skills, alcohol, drugs, depression, schizophrenia, and a host of other ills" (Jencks, 1994, p. 121). Accordingly, the largest body of research and theory to be found in this arena deals with the provision of services for the homeless, in conjunction with or separate from housing. The availability of services for the homeless has increased in recent decades (Burt et al., 2001), reflecting a widely held belief that "a continuum of services is required to meet the multidimensional needs of homeless people . . . the rationale behind [which] is the idea of moving people out of homelessness to self-sufficiency" (Johnson, 1988, p. 145). In particular, services to help find housing and the provision of physical health care have increased (Burt et al., 2001). Snow and Anderson (1993) support a services-based approach because providing only shelter and food to the homeless, though crucial, is "basically accommodative: [these basics] help the homeless endure life on the streets rather than escape it" (pp. 86–87).

Services provided to the homeless vary widely, and, like housing, they are provided by private and publicly funded organizations (Dworsky, 2008). They happen on-site at shelters or off-site in tandem with transitional housing, permanent housing, or no housing at all. The services range from treating illnesses like substance addiction and mental health problems to programs undergirded by a belief that the homeless are suffering "moral weakness and spiritual degeneration" (Snow & Anderson, 1993, p. 88). Weinreb and Buckner (1993) point out that while the variety in programs and services offered may reflect differences in clients' needs, or organizations' philosophies, "they may also indicate gaps in the availability of crucial services and inefficiencies in the use of existing resources" (pp. 403–404).

The NAEH (2003) reports that the majority of surveyed homeless individuals identified their most crucial needs as help finding a job and help finding housing. They also noted a need for transportation, case management, and physical health care, including vision and dental (NAEH, 2003).

Support services in these programs may include case management, service referrals, instruction in basic life skills, alcohol/drug abuse treatment, mental health treatment, health care (medical, dental, vision, and pharmaceutical), AIDS-related treatments, income support, education, employment and training assistance, communication services (telephone, voice mail, e-mail, Internet access), transportation, clothing, child care, and legal services. The exact mix of services and who provides them can vary greatly from one community to another, and even from one program to another in the same community. (Burt et al., 2004, p. 29)

In this section, we examine the three main bundles of services commonly available to those experiencing homelessness: case management and wraparound services, mental health and substance abuse treatment, and physical health care. We also examine the range of other interventions sometimes offered to supplement these services. This section concludes with a discussion of homelessness prevention activities.

Case Management and Wraparound Services

Case managers . . . provide critical intervention services. [A] quick and appropriate response to crisis can make the difference between residential stability and homelessness. (Oakley & Dennis, 1996, p. 182)

Intensive case management [involves] . . . attempting to meet all of their long- and short-term needs, including permanent housing, job training and placement, and linkages to other services in mental health, substance abuse, health care, and other relevant areas. (Toro, 1998, p. 129)

Case management is a crucial element of service provision for people experiencing homelessness. A case manager is a person who takes on the responsibility of helping individuals or families determine what services they need, what types of assistance they qualify for, and how to access them. These might include making referrals to treatment programs, securing passes for public transportation, helping make appointments, and providing other logistical support. Case management services "insert someone who knows the system into the life of the homeless person or family so that the multiplicity of client needs can be readily met" (Toro, 1998, p. 130). Case management services have proven helpful for "a variety of homeless populations," including single adults, families, and unaccompanied youth (Toro, 1998, p. 129). Levels of case management support also vary by program. Intensive case management involves meeting quite frequently with clients, even daily.

Case management is most successful when there is coordination and collaboration among agencies (Burt et al., 2004; Hombs, 2001; Johnson, 1988; Swick, 2005). "Currently, service referral is a component of most homeless service provision, but in the absence of more active and integrated case management, referral-based case management often results in fragmented care," which can produce barriers to and interruptions in needed services, putting people at increased risk for returning to the streets (NAEH, 2003, p. 10). Jackson (2000) found that the density of case management meetings was the most critical variable related to decreasing the length of homelessness. Programs in many cities have attempted to improve their case management services by increasing access and reducing case manager caseloads (Burt et al., 2004). Some programs assign just four families to each case worker, allowing much more frequent contacts, though this practice is quite costly (Edna McConnell Clark Foundation, 1990).

Wraparound services, those that stem from one treatment plan that involves multiple providers rather than each provider having its own plan for a client, have proven promising. Successful treatment is also more common when cities have databases, multiagency teams, and colocated programs to help this population. Data sharing allows staff members from one agency to see other treatments a client is receiving elsewhere and plan its services accordingly, avoiding duplication (Burt et al., 2004). So-called "one-stop shopping" makes services much more accessible to homeless people, who might have trouble accessing transportation. "The coordination of community resources is also essential" (Flynn, 1985, p. 198), because "federal demonstration programs confirmed the pressing need to integrate service systems from the highest levels of administration to the front lines of service provision, in order to remove barriers to care and promote efficient use of resources" (Oakley & Dennis, 1996, p. 182). This includes coordination with predischarge planning for people leaving correctional facilities, hospitals, and other institutions, particularly by using a screening tool to identify those individuals who are most at risk for becoming homeless once discharged (Lindblom, 1996).

Mental Health and Substance Abuse Treatment

No approach to the homeless problem can fail to include adequate treatment for the mentally ill and abusers of alcohol and other drugs. (Gore, 1990, p. 962)

[Our] results suggest that repeated episodes of homelessness might be reduced by providing adequate mental health services for homeless clients identified as suffering from mental health issues. (Jackson, 2000, p. 107)

Because substance abuse and mental illness commonly co-occur in the homeless population (Oakley & Dennis, 1996), it is difficult to separate the two types of treatment, and this group of services is often referred to collectively as alcohol, drug, and mental illness or ADM. Despite public perceptions of the homeless, which tend to paint these people as intractably mentally ill, Oakley and Dennis (1996) assert that "only between 5% and 7% of the single adult population needs acute inpatient psychiatric care" (p. 185). Accordingly, the Community Mental Health Services section of the McKinney-Vento Act created a block grant program that gives states funding to provide outreach, outpatient mental health, referrals, primary health and substance abuse services, case management, and supportive services to homeless individuals (Foscarinis, 1996), particularly those with dual diagnoses.

Burt (2001) finds that people with mental illness and substance abuse histories, even head-of-household single mothers, can live stable lives if they are supplied with both treatment and housing. She offers evidence that in the long run, such programs are cost-neutral; that is, the cost to provide them offsets the costs that would be required to treat people in crisis. Snow and Anderson (1993) point out that although there are agencies that aim to restore people to health rather than merely promoting their survival on the street, such as hospitals, drug and alcohol rehabilitation facilities, mental hospitals, and outpatient mental health clinics, much of this treatment "is of the stop-the-bleeding rather than cure-the-wound variety" (p. 91). Oakley and Dennis (1996) found that most people with ADM disorders want and are able to live independently in the community once they receive appropriate treatment: intensive case management of at least six months, with longer-term, less intensive follow-up for some. Stahler and colleagues (1997) summarize extant research on programs and conclude that homeless substance abusers need intensive treatment in conjunction with housing, income, and employment supports, as well as long-term follow-up care that addresses not only the maintenance of sobriety but also the effects of social isolation and alienation.

Increased ADM treatment is prescribed by many professionals who work with or study homeless populations. This treatment should include a therapeutic approach specifically targeted to the needs of homeless substance abusers. "A wide expansion of substance abuse treatment programs is needed, with improved access for those who need them" (Shane, 1996, p. 220), particularly with an emphasis on "maximiz[ing] dignity, self-respect, and potentiality" (p. 220). Because many homeless people have had negative experiences with treatment programs or facilities, "the manner of approach in working with this population should communicate equality, respect, and dignity" (Flynn, 1985, p. 198). Flaming and Tepper (2006) point out the profound marginalization and exclusion from society suffered by homeless persons, particularly those with ADM disorders. Johnson (1988) calls for empowerment of clients because "the process of empowerment reduces the impact of social problems on both client and society" (p. 167). One empowering approach requires that clients contribute to program costs once they find employment (Burt et al., 2004). Oakley and Dennis (1996) recommend involving clients in the assessment of their needs and creation of their treatment plans, relying on peer support as well as guidance from recovered formerly homeless ADM sufferers.

Many programs aimed at people with ADM issues use an outreach approach where teams of trained workers go onto the streets to make contact with individuals and try to get them into treatment (Flynn, 1985). Research shows that most chronically homeless people "are unlikely to connect even with the best housing programs unless these first contacts are effective" (Burt et al., 2004, p. 20) and that there is stigma associated with using the homeless service system (Backer & Howard, 2007). For these reasons, Oakley and Dennis (1996) recommend that contacts be made repeatedly in a patient and nonthreatening manner and that homeless individuals be offered an array of services from which to choose. Other cities have taken a more coercive approach, attempting to curtail chronic inebriate street homelessness by creating programs modeled after drug court—once arrested for public inebriation, individuals are able to opt for treatment plus transitional housing instead of jail time (Burt et al., 2004). Still other cities, like Philadelphia, combine these two approaches by sending outreach teams, consisting of a police officer, a social worker, and a local benefits technician, to try to get shelter-resistant people into housing and treatment (Burt et al., 2004).

Physical Health Care

Without state-of-the-art medicine—mental and physical examinations, accurate diagnosis, sophisticated treatment planning, pharmacotherapy, psychotherapy, work therapy, social and recreational therapy, family and community supports, adequate placement, and intensive follow-up—we do no more than guarantee chronicity and deterioration even in a sheltered environment. (Greenblatt, 1992, p. 51)

Recognizing that physical health is a serious need of people without shelter, Title VI, Subtitle A of the McKinney-Vento Act, established a grant program for the provision of physical health services to the homeless (Foscarinis, 1996). Jahiel (1992a) stresses the need for comprehensive intake services that include physicians, nurses, and social workers; prevention services including vaccinations for homeless children; and hospital coverage that provides a sheltered place to recover from illness and surgery so homeless individuals are not discharged back to the streets only to get sick again. He also advocates for the extension of medical coverage to homeless persons either through an expansion of Medicaid or the creation of new programs. Shlay and Rossi (1992) echo this call, citing a 1985 demonstration project that showed it is feasible to provide health care to homeless people.

Other Services

Other services for the homeless sometimes include the following: the provision of counseling, child care, transportation to and from treatment and employment, and training in money management, parenting, home maintenance, and landlord-tenant relationships (Johnson, 1988). Some programs offer legal assistance and HIV/AIDS prevention and treatment services as well (Burt et al., 2001). In recent years, some programs have begun to offer access to and training in how to use the Internet (Finley, 2003). A handful of researchers promote programs that offer clients help building and maintaining relationships with family, friends, and neighbors, since "these connections need to be made on a pragmatic day-to-day level if the larger structural issues in the society that go beyond housing are to be addressed" (Leavitt, 1992, pp. 32–33). Additionally, "demonstration programs have repeatedly found that meaningful daytime activity to combat isolation is crucial to housing stability," so some programs offer housing support groups, tenant associations, and so-called community living rooms (Oakley & Dennis, 1996, p. 184). One such approach presented by Pearce (1995) aims to combat isolation and promote physical health by meeting the recreational needs of the homeless with sports leagues, field trips, and summer day camps. Still other programs attempt to engage the community surrounding the service center or shelter by educating neighbors on ways of interacting with clients and involving the public in planning and fundraising activities (Burt et al., 2004).

Employment services are another solution commonly suggested for the homeless (Hardin, 1996). The McKinney-Vento Act gives funding to states for adult remedial education and job-related services like job skills training, job counseling, and assistance finding jobs (Foscarinis, 1996). Indeed, "comprehensive job support and training, provided within a homeless shelter program, can improve [homeless] mothers' job prospects" (Swick, 2004). However, Jencks (1994) reminds us of the following:

> In a competitive labor market, someone always has to be the last hired and the first fired. Training schemes can rearrange the queue, but they cannot eliminate it. That means we must try to make life at the end of the queue more endurable rather than just helping people change places. (pp. 113–114)

Homelessness Prevention Services

In this country, virtually all federal programs related to homelessness focus on serving people who are already homeless. (Burt et al., 2001)

You could spend a dollar in prevention and save four dollars on shelter care.
(Egan, 2002, p. 59)

Many researchers point to the crucial role that homelessness prevention programs can play in keeping individuals and families from losing their homes in the first place, though there is little funding for such efforts (Aron & Fitchen, 1996). As one advocate noted, "once somebody becomes homeless, it's that much harder to rehouse" that person (Egan, 2002, p. 59). Hartman (1986) points out the following: "One clear question for public policy is whether evicting someone from his or her home for failure to pay $89-a-month rent to a public agency makes sense" (p. 81) both morally and from a cost-analysis perspective—"the costs to the public of providing the same person with adequate overnight shelter are several times that" (p. 81). The U.S. Conference of Mayors (2008) survey revealed that while 13 of the 25 participating cities had adopted policies aimed at preventing homelessness, many of these were aimed generally at households in foreclosure, not specifically at those at highest risk of becoming homeless.

Advocates argue for expansion of promising programs that target very low-income households and offer services such as legal assistance with eviction proceedings, rental supports, and one-time emergency cash assistance (Hartman, 1986; Lindblom, 1996). Legal programs have been shown to help keep many people in their apartments, at least in part because so many low-income families are informally evicted by landlord threat. When these households make landlords go through formal eviction proceedings, they get a chance to assert their legal rights and often emerge victorious (Lindblom, 1996). Mihaly (1991) details successful rental support programs like ECHO Housing in California, which operates a rental deposit guarantee program to help landlords and tenants agree to a schedule for making payments on owed rent. The program encourages landlords to rent to low-income tenants by guaranteeing to make up any shortfall if a tenant defaults (Mihaly, 1991). Roy and colleagues (2008) highlight a promising practice in Flint, Michigan, where families at risk of homelessness were able to stay housed due to small ($100 monthly) subsidies given to their landlords by the state. Recently, through HUD's Neighborhood Stabilization Program, some cities have started providing services to protect the rights of tenants living in foreclosed properties, instituting mandated notification times for tenants as well as rental assistance for displaced tenants (U.S. Conference of Mayors, 2008). In May 2009, President Obama signed into law a bill reauthorizing HUD's McKinney-Vento Homeless Assistance programs, known as the Homeless Emergency Assistance and Rapid Transition to Housing (HEARTH) Act, which includes immediate protections for renters living in properties going into foreclosure, requiring 90 days' notice if the new owner plans to use the property as a primary residence, and holding the new owner to the terms of the existing lease if he or she does not intend to live there (NAEH, 2009).

Policy changes could also help households avoid homelessness. Current public assistance policies discourage home sharing by reducing benefits to people who reside in the same household and prohibiting subsidized residents from having nonfamily members live with them (Lindblom, 1996). "Some homelessness experts have even suggested a new Aid to Families with Dependent Adults program to reduce the burden on low-income parents and others who house adult at-risk persons" (Lindblom, 1996). Changes in the rent-to-income ratio have also been suggested, as 30% of income may be too much to expect low-income families to pay (Hartman, 1986). Indeed, "most homeless persons cannot afford to pay any rent at all" (Shlay & Rossi, 1992, p. 150).

Although prevention is generally assumed to be expensive, studies have shown it saves money in the long run (Egan, 2002). Roy and colleagues (2008) suggest that since so many children are taken from their families and placed into foster care without the families ever having received housing assistance, money currently spent on foster care services might be better spent providing housing assistance. Likewise, advocates argue that more funding and expansion of discharge planning services for vulnerable populations, such as individuals leaving correctional facilities or other institutions, have the potential to prevent a great deal of homelessness (Burt et al., 2004; Lindblom, 1996).

❖ SPECIAL ISSUES FOR FAMILIES

Homelessness in this era, particularly for children and families, is a symptom of larger social dysfunction. (Shane, 1996, p. 71)

The greatest challenge to ending child homelessness is building public awareness and the will for decisive action. We believe that most Americans will not tolerate this national tragedy if they understand its scope and devastating impact, and know that proven solutions exist. (NCFH, 2009, p. 3)

The question is how much responsibility we, as a society, feel for the children of people whose poverty, or pathologies, have resulted in those children having nowhere to live. (Egan, 2002, p. 59)

The passage of the McKinney-Vento Act in 1987 was the first active step the federal government took to protect homeless families and children; before that time, "services for homeless children and families [were] grossly inadequate" (Jahiel, 1987, p. 112). Though many would argue that this is still a vastly underserved population, "a strong and increasingly visible network that continues to lobby Congress and educate public officials about the conditions of homeless children" (Polakow, 2003, p. 103) has arisen in recent decades. Perhaps because they are viewed more sympathetically than adults (Jahiel, 1992c), homeless children and their families, usually their mothers, are the subject of a great deal of research and advocacy attention (see, e.g., Anooshian, 2000; Biggar, 2001; Kiesler, 1991; NCFH, 2009; Swick, 1997). Kiesler (1991) argues that homeless children should have policy priority because only by helping them can we stop the intergenerational cycle of homelessness. Rafferty (1995) points out that "reduction or elimination" of poverty and homelessness "would, in the long term, cost our society less than the persistence of current levels of poverty and its consequences" (p. 56): "The suffering and damage inflicted on these children through illness and lapsed education and trauma . . . not only reflects badly on all of us, but it is actually bad *for* us . . . we, as a society, are worse off because of it" (Egan, 2002, p. 59).

There are different ways to support homeless families, but most agree that broad policy changes are needed (Nichols & Gault, 2003). The NCFH (2009) argues that "state governments are central to ending homelessness" (p. 34). Swick (1997) advocates organization and needs assessment at the community level. At the local level, legal strategies have proven helpful. In New York City and St. Louis, Legal Aid successfully brought class-action suits against the cities and leveraged considerable increases in aid to homeless families (McChesney, 1990). Toro (1998) argues for more psychologists to become advocates because they bring professional knowledge to bear on the damaging effects of childhood homelessness, which we explored in Chapter 4. However, because of the tendency in the United States to view social problems as the result of individual actions, rather than of a breakdown of social supports, there is still no "family policy" per se in the United States (Pardeck, 2005). Some researchers believe that until the United States joins its peers in the developed world and views family support as vital to the health of our society, appropriate supports to end childhood homelessness will never be possible (Pardeck, 2005; Yon, 1995). Shane (1996) puts family preservation and strengthening near the top of his list of primary prevention strategies. Rafferty (1995) cites Al Gore's assertion that "this country must achieve a coherent and comprehensive national family policy with a strong concern with the social problems confronting children in poverty" (p. 56).

There is not as much research on specific policy approaches and programs for homeless families, but we do know that there are communities where homelessness has been reduced indicating that it is possible to address the problem. Many small pilot programs have helped families successfully transition into, and stay in, housing (Nunez, 1994b). It appears that early intervention with young families seems to work (Swick, 2004). So too does help for families once they are placed in housing—help navigating bureaucratic systems of service delivery, the "maze of agencies" (Edna McConnell Clark Foundation, 1990, p. 29).

One final point to be drawn from the existing research is that collecting and sharing data on homeless families and the services they have received or are receiving seems to streamline care systems and facilitate effective service delivery (NAEH, 2007; Rog et al., 1995). Weinreb and Buckner (1993) summarize the extant research thus: "While there is a need to improve knowledge of existing programs and demonstrate the effectiveness of various service delivery approaches, it is clear that programs for homeless families are insufficient in scale and effectiveness" (p. 402).

Although not all homeless families are alike (McChesney, 1992), they are distinct from individuals experiencing homelessness in several important ways. Accordingly, distinct policy and programmatic responses have arisen or are advocated for homeless families. Different income support programs, different housing priorities and structures, and different services are all needed to address the issues facing homeless families. As in the previous section, so too do attempts to address family homelessness fall into the three main categories of addressing poverty, increasing access to housing, and providing social services. That is, "the eradication of family homelessness in this country will require addressing its key causes: poverty, the shortage of low-income housing, and the lack of support systems for families with special needs or under particular stress" (Mihaly, 1991, p. 22).

Poverty

> *Housing alone does not resolve the interconnected problems [homeless]*
> *families battle, nor does it ensure them a future without poverty.*
> *(Nunez, 1994b, p. 15)*

> *Families are poor because the adult(s) in them are unable to earn enough*
> *money in the market economy to put the family above the poverty line.*
> *(McChesney, 1992, p. 253)*

One of the most crucial interventions for homeless families is increasing their income to decrease the effects of poverty. This can be accomplished through direct income supports, tax credits, and increasing the minimum wage. Additionally, supporting employment with related services, such as transportation subsidies, removes barriers to employment. Unlike individuals, homeless families also need quality, affordable, accessible child care in order for adults to go to work.

Income Supports

Families who are homeless can be eligible for a wide range of income supports such as TANF, Section 8 or public housing, SNAP, the Special Supplemental Nutrition Program for Women, Infants, and Children (WIC), Medicaid, and others (Taylor & Brown, 1996). Unfortunately, many of these programs are underfunded (Better Homes Fund, 1999; Rafferty, 1995). Indeed, "AFDC was not indexed [for inflation]. In a 1985 study, the Congressional Budget Office found that the real value (constant dollars) of the median states' maximum monthly AFDC benefit for a four-person family fell from $599 in 1970 to $379 in 1985, a 37% decrease" (McChesney, 1992, p. 255) that puts housing costs out of reach. In the welfare reform of 1996, AFDC was replaced by TANF, which suffers the same problems. "TANF benefits are the primary source of income for families who are homeless [but] families receiving the maximum monthly TANF benefit would have to spend 210% of their monthly income to afford a two-bedroom apartment at FMR [Fair Market Rent]" (NCFH, 2009, p. 39). Nonetheless, enrolling families in income support programs has been shown to be important: "Despite . . . grants at well below the poverty level, [our] data suggest that welfare remains a protective factor against family homelessness" (Bassuk et al., 1996, p. 645).

Additionally, these programs are often underutilized, failing to reach all who qualify for them because families do not know about the programs or how to access them (Kiesler, 1991). As Medcalf (2008) observes, "TANF represents a critical support for families with financial distress, however, it reaches only a small fraction of children in households with poverty-level incomes" (p. 9). For example, in the San Antonio area of Texas, 23% of children live in poverty but only 5% get TANF; "results of surveys . . . reveal that homeless young families are often experiencing difficulty both in accessing the TANF program and in meeting its ongoing eligibility and participation requirements" (Reeg et al., 2002, p. 2). WIC is plagued by similarly low levels of enrollment by eligible families. Advocates push for restoring federal food stamp funds to prewelfare reform levels and increasing access by holding outreach activities for residents of shelters (Better Homes Fund, 1999). States have the discretion to give priority to certain populations, and advocates believe they should use this power to assist homeless children. They also hold that the federal government should provide more information to shelters about its Child and Adult Care Food Program, which provides reimbursement for meals served to homeless children, so that more shelters will be able to provide more meals (Better Homes Fund, 1999).

Another crucial income support championed by many researchers and advocates is the Earned Income Tax Credit (EITC), a powerful tool for combating poverty. The EITC is a "tax reduction and wage supplement for low and moderate-income working families" (NCFH, 2009, p. 40) with the potential to help families avoid homelessness (Bassuk et al., 1996; Better

Homes Fund, 1999; Jencks, 1994; Mihaly, 1991; Shinn & Weitzman, 1996). The National Center for Children in Poverty calculates that if every state instituted a state-level refundable EITC set "even at 50% of the federal credit, it would lift an additional 1.1 million children out of poverty" (cited in NCFH, 2009, p. 41). Expansion of the EITC and other programs could also have preventative effects as well: "More adequate and continuous benefits . . . would prevent many families from ever becoming homeless" (Rafferty & Shinn, 1991, p. 1177). Additionally, Shinn and Weitzman (1996) argue that increasing the minimum wage would be of particular benefit to women, who tend to be employed at or below minimum wage, in low-paying, part-time, service-sector jobs without benefits (Better Homes Fund, 1999).

Job Training, Transportation, and Child Care

Lack of child care and transportation compromises the opportunity for steady work of any kind. (Better Homes Fund, 1999, p. x)

Employment services, like income supports, can help homeless families afford housing if they lead to "a major increase in income" (McChesney, 1990, p. 197). Many family shelters and transitional housing programs have job training and education services for parents (Rog et al., 1995), but researchers have found that in many instances, homeless individuals do not access these services or manage to find and maintain stable employment even after successfully completing job readiness activities (Fraenkel et al., 2009). Also, since "the typical homeless head-of-household has a tenth-grade education and reads at a sixth-grade level . . . often has a substance abuse history . . . [and] has virtually no work experience" (Nunez, 1994b, p. 111), these individuals require much more basic and intensive education and skill development than most programs are prepared to provide. Likewise, employment does not lead to immediate savings sufficient for security deposits and moving expenses, so the most successful programs must also provide transitional family income supports (Nunez, 1994b).

Another crucial employment-related service is transportation assistance, since individuals cannot get to work without transportation (Medcalf, 2008). This assistance can take the form of subsidies for public transportation, free bus and subway passes, or transportation to work sites provided by housing facilities.

Child care services are considered one type of employment support, since parents cannot work if they do not have places to send their children (Biggar, 2001; Kiesler, 1991; McChesney, 1992; Mihaly, 1991; NAEH, 2007; Shane, 1996): "Child care is a significant expense for all working families and may become a barrier to work for families who are homeless" (NCFH,

2009, p. 41). Moore (2005a) reports that some counties provide free child care for up to 15 months after families leave a shelter. Shinn and Weitzman (1996) argue that access to high-quality affordable daycare is key to increasing women's participation in the labor force, though this creates a particular dilemma. That is, according to Jencks (1994),

> single mothers now care for their children. If we make them take jobs, someone else will have to care for their children while they are at work. We will have to pay the people who watch these children more than we now pay their mothers to do the same job. That is going to cost the taxpayer more money. (Jencks, 1994, p. 110)

This issue does not frequently appear in the literature; much of welfare policy seems based on a belief that poor mothers should work outside the home. Currently, states are given federal funding through the Child Care and Development Block Grant (CCDBG) to provide child care vouchers and can also transfer up to 30% of their TANF funding to child care expenses (NCFH, 2009). They can prioritize who gets CCDBG vouchers, but only one state, Massachusetts, gives priority to homeless children (NCFH, 2009).

Housing

> *Independently of other issues, priorities in housing policies should be different for homeless families than for individual homeless adults.*
> *(Kiesler, 1991, p. 1247)*

> *The research we have surveyed suggests that homeless families also have special needs in the areas of adequate shelter facilities, stability, and adequate services without barriers to access.*
> *(Rafferty & Shinn, 1991, p. 1176)*

The basic structure of housing available to homeless families differs little from that available to individuals, and it is poorly suited for families' needs. Mihaly (1991) recommends that "families always should be sheltered in facilities that provide separate sleeping spaces that meet local health and safety codes . . . provide 24-hour shelter, and allow them to leave their possessions safely during the day" (p. 22). Rafferty and Shinn (1991) assert the following:

> Shelters must provide privacy so that children are not exposed to communicable diseases, control over light and noise so that

children can sleep and do homework, and enough space so that young children can explore their environments. Shelters must provide nutritious meals, or they must have refrigeration and cooking facilities so that families can prepare nutritious meals. (p. 1176)

But these types of facilities are hard to come by. In more than 70% of the cities in one survey, homeless families were reported to be the largest group for whom emergency shelter and other needed services were most seriously lacking (Solarz, 1992, p. 276). More recent data from Medcalf (2008) reveal a bleak situation for families: "There was a 22 percent increase from the previous year, with denial of 52 percent of emergency shelter requests from families" (p. 10). According to the NCFH (2009), there were 29,949 units of emergency shelter, 35,799 units of transitional housing, and 25,141 units of permanent supportive housing for families available, totaling 90,998 units, while Nunez (1994a) estimates roughly 600,000 homeless families.

Policies and requirements at shelters often affect families differently than homeless individuals. Emergency shelters and transitional facilities often have length-of-stay limits that result in repeated forced moves, "needlessly increas[ing] the suffering of homeless families, especially the children in them" (Shinn & Weitzman, 1996, p. 121). As we saw in Chapter 4, children's social connections and schooling are often disrupted by these moves (Rafferty & Shinn, 1991). In an attempt to address this problem, "New York City mandated shelter stays for up to one year in order to help families reduce residential (hence school) mobility" (Williams, 2003, p. 28).

Likewise, many families are forced to split up upon entering a shelter because family shelters commonly accept only women with young or female children (Rafferty & Shinn, 1991). And the neediest families are often excluded from shelter facilities precisely because of their needs. In one study, 84% of programs excluded women with substance abuse problems, 63% excluded women with mental illness, 42% excluded families with a seriously ill member, 40% of facilities excluded families with adolescent male children, and 17% percent would not provide services to victims of domestic violence (Weinreb & Buckner, 1993, p. 405). Thus, oftentimes, parents are forced to "seek alternative, precarious arrangements in order to keep their children with them" (Duffield & Lovell, 2008, p. 15).

More permanent housing options for families, some argue, is the answer to this problem. "We know that temporary housing for children is better than no housing, but stable housing, independent of family income, is critical" (Kiesler, 1991, p. 1251). This call for permanent housing solutions to replace emergency shelters is even stronger with regard to homeless families than with regard to homeless adults. "One can concentrate on children's policy both for moral and financial reasons. Our society is developing a rapidly increasing subgroup of homeless children who will become comparatively incompetent and ineffective adults" (Kiesler, 1991,

p. 1251). Some researchers believe that many of the traumas facing home-less families would be solved by permanent housing. For example, according to Kiesler (1991), "stable housing arrangements, especially for homeless families, should be the highest public policy priority. Many problems of mental and physical health will decrease or be eliminated through stable housing alone" (pp. 1248–1249). Duffield and Lovell (2008) call for the HUD definition of "homeless" to be broadened to mirror the Department of Education's definition, so that more families would be eligible for hous-ing assistance. However, though McChesney (1990) reminds us that "delivery of social services in the absence of permanent housing is an ameliorative rather than a curative approach to homelessness" (p. 197), we see in the next section how services separated from housing are still a major focus of efforts to ameliorate homelessness.

Services

There is a tremendous need for services and service coordination both during and after homelessness. While housing is essential, it must be connected to comprehensive, long-term, community-based services that permit families to maintain their housed status. (Biggar, 2001, p. 963)

In addition to approaches aimed at lessening poverty and strategies addressing housing needs, the provision of social services to homeless families is a popular remedy. The greatest volume of research and advo-cacy work exists in this area (Hart-Shegos & Associates, 1999; Shlay & Rossi, 1992). Indeed, "there is mounting support for the widespread implementation of comprehensive models . . . that educate and train fami-lies, that offer counseling, [and] that provide diverse forms of family sup-port, from child care to health care" (Nunez, 1994b, p. 47). These services might take place within transitional housing facilities or off-site at com-munity agencies. Many emergency shelters are also starting to conduct assessments and provide needed services (Rog et al., 1995).

Unfortunately, the provision of services is expensive and often difficult given the widely varying and multiple challenges confronting homeless families. Many facilities and programs are run by nonprofit organizations and volunteers, who tend to be "long on love and short on cash" (McChesney, 1990, p. 199). And designing services can be difficult since not all families have the same needs: A middle-class mother fleeing domestic violence might need short-term support and longer-term counseling, whereas chronically poor and persistently homeless families may need more supports (Swick, 2004), everything from basic services such as food and clothing to sophisticated interventions designed to buffer families from trauma, victimization, and loss. Ziesemer et al. (1994) remind us that multiple simultaneous stressors are more catastrophic than single ones, and many of these stressors are common to families living in poverty even before they become homeless. Some families have members with serious health problems, substance addictions, mental health disorders, and illiteracy; some have children in foster care, and some may never have lived independently and will need support for some or all of these issues (Edna McConnell Clark Foundation, 1990). Some have suffered abuse without support. "It is not unusual for shelter staff to be the first ones to hear of a mother's long history of physical abuse" (Weinreb & Buckner, 1993, p. 402). Given "the enormous caseloads of high-risk, multiproblem families . . . [and the] diverse problems presented by clients, caregivers must design a broad range of program models" (Hausman & Hammen, 1993, p. 366).

In order to make sure that the family's needs are met, Swick (1997) advocates "an intake process that is nurturing, comprehensive, and guided by family needs. The child, the parent, and the family's growth toward permanent, functional living guide the overall process" (p. 33). The best set of services for a homeless family comes in the form of well-matched (NAEH, 2007), comprehensive, adaptive, and responsive service plans (Swick, 1997) to help families set and achieve goals. This section explores the five main categories of services typically offered to homeless families: case management, addiction and mental health support, enhancement of social connections and empowerment, parenting support and family reunification, and physical health care.

Case Management

Case management services are one of the most popular strategies for helping families escape homelessness, particularly when paired with transitional housing (Rog, Holupka, McCombs-Thornton, Brito, & Hambrick, 1997; Stahler et al., 1997). Operating on the assumption that services for families exist in the community but are inaccessible (Rog et al., 1997), case management introduces a "benefits and entitlements specialist, expert at negotiating service bureaucracies" (Hausman & Hammen, 1993, p. 366), who can link mothers and children with TANF funding, food stamps and WIC, Section 8 housing vouchers, child care subsidies, and other programs. Case workers make a plan for each family, help with program referrals and contacts, and monitor the family's progress, often making home visits and also providing training in basic household skills like budgeting and problem solving (Rog et al., 1995). Some case managers help families connect with religious institutions and recreational activities (Edna McConnell Clark Foundation, 1990). Others accompany families while they visit agencies, make court appearances, take their children to medical appointments, and even go to routine places like the grocery store (Nunez, 1994b).

Frequency of case management meetings varies by program and by location. Rog and colleagues (1995) found that in Denver, Nashville, and

Seattle, families received "moderate" levels of case management, one hour every two weeks, whereas in Portland, families received one hour every week on average. Unfortunately, caseworkers in Rog and colleagues' 1997 study reported spending three-quarters of their time completing paper-work, making phone calls, going to meetings, conferring with colleagues, and traveling to visit families, dramatically reducing the amount of time they were actually able to spend with families. The ability of a case manager to develop trusting relationships with her clients is crucial to successful interventions (Nunez, 1994a, 1994b) and is more probable when caseloads are lower. With fewer families to attend to, case managers with low case loads can spend time getting to know families and building relationships that engender trust. Intensive case management models involve dramati-cally reducing caseloads—sometimes from 40 families per caseworker to 4—so that frequent meetings and high levels of support can be given to the highest-risk families until they are stabilized. Some of the highest-risk homeless families are those who "have severe health problems, are headed by teenage mothers, have children in foster care, or those who have never lived on their own" (Edna McConnell Clark Foundation, 1990, p. 35).

Jackson (2000) finds that intensive case management may make a significant difference in decreasing the duration of families' homeless-ness and preventing repeated episodes of homelessness. But intensive case management is also expensive and therefore not available to many families. "Even when available, support and services are generally fragmented and temporary . . . more often than not a homeless family has no one contact person or caseworker to turn to during their ordeal" (Nunez, 1994b, p. 90). And whether intensive case management is really necessary for most families is debated. "No clear pattern has yet emerged" (Rog et al., 1997, p. 80) between family needs, the intensity of case management, and outcomes. Shinn and Weitzman (1996) discov-ered that "once families had subsidized housing and income support from welfare, case management services made only a small additional difference" (p. 115).

Mental Illness, Substance Abuse, and Counseling

If a portion of the multiple stresses which plague homeless families were substantially alleviated, the psychological risk for children would be greatly reduced. (Neiman, 1988, p. 21)

⌒◦⌒

Our findings of severe developmental delays in [homeless] preschoolers, and of anxiety, depression, and learning difficulties in school-age [homeless] children show that their problems cannot wait. (Bassuk, 1992, p. 263)

⌒◦⌒

ADM problems, as well as subclinical mental health issues, are well documented in homeless families, though not at rates higher than in other low-income families (Goodman, 1991). Not surprisingly, then, researchers and advocates call for ADM treatment to be available to homeless families in shelters and off-site (LaVesser, Smith, & Bradford, 1997). Rog and colleagues (1995) found that 67% of homeless families in their study received mental health or substance abuse services (p. 509). Indeed, many programs require participation in ADM programs. At the same time, many homeless mothers who are preoccupied with basic survival find required participation in treatment programs so stressful or threatening that they decline to participate (Weinreb & Buckner, 1993), even if it means sacrificing shelter. Because substance abuse can often lead to having one's children placed in foster care, some programs attempt to address addiction and family reunification issues together, making sobriety for the sake of getting one's children back the goal (Nunez, 1994b). Because research has also shown that the effects of a combination of stressors is much greater than the sum of each separate stressor (Neiman, 1988), Goodman (1991) points out that the combination of family substance abuse and homelessness produces extreme trauma that is likely to have long-term effects on families even after they return to housing. The Better Homes Fund (1999) calls for the Comprehensive Community Mental Health Block Grant program to give priority to homeless children and their mothers.

Although, as McChesney (1990) points out, "delivering mental health services will not decrease the total number of homeless families" (p. 197), and the Urban Institute (2000) reports that helping families deal with emotional problems is much easier once families are permanently housed, counseling is nonetheless a popular service delivered to this population. As we reported in Chapter 4, the experience of being homeless creates significant trauma, particularly for children, and counseling can help victims deal with its effects (Goodman, 1991). Even for those homeless individuals who do not suffer from chronic mental illness, mental health treatment is often needed for "temporary personal crises such as divorce or separation, domestic violence, or death in the family" (Ropers, 1988, p. 179). Individual members of a family may need counseling and the family unit may need group counseling to improve communication and cohesion (Daniels, D'Andrea, Omizo, & Pier, 1999; Weinreb & Buckner, 1993). Some argue for the teaching of coping strategies like social problem solving, relaxation training, and behavioral self-control to help children (Menke, 2000) and adults (Daniels et al., 1999) handle the stresses of being homeless.

In particular, trauma caused by violent victimization is common in homeless families (Better Homes Fund, 1999). Women escaping partner violence are not the only victims. Tyler and Melander (2009) found high rates of partner violence experienced by both men and women in their study, prompting them to recommend extreme sensitivity on the part of service providers to the potential mental health outcomes of violence, such as post-traumatic stress disorder. Victims of partner violence who are homeless are also at high risk of revictimization, so Tyler and Melander (2009) advocate training for shelter personnel and changes in laws to allow greater protections, as well as additional research into ways to break the cycle of violence. D'Ercole and Struening (1990) point to the high likelihood of homeless women having experienced physical or sexual abuse at some point in their past as a reason for caregivers to be particularly sensitive to the effects of trauma these women might be experiencing, advocating a low-demand drop-in center approach—one where women can first "drop in" and participate in whatever programs they want, without signing up for long-term programs or being held to participation requirements—for establishing trust. Bassuk and colleagues (1996) call for health care providers to incorporate screenings for indicators of abuse and assault into routine exams with homeless women, both alone and with children, and to forge connections with mental health treatment providers to allow for coordination of referrals and services.

Social Connections and Empowerment

Oakley and Dennis (1996) demonstrate the need for persons experiencing homelessness to engage in meaningful activity to combat isolation and forge social connectedness. Formal and informal social connections are believed to be crucial for homeless families (Rabideau & Toro, 1997). Without them, "it is extremely difficult for families to exit homelessness, and almost impossible for them to remain housed" (Jackson, 2000, pp. 18–19). Daniels and colleagues (1999) advocate for group therapy as an efficient way to give homeless youngsters and their parents increased social support. Some counselors and case managers are adept at helping mothers find supports within their existing social networks. The director of one New York City program, disagreeing with well-established research, asserts that most homeless women do indeed have at least one person on whom they can rely. What is often lacking is appropriate guidance in identifying and reaching out for that support, and a "strategy of finding alternative supports may be pivotal to family stabilization" (Hausman & Hammen, 1993, p. 367). This is particularly critical for the mother of an infant, because having a safe place where her child can live for even a few days can protect her from having that child placed in foster care. Toro and Wall (1991) emphasize the need for services to help families "repair relationships and maintain productive roles in the community" (p. 484). Stahler et al. (1997) also emphasize the need for aftercare, less intensive supports that help families maintain the social connections they forged while in treatment.

Empowering homeless families is also crucial. Too many programs "actually do more harm than good" because they are "based on a deficit model of human services" (Swick, 2005, pp. 198–199). In contrast, though few in number, family-centered programs "recognize inherent strengths within all families and value the priorities that each family establishes" (Taylor & Brown, 1996, p. 21). These programs operate from the assumptions that the caregivers in the family are competent, family preservation is essential, families are capable of making decisions about their own treatment, and "families have rights and beliefs that need to be recognized and respected" (Taylor & Brown, 1996, p. 21). D'Ercole and Struening (1990) cite Margot Breton's "sistering" program, which emphasizes self-help to combat learned helplessness and encourages homeless women to establish "a sense of dignity and worth" (p. 150). Cultural sensitivity can also empower the family by validating clients' cultural and ethnic identities (Stahler et al., 1997; Taylor & Brown, 1996).

Fraenkel et al. (2009) detail a study using group narrative therapy to promote both family empowerment and social connections with other families. This technique, which was well-received by study participants, involves having families tell narratives of how they came to be homeless and envision preferred futures. By encouraging positive expectancy—a sense of hope about the future (Stahler et al., 1997)—and focusing on externalization—encouraging families to identify themselves as separate from the circumstance of being homeless—this therapy seems "uniquely suited to address the impact of stigmatizing language and images of 'the homeless' and to help families recover and enlarge other ways of viewing themselves" (Fraenkel et al., 2009, p. 329). Fraenkel and team (2009) note that this approach asks professionals to act more as facilitators than directors of treatment, increasing the empowerment of family members as they take a central role in their own treatment. The experience of "being witnessed bearing testimony" (p. 330) has well-documented therapeutic benefits for trauma survivors, and speaking to other homeless families allows for a sense that one is not alone, as well as for cohesiveness and bonding.

Parenting Support and Family Reunification

The help a mother receives benefits not only her directly, but benefits her children as well. (Rabideau & Toro, 1997, p. 13)

Homeless families are at increased risk for child abuse and neglect charges (Nunez, 1994a, 1994b), so the provision of services specifically targeting the needs of parents is crucial to this population (Shane, 1996). Although many shelters and transitional facilities are committed to providing services in the area of parenting skills to mothers, they differ in approach. Some require participation in formal parenting classes, while others consider this too much stress for a woman in crisis and focus instead on strengthening self-esteem until the woman is ready to voluntarily participate (Hausman & Hammen, 1993). Daniels and colleagues (1999) call for interventions "intentionally designed to affirm and enhance homeless mothers' parenting skills as a fundamental empowerment strategy" (p. 169) leading to improved parenting. Rabideau and Toro (1997) report that the amount and quality of social support mothers receive is an important predicting factor in their children's self-perceptions, concluding that "maternal social support may serve as a protective factor that facilitates resiliency in homeless children" (p. 13). Likewise, Neiman (1988) calls for strengthening social supports for parents in order to increase their abilities to support their children's emotional needs.

Supporting mothers may help reduce instances of child abuse and neglect. One national program using home visits for new mothers was successful in preventing child maltreatment, and some researchers would like to see such visits made to parents with newborns and infants in shelters (Better Homes Fund, 1999). Nunez (1994b) profiles one example of a crisis nursery, which aims to prevent child abuse and neglect by giving parents "a respite from their children in times of extreme stress and upheaval" (p. 139). Prospect Family Nursery in the South Bronx operates 24 hours a day, seven days a week, and allows homeless parents and those at high risk for becoming homeless to leave their young children up to 72 hours per stay, for up to 30 days per year, and does not require legal separation. After families pick up their children, they are visited by an aftercare worker who helps establish connections to community supports. There is also a 24-hour hotline to provide support to parents (Nunez, 1994b).

Likewise, Nunez (1994b) describes a New York City program specifically designed to help reunify homeless families with children who were taken from them and placed in foster care, as well as to prevent foster placements from occurring in the first place. Though undoubtedly expensive and unique, this program offers a promising alternative to the traditional system, which separates parents from their children in often irreparable ways. The NCFH (2009) advocates for more funding for wraparound services—ongoing supports after intensive treatment has ended, like links to income support programs, employment services, child care, and recreation—that may prevent the placement of homeless children into foster care.

Physical Health Care

Physical health care is cited as an urgent need of homeless families, especially children (Menke & Wagner, 1997). Shane (1996) cites research from Philadelphia suggesting that the first six months of homelessness are the most dangerous and calls for preventive services, early detection and care of illness, and treatment for existing medical conditions to improve health outcomes for homeless adults and children. The American Academy of Pediatrics (2005) calls for pediatricians to be aware of the special mental and physical health problems faced by homeless children and to use "appropriate screening to identify family, environmental, and social circumstances, as well as biological factors" in pediatric assessments (p. 1097). Particularly for families, such services as prenatal and postnatal care (Shane, 1996), childhood immunizations, health education for parents (Nunez, 1994b), regular physicals, and lead poisoning screenings (Mihaly, 1991) are especially important. In addition to treating acute illness, other researchers acknowledge the need for appropriate recreational activities and facilities to support children's healthy physical development (Neiman, 1988).

Although "Medicaid is the primary way that children who are homeless receive health insurance" (NCFH, 2009, p. 43), two-thirds of eligible children are not enrolled. For this reason, many advocates call for expansion and outreach designed to increase enrollment in Medicaid and State Children's Health Insurance Programs (SCHIP). Expansion of presumptive eligibility would also help enroll homeless children. Presumptive eligibility means that in certain low-income areas, programs are able to enroll a child to start receiving coverage immediately based on the family's reported income, and they have a month to verify that income. Fourteen states have presumptive eligibility for Medicaid and nine for SCHIP (NCFH, 2009). Likewise, expansion of the Medicaid reciprocity model, which allows recipients in one state to receive Medicaid in another state without reestablishing eligibility, would make health benefits more accessible to homeless families (American Academy of Pediatrics, 2005). The NCFH (2009) points out that enrolling families in Medicaid is more cost-effective to society than paying for expensive visits to the emergency room.

Food insecurity, also shared by many housed families living in poverty, is believed to be especially problematic for homeless children. The NCFH (2009) notes that although "SNAP has been called 'the single most effective program in lifting children out of extreme poverty,'" (p. 17), it and other programs, such as WIC and the Summer Food Service Program, fail to reach enough homeless families and children. Additional outreach and enrollment efforts are needed (NCFH, 2009), as well as modifications to existing food packages that "meet the needs of families with no access to refrigeration or storage" (Mihaly, 1991, p. 24). Some cities require higher nutritional standards for meals provided to homeless families than to individuals (Nunez, 1994b), under the assumption that childhood nutrition lays a foundation for academic and socioemotional success, as well as physical health in adulthood. Additionally, Shlay and Rossi (1992) cite evidence that the availability of food subsidies may actually prevent homelessness by allowing "precariously housed persons to put most of their income into housing" (p. 151).

Prevention

Although most of the remedies discussed herein are intended for people already experiencing homelessness, there is a call in the literature to provide similar services—income supports, counseling and ADM treatment, health care, child care, and job training—to housed extremely poor families, in order to prevent homelessness from occurring in the first place (Bassuk et al., 1996). Providing services to help families negotiate with landlords, one-time emergency rent or utility assistance, transportation vouchers, and access to employment can help families stay housed (NAEH, 2007), avoiding their entrance into "a lifetime of deprivation and violence . . . this cycle of intergenerational homelessness" (Bassuk, 1992, p. 263).

❖ SPECIAL ISSUES FOR YOUTH

Just as some approaches to addressing homelessness are appropriate for individual homeless adults while others are suited to the needs of homeless families, another distinct set of responses exists for homeless single adolescents, the nation's unaccompanied youth. These young people are often too young to stay in adult shelters but not welcome at family shelters because they are homeless without their parents. The main areas in which responses to youth homelessness have been developed are housing and services.

Housing

Adolescence and its transition to adulthood is a challenging time for youth under the best of circumstances. Adolescents who are homeless must take on the adult tasks of securing housing, a livable income, and seeing to their future at a time when their capacity for rational thought and decision making is inconsistent and still developing. (NAEH, 2006, p. 3)

Homeless youth have special needs, but above all, they need more housing availability (Rothman, 1991). Russell (1998) demonstrates that "public policy has tended to be unidimensional with regard to . . . interventions" for this population, "favoring either institutionalization or family reunification" (p. 318), but most researchers and practitioners agree that a wider range of solution strategies is required. Pires and Silber (1991) point out that, much like the impact it had on the adult population, the deinstitutionalization movement of the 1970s came without increases in community-based housing for youth, and "too many of these formerly institutionalized youth have become homeless" (p. 97). When Whitbeck and Hoyt (1999) asked runaway youth about what they needed, the most discernible theme was available shelter. Facilities that do not require parental contact or deny shelter based on age or gender (Hallett, 1997) were specifically mentioned as being critical. A desire to stay off the streets and avoid getting involved in the substance use and crime associated with street life, and instead to "initiat[e] a nonhomeless trajectory," was clear in the youth Hagan and McCarthy (1997) interviewed (p. 209).

The first housing for homeless children came, in the United States as well as Western Europe, in the form of "cottage-like reformatories located in rural areas" (Karabanow, 2004, p. 17), where children were educated and instilled with "Westernized notions of family, work, and religion" (p. 17). In 1974, congress enacted the Runaway Youth Act (RYA), which gave grants for runaway shelters (Janus et al., 1987) with social workers and nurses on staff (Rotheram-Borus, 1991). In its first year, the funding from the RYA provided shelter for 33,000 youths. These days, shelters are likely to have a social worker on site whose primary goal is reunifying youth with their families, as well as some supervisory staff, but the full-service model is largely a thing of the past (Rotheram-Borus, Parra, Cantwell, Gwadz, & Murphy, 1996).

Housing for unaccompanied youth takes many forms: safe houses, drop-in centers, temporary shelters, and permanent supportive housing (Baron, 2003). Pennbridge, Yates, David, and Mackenzie (1990) recommend both the expansion of emergency shelters for youth as well as development of long-term, transitional living facilities to "support the multiproblem, disconnected, older youth as they seek to develop independent living skills and become self sufficient adults" (p. 164). Robertson (1992) calls for "a continuum of living accommodations for youths" (p. 294), including drop-in day centers, emergency shelters, and transitional facilities. The NAEH (2006) points out that nonhomeless youth often move between forms of housing like college dormitories, shared apartments, and their parents' homes while making the transition to adulthood and argues that housing options for homeless youth should exhibit similar flexibility. Some model programs like Bridge House in Boston allow youth to start in a minimum-requirement short-stay shelter before giving them the option of joining a more intensive, longer-term transitional facility (Pires & Silber, 1991). In this section, we examine the three primary forms of housing available to unaccompanied homeless youth: emergency shelters, transitional housing, and permanent housing. We also look at some best practices, recommended by researchers and advocates, that can be applied to all types of youth housing.

Emergency Shelters

At the least intensive end of the housing spectrum are emergency shelters, sometimes called walk-in/drop-in centers, which offer short-term shelter, food, clothing, and sometimes counseling and medical assistance (Slavin, 2001). These facilities generally have few admission requirements—their goal is simply to get adolescents off the streets. For some, these shelters, along with the family preservation services they provide, are enough to return youth to their families (Pires & Silber, 1991). Like adult shelters, emergency or temporary shelters for youth usually have length-of-stay maximums that result in high mobility (Williams, 2003). Rotheram-Borus (1991) and others have argued for more flexibility in federal time guidelines that would allow youth to stay longer in these shelters. Likewise, some states have changed their laws to allow for the creation of shelters for adolescents between ages 14 and 21, to avoid these children having to resort to the adult shelter system, where youth "feel neither safe nor welcome" (Pires & Silber, 1991, p. 103) and are much less likely to receive supportive services appropriate to their needs. Unfortunately, there are not enough of these shelters to meet the need. Though as many as 300,000 youth per year in the 1990s reported making use of these facilities, in 1987, 65% of temporary shelter requests by youth in Los Angeles had to be turned down for lack of space (Rotheram-Borus, 1991, pp. 24–25).

"The original runaway shelter policy was grounded in a mental model that predicted shelters would move children in linear progression from street to shelter to home. Shelters were assumed to have a stabilizing effect on youth and . . . the entire macro runaway population" (Staller, 2004, p. 387). However, for many youth, returning home is simply not an option, either because they are unwelcome or because returning would place them in danger of continued physical or sexual abuse (Shane, 1996). Family reunification is not a realistic goal for many of these youth. Some experts recommend a family reconciliation model instead (Pires & Silber, 1991), where youth are helped to reestablish and maintain familial ties without ever moving back home. In actuality, many more services for these youth are needed, as well as transitional facilities that allow youth some feeling of autonomy while preparing them to live on their own.

Transitional Housing

For those youth for whom returning home is not possible, foster care is one transitional option, but it is not widely successful. Fox and Duerr Berrick's comprehensive 2007 review of research on foster children's reports of their experiences found that these foster care experiences were very negative. Many reported being separated from biological siblings and not being given enough opportunities to maintain relationships with them (Fox & Duerr Berrick, 2007). More than one-fifth of foster children surveyed said they did not have their own bed or adequate bathroom facilities and 14% reported not having enough food to eat (p. 37). Even more alarmingly, since foster placements are often made to protect children from abuse, 40% of respondents in one survey and 25% in another survey reported having been subjected to "severe physical punishments" in their foster homes, and 15% of children in one survey said that someone in the foster home had tried to take advantage of them sexually (p. 34). Children placed in these homes often run away, preferring homelessness to enduring foster care.

Transitional housing is another alternative for youth unable to go home. Group homes are the most common type of transitional housing, though youth are sometimes resistant to the rules and regulations associated with this type of housing (Pires & Silber, 1991). They often enter group homes but then run away when they become overwhelmed with the rules, only to return days or weeks later to try again. Some group homes anticipate this cyclical pattern of entering the home and then running away and build in time for youth to grow accustomed to living in a structured environment. "Experienced shelter providers anticipate such cycles and perceive their role as helping the youths to increase their tolerance of rules over time" (Rotheram-Borus, 1991, p. 28).

Because so many unaccompanied youth living on the streets are also dealing with substance abuse, exploitation, and health issues like HIV, some transitional facilities have a treatment component (Slavin, 2001). Unfortunately, these facilities are few and far between, and they often have long waiting lists (Williams, 2003). Experts call for more funding for medium-term housing that provides the comprehensive social services needed to address these addiction, sexual exploitation, and health issues. Such housing would provide counseling, physical health services, and referrals to other agencies (Baron, 2003; Farrow et al., 1992; Slavin, 2001).

Permanent Housing

Although "housing for young people, homeless or otherwise, is, by nature, transitional" (NAEH, 2006, p. 3), permanent supportive housing is one model that has been tried in some cities. Denver has two programs, one for youngsters in or about to leave state custody, who are very vulnerable to becoming homeless; the other is housing for street youth with disabilities (Burt, 2007). Janus and colleagues (1987) call for the establishment of more long-term facilities where youth can live independently while pursuing counseling and other supportive services. Robertson (1989) also calls for more long-term placements like voluntary group homes, and Baron (2003) notes the importance of youth having places to go to "distance themselves from the offenders, the poverty, the deviant subsistence strategies, and the culture that all lead to violence and victimization" (p. 40) on the streets. There is emergent evidence to suggest that youth have had good experiences with permanent housing. For example, Levin, Bax, McKean, and Schoggen found in 2005 that although only 3.9% of youth in their survey had accessed permanent housing, they rated it five out of five in terms of quality.

Best Practices

Researchers and advocates have identified six practices that work well and can be instituted across the spectrum of different types of housing available to homeless youth. These include paying attention to the placement of facilities, paying attention to the issues of recidivism among runaways, establishing a caring community, conducting outreach to youth on the streets, targeting youth in danger of becoming homeless, and undertaking public awareness campaigns.

The first practice experts recommend is providing ample attention to the placement of youth housing facilities, whether they are emergency, transitional, or permanent in nature. When facilities are being built or chosen, there are important issues to balance and try to account for. If, for example, the decision is made to locate in a less stable neighborhood in order to attract more homeless youth, special attention needs to be paid to security measures and making sure youth are protected from victimization and crime. If programs are placed in more stable neighborhoods, special efforts need to be made to help youth learn about them.

Experts also recommend that programs providing housing to homeless youth pay special attention to the issue of recidivism. Homeless youth tend to run away, return home, and run away again. This evidence supports the idea that a "positive feedback loop" keeps youth cycling between home and shelters, including one study that showed 74% of homeless street youth had run away from home more than once (Staller, 2004, p. 385). Programs can account for this cyclical behavior by anticipating it and designing systems of care that do not depend on youth spending long periods of time in shelters or prohibit them from leaving and coming back.

Another important practice is the establishment of a safe and caring environment. Throughout the research on homeless youth, the idea that any facility or program needs to make youngsters "feel safe, cared for, and part of a community" is pervasive (Karabanow, 2004, p. 1). Pires and Silber (1991) cite successful programs that create "a strong family atmosphere in which youth are both valued and challenged to succeed" (p. 100). Such spaces create "an environment in which young people gain strength, courage, resiliency, and optimism regarding present and future endeavors" (Karabanow, 2004, p. 1).

Street outreach, which sends workers out onto the streets to locate youth and let them know about services and facilities available to them, is considered by many to be a crucial component of providing shelter to homeless youth. Because street youth are presumed to be less knowledgeable than adults about the services available to them, as well as more vulnerable to the exploitation and victimization of street life, many experts recommend programs that send workers out to find and educate them (Baron, 2003). As we reported in Chapter 4, Whitbeck and Hoyt (1999) state that "runaways, particularly young women, are in immediate danger once they are on their own," and "aggressive outreach programs need to be established . . . to identify runaways and provide immediate and secure shelter the first time they run away" (p. 169). Levin and colleagues (2005), Pearce (1995), and Slavin (2001) echo the call for outreach services.

Some programs operate outreach vans that target areas of cities where street youth are commonly seen. These vans are staffed by outreach workers trained in crisis management with teenagers. Staff members provide emergency supplies such as food, clothing, and blankets; offer AIDS prevention education; and make referrals to agencies for any services young people might request (Pires & Silber, 1991). Unfortunately, the freedom of life on the street is powerfully attractive to many youth, particularly those who come from overly rigid homes (Janus et al., 1987). To counteract this lure, Levin and colleagues (2005) recommend that outreach "be implemented in an 'adolescent and youth friendly' matter . . . designed to publicize the availability of youth services and encourage [youth] to access them . . . [and] address the factors leading to their current homelessness" (p. 57). The primary goal of street outreach is "to provide a contact point for disconnected, homeless youth" (Pennbridge et al., 1990, p. 162).

Some homeless shelters also run programs targeted at youth who are not yet homeless but are at risk of running away or being told to leave home. Youth who have experienced "serious family disruption, have been arrested for shop-lifting, prostituting, or drug-related crimes, or have been removed from a foster home, group home, or residential treatment facility" are very vulnerable to becoming homeless (Pires & Silber, 1991, pp. 44–45) and are the target of some of these programs. Rothman (1991) notes that one additional and vitally important piece of the puzzle of supporting homeless unaccompanied youth is increasing public awareness about the problems and needs of this group. Doing this can help get homeless youth connected with social services even before they enter into housing facilities. In our next section, we examine in detail the services that are usually offered to meet the needs of homeless unaccompanied youth.

Services

The homeless youth population is diverse and one must be aware of the differences among subgroups so services can be matched to the adolescent's specific needs and difficulties. (Boesky et al., 1997, p. 20)

⌁

The goal of social service agencies must be to reintegrate street youth into mainstream culture while signaling the importance of their unique and alternative attributes. This orientation is a delicate balance between street ethics and mainstream culture's values. (Karabanow, 2004, p. 84)

⌁

Like their adult counterparts, homeless youth have diverse needs and are generally treated with services in conjunction with or independent of housing. They need food and basic supplies and are often offered case management, physical health services, counseling, and mental health/substance abuse services. These young people also have some specific needs, including family reunification services, sex education, and protection from exploitation and abuse on the streets. However, they are a diverse population, making one-size-fits-all interventions impossible (McCaskill et al., 1998; Rothman, 1991).

At the same time, the overall characteristics of young homeless people have changed a great deal since the RYA, which has (1) "placed many new demands on service providers [and] altered considerably the profile of today's runaway and homeless youth program" (Pires & Silber, 1991, p. 19) and (2) increased the need for funding to serve this population. Unfortunately, until funding increases, agencies will continue to struggle to anticipate and meet the needs of today's homeless young people. Because funding is lacking, many service providers are forced to pay poorly and recruit primarily untrained personnel (Rotheram-Borus, Parra, Cantwell, Gwadz, & Murphy, 1996), compromising the quality of services they can provide to homeless adolescents.

Karabanow (2004) identifies four main ideological assumptions underlying programs that serve homeless youth: (1) the "correctional and institutional" view that sees homeless youth as delinquents and aims to protect society by correcting their "personal pathologies"; (2) the "rehabilitation" approach that views unaccompanied youth as deficient or harmed and aims to correct them; (3) "street education," which assumes that teens are forced onto the streets by difficult living conditions; and (4) "prevention," which "involves strategies of education and advocacy in order to find solutions to the root causes of homelessness" (p. 88). Rothman (1991) sees three categories: "heavy hands," which presumes that children need discipline and toughness because they are rebellious; "helping hands," which assumes that street youth are confused or have been exposed to harm and aims to use counseling and social support to help them find direction in their lives; and "hands off," which assumes that runaway youth are "engaged in the experimenting and deviating activities characteristic of adolescence" and that "radical nonintervention" is the best approach (p. 5). Although radical nonintervention is not a theme appearing in much of the service literature, drop-in centers are based on the similar idea that youth will seek help when they want it.

Janus and colleagues (1987) would like to see treatment for homeless youth based upon how long each young person has been away from home, with intensifying services as youth have been away longer, but service provision is not always organized this way. This section examines the three categories of service commonly offered to homeless youth: substance abuse and mental health treatment, specialized counseling and family reunification, and sexual health education and victimization prevention. It also looks at miscellaneous services sometimes offered to youth and examines best practices for service providers working with this vulnerable population.

Substance Abuse and Mental Health Treatment

Pires and Silber (1991) found that many of the homeless youth in the centers they studied had problems with substance abuse. However, most adolescent substance abuse treatment programs are based on adult models, which Rotheram-Borus, Parra, Cantwell, Gwadz, and Murphy (1996) note is inappropriate given that "adolescent substance abuse seems to be quite different from that of adults" (p. 388). Many programs are modeled after spiritual self-help groups like Alcoholics Anonymous, which, though effective for adults, have not proven effective for youth. Likewise, mental health treatment for youth is an underexplored arena. Pires and Silber (1991) report that "at many of the programs we visited, the distinction between substance abuse and mental health counseling is intentionally blurred because staff believe that drug use among youth is so integrally related to their psychological pain and suffering" (p. 51).

Specialized Counseling and Family Reunification

First and foremost, counseling for adolescents on the street needs to be delivered by professionals familiar with the challenges of adolescence generally, that is, counselors who are "cognizant of the most recent research and theory concerning teenage attitudes, confusions, and strivings" (Rothman, 1991, p. 36). However, because youth become homeless for such a wide variety of reasons, including abuse, neglect, and persistent poverty (Pires & Silber, 1991), careful screening and differential diagnosis are still very important for their therapeutic needs (Caton, 1986; Rothman, 1991). Although many of these adolescents have taken on adultlike roles and attitudes, it is important for therapeutic interventions to recognize that in many cases, these young people missed out on opportunities for normal socialization and coping mechanisms, which will need to be taught in "alternative" ways (Whitbeck & Hoyt, 1999). Rothman (1991) identifies a need for specialized counseling that offers a young person an individual blend of counseling types for his specific challenges. Additionally, he points out that unaccompanied youth "may need sustained counseling regarding self-image, self-confidence, and interpersonal relationships . . . [because] as a group this population appears to be in considerable need of ego and environmental support" (p. 36).

As noted earlier, for some youth who have been physically or sexually abused, returning home is not an option (Hammer et al., 2002; Rothman, 1991). However, many programs have family reunification services for those children who might be welcome back home. This approach would likely fall into Karabanow's (2004) category of "rehabilitation," as it assumes that personal deficits, caused by the family or by some other hardship, have led to the youth being homeless. In this view, the family system and/or the individual adolescent can be fixed and the problem resolved. Following assessment to ensure that it is the appropriate goal, family therapy, which may include conflict resolution, mental health and/ or substance abuse treatment for all family members, and parenting skills for the parents of homeless youth (Hammer et al., 2002), is a common route to reintegrating children into their homes (Pires & Silber, 1991). Farrow and colleagues (1992) note that "sexual identity concerns and family rejection constitute a major causative factor" (p. 724) in youth homelessness, and they advocate for professionals to be trained to help families cope with these issues as well. In cases where family therapy does not successfully lead to reunification, sometimes the preservation of family ties is possible, so youth can continue positive relationships with their families even without returning to live with them (Pires & Silber, 1991). Some programs also offer continued counseling services for weeks or months after youth return home (Pires & Silber, 1991). Shane (1996) calls for emancipated minor programs and greatly improved foster care services for those youth who cannot return home, while Boesky and team (1997) advocate independent living for older teens in this situation.

Sexual Health Education and Victimization Prevention

Because of their patterns of sexual behavior, homeless adolescents are at great risk for HIV and other sexually transmitted infections (STIs). Teenagers as a whole have high rates of STI (Noell, Rhode, Seeley, & Ochs, 2001), and homeless teenagers are no exception. As we reported in Chapter 4, many homeless youth engage in "survival sex," which is the selling of sex in order to provide money for basic needs (Greene et al., 1999), repeatedly exposing themselves to STIs including HIV. These young people often lack knowledge of the risks of unprotected sex, particularly with strangers, or the resources to protect themselves from STIs. For this reason, teen homeless shelters and drop-in centers often focus on sexual health education as well as STI prevention and treatment. This population also needs education on and access to contraception and pregnancy testing (Rothman, 1991).

Additionally, because many young people, both male and female, are prone to falling victim to prostitution when they leave home, many providers offer services directly aimed at preventing their entrance into this lifestyle or helping them get out of it. Many street youth suffered sexual abuse at home and are therefore at great risk of revictimization on the streets (Baron, 2003; Pires & Silber, 1991). Because it is common for children to come to runaway centers for help when they have been maltreated,

Kurtz, Kurtz, and Jarvis (1991) stress the need for staff at these sites to have up-to-date education on child abuse and neglect laws, as well as training in methods of detecting and exploring the maltreatment histories of these young people. Janus and colleagues (1987) stress the importance of long-term therapeutic services for victims of sexual and physical abuse to help them overcome the trauma and to prevent them from being exploited again.

Other Services

Other services that are offered for homeless youth include alternative education, like GED programs, employment training, and basic life skills training (Pires & Silber, 1991). Youth also benefit from having access to transportation, laundry facilities, showers, storage areas for belongings, and peer counseling (Levin et al., 2005). Youth often require legal support, particularly in locating legal documents they need in order to apply for benefits or enroll in school, particularly those youth seeking emancipation (Levin et al., 2005). Duffield and Lovell (2008) stress the importance of policy changes that would allow unaccompanied youth to be eligible for assistance like food stamps and Medicaid. Beyond basic life skills, homeless youth also benefit from being given the chance to identify and navigate services themselves (Aviles & Helfrich, 1991). Pearce (1995) notes the positive potential of healthy leisure opportunities, like recreational sports and street theater productions, that allow street youth to find their positive qualities and see the potential in their lives.

Best Practices

As we saw earlier with best practices that can be applied across a range of housing options, experts have recommendations for providers of various services to youth. These include engendering trust, empowering youth, and making sure programs are relevant to young people's needs. Other practices of note are focusing efforts on the hardest-to-help youth and making sure service delivery is coordinated within and across agencies.

Homeless youth tend not to be trusting of outside help, having had negative experiences with adults either within their families or in social service organizations. "The very issues that make it difficult for a youth to remain within his or her family also make it difficult for the runaway to respond to outside help" (Janus et al., 1987, p. 106). But how best to engender trust when providing services to homeless youth can be difficult to discern. Some researchers (Rothman, 1991) stress that service providers can promote trust by setting and enforcing consistent boundaries and expectations. Kurtz and colleagues (2000), in turn, found that while youth consistently emphasized the role of trust in their helping relationships, they identified workers being able to extend empathy without pity or objectification as the key element to gaining their trust. For this reason, they advocate for long-term interventions that are process-oriented rather than outcome-oriented. "Mounting distrust seems to be a consequence for youth who experience one such [short-term] helping encounter after another. Who can they count on not to let them down? Who can they really trust?" (p. 400). Youth in the study who had positive experiences identified "multiplex" trusting relationships with caregivers, those where the youth could expect nonjudgmental, unconditional support on many different levels from the same person. "Caring, stable relationships seemed to be what they were seeking and found most beneficial" (Kurtz et al., 2000, p. 399). Likewise, Pires and Silber (1991) discovered that one hallmark of successful youth programs was a strong sense of family among staff and clients. Homeless youth in Whitbeck and Hoyt's 1999 study identified the best worker as someone who is "just like a friend" (p. 167). Van der Ploeg (1989) notes that although many homeless youth have had repeated therapeutic interventions, it is likely that each intervention helped a bit and that persistence may be the key to gaining young people's trust and getting them off the streets.

In addition to creating situations where unaccompanied youth can develop trust in their service providers, many experts also recommend empowering youth to make decisions about their own treatment (Farrow et al., 1992). Bass (1995) and Rothman (1991) suggest involving individual youth in writing their own treatment plans and having them sign treatment contracts in order to encourage empowerment and integrity. King, Ross, Bruno, and Erickson (2009) and Karabanow (2004) support programs that use identity reconstruction to allow homeless youth to construct themselves as more than the experience of being homeless. These empowering experiences increase the likelihood of positive outcomes for youth participating in the services and also provide a training ground for the independent decision making they will face as adults.

Programs attempting to provide services to homeless youth also need to make sure to stay up to date and relevant. Pires and Silber (1991) note that, particularly when working with young people, service providers need to stay current on issues affecting adolescents and be prepared to reevaluate policies and programs regularly to keep them "relevant and dynamic" (p. 150). Stanistreet (2008) reminds us that homeless youth, like other youth and older people, are attracted by activities they find enjoyable: "Having fun turned out to be the best way of getting people through the door" (Stanistreet, 2008, p. 16). Providers who are aware of what today's young people do for fun are more likely to have success in attracting and keeping them participating in programs.

Burt (2007) describes the often politically unpopular strategy of programs aiming to help the "hardest-core" homeless youth they can find, rather than those with fewer needs, and insists that it is a best practice.

"This may sound counterintuitive," she explains, but these interventions "yield the most impact for the investment . . . because these are the people who are pretty much guaranteed *not* to solve their own problems if left to their own devices" (p. 7). She points out that as youth are leaving correctional or juvenile facilities, substance abuse programs and psychiatric hospitalization are the most "potentially fruitful" intervention points for preventing homelessness (Burt, 2007, p. 8). Other programs mix high-risk and relatively stable homeless adolescents in an attempt to allow them to support one another (Pires & Silber, 1991).

As with adult clients, one best practice identified by many researchers (e.g., Pires & Silber, 1991; Robertson, 1992; Rothman, 1991) is the integration of services: establishing one centralized point of intake into the homeless services system, providing comprehensive care, and promoting communication between care providers. Rotheram-Borus (1991) points out that in addition to the benefits of providing education, getting street youth enrolled in school can help provide a structured, predictable place to go "to bond with caring adults" (p. 29) who can help ensure the coordinated delivery of other services. We explore this further in Chapter 7, when we turn the spotlight on the role of schools in helping homeless youth.

Prevention

Although "we do not have much research evidence capable of guiding us toward the most effective interventions to prevent or end youth homelessness" (Burt, 2007, p. 9), Bass (1995) points out that research has identified certain factors that increase the risk of a young person running away from or being told to leave home. These include abuse and neglect, parental substance abuse, and placement in foster care (Bass, 1995). Prevention services should aim to identify children living in these conditions while they are still living at home and try to heal their family systems (Rotheram-Borus, 1991). Some homeless teen drop-in centers perform outreach activities with nonhomeless youth who are at risk, hoping to establish helping relationships before youth leave home (Pires & Silber, 1991).

Special Populations

Within the larger group of homeless youth, there are three subpopulations whose needs deserve special attention. Parenting minors straddle a line between being homeless youth but also the heads of homeless families, and they often fail to qualify for services directed at either group. Youth who have run away from or aged out of the foster care or child welfare systems or become homeless after leaving mental health or correctional facilities, sometimes called "systems youth," require targeted services as well. Finally, LGBTQ youth also comprise a subpopulation in dire need of specialized attention. This group of very vulnerable young people needs safe havens and counseling specific to issues surrounding sexuality and acceptance.

Parenting Minors

Unaccompanied youth with children comprise a particularly vexing and vulnerable segment of this population. Indeed, the line between homeless youth and homeless family, with respect to research, policy, and practice, can be blurry. There is a need for special housing where young mothers will not have to separate from their children. A few programs have been successful in providing housing for teenage mothers and their young children (Pires & Silber, 1991), often by providing round-the-clock access to child care and parenting support.

In 1996, when TANF replaced the long-standing AFDC program, it caused a new problem for homeless teen parents by "prohibit[ing] a state from spending TANF federal funds on assistance to an unmarried, minor, custodial parent unless the teen lives with a parent, legal guardian or other adult relative" (Center for Law and Social Policy, 2002, p. 1). Although the law makes mention of states' requirement to provide alternative living situations if parenting teens are unsafe with their parents or if their parents are unavailable, no funds are made available for this type of housing. In 2002, Reeg and colleagues found that nearly one-third of TANF-receiving homeless teenagers who had been subject to this rule reported that it put them in an unsafe situation. A reworking of this rule, or greatly increased funding to provide alternate arrangements, is needed to protect these young people and their children.

Foster Children and System Youth

Children who are placed in foster care are at high risk of becoming homeless, either because they find their foster placements unsupportive (Karabanow, 2004) and run from them or because they are not prepared for independent living when they age out of their placements (Rotheram-Borus, Parra, Cantwell, Gwadz, & Murphy, 1996). Likewise, youth in juvenile detention or other institutions are at high risk of becoming homeless once they are released (Farrow et al., 1992). The majority of youth in foster care or other forms of state custody no longer qualify for services after they turn 18, but "most youths . . . who are in foster care do not magically become adults with stable employment and housing on their 18th birthday" (Rotheram-Borus, Parra, Cantwell, Gwadz, & Murphy, 1996, p. 385). Lindblom (1996) advocates allowing foster families to continue receiving benefits until young persons turn 21, in hopes that three extra years of housing will help reduce the link between aging out and homelessness. In addition, Lindblom proposes special training for foster parents in how to prepare children for independent living, support groups for foster children, and life skills training (Lindblom, 1996).

For youth exiting foster care between the ages of 18 and 21 (or, in some programs, 23), transitional facilities have proven helpful. Often group homes with trained youth workers provide supervision and help young people progress toward the goal of independent living (Lindblom, 1996). Youth who receive this type of housing are less likely to become homeless and are more likely to go to college and have access to health care, and they are less likely to be involved in the criminal justice system (Burt, 2007). These programs are expensive, but "the costs associated with not making a successful transition to an employed adult are high for society" (Rotheram-Borus, Parra, Cantwell, Gwadz, & Murphy, 1996, p. 385). Many argue that more funding is needed for this type of program (NAEH, 2006) or other initiatives such as providing Section 8 vouchers to emancipating foster youth (Lindblom, 1996).

Lesbian, Gay, Bisexual, Transgender, and Questioning Youth

Many youth become homeless because of their sexuality, either having run away or having been told to leave (Farrow et al., 1992). Some "national studies estimate that as many as half of all homeless youth are lesbian or gay, many of them tossed out by parents who scorn homosexuality for a variety of reasons" (Jacobs, 2004), though other surveys identify closer to 25% of the homeless youth population as homosexual (Woronoff et al., 2006). LGBTQ youth have higher rates of physical illness, substance abuse, and psychological problems than their heterosexual peers, and these issues are exacerbated when youth become homeless (Cochran, Stewart, Ginzler, & Cauce, 2002; Russell, 1998). These homeless youth are at greater risk of exploitation than their heterosexual homeless peers (Kruks, 1991). Shelters need to be extremely sensitive to the needs of this subset of homeless youth.

Many LGBTQ youth report having been harassed and bullied within youth homeless shelters because of their sexual identity. These experiences leave them wary of using services designed for heterosexual youth (Russell, 1998). "There was a clear consensus among participants that the child welfare system is not a safe place for LGBTQ youth, and that as a result LGBTQ youth may be more likely to attempt to forge a life on the street rather than seek services and support from the system" (Woronoff et al., 2006, p. 36). Accordingly, some advocates call for special shelters for LGBTQ youth (Russell, 1998). In the absence of special shelters, LGBTQ youth should be referred, whenever possible, to shelters with nondiscrimination policies that include sexual orientation and gender identity (Woronoff et al., 2006). Staff at all shelters should be trained in how to respond to the needs to this population and how to ensure the safety of LGBTQ youth in shelters and social service programs (Woronoff et al., 2006).

Within the homeless population, there are subgroups requiring special attention. These include parenting minors, who need expansions of existing rules that allow them to access welfare payments and food supplements, as well as shelters designed to support mothers caring for babies and young children. Youth who end up homeless from the foster care system, as well as those who come from state facilities like mental institutions and detention centers, need special programs targeting the development of their independent living skills and an extension of benefits beyond age 18. Finally, LGBTQ youth need special shelters with staff trained to ensure their physical and emotional safety as they struggle for acceptance. Like the adult homeless population, homeless unaccompanied youth have a wide range of experience and require a wide range of solutions.

❖ CONCLUSION

In this chapter, we reported that attempts to address homelessness in the United States generally fall into one of three categories: addressing poverty, increasing the stock of housing, and providing social services. Strategies that attempt to lessen homelessness by lessening poverty tend to call for increasing income supports—welfare payments and other direct subsidies—or increasing and improving employment opportunities. Strategies that use housing to address the issue of homelessness generally focus on providing emergency shelter, transitional housing, rapid rehousing, permanent housing, and supportive permanent housing. Finally, the most research and advocacy has been done on the provision of social services for single adults, families, and unaccompanied youth experiencing homelessness. Case management is the most common service offered, often with wraparound services. Drug and alcohol treatment and mental health support are common as well. Physical health is the final category of services most often offered, though a long list of other services is also available less frequently.

We also documented that efforts are in place to address family homelessness by trying to decrease poverty through income supports, tax credits, job training, and an increase in the minimum wage. Additionally, most U.S. cities also provide emergency, transitional, and permanent housing for homeless families. We saw that social services are by far the most widely used approach to addressing family homelessness in this country.

Finally, we noted that homeless youth are a complex and multifaceted group who require different strategies from homeless single adults and homeless children within families. Providing flexible, accepting housing is a crucial element. In addition, homeless youth require social services targeted to their particular needs. We examined these services as well as some best practices for service providers working with this vulnerable population: establishing trusting relationships between youth and caregivers, empowering youth, keeping programs relevant to young people's interests, targeting the hardest-to-reach youth, and coordinating services across providers.

PART IV

The Role of Schooling in Helping Homeless Children and Youth

6

The Legal Framework and Ensuring Access

Schools were generally insulated from the concerns of homelessness in earlier periods of our history. Today, however, with the phenomenon of homeless families with school-age children, as well as a growing population of independent school-age youth, homelessness has been brought to the schoolhouse door. (Stronge, 1992a, p. 4)

Homeless children need education most desperately of all. They are even more undereducated and at risk of severe, generational poverty than are other poor children. (Nunez, 1994b, p. 57)

❖ INTRODUCTION

To prevent youth from being trapped in a cycle of homelessness an educational intervention is necessary. (Tierney et al., 2008, p. 33)

School can be an oasis for homeless youth, where they can find security and support and obtain the skills they need to survive safely on their own. (Julianelle, 2007, p. 8)

In the final two chapters of the book, we turn the spotlight directly on schools and districts, exploring ways that they can help children and adolescents overcome the negative consequences of homelessness and ensure successful educational experiences and outcomes. We ground that analysis in the following series of observations. First, as should be abundantly clear by this point in our narrative, the problem of homeless minors is a critical issue. It represents an "immense crisis" (National Law Center on Homelessness and Poverty, 2004a, p. 2): "Homelessness is an overwhelming problem, especially if you are a child or adolescent disconnected from all that is familiar, all that is stable, reassuring, and safe" (Tucker, 1999, p. 89). Second, as Tierney and colleagues (2008) assert, the "magnitude of numbers reflects the urgency of addressing the issue" (p. 4). We do not have the luxury of time. Third, as we saw in the analysis in Chapters 4 and 5, the needs of homeless children and youth cannot be met by the educational system alone (Rafferty & Shinn, 1991). That is, since "the best way to improve the educational attainment of homeless youth is to ensure that they are no longer homeless" (Hallett, 2007, p. 3), "some of the issues homeless youth confront are beyond the capacity of the education system to remedy" (Tierney et al., 2008, p. 2). At the same time, schools have a part to play (Daniels, 1992). The school is a "valid locus for facilitating intervention" (Levine et al., 1988, p. 103). Or, as Moore (2005b) makes our fourth point, "*one* promising avenue in seeking to decrease the problems associated with homeless youth is through the school system" (p. 13, emphasis added). Or from the other side of the ledger, "without education there is little hope" (Nunez, 1994b, p. 57):

> Schools cannot fill all the gaps in the lives of homeless children. They can, however, play a significant role in meeting the needs of homeless children by providing an environment that supports their physical, emotional, and social development. (Rafferty, 1995, p. 55)

> School can be an oasis of stability and support for children and youth experiencing homelessness. School can provide opportunities for homeless children and youth to obtain the skills they need to escape poverty and avoid homelessness as adults. (Duffield & Lovell, 2008, p. 9)

Fifth, all evidence suggests that the struggle will be intense. Addressing the needs of homeless minors has been and will continue to be an uphill battle (Jozefowicz-Simbeni & Israel, 2006), a "profound challenge of great complexity" (Masten et al., 1997, p. 43). To begin with, "homeless children have the education deck stacked against them" (NCFH, 2009, p. 27). And "of all the varieties of educational disadvantage, issues involving students who are homeless . . . are perhaps some of the most difficult for public school educators in the U.S. to address (James, 2005, p. 199). These students present "a difficult set of issues for educational institutions" (Gibbs, 2004, p. 26) and "enormous challenges" (Lindsey & Williams, 2002, p. 16) for educators. Sixth, change is required if schools are to be successful in meeting this challenging assignment: "Schools must make serious changes in procedures that have been in place for many, many years. The circumstances of the children's lives will not and cannot change to make it easier for the school. The school must change policies, procedures, and assumptions to meet the needs of these children" (Medcalf, 2008, p. 32).

Seventh, we are handicapped by a near absence of research specifically on homelessness about how to proceed. While we have an extensive library of work on what homelessness entails (see Chapter 4), there is remarkably little research on what schools can do to effectively address the problem (Mawhinney-Rhoads & Stahler, 2006; Tierney et al., 2008). To be sure, there are "best guesses," "logic models," and "stories" about programs, but remarkably little empirical evidence about what works, why, and in what contexts (Hallett, 2007; Markward & Biros, 2001).

> Current support for reforms is largely based on speculation in the absence of any empirical evidence of efficacy and effectiveness . . . further research is vitally needed to determine how well all reform efforts have met homeless children's needs and what service mix is effective or should be modified. (Mawhinney-Rhoads & Stahler, 2006, p. 302)

As a consequence, it is necessary to augment the education solution portfolio for homeless children and youth with research on related populations (e.g., students on the wrong side of the achievement gap, highly mobile youngsters, and students from low-income families).

Eighth, we need to remember a central caution ribboned throughout the book: Homeless children and youth are not "a static group who are all the same" (Hallett, 2007, p. 6). This is a heterogeneous group (Alker, 1992; Milburn et al., 2009): "The outstanding characteristic . . . is diversity" (Ziesemer & Marcoux, 1992, p. 84). Needs vary by residency (Auerswald & Eyre, 2002; Tierney et al., 2008), gender (Tyler et al., 2004), age (Moore, 2007), "path into homelessness" (Hallett, 2007, p. 6) or cause (Terrell, 1997), and time homeless (Powers & Jaklitsch, 1992). Since "not all homeless youth are alike, solutions must account for individual differences" (Hallett, 2007, p. 6). And, finally, when all is said and done, "much of the action in providing access and success in education rests with schools and school district officials" (Helm, 1992, p. 29): "For even after facilitating decisions are issued by the judiciary, and even after enabling legislation is passed by Congress and state legislatures, the reality of effecting 'meaningful change' rests with school districts, principals, teachers" (Quint, 1994, p. 7).

In the balance of the chapter, we complete two assignments. We describe the law that has provided the impetus and the architecture for the nation's engagement with the education of homeless children and youth. We then examine issues related to student access to schooling.

❖ THE LEGAL FRAMEWORK FOR ACCESS AND SUCCESS

The Stewart B. McKinney Homeless Assistance Act (1987) requires states to ensure that every homeless child—whether the child is in a homeless family, or is an unaccompanied homeless child—has access to the same free and appropriate public education provided any other child resident of the state. (James et al., 1991, p. 305)

The sole purpose of subtitle VII-B of the federal McKinney-Vento Homeless Assistance Act is to improve educational access and success for children and youth experiencing homelessness. (Julianelle, 2007, p. 22)

It is not our intention to provide an extensive analysis of the law that opened the school doors for homeless children and youth.[1] Nonetheless, it is useful to provide some backdrop on the legal structure that creates the context for schools to address issues of educational access and success. The story begins in the mid-1980s. Prior to this time, government efforts to address the educational impacts of homelessness were almost exclusively local in nature. The federal government exercised only a very limited role (Moore, 2005b). Startled by (1) the increasing extent and visibility of the homeless problem in general in the 1980s (see Chapter 2); (2) the dramatic change in the homeless population, in particular the increasing number of homeless families (see Chapter 3); and (3) data showing that the majority of homeless children and youth were not attending school, demand for more centralized action began to increase.

In response to these pressing realities, the Stewart B. McKinney Homeless Assistance Act—"the first comprehensive legislation to aid the homeless" (Rafferty, 1995, p. 40)—was passed in 1987. It has subsequently been amended a half dozen times, evolving into what is known today as the McKinney-Vento Act (Funkhouser et al., 2002; Gargiulo, 2006). In addition to a general recognition of the problem of homelessness and a willingness to engage the issue, the important points for educators in the law are as follows: (1) a specific acknowledgment of the problems of homeless children and youth (one of the sections of the law deals solely with this issue), (2) the provision of a framework for improving the well-being of homeless minors, and (3) a plan to use education as an improvement tool in the battle to end homelessness.

In its current, improved form (Biggar, 2001; Funkhouser et al., 2002), the Education of Homeless Children and Youth part of McKinney-Vento is designed to accomplish a number of objectives, all based on the core concept of "ensuring that homeless minors have equal access to the same free and appropriate public education as their non-homeless peers" (Funkhouser, 2002, p. 17), including all compensatory and special programs (Duffield et al., 2007; Ely, 1987; Helm, 1992). It attempts to accomplish this overarching goal in two ways: (1) by working to remove barriers to the enrollment and attendance of homeless children and youth (e.g., residency requirements, difficulties with transportation) (Biggar, 2001; Ely, 1987; Ziesemer & Marcoux, 1992) and (2) by creating conditions (e.g., enhanced parent participation, interagency collaboration) that promote the educational success of these young people (Alker, 1992; Duffield et al., 2007; Moore, 2007)—what together homeless advocates call the "enroll, attend, and succeed" package (Moore, 2005b).

Specific actions (mandates) are required of both states and school districts (First, 1992). Limited funding in the form of grants is available to help educators achieve the objectives of the Act (Alker, 1992; Eddowes & Hranitz, 1989; Moore, 2005a).[2] Language in the Act directs that homeless children and youth should enjoy benefits in the company of their housed peers; that is, they "should not be separated from the mainstream school environment because of their homelessness" (Funkhouser et al., 2002, p. 18):[3] "McKinney-Vento indicates that services should be provided in a way that allows homeless children to remain in the mainstream setting with their peers to avoid being ostracized, segregated, and harassed" (Jozefowicz-Simbeni & Israel, 2006, p. 40). There is also an assumption that mobility is harmful (Williams, 2003) and that it should be "minimized to mitigate school disruption and its effect on academic success" (Jozefowicz-Simbeni & Israel, 2006, p. 40).

More specifically,

> the McKinney-Vento Act requires that every state educational agency (SEA) establish an Office of State Coordinator for the Education of Homeless Children and Youth. This office is charged with critical responsibilities with respect to the implementation of the Act, including providing technical assistance, resources, coordination, data collection, and overseeing compliance for all local educational agencies (LEA) in the state. (Duffield et al., 2007, p. 12)

It also mandates the following:

♦ Immediate school access and enrollment for students who are homeless, even if they do not have required documents such as school records, medical and immunization records or proof of residency;

- Continuation of the pupil's education in the school of origin for the duration of homelessness (to the extent feasible), except when this is contrary to the wishes of the student's parent/guardian, or transfer of the student into the school serving the attendance area in which the child is currently residing. The school of origin, however, remains responsible for providing special education services to the pupil even when the student no longer resides in that attendance zone;
- Transportation for students who are homeless to and from the school of origin at the request of the parent/guardian;
- Designation of an individual to serve as a liaison for students who are homeless. This person is responsible for ensuring that children experiencing homelessness are identified, provided full and equal opportunity to succeed, and receive all services for which they are eligible; and
- Development or revision of all school policies, regulations, and procedures necessary so as to remove barriers to the enrollment and retention of pupils [who] are homeless. (Gargiulo, 2006, p. 359)

❖ ENSURING ENROLLMENT AND ATTENDANCE

Traditionally, homeless children have been excluded from the nation's public schools. (Eddowes & Hranitz, 1989, p. 198)

Frequent absenteeism is common among homeless students. (Shane, 1996, p. 36)

Action to improve school attendance can meaningfully support highly mobile students, since absenteeism poses the sharpest challenge to students' ability to keep up with their classmates. (Williams, 2003, p. 38)

Setting the Stage

In recent decades, the homeless families have had to surmount a variety of obstacles for their children to receive an education, including barriers to accessing school. (Mawhinney-Rhoads & Stahler, 2006, p. 291)

We begin with the logic chain that undergirds our analysis of the participation of homeless minors in the education process. First, starting at the end point, as we have reported in Chapter 4, "regardless of the cause of their homelessness, all students benefit from continuity in their education" (National Center for Homeless Education, 2006b, p. 1). Second, and back to the first links of the chain, homeless minors have significant problems with school enrollment and attendance. In particular, absenteeism is often a problem among homeless students (Funkhouser et al., 2002; Shane, 1996). Third, enrollment and attendance problems can be traced to two sources: the condition of homelessness itself and school policies, structures, and practices (Rafferty, 1995). Stronge and Lindsey and Williams captured this reality nicely when they observed the following:

> Problems associated with homelessness (e.g., financial barriers, transiency) and problems associated with the organization of schools (e.g., residency requirements, transportation) combine to pose formidable barriers to their education. (Stronge, 1992a, p. 19)

> While many of these obstacles stem from the learning difficulties and emotional problems of the individual youth, certain school policies have created systemic barriers to their access to school. (Lindsey & Williams, 2002, p. 24)

We have already reported in considerable detail in Chapter 4 on how conditions of homelessness impede the education of homeless children and youth. Here we focus on the second source of the difficulty, on how the school system itself hurts homeless children (Nunez, 1994b) through its "organizational procedures" (Korinek et al., 1992, p. 138) and its "policies and practices" (Medcalf, 2008, p. 24), that is, on the "significant barriers to homeless children attending school that are inherent in school systems" (Hicks-Coolick et al., 2003, p. 200). We remind the reader that we are examining two issues, student enrollment and, once students are enrolled, attendance.

Enrollment

On the enrollment front, while victory has not been secured and vigilance is still the watchword, there is good news to share, at least for the K–12 part of the educational system. Indeed, as Stronge (1992a) reports, "the problem of access to education may have moderated in recent years as school officials have become more sensitive to the plight of homeless students and have modified enrollment procedures to better accommodate the students' educational needs" (p. 20). At the time of the passage of the McKinney Act in 1987, it was estimated that between 33% and 43% of school-age homeless children and youth were not enrolled in school (Eddowes & Hranitz, 1989; Mihaly, 1991, p. 8). Since enactment of the McKinney Act, the situation has improved dramatically, with enrollments for homeless minors calculated as follows: 1997 at 73%, 2003 at 84%, and 2004 at 87% (Dworsky, 2008, p. 1; Tierney et al., 2008, p. 9; U.S. Department of Education, 2000, p. 5).

The less-than-sanguine news on the enrollment front is found in the preschool area (Solarz, 1992; Stronge & Hudson, 1999), "an age group that is greatly underserved" (U.S. Department of Education, 2000, p. 5). When we add these homeless children into the equation, the 87% enrollment figure drops to 67% (U.S. Department of Education, 2000, p. 5). According to Nunez (1994b), homeless preschool children are enrolled in preschool not only less frequently than the general population but also less frequently than poor, housed students. Biggar (2001), for example, documented that at the turn of the century, homeless children were "enrolled in preschool at less than half the rate of other children (21% versus 53%; p. 961). Similar information has been provided by staff from the U.S. Department of Education (2000), who reported an enrollment of only 15% for homeless preschool children.

Attendance

The picture here is also brighter today than it was a quarter century ago when McKinney became the law of the land. Nonetheless, quite a few dark clouds persist (Better Homes Fund, 1999). The bright side first: "More homeless kids are attending school" (Myers & Popp, 2003, p. 3). Indeed, "77 percent of enrolled homeless children and youth (K–12) attend school regularly" (U.S. Department of Education, 2000, p. 5), up from 55% in 1997 (Myers & Popp, 2003, p. 3; U.S. Department of Education, 2000, p. 9). On the dark side of the picture, nearly one in four homeless minors are not attending school regularly (Funkhouser et al., 2002, p. 13). Given the importance of continuity in the academic achievement algorithm (Duffield et al., 2007; Williams, 2003) and because these students who are at risk are more school dependent than the general student population, absences are especially damaging to the success of homeless children and youth.

The Nature of the Problem: Focusing on Schools

Barriers to school attendance and academic success for homeless children are numerous. (Anooshian, 2005, p. 147)

Homeless children and youth face a number of barriers to accessing an appropriate education, and as a result, they are often precluded from achieving academic success. (Duffield et al., 2007, p. 11)

Residency, Guardianship, Immunization, and School Records

As explained earlier, "school-related barriers" (National Law Center on Homelessness and Poverty, 1995, p. i) comprise one of the two domains of impediments to the participation of homeless minors in school. This domain includes a collection of structures and "policies, procedures, and practices" (Vissing, 2000, p. 50) that makes it difficult for children from homeless families and adolescents away from home on their own to enroll in and attend school (Berliner, 2002; Gibbs, 2004; Medcalf, 2008; National Law Center on Homelessness and Poverty, 1995). As Medcalf (2008) reminds us, "the average person cannot even recognize what can and does pose enrollment and/or attendance barriers for someone who is homeless. What is perfectly fair and appropriate to expect from the average family can pose serious barriers for the homeless that are all but impossible to overcome" (p. 24).

Historically, "the most pervasive and persistent barriers" (Biggar, 2001, p. 959) include policies addressing residency, guardianship, immunization, school records, access to special services, and transportation (Cunningham, 2003; Daniels, 1992; Hightower et al., 1997; Polakow, 2003). At the same time, it is essential to note that major progress has been made over the last 25 years in dismantling these impediments to matriculation and attendance. Each successive reauthorization of the McKinney-Vento Act, in particular, has blasted away at these obstacles, opening the school door to increasing numbers of homeless minors and fostering ongoing participation once enrolled.

Documentation is at the heart of many of the traditional barriers to enrollment (National Coalition for the Homeless, 2008). That is, parents and homeless adolescents have been expected to produce records that either make little sense for the homeless (e.g., proof of residency) or can be exceptionally difficult to produce on demand (e.g., medical records) (Kling et al., 1996; Swick, 2004). And, as Powers and Jaklitsch (1992) remind us, "homeless youth who do not live with their families face even greater obstacles in obtaining records" (p. 116; see also Funkhouser et al., 2002; Lindsey & Williams, 2002; National Coalition for the Homeless, 2008).

The McKinney-Vento Act has been a major asset for homeless in the area of documentation. It exempts homeless children and youth from many documentation requirements, allowing students immediate access to the school while record issues are resolved. Nonetheless, victory here has not been secured. Entrenched habits (norms) and ways of doing the business of enrolling students (i.e., practices and procedures) that disadvantage the homeless persist: "bureaucratic rigidities" (Mihaly, 1991, p. 8) remain. This appears to be the case because the McKinney-Vento Act requires solutions that run counter to the policies and practices used in enrolling nonhomeless students. In 2009, for example, the NCFH revealed that roughly a quarter of McKinney-Vento subgrantees acknowledged that documentation problems were still evident in their districts.

A residency requirement—proof of residency inside the attendance zone of the school—was "the most apparent barrier" (Mawhinney-Rhoads & Stahler, 2006, p. 291) for the homeless before the McKinney-Vento Act went into effect (Yon, 1995).

> In 1987, residency laws were the major barrier to the enrollment of homeless children. Children with no fixed address had extreme difficulty in proving residency in a school district. Families who moved to a shelter in another district in the middle of the school year were unable to demonstrate intent to reside permanently in the district in which they were temporarily living and often were unable to continue their child's education in the original district due to distance or inadequate transportation. Because school funding is based on residency requirements, many schools were unwilling to be flexible on this issue. (Alker, 1992, p. 24)

Helm (1992) also portrays the essence of the residency obstacle before the McKinney-Vento Act:

> Residency requirements cause a two-pronged problem for homeless families with school-age children. First, a family moving—or moved by a social service agency—to what may be temporary quarters in a shelter, motel, or apartment with a family or friends in another school district are not considered residents either of the district in which they previously attended school or in the district where they temporarily live, because they have not established permanent residency there. Both the school districts, in denying admission to their schools, would (prior to the McKinney-Vento Act) have claimed accurately that they simply were implementing state laws.
>
> Second, homeless families not infrequently are split up among two or more residences, with some children being sent to relatives, others perhaps to live with friends, and sometimes one or more becoming wards of the state. They may find themselves in several different school districts, and if the state law requires evidence of permanent residency in the district, it is easy to see that the children and their parents or guardians cannot meet that requirement. (p. 30)

This was the most visible barrier that came under the guns of the original (1987) McKinney Act (Biggar, 2001; National Law Center on Homelessness and Poverty, 1990). Under the law, states were mandated to "review and revise residency requirements to ensure access of homeless children and youth to school" (Helm, 1992, p. 36). Since that time, school districts have been prohibited from using residency laws to bar homeless children from school (Mihaly, 1991) and more recently from the school of origin when students move. Consequently, "residency problems [have] to a great extent been addressed" (Markward & Biros, 2001, p. 184). Remaining obstacles in this area center on awareness of mandates (Biggar, 2001) and the struggle of school personnel to successfully carve out a meaningful exemption to a district's regular enrollment policies. Hallett (2007) makes this latter point when he observes that "school personnel are trained to deny enrollment to students outside of the school boundaries and frequently do not ask the appropriate questions to determine if the child is protected under McKinney-Vento" (p. 1).

Before 1987, homeless minors without documentation of *required immunizations* would regularly be denied matriculation (Better Homes Fund, 1999; Mihaly, 1991; Solarz, 1992).

> Proof of vaccination [was] required before enrollment. Homeless children and families who are often transient and carry minimal belongings, frequently lose medical records. Additionally, many children in homeless families do not receive adequate access to health care professionals and therefore will not have required vaccinations. Lack of medical records or lack of access to medical care (and therefore not receiving required vaccinations) result[ed] in schools denying a student access to education. (Mawhinney-Rhoads & Stahler, 2006, p. 292)

> Most if not all states mandate that students receive and present records of immunization against common communicable diseases before or very shortly after being admitted to school. Homeless children, depending on the length of time their families have been homeless, may have difficulty meeting this requirement in several ways: (a) The parents may not know about immunization requirements, (b) the parents may not be able to afford immunization or know about public health immunization programs, (c) the parents may have difficulty contacting the appropriate physician or public health office for copies of immunization records, and (d) the schools in which the children were previously enrolled may be slow in responding to requests for school records from the school in which the family is trying to enroll their children. Without proof of immunization, most schools are required by law to exclude children trying to enroll or already enrolled. (Helm, 1992, p. 31)

Since McKinney, however, as Funkhouser and colleagues (2002) affirm, "states have made significant progress in resolving issues having to do with immunization records for homeless students" (p. 8). Homeless youth can enroll in schools immediately even without required documentation (Tierney et al., 2008). Remaining barriers here parallel those for documentation of residency—awareness and the ability/willingness to deal with exceptions to deeply entrenched school policies and practices.

Proof of guardianship has been and to some extent remains a barrier to the enrollment of homeless minors. It can be a particularly knotty problem for homeless youth who have either run away from or been asked to leave home (or foster care) and therefore have no access to their former legal guardians and, in almost all cases, have no state-provided current legal guardian (Alker, 1992; Julianelle, 2007; Tierney et al., 2008). It also histori- cally has been a considerable problem for children and youth who are living with friends because homelessness forced the family to splinter (Biggar, 2001; Mawhinney-Rhoads & Stahler, 2006; Rafferty, 1995). These "others" are not legal guardians who can act on behalf of these minors (Solarz, 1992), that is, enroll them in school (Rafferty, 1995). Collectively, then, "guardianship is another problem because homelessness sometimes separates families and makes it difficult, if not impossible, for students to obtain required signatures for school enrollment. This can especially be a problem for independent homeless youth" (Stronge, 2000, p. 5).

The guardianship issue remains a problem because while the law requires schools to enroll homeless children and youth in the absence of a "legal" guardian (Tierney et al., 2008), educators are not always vigilant in identifying the homeless and are, therefore, likely to apply extant policies and practices that disadvantage these displaced students.

Once students are enrolled, other barriers to participation sometimes arise. *Fee requirements* to participate in selected activities (e.g., field trips, cocurricular activities) have been shown to be an obstacle to the full engagement of homeless children and youth in school (Wilder et al., 2003). More problematic are delays in the *movement of school records* (Helms, 1992; Penuel & Davey, 1998; Shane, 1996). Or as Rafferty (1995) pens the issue, "one major barrier to accessing appropriate programs and services is the untimely transfer of school records" (p. 47), "delays that prevent children from accessing timely transfers in local schools" (p. 46). These gaps even when they do not prevent enrollment often "impede the ability [of school personnel] to place children in appropriate programs" (Polakow, 2003, p. 100): "Time lapses lead to service lapses" (Bowen, Purrington, Layton, & O'Brien, 1989, p. 51) as "the transfer of school records takes time and prevents new school personnel from preparing an appropriate learning program for the student" (Pawlas, 1994, p. 80).

Transportation

Almost every analyst who reviews these issues finds that transportation has been the most critical obstacle—and "the most frequently cited barrier" (Rafferty, 1995, p. 46)—to participation in school by homeless children and youth (James & Lopez, 2003; Tower & White, 1989; Williams, 2003). Initially this was the case because while the original McKinney Act attacked most of the barriers to enrollment, insufficient attention was devoted to transpor- tation (Helm, 1992), especially the requirement to use resources to keep students who were bouncing across various living situations and venues "to remain in their own schools, with familiar teachers, curriculum, and peers" (Rafferty, 1995, p. 54), that is, in their "schools of origin." "The original McKinney Act, passed in 1987, did not recognize transportation as an education-related problem" (James & Lopez, 2003, p. 127). However, reauthorization of the Act in 1990 (and subsequently) considerably strengthened the law on the transportation front (James & Lopez, 2003). As it exists now, the Act requires that school districts provide transportation to enable children and youth to remain in their school of origin (the school a student attended when permanently housed or the school in which the student last enrolled) (James & Lopez, 2003). "It requires this, even if the school of origin is in a different district from the one in which the student experiencing homelessness resides. If a student requests transportation to a school of origin in a different district, McKinney-Vento requires both districts to negotiate provision of the transportation services across district lines or split the cost and responsibility equally" (James & Lopez, 2003, p. 127). And the provision of transportation is required even if the district does not have a transportation system for nonhomeless students.

While these changes significantly lessened the grip of the transportation barrier, they did not reduce its power completely (Bowman & Barksdale, 2004; Iowa Department of Education, 2004a; Masten et al., 1997). Indeed, "transportation remains the major enrollment barrier for homeless children and youth" (Funkhouser et al., 2002, p. 8), and "getting homeless youth to the school itself remains problematic" (Tierney et al., 2008, pp. 28–29): "In the 2005–2006 school year, school districts receiving McKinney-Vento subgrants reported numerous barriers, including eligibility for services, transportation, school selection, and immunizations. Of these, transportation was by far the most commonly reported barrier, with 78% of all subgrant districts reporting this as a significant barrier" (NCFH, 2009, p. 44): "Over half of the districts nationwide report that transportation barriers still exist for homeless youth" (Tierney et al., 2008, p. 26). This is the case on one front because the fluid nature of homelessness makes locating homeless minors difficult. And, of course, unidentified students cannot be transported anywhere, to school of origin or elsewhere. Also, unlike with some of the other barriers, there are significant costs, both "financial and logistical" (Duffield & Lovell, 2008, p. 5), associated with attacking the transportation issue. As Medcalf (2008) confirms, "transportation is often one of the barriers that is most difficult to overcome because of the costs to school districts and cities" (p. 109).

Collectively, then, from a macroperspective, "three factors combine to make transportation such an intractable problem: transportation is primarily a local issue; provision of transportation for homeless children and youth often requires new resources; and the mobility of families experiencing homelessness makes the logistics of providing transportation difficult" (James & Lopez, 2003, p. 128).

Although the McKinney amendments require schools to provide transportation for homeless students, often children and youth staying in shelters not on regular school bus routes are unable to get to school unless the school district transportation system, shelter staff, or parents can arrange other forms of transportation. Most homeless families do not reside in shelters and, therefore, face even greater difficulties. They may be temporarily staying with relatives or friends or in campgrounds, motels, and other places not on existing bus routes. While the intent of the McKinney legislation is to allow children to stay enrolled in their school of origin, transportation to and from out-of-district temporary shelter and school sites is expensive and logistically difficult. Policies, if they exist at all, are often unclear about which district is responsible for providing transportation. (Ritter & Gottfried, 2002, p. 43)

On a less strategic, more concrete level, Medcalf (2008) reveals how transportation remains a problem for homeless children and youth:

The third barrier for homeless children is the simple matter of transportation for reaching school and maintaining regular attendance. . . . For students in shelters, or other non-traditional housing, traveling to and from school can pose a tremendous problem. Even if schools are within walking distance for older students, many of the neighborhoods where homeless people find shelter are not safe. Parents are usually reluctant to allow their children to walk to school. The requirements spelled out in the McKinney-Vento Act are that transportation must be requested by the parent or guardian and must be deemed "feasible" by the school district for the student to receive the services. Most homeless parents do not realize that they even have the right to request that their child be taken to another school. Therefore, most homeless children are not transported to the school they were attending before they became homeless. They attend the school that is most convenient to the shelter. Even with these requirements, most states have regulations that may prohibit buses from picking up students who live within a certain distance from the school they attend, often between one and two-and-a-half miles. (p. 26)

Solution Strategies

Without permanent housing, homeless children inevitably face significant educational problems. But until this underlying problem is addressed, [we] must work to eliminate barriers that now shut homeless children out of school. (National Law Center on Homelessness and Poverty, 1990, p. 30)

⌐◠◡◠⌐

School administrators have an important role to play in minimizing educational disruption when children become homeless, by ensuring they get timely and appropriate assistance to either continue attending their current school, or transfer into local appropriate classroom placements with minimum delay. (Rafferty, 1995, p. 125)

The goal with homeless students should be to remove as many barriers as possible to their learning. (Tower, 1992, p. 57)

In Chapter 4, we exposed the devastating impact that homelessness can have on children and adolescents. If there is any hope of mitigating these effects, we need, to begin with, to ensure that these students are enrolled in and attend school on a consistent basis. That is, students cannot benefit from school if they are not enrolled. And they do not benefit from enrollment if they fail to attend. Concomitantly, we know that when "school personnel work to keep children from homeless families in school the children . . . garner powerful rewards" (Williams, 2003, p. 35). Thus, the task at hand is to remove or at least mitigate impediments to enrollment and attendance (Swick, 2000; Ziesemer et al., 1994). Fortunately, the seeds of improvement are often to be found in the descriptions of the barriers themselves. Equally helpful, the law for addressing the education of homeless children and youth (the McKinney-Vento Act) provides a robust platform for action. The battle is no longer focused on creating new laws so much as it is implementing the mandates and the spirit of the McKinney Act effectively, to make the requirement of "address[ing] the consequences of involuntary and unpredictable residential mobility and provid[ing] continuity and stability through ensuring school stability" (James & Lopez, 2003, p. 131) a reality.

Support and Policies

The first cluster of moves here is to energize support and to craft appropriate district policies and procedures, to set the framework for success. On the initial part of this agenda, support, James and Lopez (2003) argue that the "uncompromising support of the district's top officials" (p. 137) is essential to win enrollment and attendance battles (Ely, 1987). Slack commitment is a recipe for failure. If homeless students are not a priority for the district's leaders, they are unlikely to be a priority for others (Berliner, 2002). Support means, according to homeless advocates, assuming a proactive stance in moving on the barrier problem (Herrington, Kidd-Herrington, & Kritsonis, 2006). It also means ensuring that plans to foster success are in place.

On the remaining dimension of the agenda, policies and procedures, it is imperative that the operating systems of the district be revised to shape and buttress efforts to guarantee the enrollment and attendance of homeless children and youth (Iowa Department of Education, 2004b): "Schools must make every effort to ensure that the children experiencing homelessness enjoy success in their schooling. To realize this success, educators must craft appropriate school district policies" (Williams, 2003, p. 3); that is, that "local policies that reinforce the McKinney-Vento legislation [be] established" (Bowman & Barksdale, 2004, p. v). In particular, districts "must review and revise policies, practices, and procedures to remove barriers to access . . . for homeless children and youths" (James & Lopez, 2003; Medcalf, 2008, p. 108; Tierney et al., 2008). New policies that ensure participation once students are enrolled will also be required (Bowman & Barksdale, 2004).

Homeless Liaisons

A second set of moves is needed to make certain that responsibility for the well-being of homeless children and adolescents is fixed in one place in the district, rather than being so diffused that no one is really account-able. The legal requirement is for each district to have "personnel who are directly responsible for homeless children in the district" (Medcalf, 2008, p. 25; Parrish, Graczewski, Stewart-Teitlebaum, Van Dyke, Bolus, & Delano, 2003), usually a homeless liaison or coordinator. The practical necessity is to put this person on point for creating and invigorating systems and procedures that serve homeless children and adolescents and their families.

Facing outward, this position "is vital to making those who are home-less comfortable and to providing for their specialized needs" (Medcalf, 2008, p. 109). Facing inward, the liaison is the critical lineament in the plan to help local school personnel engage a wide range of interventions to meet the needs of homeless minors (Duffield et al., 2007). Liaisons are also essential in getting the various academic departments (e.g., Title I, special education) and service units (e.g., transportation) to attend appropriately to the needs of homeless minors and to work collaboratively in the service of these students (Julianelle, 2007).

> Liaisons are LEA staff responsible for ensuring the identification, school enrollment, attendance, and opportunities for academic suc-cess of students in homeless situations. Some of these activities may be accomplished by the liaison himself or herself, while others are accomplished by coordinating the efforts of other staff and commu-nity partners. National evaluations indicate that liaisons are a neces-sary common denominator for successful district efforts to identify and support students experiencing homelessness. . . . The U.S. Department of Education's 2006 Report to Congress on the imple-mentation of the EHCY Program describes the demonstrated bene-fits of having a local liaison in every school district, including increased identification of homeless children and youth, increased

service provision, better coordination among school district programs, increased awareness of homeless children and youth among
school and school district staff, and increased awareness of issues
related to homeless education in the community. By linking students and their families to school and community services, liaisons
play a critical role in stabilizing students and promoting academic
achievement at the individual, school, and district level. (Duffield
et al., 2007, p. 13)

Specifically, on the issue in play here, matriculation, homeless liaisons are
responsible for ensuring that "homeless children and youths are identified
by school personnel and through coordination activities with other entities
and agencies [that] homeless children and youth enroll in schools of that
local educational agency" (Julianelle, 2007, p. 26).[4]

Identification Strategies

A third domain of action is comprised of efforts to create systems and
processes to locate and account for homeless children and youth (Bowen
et al., 1989; Iowa Department of Education, 2004b; Taylor & Brown, 1996),
to "improve the data collection, identification, and outreach efforts of local
education agencies" (Julianelle, 2007, p. 43), devoting special attention to
the hard-to-find homeless (by choice or residency patterns that make them
almost invisible; Myers & Popp, 2003; Tierney et al., 2008): "Identifying
homeless children and youth is a crucial step to ensure that these students
enroll in school and have the opportunity to reach high academic standards. Many districts are not aware that they have homeless students; nor
do they know which children to count as 'homeless'" (Funkhouser et al.,
2002, p. 9). Analysts maintain that training on data collection strategies can
be especially helpful in meeting the identification assignment (Iowa Department of Education, 2004b; Julianelle, 2007); so too, they maintain, can the
creation and use of a sophisticated database (Bowman & Barksdale, 2004;
Iowa Department of Education, 2004b).

Duffield and colleagues (2007) help us understand the following:

There are really two aspects to the obligation to "identify" homeless children and youth. One is simply to understand which students within the school may meet the definition of "homeless" so
that each of them may be afforded full access to services and so that
the school is able to obtain an accurate count of the number of
students experiencing homelessness. The other is to locate potential students not currently within the school system who are homeless and school-age, to ensure that they are enrolled or rejoined to
appropriate school programs. This second effort at identification is
often referred to as "outreach." (pp. 19–20)

On the first issue, school personnel need to be "sentinels" (Sullivan & Knutson, 2000, p. 1287) for homeless children and youth (Herrington et al., 2006; Myers & Popp, 2003; Swick & Bailey, 2004). They require training (1) to understand potential identifiers of homelessness and (2) to conduct informal interviews with children and parents.

On the second issue, outreach, "enrollment programs can take many forms" (Johnson, 1992, p. 164). The district can be proactive in disseminating information about school services at the places homeless children and their families and unaccompanied youth are likely to see it (Duffield et al., 2007). "Some schools simply provide shelters with all the necessary enrollment forms so that parents know that their children are welcome and expected. [In] other schools, the guidance counselor visits shelters for homeless persons on a daily basis to help ensure that homeless students are enrolled in school" (Johnson, 1992, p. 164). This is especially important "because many families experiencing homelessness do not know that their living situation qualifies their children for educational protections and services" (Duffield & Lovell, 2008, p. 12).

> Whether because of previous experiences, misinformation, or fear of the system, many homeless parents do not pursue the enrollment of their children in public school. Ultimately these parents assume that the school does not want their children. Through outreach enrollment programs, schools can send a different message to homeless parents and their children. (Johnson, 1992, p. 164)

Liaisons can also work closely with service providers such as "shelter directors to [in turn] work with parents to ensure that children attend school" (Rafferty, 1991, p. 130). They can join coalitions that provide services to homeless families and youth with an eye on promoting better identification and enrollment procedures (Bowman & Barksdale, 2004; Duffield et al., 2007) for homeless minors.[5] Finally, as we examine in considerable detail in the final chapter, by doing "outreach at youth shelters, drop-in centers, and street locations where homeless youth gather" (Duffield et al., 2007, p. 38), educators can enhance identification and enrollment efforts.

Barrier Removal

Finally, schools can directly attack the barriers described earlier that discourage enrollment and attendance (e.g., residency requirements). Resources in this area are on the websites of all the leading homeless agencies, such as the National Center for Homeless Education and the National Law Center on Homelessness and Poverty. In addition, Bowman and Barksdale (2004), Duffield and team (2007), Funkhouser and colleagues (2002), and the Iowa Department of Education (2004b), among others, provide explicit strategies to neutralize documentation and transportation obstacles to the matriculation and participation of homeless children and youth. For example, Funkhouser et al. (2002) offer the following recommendation in the area of documentation:

> To ensure that homeless children and youth can enroll in school immediately, districts can minimize enrollment barriers through policy. . . . They can use a systematic process for records transfer and assign a staff member the responsibility to oversee this process. Many have found that when a liaison or other specified contact person leads a homeless student through the enrollment process—going with the student from the shelter to the school and completing forms and requirements, such as a doctor's appointment if immunization records cannot be found—the length of time it takes to access a student's records decreases significantly. (p. 10)

And Bowman and Barksdale and Duffield and colleagues provide the following integrated attacks on the transportation barrier:

- ◆ Establish strong networks of community support.
- ◆ Develop a strong partnership between the homeless education program and the department of pupil transportation.
- ◆ Establish interdistrict collaboration.
- ◆ Establish formal procedures for equity, transparency, and consistency.
- ◆ Establish policies to support the federal legislation.
- ◆ Establish a database and system for data collection.
- ◆ Seek economical and creative solutions.
- ◆ Keep in mind the safety of the child.
- ◆ Inform policy-makers of the need for school stability for highly mobile children. (Bowman & Barksdale, 2004, pp. 14–18)
- ◆ Coordinate with local housing authorities and community-based organizations to house students near their schools of origin.
- ◆ Reroute school buses (including special education, magnet school, and other buses) and ensure that school buses travel to shelters, transitional living programs, and motels where student reside.
- ◆ Develop interdistrict transportation agreements to coordinate interdistrict transportation and avoid delays and disputes.
- ◆ Designate a district-level point of contact to arrange and coordinate transportation.
- ◆ Provide sensitivity training to bus drivers and arrange bus stops to keep students' living situations confidential.
- ◆ Provide passes for public transportation, including passes for caregivers when necessary.
- ◆ Collaborate with local public and nonprofit agencies and service providers to develop transportation plans or provide transportation.

◆ Take advantage of transportation systems used by public assistance agencies and coordinate with those agencies.
◆ Reimburse parents, guardians, or unaccompanied youth for gas if they are able to provide their own transportation.
◆ Obtain corporate or other sponsorship for transportation costs. (Duffield et al., 2007, p. 25)

❖ CONCLUSION

This chapter and the next highlight the place of the school in the algorithm to mitigate the effects of homelessness. The next chapter spotlights actions to ensure student success once homeless minors are enrolled in and regularly attending school. Here we underscored strategies to ensure matriculation and access. We reviewed the legal framework for educational activity and we examined ways that schools have contributed to enrollment problems as well as a platform of actions to help overcome barriers to access.

❖ NOTES

1. In-depth treatment of the legal dimension of educating homeless minors has been provided by an assortment of scholars. See especially the work of Duffield (2000), Duffield and team (2007), the National Law Center on Homelessness and Poverty (2004a), Ely (1987), First (1992), Helm (1992), and Jackson (2004).

2. Since the overall pot of funding is quite small and only a tiny percentage of school districts nationwide apply for these resources (Hightower et al., 1997; Wilder et al., 2003), it is obvious that it is the mandate, not the resources, that is at the center of opening educational opportunities for homeless children and youth.

3. While this idea is widely accepted (Pawlas, 1994; Tierney et al., 2008), it is not uncontested. A number of analysts hold that schools that attend specifically to the needs of homeless minors have a role to play in helping displaced young people be successful on the educational playing field (Hallett, 2007; Mawhinney-Rhoads & Stahler, 2006).

4. For a rich description of the responsibilities of these homeless liaisons, see Duffield and colleagues (2007).

5. It is important to point out, however, that linkages between schools and law enforcement agencies can actually create barriers to the identification of homeless youths if these youngsters sense that they will be forcibly returned to their homes (Julianelle, 2007).

7

Ensuring Success[1]

Without the active participation of teachers, administrators, parents, policy makers, and advocates, the rights conferred by the McKinney Act are merely theoretical. (Duffield, 2000, p. 204)

Children and youth need to learn to overcome the potentially cyclic and devastating effects of a homeless situation. An appropriate education is the most promising intervention available. (Heflin, 1991, p. 4)

It is important to remember that the school can be a vitally important part of the homeless child's life. School experiences can actually enable children to cope with their homelessness. (Tower & White, 1989, p. 32)

❖ INTRODUCTION

School should be an oasis for homeless children and youth—a stable place where they receive sustenance, guidance, and support in learning the skills they will need to escape poverty as adults. (Duffield, 2000, p. 204)

We can, at the very least, offer the uprooted child a welcome mat to the security of the classroom. (Gewirtzman & Fodor, 1987, p. 244)

At the outset of our journey into the role of education in the homeless narrative in Chapter 6 (the "access" story line), we presented some general insights about the role of schooling in helping homeless children and youth. We remind the reader that these points apply to our discussion of education "success" here in Chapter 7 as well. In addition, before we delve into the success story line, we present some further guiding observations.

School as a Source of Hope

While acknowledging that homelessness is a complex and layered phenomenon, there is a well-established claim in the literature that schools must be a hallmark element in any attack on the homeless problem. Josefowicz-Simbeni and Israel (2006) assert the following: "Ensuring that homeless children and youths receive an education on par with their peers is necessary in addressing the needs of homeless people in the United States" (p. 38). There is also a firm belief in the literature that schools can be effective in "mitigat[ing] the educational impacts of homelessness" (Duffield & Lovell, 2008, p. 9), that "public education can play a significant role in meeting needs of homeless children and adolescents" (Reganick, 1997, p. 134):

> Awareness of homeless children, making the initial identification, assessing the special needs of the homeless student, allowing flexibility both in time and program can make all the difference and ultimately save a child. (Gibbs, 2004, p. 28)

> Hope persists for homeless adolescents to have viable futures. That hope lies in education. (Powers & Jaklitsch, 1992, p. 130)

There is also empirical evidence to support these beliefs; that is, school staff can translate hope into tangible outcomes, and through the efforts of dedicated teachers and administrators, homeless children can reach ambitious learning targets (Landsman, 2006; Medcalf, 2008; Powers & Jaklitsch, 1992). In particular, "teachers—by virtue of their understanding of and close contact with students—are in an excellent position to make a significant difference in the lives of the homeless students in their classrooms" (Tower & White, 1989, p. 35).

A Recognition That Schools Need to Do More

As we noted in Chapter 6, it is consistently reported that schools need to do more to assist homeless children and youth, that current arrangements "must be changed and schools must take the lead in making the difference for these children" (Medcalf, 2008, p. 109). Explicit in this narrative is the proposition that schools are currently not doing enough, that "far more work is needed" (Funkhouser et al., 2002, p. 59). That is, "despite federal legislation ensuring educational opportunities, the educational needs of children who are homeless are frequently unfulfilled" (Gargiulo, 2006, p. 357). The claim by an assortment of analysts is that schools are "failing to serve a large percentage of homeless young people" (Julianelle, 2007, p. 26), "that in many schools [their] needs are largely ignored" (Wilder et al., 2003, p. 9), and that "far more initiatives are needed to enhance educational opportunity for homeless students" (Markward & Biros, 2001, p. 184).

Explanations for underservice ribbon the literature. The central line of analysis, however, traces the problem to the fact that the overwhelming bulk of energy in the first two decades since the passage of the McKinney-Vento Act has flowed to the issue we explored in Chapter 6, "access" to schooling (National Law Center on Homelessness and Poverty, 1990; Wood, Valdez, Hayashi, & Shen, 1990). While the topics of "success" and "access" are often cojoined, enrollment and attendance issues receive the lion's share of attention (Stronge, 1992b): "Most time and energy goes into identifying and enrolling homeless children and youth; the nature and quality of the service these students receive once they have arrived at school, if considered at all, may be viewed as a secondary issue" (Funkhouser et al., 2002, p. 55). This results, as Tierney and associates (2008) point out, in a significant gap in the battle plan being directed to the education of homeless children and youth.

> To be sure, enabling homeless youth to enroll in and receive transportation to school is important, but this only begins to address their educational needs. . . . While schools and districts have a better sense of the number of homeless youth and the schools where they attend—albeit sporadically—solutions on how to help these students have remained elusive. (p. 11)

Our position for this chapter, then, is as follows:

> The passage of the McKinney-Vento Act provided federal protection for homeless youth and families in terms of getting students enrolled, securing transportation to school, and acquiring necessary supplies. The next step is to consider the services that are needed for students as they arrive on the school campus. (Hallett, 2007, p. 3)

We need "to help ensure that homeless children not only have access to school but that they are able to obtain an adequate education while in school" (National Law Center on Homelessness and Poverty, 1990, p. 32).

Also of importance in explaining the limited attention to success factors is the absence of research on the effectiveness of proposed interventions and strategies (Mawhinney-Rhoads & Stahler, 2006). While researchers and advocates promulgate ideas, there is very limited research on the impact of these reforms in the context of the homeless problem.

Explanations for the limited attention to success factors are also linked to organizational roadblocks (Gibbs, 2004) and "institutional rigidities and other factors that influence the ability of schools to respond to the needs of homeless children" (Shane, 1996, p. 20). The logic here is animated by the fact that "the education of homeless [children and] adolescents pose numerous challenges to school personnel" (Lindsey & Williams, 2002, p. 2); "these youth present myriad problems that school systems are often ill-equipped to handle" (Ritter & Gottfried, 2002, p. 1), especially unaccompanied youth (Funkhouser et al., 2002; Julianelle, 2007). There is an absence of congruence between how schools work and what homeless children and youth need, a mismatch that too often is resolved in the favor of the organization, not the homeless students (Herrington et al., 2006; Tierney et al., 2008; Williams, 2003). Thus, "educators attempting to meet the educational needs of homeless children must face the reality that, in general, the public school system is not designed to meet these needs" (Medcalf, 2008, p. 23).

The final point in our preface to action is that schools must improve: "The public school system must figure out how to address the needs of this vulnerable student population" (Hallett, 2007, p. 3)—"educational services that promote academic success must be implemented" (Rafferty, 1991, p. 125). If schools fail to do so, "then education will become irrelevant and the avenues out of [homelessness] and poverty will be foreclosed" (Tierney et al., 2008, p. 23):

> If school systems do not provide special educational interventions to address the particular educational barriers that these children face, then it is likely that these children will stay marginalized in the lowest economic rung of society. (Mawhinney-Rhoads & Stahler, 2006, p. 289)

> Providing educational services to homeless students may not eradicate homelessness, but refusing to provide educational services for homeless students will most certainly perpetuate it. (Wilder et al., 2003, p. 14)

In the balance of the chapter, we discuss what schools can do to ensure the success of homeless children and youth. Colleagues who have labored on this issue have provided insights about how to organize the material. For example, Stronge (2000), arguably the best-known scholar in the area, discusses "building awareness, securing parental involvement and support, providing early childhood education opportunities, addressing special needs of special populations, and coordinating and collaborating in-service delivery" (p. 6). Wilder and team (2003) list the following service categories: "tutoring or academic support programs, mentoring, prosocial skills training, educational supplies, access to technology and research facilities after school hours, help with homework, and vocational and life skills training" (p. 10). In his framework, Williams (2003) explores family involvement. Our analysis produces the following categories of action: (1) developing awareness about homelessness and homeless children and youth, (2) attending to basic needs, (3) creating an effective instructional program, (4) developing a stable and supportive environment, (5) providing additional supports, (6) collaborating with other agencies and organizations, and (7) promoting parent involvement.

Before we begin, however, we provide one last note. Our success factors are, by necessity, pulled apart for analysis. However, we want to be clear that it is the ability to weave these elements into a coherent design package that is critical (Iowa Department of Education, 2004a), the capability and commitment to "mount an organizational response rooted in a systematic approach" (Williams, 2003, p. 14). Or, as Funkhouser and colleagues (2002) corral the issue,

> Homeless students will be best served when promising practices are implemented as part of a comprehensive and coordinated homeless education program. Promising practices that are implemented in isolation are likely to result in some homeless students falling between the cracks. (p. 66)

A "holistic plan" (Hallett, 2007, p. 6) includes "the development and implementation of a broad range of interventions" (Josefowicz-Simbeni & Israel, 2006, p. 43) and a "continuum of services" (Ziesemer et al., 1994, p. 666). It underscores the use of "additional support" (Wood et al., 1990, p. 865) and services. It incorporates interventions that "address the complexity and diversity of homeless students' needs—educational, emotional, behavioral, and physical" (Williams & Korinek, 2000, p. 184). It privileges collaboration inside the school (e.g., coordination between Title I services and McKinney-Vento services) and between the school and other parties working to promote the academic and social–emotional well-being of homeless children and youth (Lumsden & Coffey, 2001; Swick, 1997, 2005). A comprehensive platform of action is scaffolded on a multilevel design (Schmitz, Wagner, & Menke, 2001). It is more than an assemblage of ideas and strategies; it is an aligned and coordinated plan (Williams, 2003). It includes both short- and long-term elements (Williams, 2003) to address the needs of youngsters from preschool through linkages to higher education (Stronge & Hudson, 1999; Tierney et al., 2008). It highlights ongoing monitoring and assessment (Ziesemer et al., 1994) and features accountability procedures to ensure that educators are "measured by whether homeless students are educated appropriately" (Funkhouser et al., 2002, p. 11).

❖ DEVELOPING AWARENESS ABOUT HOMELESSNESS AND HOMELESS CHILDREN AND YOUTH

It is important for teachers to be aware of and to understand the problems faced by homeless adolescents. (Powers & Jaklitsch, 1992, p. 126)

Raising the awareness of teachers, administrators, and others, and equipping them with an understanding of homelessness and its effects on the personal and instructional needs of homeless students is an important first step in planning and providing effective educational services.
(Stronge & Hudson, 1999, p. 10)

A well-developed, ongoing, multidimensional program of staff development experiences to facilitate within-school and within-district awareness, understanding, and capability to respond to identified needs of homeless students characterizes effective school programs serving these students.
(Williams & Korinek, 2000, p. 188)

Logic Model

Teachers must be armed with knowledge about the homeless to meet the needs of increasing numbers of homeless students. (Tower & White, 1989, p. 6)

For educators, significant knowledge of the typical needs of homeless children and practices that address these needs is essential for effectively assisting these children and students. (Eddowes & Butcher, 2000, p. 31)

Post-"access" assistance for homeless children and youth must begin with the education of professional staff (Julianelle, 2007): "Though the goal is to educate, the process must first focus on educating the educators" (Nunez & Collignon, 1997, p. 60). This education should include both awareness training and professional development for how to work effectively with these students who are at risk: "Carefully planned staff development programs are necessary to sensitize school personnel to the effects of homelessness and to enhance their ability to educate homeless children and youth" (Korinek et al., 1992, p. 145). The logic chain here runs as follows: First, it is difficult to assist these young persons when one is unaware of the existence of homeless children or of the special problems and needs of these children and adolescents. That is, "school personnel who are not aware of the specific needs of homeless youth will be less equipped to serve them appropriately" (Julianelle, 2007, p. 25). The provision of help is equally problematic when educators are not familiar with the services they are required to make available to displaced students. In a similar way, quality assistance is difficult to render when teachers and leaders lack knowledge of the resources that can and should be marshaled to benefit homeless students—and their families as appropriate. "Without proper training staff may not recognize or relate to homelessness" (Iowa Department of Education, 2004b, p. 4): "Without training, staff will be wearing blinders" (Gonzalez, 1992, p. 199).

Second, currently most educators do not have a good understanding of homelessness in general or of the needs of homeless children and youth in particular (Eddowes, 1992; Herrington et al., 2006; Stronge & Hudson, 1999). They lack "awareness of the severity of the problems of homeless youth" (Cunningham, 2003, p. 7) and "remain unaware of the serious consequences of homelessness for school-age children and youth" (Funkhouser et al., 2002, p. 8): "Teachers often know little if anything about homeless students' circumstances or how homelessness affects children's education" (Nunez, 1994b, p. 66). Neither are they well trained on the most effective strategies to help these students (Shane, 1996; Yon, 1995).

Third, "lack of awareness of the problems posed by homelessness" (Stronge & Hudson, 1999, p. 9) and lack of understanding of how to help homeless young people have important consequences (Crowley, 2003; Funkhouser et al., 2002). For example, Whitman and colleagues (1990) found that "this lack of awareness often leads to inadvertent insensitivities" (p. 518) on the part of professional staff (Rafferty, 1995). This has been linked to "alienation of homeless families" (p. 519) from the education process. Stronge (2000) documents that "studies have consistently recorded a persistent pattern of insensitivity toward homeless students" (p. 7), a condition, he argues, "that stems from lack of awareness" (p. 7). Shane (1996), in turn, reports that "professional ignorance about the needs of individual [homeless] children and the extent of the problem within a school or school system [have been] found to be impediment[s] to the provision of appropriate educational services" (p. 34). Where lack of awareness is common, teachers often "make school a less inviting place for homeless children" (Johnson, 1992, p. 169) and "fail to reach homeless children" (Nunez, 1994b, p. 169). Students, in turn, may experience rejection (Anooshian, 2000; Swick, 2000).

Finally, knowledge of the condition of homelessness and understanding about how to help homeless students be successful in school can pay significant dividends: "Educators can positively affect the lives of homeless children and their families" (Swick, 2004, p. 120). Knowledge allows educators to be more (1) adept at identifying homeless youngsters, (2) "responsive to the challenges impeding their functioning" (Swick, 2004, p. 120), and (3) skillful in planning and delivering targeted educational interventions. On this last point, Powers and Jaklitsch (1992) maintain that "an understanding of the problems faced by homeless adolescents and recognition of the difficulties in working with them may shed light on how to plan for and more effectively meet their educational needs" (p. 119).

Awareness of Conditions and Laws

Before improved educational opportunities can become a reality, the lack of awareness and its related problems need to be addressed. (Stronge, 2000, p. 7)

Effective compliance with McKinney-Vento by school districts depends on school personnel's knowledge, awareness, and understanding of the social, emotional, financial, and educational consequences encountered by students and families who experience homelessness. (Iowa Department of Education, 2004b, p. 17)

By providing opportunities for school personnel to better understand the needs of homeless children, schools can promote an environment in which homeless students feel accepted. (Johnson, 1992, p. 170)

Scholars in this arena maintain that the first educational move for adults is enhanced awareness of the condition of homelessness and of the problems displacement causes for families and young persons (Julianelle, 2007; Rafferty, 1997; Rotheram-Borus, 1991): This "is the beginning of the teacher's response to the problem" (Tower & White, 1989, p. 8). Tower and White (1989) capture this eloquently when they assert that "the most important thing teachers can do for their homeless students is to become educated on the subject of homelessness" (p. 34): "The more prepared the teacher is, the more comfortable he or she will be in dealing with homeless children and their families" (p. 57). Noted scholar and advocate for homeless students James Stronge makes a similar point when he posits that "awareness-raising activities that target school personnel are essential to avoid further isolation of homeless students and to promote specific strategies to meet their needs" (Stronge & Hudson, 1999, p. 10).

Awareness training needs to center on the material presented in Chapters 1 through 4: "basic knowledge about homeless students and their families, what they experience, and why they find themselves in this situation" (Tower & White, 1989, p. 7), what Finley (2003) refers to as "empathetic understanding of the lives of unhoused people" (p. 522). The focus is on sensitizing educators to the needs of homeless families and young persons (Baron, 2003; Quint, 1994; Reganick, 1997)—"knowledge of the issues in being homeless [and] sensitivity to the realities parents and children face" (Swick, 1997, p. 30).

One important dimension of awareness is learning the "subtle clues that suggest that a student or parent may be experiencing homelessness" (Duffield et al., 2007, p. 220). On this score, Gargiulo (2006) provides the following "indicators of possible homelessness in children" (p. 358):

- ◆ Chronic absenteeism/frequent tardiness
- ◆ Inconsistent personal hygiene
- ◆ Habitual tiredness in school
- ◆ Complaints of hunger—evidence of hoarding food
- ◆ Lack of school supplies
- ◆ Inadequate/inappropriate school apparel
- ◆ Incomplete homework assignments
- ◆ Reluctance or inability to provide address or telephone number
- ◆ Unresponsive parent/guardian—notes from school go unsigned
- ◆ Unwillingness to go home after school (p. 358)

A second dimension of awareness is information about the needs of homeless children and their families and unaccompanied youth (Bowen et al., 1989; Stronge, 2000; Swick, 2005). As Masten and associates (1997) inform us, "teachers need to be prepared for the multifaceted needs of these children" (p. 43), and this preparation begins with awareness. Here, Stronge (2000) maintains that enhanced teacher "awareness of the need for emotional . . . support for students" (p. 18) is critical.

It is also important that educators become informed about the legal protections provided to children under the McKinney-Vento Act, knowledge that is not widespread in education today (Duffield & Lovell, 2008). As we reported earlier, "teachers need to know what the law requires of them" (Wilder et al., 2003, p. 11). Awareness of these requirements is a first step in ensuring that they are met (Funkhouser et al., 2002; Herrington et al., 2006; Myers & Popp, 2003).

The other major dimension of the awareness puzzle is knowledge of "the types of things teachers and school administrators might do to help [homeless] youngsters' development" (Daniels, 1995, p. 351). We turn to this topic immediately here.

Awareness of Appropriate Educational Responses

Raising the consciousness of members of the school staff is not enough. Community members also must be educated to increase the capacity of the system to respond to the needs of homeless students.
(Stronge & Hudson, 1999, p. 10)

*The sheer numbers of homeless students make it mandatory that teachers
prepare to teach them. (Tower & White, 1989, p. 6)*

While it is important that educators develop an awareness of the context of homelessness and the educational requirements to serve displaced children and youth, this knowledge is insufficient. Teachers must also develop an understanding of "homelessness and its impact on the learning process" (Duffield et al., 2007, p. 31). Teachers and school leaders need to forge "the capacity to respond to problems in the education of homeless children" (Rafferty, 1995, p. 41). They must know what to do to ensure that these students are successful; they need concrete "strategies for working with students who are homeless" (Hightower et al., 1997, p. 32). In particular, they must learn "to deal with the issues of educational disadvantage that accompany this population" (James, 2005, p. 201). While we discuss some of these strategies here, the central message is that the platform for action is comprised of the ideas we discuss in the balance of the chapter (e.g., developing a stable and supportive environment, promoting parent involvement). The general theme has been laid out by Masten and colleagues and by Bowman and Barksdale:

> If schools are expected to provide an "appropriate" education, teachers will need to know a great deal more about the nature of the academic problems these children may have and the most promising means of addressing them. (Masten et al., 1997, p. 28)

> Individuals involved in the education of homeless children and youth need greater awareness of the strategies that foster educational achievement and wellbeing of homeless children and youth. (Bowman & Barksdale, 2004, p. 18)

More specifically, analysts maintain that educators must become informed about and develop "a keen knowledge of" (Vissing, 2000, p. 58) the resources and services that can advantage homeless children and youth (Anooshian, 2000; Duffield et al., 2007): "School personnel serving these students must know school and community resources that are available to support their work" (Myers & Popp, 2003, p. 2). Or, as Vissing (2000) tells us, they "need to become ferrets of community intervention information" (p. 49). Relatedly, principals and teachers need to become knowledgeable about ways in which they can advocate for their homeless student population in the larger community (Crowley, 2003).

Also in the arena of awareness, teachers have an obligation to help their housed students understand homelessness and what it means for their displaced peers (Daniels, 1995; Rafferty, 1995; Solarz, 1992). This is necessary, Swick (2000) asserts, because "the empowerment of students in understanding homeless students and specifically the situation(s) of their homeless peers is critical to developing an effective school and community environment" (p. 171).

❖ ATTENDING TO BASIC NEEDS

Many homeless children, however, have difficulty concentrating, attending regularly, or feeling motivated to participate in school activities because basic needs have not been adequately addressed. (Korinek et al., 1992, p. 153)

Many homeless youths have difficulty meeting basic needs. (Ringwalt, Greene, Robertson, & McPheeters, 1998, p. 1325)

The lack of such resources [school clothes and supplies] has been identified as an ongoing and major barrier to school attendance for homeless students nationwide. (Rafferty, 1995, p. 51)

To make homeless children and youth's school experiences more positive and productive, school personnel should take action to meet the basic and personal needs of their homeless student population. Meeting these needs is often a prerequisite for normal development and success in school. (Hightower et al., 1997, p. 18)

The Core Narrative

In a later section, we discuss the importance of providing supplemental services to help homeless children and youth succeed in school. We examine the topic of basic need services here, however, because in many ways, ensuring that these services are available sets the stage for the effectiveness of the other "success" interventions we detail in later sections.

The sections of the narrative fall out as follows. First, research informs us that "the nature of homelessness deprives many children of basic physiological necessities" (Johnson, 1992, p. 153). That is, "homeless children attending school do not have their basic needs met" (Biggar, 2001, p. 949). More specifically, "most homeless children do not have access to or a means for acquiring clean clothes, items for personal hygiene, or basic school supplies" (Medcalf, 2008, p. 27; Reeg et al., 2002; Swick, 2009). Second, this reality impacts students' motivation negatively. That is, "many homeless children refuse to go to school because they are embarrassed about their lack of adequate clothing and school supplies, and their poor hygiene" (Yon, Mickelson, & Carlton-LaNey, 1993, p. 411). Third, even when they attend school, the lack of basic goods can undermine effort and achievement. Because "a child is not ready to learn without these basics" (Gonzalez, 1992, p. 197), her "ability to perform well in school is severely limited" (Medcalf, 2008, p. 27).

> The lack of clean, presentable clothing and adequate school supplies also affects homeless students' school experiences. Without these commonplace resources, a homeless child or youth feels conspicuously different and vulnerable and often experiences the ridicule or rejection of classmates. Furthermore, a child's work suffers when he or she does not have the appropriate supplies to complete homework assignments or participate in classroom activities. (Hightower et al., 1997, p. 19)

> Homeless children, however, have difficulty concentrating, attending regularly, or feeling motivated to participate in school activities because basic needs have not been adequately addressed. (Johnson, 1992, p. 153)

Fourth, before "school personnel can even begin to help these children start the learning process, they must help them meet the basic necessities for survival and well being" (Medcalf, 2008, p. 27): "The satisfaction of basic needs is essential in freeing the child to pursue social and academic interests" (Eddowes & Butcher, 2000, p. 33; see also James et al., 1991; Reed-Victor, 2000; Reed-Victor et al., 2003). Fifth, schools can create a platform for success by working proactively to address "basic needs (clothing, supplies, health)" (Daniels, 1992, 1995; Iowa Department of Education, 2004b, p. 43). This, of course, demands that they "become aware of such basic services as food, health, and clothing needs" (Gonzalez, 1992, p. 197). Sixth, "many schools have adopted policies and practices to provide homeless young people with access to [basic needs] resources" (Julianelle, 2007, p. 3), supports that one "usually assumes children receive at home" (Nunez & Collignon, 1997, p. 57). Others need to follow their lead.

> Many school systems help homeless children obtain the basic clothing, food, shelter, medical care, and school supplies they need to attend and succeed in school. Innovative programs alleviate the difficult circumstance homeless children frequently confront. (Hightower et al., 1997, p. 19)

A Taxonomy of Needed Basic Services

The public school system can offer a wealth of resources that can assist homeless youth in meeting their needs, including: school meals; laundry and cooking facilities; showers and personal hygiene supplies; lockers; [and] clothing banks. (Julianelle, 2007, p. 3)

School Supplies

In order to engage productively in school, oftentimes students require school supplies that the homeless child or youngster "may not have access to as a result of residential instability" (Tierney et al., 2008, p. 10) or that "may be inaccessible for financial reasons" (Shane, 1996, p. 36). The simple truth, then, is that "many [homeless students] lack basic school supplies" (National Center for Homeless Education, 2006a, p. 1). Schools that are proactive in helping their homeless students will generally make these supplies and related study materials available (Daniels, 1992; Eddowes, 1992; Polakow, 2003; Vissing, 2004).

Clothes

In a similar vein, many homeless children and youth lack adequate, clean, and appropriate clothing (Johnson, 1992; Reganick, 1997; Tower, 1992; Wilder et al., 2003).

Inadequate apparel is a further problem . . . homeless children often are unable to get new clothing. In many social and educational settings, clothing styles become important peer-valuation indicators. Without peer-acceptable clothing, the social environment in a school may be untenable, especially for insecure and already frightened children. (Shane, 1996, p. 36)

And as we reported earlier, from a "child's viewpoint not having appropriate clothing [is] a perceived barrier to school attendance" (Newman & Beck, 1996; Penuel & Davey, 1998, p. 9). Schools that are prepared in addressing the homeless problem attend to this second basic need (Duffield et al., 2007; Vissing, 2004). Through various collection procedures, generally in partnership with other social agencies (Daniels, 1992; Hightower et al., 1997), they amass "clothing banks" (Julianelle, 2007, p. 18) for homeless students (James et al., 1991; Reed-Victor et al., 2003; Swick, 1997). In these schools, "clothing can become a regular part of day-to-day activities" (Nunez & Collignon, 2000, p. 120).

Food

Analysts help us see that hunger is an especially virulent condition of homelessness (Hyde, 2005; Quint, 1994; Ritter & Gottfried, 2002). They document that many homeless children and youth do not receive enough to eat (see Chapter 4). They are often hungry at school (Anooshian, 2000; Shane, 1996). These same analysts also note that "without adequate food homeless children face even greater difficulty in school" (National Law Center on Homelessness and Poverty, 1990, p. 32). They are often inattentive: "Many homeless children come to school without breakfast and possibly no snack or lunch. These further interfere with school-related activities, concentration, ability to learn, and tolerance levels" (Shane, 1996, p. 36).

Schools can make a significant dent in this problem, once it is recognized and once commitment is secured. Case studies reveal that educators have three avenues to pursue in this area, all revolving around the core idea of making food a routine part of the school culture (Masten, 1992; Rew, 1996). First, they can be diligent in ensuring that all homeless minors are receiving "school meals" (Julianelle, 2007, p. 18), that is, breakfast and lunch from the free and reduced meal program (Eddowes, 1992; Swick, 1997). As Duffield and team (2007) remind us, "under the Child Nutrition and WIC Act of 2004, homeless students are automatically eligible for free meals and do not have to submit an application" (p. 15). School personnel need to be aggressive in moving homeless minors to take advantage of this entitlement, especially adolescents.

Second, school staff can make sure that nutritious snacks are readily available to homeless students (Reed-Victor et al., 2003). On this front, Duffield and Lovell (2008) report that "many schools have established food closets to meet the needs of homeless children" (p. 14). Others have instituted "snacks" as a part of school and afterschool activities (Daniels, 1992; James et al., 1991).

Third, educators can be sure to send homeless students home with food for their families (Polakow, 2003; Tierney et al., 2008).

Hygiene Items

In addition to school supplies, clothing, and food, advocates suggest that schools create a "welcoming and supportive environment for homeless youth in which the immediate need for hygiene can be met" (Duffield et al., 2007, p. 38). Two domains are highlighted in this area: the provision of "facilities for personal hygiene" (Eddowes, 1992, p. 112), such as showers and laundry facilities (Julianelle, 2007; Williams, 2003), and the distribution of "personal hygiene supplies" (Julianelle, 2007, p. 18), such as first-aid materials and toiletries like deodorant, toothpaste, shampoo, and so forth (Nunez & Collignon, 1997; Woods, 1997; Woods & Harrison, 1994).

Health Services

We reported in Chapter 4 that the impact of homelessness on children's health is consistently negative, often devastatingly so. As we noted there, these students lack many of the medical services that housed minors often take for granted. Or, as Hicks-Coolick and colleagues (2003) tell the story, "health care for homeless children is not available on a regular basis, and when available is not in a child-friendly environment" (p. 202). Thus, homeless children "may come to school in need of medical attention" (Reed-Victor et al., 2003, p. 6) and unable "to listen, concentrate, or fully participate in learning activities" (Johnson, 1992, p. 156). Schools, then, "can increase the likelihood of school success for homeless students by providing comprehensive school health services" (Johnson, 1992, p. 156), including vision, hearing, medical, dental, and psychological counseling (Swick, 1997; Yon et al., 1993).

❖ CREATING AN EFFECTIVE INSTRUCTIONAL PROGRAM

Less has been written about specific instructional practices. (Popp, 2004, p. 18)

Programs for homeless students may also require many of the varied strategies used for effective instruction, practice, and evaluation of at-risk learners. (Korinek et al., 1992, p. 147)

In this section, we turn the spotlight on the instructional program (teaching and curriculum), exploring how teacher actions can help ensure the academic success of homeless children and youth. We begin with five important notes. First, very little has been written about the types of instructional strategies that work best for these young people. Almost all the work on the success part of the access and success narrative addresses the larger context in which classroom actions are nested, that is, the other factors we investigate in this chapter.

Second, because of this, it is necessary to some extent to develop answers to the effective instructional program question from the research on what works for other groups of students at high risk of school failure (e.g., housed but highly mobile students, youngsters on the wrong side of the achievement gap; Korinek et al., 1992).

Third, insights about effective teaching strategies for academic success also dot other sections of this chapter. For example, we have already discussed the importance of teacher professional development. Later, we examine the provision of additional instructional time and working with parents and the larger community to enhance academic success.

Fourth, the answers vary depending on the way schools cluster homeless children for learning. If young persons are integrated into the regular classroom, for example, a focus on mixing students for work by SES is a useful strategy. If, on the other hand, districts rely on special classrooms or schools for the homeless, then the use of "diagnostic and prescriptive teaching methods that enable teachers to design an individualized lesson plan for each student" (Pires & Silber, 1991, p. 133) makes more sense.

Fifth, with some adjustments, it appears that what homeless children and adolescents need is not some unique set of interventions, that is, something different than best practice for youngsters in general and students who are at risk in particular. What is needed is more of the best. Accommodation moves that are required will tend more to structural arrangements than instructional practices. For example, in the area of accommodation, it is recommended that assessment systems for incoming homeless youngsters be modified to ensure expedited review and placements in various programs (e.g., special education; National Center for Homeless Education, 2006b):

> Expedited evaluation services can help ensure that homeless students promptly receive needed services. Evaluation may determine the need for such special programs as bilingual education, special education, or programs for gifted/talented students. Evaluation may also determine the appropriate focus of regular classroom placement. For instance, evaluation may help a teacher immediately determine the appropriate reading program for a child or identify the skills that should be the focus of math instruction for the child. (Johnson, 1992, p. 172)

Instructional Strategies

There is a growing research literature showing that student performance is determined as much by the characteristics of students' peers as the characteristics and performance of their teachers and administrators.
(Harris & Herrington, 2006, p. 222)

Research suggests that homeless children and youth may be advantaged by two instructional approaches. First, individualized instructional programs appear to be helpful for highly mobile students (Eddowes & Butcher, 2000; Eddowes & Hranitz, 1989; Ziesemer & Marcoux, 1992). Second, cooperative learning platforms allow homeless students to master important academic content (Gonzalez, 1992; Ritter & Gottfried, 2002) while developing much-needed social–relational skills as they interact with peers from a range of economic and social backgrounds. That is, "appropriate use of cooperative learning . . . may facilitate social integration" (Korinek et al., 1992, p. 145). And, as Johnson (1992) reminds us, "by integrating homeless students with nonhomeless peers, the potential is less for stigmatizing and isolating homeless students" (p. 162). Finally, cooperative learning strategies feature the type of active participation from which many homeless students can benefit (Eddowes & Butcher, 2000; Hightower et al., 1997). Collectively, then, researchers conclude that "activities promoting cooperative learning would be helpful. Cooperative learning groups can include children with different backgrounds and talents. These groups positively affect intergroup relations and the ability to relate with others. They can be a valuable asset in assisting homeless children to develop friendships in school" (Eddowes, 1992, p. 103).

There is also evidence that breaking assignments for homeless children and youth into discrete pieces of work is a good instructional strategy (Gewirtzman & Fodor, 1987; Tower & White, 1989; Woods & Harrison, 1994). Such an approach recognizes the likely transience of homeless youngsters and helps "ensure completion before departure" (Ziesemer et al., 1994, p. 667).

> Because homeless students' class attendance is often intermittent or brief, teachers should present lessons in short units that allow students to complete and master material. Likewise, weekly or even daily report-cards-in-progress acknowledge spotty attendance patterns in recording students' social and academic performance. They also provide students with a record they can take to a new school if they must transfer abruptly. (Berliner, 2002, p. 2)

Scholars suggest that lessons "open and close on the same day" (Woods & Harrison, 1994, p. 124) and that individualized contracts be established for short durations and be renewed frequently (Nunez, 1994b; Nunez & Collignon, 1997). Researchers and advocates alike routinely argue for a "strength-based approach" (Lindsey et al., 2000, p. 137) to instructional planning, as opposed to an overreliance on a problem-oriented perspective (Barry et al., 2002; Hyde, 2005; Wilder et al., 2003).

Almost all analysts in the domain of homeless education conclude that "homeless adolescents are in need of practical 'life skills' in the areas of employment, money management, housing, household management, health, and community resources" (Aviles & Helfrich, 1991; Powers & Jaklitsch, 1992, p. 127). Also included in the broad category of "life skills" (Pawlas, 1994, p. 81) are the following: "listening, following instructions, social skills" (p. 81; Nabors, Proescher, & DeSilva, 2001; Rew, 1996), intrapersonal skills (Lindsey et al., 2000), and interpersonal skills (Raleigh-DuRoff, 2004), or what Lindsey and associates (2000) refer to as "skills for interacting with other people in more constructive ways" (p. 137). Coping skills and problem-solving skills, it is argued, often require explicit attention in instructional programs for homeless children and youth (Wilder et al., 2003).

Finally, because students placed at risk in general and homeless students specifically are much more school dependent than their peers, it is imperative that these youngsters be assigned to the most effective teachers in the school.

Curriculum Frameworks

In essence, locally based models that are tailored to the unique local context, not one-size-fits-all or national reforms, are what will ensure homeless student success. (Mawhinney-Rhoads & Stahler, 2006, p. 302)

∽◯╬◯∼

Credit recovery programs can greatly accelerate students' graduation. Particularly for older homeless youth, this flexibility can be the key to their success. (Julianelle, 2007, p. 30)

∽◯╬◯∼

Providing flexibility in school policies and procedures such as course offerings can be paramount to getting adolescents in school and keeping them there. (Stronge, 2000, p. 12)

∽◯╬◯∼

We begin here by returning to our introductory notes. Specifically, we conclude that, by and large, homeless youngsters do not need a different or separate curriculum. What they need is access to the same high-quality curriculum available to their peers. At the same time, because "homeless students are almost certain to be at a disadvantage in doing required schoolwork" (Vissing, 2004, p. 35), what does seem to help is a willingness of schools to "restructure their schedules, social organization, and functions in order to best meet the needs of children who have no idea of place" (Quint, 1994, p. 15). One important action is to accelerate students along with their peers while concomitantly addressing remedial needs. That is, homeless students should not be put into closed remediation loops in which they never catch up with peers. Schools that work well for homeless children and youth need to accelerate and address deficiencies at the same time.

A second helpful guideline is for "districts to develop shared frameworks [across schools] for learning" (Penuel & Davey, 2000, p. 74). If they do so, then students who change schools often and are confronted with varied curriculums "are given [a] fairer chance of doing well in school" (Penuel & Davey, 2000, p. 74).

Homeless students, it is held, will also benefit from more flexible ways to traverse through the curriculum (Julianelle, 2007; Vissing, 2000). Because "high school students are often not able to keep up with classes and lose credits because of missing school [thus] making it impossible for them to graduate in a regular program" (Van Ry, 1992, p. 75), Duffield and team

(2007) propose that schools "develop course credit and schedule flexibility so that school time can be recovered promptly" (p. 38). Partial credit programs and credit recovery programs seem to be especially helpful (Parrish et al., 2003; Ziesemer & Marcoux, 1992). Credit recovery allows homeless students to fill in gaps in coursework. Partial credit programs allow them to gain credit for part of a course. In a related way, "flexible assessment schedules [allow schools] to accommodate children and youth who enter schools at times outside the regular assessment cycle" (Hightower et al., 1997, p. 25). So too do policies that provide flexibility for homeless youngsters to complete schoolwork and school projects at school (Gargiulo, 2006; Myers & Popp, 2003). "Flexible graduation criteria" (Vissing, 2000, p. 56) are also helpful for ensuring the academic success of homeless adolescents.

Finally, reformers advocate for curriculum designs that provide homeless students with alternative pathways to success and/or recover from leaving school prematurely. One set of designs is referred to as "alternative programs" and a second is known as "dropout recovery." Julianelle (2007) amplifies on the importance of alternative programs:

> Most homeless youth have many more responsibilities than their housed peers, as they struggle to meet basic needs and make decisions without parental guidance. In some cases, these responsibilities may make attending a traditional high school difficult. Particularly those young people who are working full-time, are pregnant or parenting, or are older than typical high school students may prefer alternative educational programs. For them to meet their educational goals, they must have access to alternative programs that meet their needs. (p. 31)

Because many homeless youngsters have already left school, strategies to reengage them are also essential (LaVesser et al., 1997; Nunez, 1994b; Rafferty, 1991).

❖ DEVELOPING A STABLE AND SUPPORTIVE ENVIRONMENT

Perhaps the best way to give homeless children an opportunity to feel good about themselves is to provide in the school setting the safety and stability not available to them outside of the classroom. (Tower & White, 1989, p. 31)

Until they believe that an educational setting is a secure, positive, and predictable place, they may not have the confidence necessary to be successful students. (Eddowes & Butcher, 2000, p. 28)

Students who are homeless like most pupils need a warm and nurturing
learning environment, a place which offers structure, stability, and security.
(Gargiulo, 2006, p. 360)

The challenge of educating homeless children and youth invokes concerns for
the socioemotional well-being of the students, as well as for the more
traditional emphasis on academic progress. (Stronge, 1992a, p. 21)

The Goal

One of the clearest social policy implications of this research is of a pressing
need for children who are homeless to be enrolled in a stable and supportive
school program. (Rescorla et al., 1991, p. 219)

Schools can successfully address the needs of homeless students if they
develop an environment that will provide the homeless children with the
support they need. (Gonzalez, 1992, p. 197)

Ensuring "success" for homeless children and youth will necessitate
the creation of a robust instructional program. But as is the case for other
groups of students at risk (Murphy, 2010), "dealing with homeless students is not just an academic issue" (Tower & White, 1989, p. 26). Success
will also be dependent upon the ability of school staff to create a caring
and stable culture, both in classrooms and the school as a whole.

> A thoughtfully planned classroom environment can foster a home-
> less child's ability to deal with the adverse circumstances that exist
> in his/her life. (Eddowes & Butcher, 2000, p. 37)

> In a world of disequilibrium, the school takes on the character of a
> safe haven; it may be the only place a [homeless] child can feel safe.
> (Eddowes, 1992, p. 102)

What makes climate so important, as we documented in Chapter 4, is
that many homeless children bring a portfolio of troubles and worries that
hinder sustained engagement in the school's academic program. Because
of this, many of these minors have learned to be distrustful of others
(Herrington et al., 2006; Tower & White, 1989). They are likely to "suffer
from low self-esteem and isolation" (Vissing, 2000, p. 54) and have little
self-confidence (Eddowes, 1992), feelings often exacerbated rather than

abated at school (Mihaly, 1991; Tower & White, 1989). They often "have no sense of belonging and no sense of hope. Most of them are frightened and feel very much alone" (Quint, 1994, p. 78). They often "perceive themselves as less capable than peers with homes" (Eddowes, 1992, p. 102). They may also be marked by "a profound sense of shame and fear" (Polakow, 2003, p. 102) and anger (Anooshian, 2000).

The antidote, researchers assert, is to make the school an "oasis" (Ziesemer & Marcoux, 1992, p. 79) of stability and caring in what can oftentimes seem like a random, chaotic, and inhumane world (Ziesemer & Marcoux, 1992). According to nearly everyone associated with homeless education, the message is that "efforts should be directed toward improving a stable school environment for homeless children" (Rubin et al., 1996, p. 293), a supportive environment that stimulates emotional and physical growth (Reganick, 1997).

Goals in this area are expressed both in student terms and objectives for the school. On the student front, the primary goal is to offset stress and feelings of inadequacy by nurturing "a sense of acceptance and belonging" (Gargiulo, 2006, p. 360) and a sense of hope (Raleigh-DuRoff, 2004). Thus, according to Ziesemer and associates (1994), "efforts need to be made to . . . make certain that [homeless] students become members of the school community" (p. 667), thus "replacing social isolation with social connections and support" (Anooshian, 2005, p. 148).

On the school front, the goal is to create a climate in which homeless students feel welcomed (Duffield et al., 2007; Julianelle, 2007). The objective is to develop a positive, caring, safe, stable, supportive, and well-structured environment at both the school and classroom levels (Baggerly & Borkowski, 2004; Pawlas, 1994; Swick, 2005). Schools need to understand "the importance of a warm, structured, and capacity-building environment" (Stronge & Hudson, 1999, p. 11), and they must work to realize "the potential to provide developmental havens of safety, stability, and care for children living in poverty whose lives are complicated by homelessness" (Masten et al., 1997, pp. 43–44).

Because for many homeless children and youngsters "school may be the one stable element in their lives" (Lindsey & Williams, 2002, p. 17), researchers consistently report that there is a "pressing need for children who are homeless to be enrolled in a stable and supportive school program" (Rescorla et al., 1991, p. 219), one that is characterized by safety and orderliness (Julianelle, 2007): "The first task is to provide a structured, stable, nonthreatening environment" (Gewirtzman & Fodor, 1987, p. 243). They also contend that schools should create "flexible and humane environments" (Rew, 1996; Vissing, 2000, p. 50), yet ones that are defined by the routines and structures that many homeless students require. That is, "because of the lack of structure within the lives of many homeless children, a consistent, predictable school setting can lessen fear and anxiety and contribute to the progression of healthy, cognitive, social, and emotional development" (Eddowes & Butcher, 2000, p. 35): "School stability . . . should be a goal" (Crowley, 2003, p. 35). So too should having a "structured environment" (Raleigh-DuRoff, 2004, p. 567) with "relatively stable schedules" (Stronge & Hudson, 1999, p. 12).

Scholars are consistent on the cardinal place of care in the "cultural ethos" (Quint, 1994, p. 108) that envelops homeless minors (Rew, 1996), what Gargiulo (2006) refers to as an ethic of care. On the topic of nurturing, schools are urged to develop cultures that are "warm and intimate" (Quint, 1994, p. 33) and to be responsive to the needs of homeless young persons (Medcalf, 2008), not simply ones into which the homeless are fitted. A nurturing environment, analysts aver, is one in which adults have "a sense of ownership for [homeless] students" (Ziesemer & Marcoux, 1992, p. 84).

Advocates for homeless minors maintain that because "shelters and other temporary living arrangements rarely provide young children with little, if any, space to call their own" (Eddowes & Butcher, 2000, p. 34; Quint, 1994), a school environment that is "sensitive to the importance of personal possessions of homeless children" (Myers & Popp, 2003, p. 6) is desirable. Specifically, "a place should be provided for each child's personal belongings" (Eddowes, 1992, p. 110):

> Due to the transient nature of their living situations children who are homeless are rarely alone. Consequently, at school they need quiet places to retreat and an individual cubby for their own possessions. (Kling et al., 1996, p. 6)

In a paradoxical way, the goal of the school is to become more institutional and less institutional at the same time. Institutions by definition are places that assume control over many dimensions of their clients' lives. For schools to work well for homeless children and youth, it is clear that they will need to extend their reach to address the full array of needs displaced minors carry with them to the schoolhouse—safety, health, education, nutrition, and so forth. At the same time, for homeless children and adolescents to flourish, schools need to develop environments that are less institutional and less bureaucratic. They must find ways to jettison the core elements of institutions (e.g., impersonality, division and specialization of work) and replace them with the defining elements of community (e.g., empowerment, high personalization). Or as Quint (1994) argues, the school must "attempt to act more like a family than an institution" (p. 90) if educational success for homeless children and adolescents is to become the norm.

Social Networks

Intervention approaches must recognize that healthy development depends on positive relationships. (Anooshian, 2000, p. 95)

~◠◡◠~

Helping [homeless] children form social support networks with peers and caring adults can buffer some of the effects of stress. (Ziesemer et al., 1994, p. 667)

~∽∾~

Stripped to the essentials, the case can be made that the hallmark element in all efforts to create the caring, stable, supportive environment outlined earlier is the development of "multiple support networks" (Tierney et al., 2008, p. 25) that stretch across multiple groups—student peers, teachers, and other adults (Ennett et al., 1999; Reed-Victor et al., 2003). Entering the battle for student success here helps schools see that the paramount "concern is with the scarcity of social attachments and high-quality social interactions experienced by homeless children" (Anooshian, 2000, p. 81). School personnel must understand that building webs of meaningful social relationships is the most efficacious strategy available to build a culture that advantages homeless students (Anooshian, 2005; Raleigh-DuRoff, 2004; Williams, 2003). Thus, "the primary message is that educators should devote considerable efforts to helping homeless children build positive relationships in school settings" (Anooshian, 2000, p. 80). We explore this critical strategy here, beginning with the importance of positive relationships among homeless children and adolescents and student peers and moving next to linkages with important "nurturing adults" (Reed-Victor et al., 2003, p. 2) in the school.

Students

One way to help homeless children in their relationships with peers is to educate all students in the classroom about homelessness.
(Tower & White, 1989, p. 30)

~∽∾~

Anooshian (2000) sets the stage here when he reminds us that "successful strategies for educational success will require significant efforts in supporting positive peer relationships for homeless children" (p. 88). In the quest to forge these peer relationships, four issues dominate the homeless education literature. The first is a thick line of analysis focusing on ways that teachers and other school personnel can build the foundation for peer relationships. School staff members accomplish this primarily, analysts argue, by educating nonhomeless students "about homelessness and the difficulties that children in homeless situations encounter" (Gargiulo, 2006, p. 360), by being "consistently vigilant to what can help their students understand homelessness" (Tower, 1992, p. 54). Thus, reviewers regularly conclude that "educating peers about homelessness is an important strategy for providing supportive environments for homeless children" (Anooshian, 2005, p. 147). Such awareness training is necessary, analysts assert, because ill-informed youngsters have been known to make "disparaging remarks about clothing, personal hygiene, or living conditions of homeless students" (Medcalf, 2008, p. 27; Polakow, 2003; Quint, 1994).

> Unfortunately, homeless children who overcome other barriers to regular school attendance often experience more negative labeling and rejection than social support. (Anooshian, 2000, p. 84)

> Another major category to emerge regarding their school experiences related to the respondents' feelings of shame and embarrassment when their classmates found out that they were homeless and then teased them about it. Specific reference was made to being called names, feeling so frustrated that they would react in an aggressive and hostile manner, and feeling the need to leave school quickly after classes were dismissed to avoid being confronted by others. (Daniels, 1995, p. 350)

It should come as little surprise to learn that such behavior can create "a formidable barrier to socially integrating homeless children into classrooms" (Anooshian, 2005, p. 147) and the resultant poor peer relationships are linked to "widespread negative outcomes" (Anooshian, 2000, p. 84). To the extent, then, that "part of the homeless experience involves being stigmatized and often taunted by other children" (Tower & White, 1989, p. 7), "conducting campuswide sensitivity and awareness activities" (Julianelle, 2007, p. 21) can "minimize some of the pressure homeless students feel from their peers" (Tower & White, 1989, p. 7): "The need for the education of fellow classmates cannot be overemphasized. As human beings, we tend to reject and stigmatize what we do not understand. If other children understand the issues faced by homeless children, they might be better able to help them integrate" (Tower, 1992, p. 60).

With student understanding in place, teachers can turn their attention to the second recommendation in the student social network literature: building a nurturing environment by creating systems of peer supports (Helge, 1992; Rotheram-Borus, 1991). The most regularly voiced recommendation here is the development of a system of peer mentoring, that is, buddy programs that match newly enrolling homeless students with peer helpers (Johnson, 1992; Korinek et al., 1992; Pawlas, 1994). The role of this "special friend [is] to assist the child in acclimating to the new environment" (Gonzalez, 1992, p. 207), "to assist students who are homeless to become familiar with the school and useful rules and routines" (Gargiulo, 2006, p. 360). Hightower and colleagues (1997) extend this suggestion by asking teachers to ensure "that homeless students in turn become buddies to other new students" (p. 49).

Third, although not featured as much as other ideas in the homeless literature, we know from related bodies of work on other students who are at risk that the creation of peer social relationships can be nurtured by using group approaches to instruction. In particular, cooperative learning formats that require students to construct answers collectively and that privilege both individual and group measures of accountability offer real promise to foster strong peer relations, and, as we noted earlier, to strengthen academic achievement as well.

Finally, researchers reveal that finding ways for homeless students to be meaningfully involved in classroom and school activities facilitates the development of social skills and peer relationships (Douglass, 1996; Hallett, 2007; Moore, 2007). These opportunities for involvement can take a variety of forms. For example, at the classroom level, Duffield and colleagues (2007) suggest that it is a good idea to ensure that homeless students have a "class job/role" (p. 28). At the school level, Wilder and team (2003) list the following examples of activities that homeless students can pursue, all of which offer the promise of strengthening the school culture by deepening student social relationships: "tutoring younger students, participating in athletics, participating in service learning, joining after-school clubs and study groups, acting in drama productions, taking art classes, joining music groups, and attending other extracurricular activities" (p. 13). Quint (1994) and other scholars discuss the importance of involvement in leadership activities at the school level, especially participating in the planning of school services (Powers & Jaklitsch, 1992; Swick, 2000). Still other analysts point to the usefulness of engaging homeless youth with peers in service learning projects and recreational activities (Anooshian, 2000; Hallett, 2007).

Adults

We unpack homeless young persons' "relationships with competent and caring adults" (Hart-Shegos & Associates, 1999, p. 10) into three dimensions: liaisons, teacher advocates, and mentors. We begin with Julianelle's (2007) cogent observation about the "one basic principle for establishing partnerships with homeless youth—schools must build trust with [these] youth" (p. 19).

Liaisons

There is a general consensus that at the systems level (i.e., the district) there needs to be someone whose assignment is to worry about and help structure the success of the homeless school population. There is support for the importance of this role at the school level as well. These advocates, known as liaisons in the McKinney-Vento legislation, are point persons for ensuring that the homeless population is well served by the school system and other community agencies (Hightower et al., 1997; Iowa Department of Education, 2004b). They are "the backbone of the school response to homelessness" (Duffield & Lovell, 2008, p. 13).

Liaisons nurture relations with homeless students as they perform an assortment of tasks to assist these young persons and oftentimes their families. Outside the school system, they advocate "before local, state, and national politicians for solutions to the variety of social problems associated with homelessness" (Penuel & Davey, 2000, p. 74): "It is the liaison who serves as an advocate for the student at both the ground level and in the realm of state and local policymaking" (Williams, 2003, p. 30). Relatedly, they "work hard to raise public awareness about homelessness" (Funkhouser et al., 2002, p. 64).

Liaisons are also the central coordinating agent in the larger community (Hightower et al., 1997; National Center for Homeless Education, 2006c; Tierney et al., 2008). In particular, it is their responsibility to collaborate with community groups and social service agencies that are in the business of providing "education and related services to homeless children and youth" (Iowa Department of Education, 2004b, p. 47). They are also the people who make sure that "schools are in compliance with federal and state mandates" (Tierney et al., 2008, p. 10). Finally, liaisons are essential in providing "a link between home and school" (Funkhouser et al., 2002, p. 56) for homeless students. In particular, "it is the liaison's job to get to know the families" (Williams, 2003, p. 31) of homeless students and to show that by helping the family, the school can help the student.

Liaisons are responsible for ensuring that homeless children and youth navigate the pathways to school access and success (Tierney et al., 2008), "to ensure that they are enrolled and have opportunities to succeed in school" (Duffield & Lovell, 2008, p. 13). In the area of access, they are responsible for identifying, involving, and assuring transportation (Funkhouser et al., 2002; Korinek et al., 1992). On the issue of success, liaisons are the educators who must see to it that homeless children and youth receive all the services and assistance to which they are entitled (Hightower et al., 1997; Iowa Department of Education, 2004b): "The homeless liaison [is] the critical link between homeless children and youth and the services to which they are entitled" (Funkhouser et al., 2002, p. 64). They are also expected to help ensure that all school support services (e.g., Title 1, special education) are integrated around homeless children and adolescents. Liaisons are the people who must ensure that school-based staff are educated about homeless issues in general and the needs of homeless minors in particular, as well as seeing to it that classrooms are recultured to support these students who are at risk (Duffield, 2000; Tierney et al., 2008). They are the "educators of school personnel" (Swick & Bailey, 2004, p. 213).

Teachers

Often the most essential element of a supportive and nurturing environment for the homeless child is a caring relationship with his teachers (James et al., 1991; Swick, 2005; Vissing, 2000). In important ways, teachers can help provide what "is missing when students do not have a secure place to live" (Landsman, 2006, p. 29), "the warmth and nurturing these students so desperately need" (Tower & White, 1989, p. 7). Thus, teachers are asked to become "compassionate advocates" (Landsman, 2006, p. 31) for homeless students.

In classrooms where teachers are effective advocates, they are "sensitive to, and aware of, the needs of homeless students while being careful not to stigmatize them or set them apart" (Duffield et al., 2007, p. 32). They show respect for homeless children by taking time to understand what these young persons experience (Eddowes & Butcher, 2000); by helping others, especially other children in the class, understand homelessness; by being "good listeners" (Swick, 1997, p. 29); by "doing some creative digging to find out what's happening in their lives" (Landsman, 2006, p. 29); and by "valuing [their] ideas and suggestions" (Eddowes & Butcher, 2000, p. 36). And they maintain high expectations and accountability "but show compassion and flexibility in helping [homeless] students succeed" (Landsman, 2006, p. 27; Lindsey & Williams, 2002).

Mentors

A well-thought-out mentoring program that creates social bonds between adults and homeless children can also be a central plank in the plan to create a stable and nurturing school environment (Myers & Popp, 2003; Popp, 2004; Swick, 1997). And Johnson (1992) notes, "like buddy programs, mentor programs are designed to help children feel a sense of acceptance at school, a sense of belonging. Whereas buddy programs provide the new students with the attention of a peer, mentor programs provide the attention and support of an adult" (p. 167). According to research, "having one positive relationship with a supportive adult is key to helping [homeless] young people make healthy decisions about their lives and deal constructively with adversity" (Penuel & Davey, 2000, p. 68).

> Studies that have examined factors contributing to the resiliency of at-risk youth who have overcome adversity and have succeeded despite poverty and dysfunctional home conditions have reported a clear and consistent finding: Resilient youth somehow have found and maintain a positive relationship with adults other than their parents. This finding has led to an increased appreciation of the mentoring concept, which is based on a young person building a one-on-one relationship with a caring, nurturing adult. Because homeless youth are particularly distrustful of adults, especially adult authority figures, mentoring programs may be extremely valuable if carried out in a nonthreatening, nonauthoritarian manner. (Powers & Jaklitsch, 1992, pp. 126–127)

Mentoring for homeless students has also been linked to "enhanced engagement and success in school" (Julianelle, 2007, p. 4) and "making school a safe and supportive place" (Julianelle, 2007, p. 19).

Mentors can come from an array of places. In schools, counselors, school leaders, teachers, other professional staff, and support personnel can assume mentoring responsibilities for homeless children and youth (Baggerly & Borkowski, 2004; Daniels, 1995; Julianelle, 2007). From outside the school, "mentoring can be a volunteer program involving business people, college and high school students, and community members as role models" (Helge, 1992, pp. 221–222). Beyond the key ingredients of caring and commitment (James & Lopez, 2003), core elements of effective mentoring programs for homeless children and youth include training for the role, the creation of a framework for an ongoing relationship (Hallett, 2007) to provide consistency (Julianelle, 2007; Wilder et al., 2003), and the development of "structured opportunities" (Penuel & Davey, 2000, p. 68) for mentoring to occur.

❖ PROVIDING ADDITIONAL SUPPORTS

> *To compensate for the disruptions associated with homelessness and its ancillary problems, homeless children need more than equal access to the classroom. (Rafferty, 1995, p. 55)*

> *Students experiencing homelessness require additional support from teachers and administrators to ensure that social, developmental, and academic goals are met. (Myers & Popp, 2003, p. 1)*

> *Given their mobility, homeless students, regardless of interest or ability, may lag behind their peers academically. Supplemental academic support may provide the key to their school success. (Hightower et al., 1997, p. 25)*

There is considerable agreement in the literature that if educators are to be effective in helping homeless youngsters succeed, schools will need to provide more than the basic package of services (Rafferty, 1991): "After-school and extended programs [have been] identified as one of the major needs of homeless students" (Rafferty, 1995, p. 47).

> When children are homeless, many of the requisites necessary for normal child development and learning are missing. That is the time for school programs to provide additional support for homeless families to help the children develop and learn despite the turbulence in their lives. (Eddowes, 1992, p. 99)

In addition, there is evidence that homeless children and youth are not on equal footing with their peers in this area. That is, "homeless students are at a disadvantage in terms of access to school services that supplement the standard education program" (Funkhouser et al., 2002, p. 8).

According to the scholarship in this area, additional supports serve many ends for homeless students. First, oftentimes these services offer homeless minors a secure and safe place to be, an alternative many times to the street: "For many homeless students, the most important facet of extended-day programs is that they extend for a few more hours the safe haven provided by school—a few more hours of peace, and fewer hours of worry or fear" (Johnson, 1992, p. 162). Second, scholars such as Emerson and Lovitt (2003) maintain that supplemental services "are important to keeping children in school" (p. 200). Third, if crafted well, these programs can enhance "the social skills needed to survive in and out of school" (Emerson & Lovitt, 2003, p. 200), build self-esteem (Johnson, 1992; Nunez, 1994a), and lengthen academic learning time and deepen achievement (Mawhinney-Rhoads & Stahler, 2006). In short, then, the goal in crafting a system of additional supports is (1) to embed students in a safe environment and a dense web of interpersonal relationships and (2) to provide additional academic scaffolding. Together these supports help offset the cognitive and social–emotional problems accompanying homelessness— they help to keep these young people in school and to ensure maximum academic and social development.

Scholars in the area of homelessness also provide frameworks for thinking about the provision of additional supports. Three types of assistance are often highlighted: basic need supports (e.g., clothing, health services), special academic services (e.g., tutoring), and nonacademic activities (e.g., clubs and recreational activities; Hightower et al., 1997; Julianelle, 2007; National Law Center on Homelessness and Poverty, 1990), collectively defined as "educational and support services" (Rafferty, 1995, p. 54). Earlier, we examined the domain of basic need supports. In this section, we attend to academic assistance and nonacademic supports.

Analysts also provide a two-dimensional taxonomy of avenues to provide these services (Dworsky, 2008; Hicks-Coolick et al., 2003; Stronge, 1992b). Pathway number one features "in school" supplemental activities (e.g., special education and extracurricular programs). The second pathway highlights "out-of-school" supplemental services (e.g., homework assistance at a center and community-based recreational clubs; Gargiulo, 2006; Mawhinney-Rhoads & Stahler, 2006).

Academic Support Services

In this domain, the spotlight is clearly on additional academic learning opportunities for homeless children and youth (Bowen et al., 1989; Medcalf, 2008). Stronge (1992b) informs us that academic support services generally focus on two areas of assistance: (a) helping students with academic work related to their regular school day academic program, and (b) supplemental assistance designed to enhance academic performance in a targeted skill area. Illustrative academic support services include tutoring and remedial assistance, help with homework, provision of a place to study, and preparation assistance for a high school equivalency examination. (p. 242)

Funkhouser and team (2002) add "after-school extended learning programs, homework assistance programs, and enrichment programs" (pp. 57–58).

Extant Supplemental Supports

Some of the extra assistance needed by homeless children and youth is already in the system. The task is to ensure that displaced students partake of these services (e.g., special education). Analysts often begin by documenting that homeless students are routinely underserved by existing systems of additional assistance (Medcalf, 2008; Stronge, 1992a). They then point out "the importance of linking homeless students [more effectively] . . . to existing services and school programs" (Jozefowicz-Simbeni & Israel, 2006, p. 42). They call for enhanced vigilance on the part of educators to "integrate support services within schools" (Penuel & Davey, 2000, p. 71) for homeless students. And they argue that "it is the role of teachers to make available to the homeless student whatever educational services they can access" (Tower & White, 1989, p. 27). In particular, given the inadequacy of funding under the McKinney-Vento Act, analysts underscore the responsibility of school to employ both targeted program resources *and* general education funds to help homeless students flourish in school (Julianelle, 2007; Stronge, 2000).

From the portfolio of internal supplemental supports, reviewers often underscore the issues raised earlier—access to the service and coordination with other programs—in the area of special education (Duffield et al., 2007; Williams, 2003). To begin with, they confirm that because of the impacts of dislocation, homeless children and youth are much in need of special education services: "The conditions under which homeless students live undoubtedly exacerbate the negative effects of any disabilities they may have. Consequently these students may be more in need of special education than students with the same disabilities who are not homeless" (Korinek et al., 1992, pp. 139–140). Next, they document that homeless minors are often underserved in special education programs (Cunningham, 2003; Medcalf, 2008; Shane, 1996); that is, "needs do not lead to greater access to special services" (Medcalf, 2008, p. 118). Korinek and colleagues (1992) explain this by noting that "several factors mitigate against homeless students with disabilities receiving special education services" (p. 135). Stronge (2000) elaborates:

> Factors such as transiency, difficulty in transferring records, etc., make it difficult to access specialized educational services on a timely basis. Even the stipulations within special education statutes designed to bring services to eligible students can serve as formidable barriers to their education. For example, special education procedural due process rights found in the Individuals with Disabilities Education Act (IDEA, PL. 104–476) can result in service delivery timelines that are incompatible with homeless lifestyles. (p. 12)

And Korinek and team (1992) report, "even when school personnel are well intentioned, the length of the special education referral and eligibility process may effectively prevent homeless students from receiving services" (p. 140).

These same scholars also expose inadequate coordination and integration between special education services and the homeless program and other in-school supplemental programs (e.g., Title 1). They document a "promulgation of 'special' programs and services which target each category of student need. This [they contend] has resulted in duplication of services and fragmented delivery systems" (Williams & Korinek, 2000, p. 184), fragmentation that is particularly disadvantageous for homeless children and youth.

Analysts, however, go beyond cataloging problems in providing internal supplemental support. They offer a series of ideas to ensure that these extant school-based assistance programs better serve homeless children and youth. On a broad level, they advocate for much more "instructional collaboration . . . in schools that serve large numbers of homeless youth" (Korinek et al., 1992, p. 150). They maintain that "working together daily, professionals will be more likely to share their observations and intervention ideas. As a team, they may be more successful in quickly identifying student needs and in mobilizing available school and division resources to aid these students" (Korinek et al., 1992, p. 150). Reviewers hold that "administrative, instructional, and support staff work[ing] together" (Williams & Korinek, 2000, p. 186) to help homeless children and youth is a key to their success. Relatedly, they propose a "cross program approach" (Iowa Department of Education, 2004b, p. 44) to serving homeless young persons, extending collaboration to district-based educators as well.

On the more concrete level, analysts advocate for speeding up processes that are used to admit homeless students to supplemental academic programs (Duffield et al., 2007), what Reed-Victor and associates (2003) call "expedited evaluations" (p. 4): "Expediting evaluations can be accomplished through accessing and using reports from other agencies and schools, using interdisciplinary team approaches, and determining eligibility as quickly as possible so that appropriate service can be provided right away" (p. 4). The speeding-up process can also be accomplished by "moving the evaluation [of homeless children and youth] up on waiting lists, recognizing that their mobility places them at risk of long delays in evaluations" (Duffield et al., 2007, p. 52).

A number of authors who explore the power of educators to help homeless minors succeed highlight the importance of developing robust counseling services for these children (Baggerly & Borkowski, 2004; Hallett, 2007; Timberlake, 1994). In particular, advocates for the homeless believe that "special counseling services should be offered to adolescents that will help them deal with the physical, social, and emotional stresses of being homeless" (Powers & Jaklitsch, 1992, p. 127), with a primary focus on "socioemotional support, including dealing with such concerns as social acceptance, self-esteem, and stress" (Stronge, 1992b, p. 243).

The logic chain for the counseling intervention parallels that found with other supports. To begin with, it is suggested that "for some students the trauma of homelessness may be overwhelming. These students may have little capacity to focus on learning tasks because of the many feelings associated with homelessness" (Johnson, 1992, p. 168). Moving on, then, it is asserted that "because homelessness frequently creates personal and family stress, dealing with emotional and social issues can be paramount to making education meaningful for homeless students" (Stronge, 2000, p. 6). It is also found that at times, school personnel act in ways that stigmatize homeless young persons, thus compounding homelessness-induced problems (Daniels et al., 1999).

The call, then, is for counseling services to help alleviate these difficulties: "Homeless students often feel uncomfortable in the school environment. They need a counselor who can build a trusting relationship with them and support them in negotiating the various social and emotional challenges inherent in their situation" (Swick, 2000, p. 174): "In light of the unique barriers many of these students manifest in terms of being able to develop personally and academically, school counselors hold a pivotal position within the organizational structure of the schools to offer assistance in helping homeless children better realize their psychological and academic potential" (Daniels, 1992, p. 108). Counselors, it is held, are in unique "positions to identify and assist students who are experiencing various academic, personal, and social difficulties as a result of being homeless" (Daniels, 1995, p. 347). The final piece of the logic chain, the end game for students, is the development of a "personal sense of industry, learning new coping strategies to deal with stress . . . and positive peer affiliation and friendships (Daniels, 1992, p. 110). Overall, then, school counselors can help "ensure that the social–emotional needs of homeless children are adequately addressed by offering these students an opportunity to express appropriately their feelings and frustrations, resulting in improved school behavior, self-esteem, and interpersonal relationships" (Johnson, 1992, p. 169).

Additional Supplemental Supports

The literature on assisting homeless children and youth also addresses the provision of supports in addition to systems already in place in schools. It is held by some, for example, that extended academic work, both in terms of remediation and acceleration, be made available in the *summer* for homeless students (Dworsky, 2008; Iowa Department of Education, 2004b; Nabors et al., 2001) and that "homeless students be prioritized for summer school programs" (Rafferty, 1991, p. 144). In a similar vein, analysts propose that much more energy be invested in developing extended learning opportunities *before and after school* for homeless students (Johnson, 1992; Myers & Popp, 2003; Nunez, 1994b).

Some analysts advocate for the development of robust *mentoring* programs that link homeless students with a specific adult in ongoing relationships to promote academic success (Swick, 2000; Tierney et al., 2008). More common still are calls to develop *tutoring* programs (Eddowes, 1992; Hightower et al., 1997; Pawlas, 1994), using peers, older students, and adults (Johnson, 1992; Quint, 1994) to help homeless children and youth "keep up with their schoolwork" (National Law Center on Homelessness and Poverty, 1990, p. 32) and make up for lost instructional time (Hart-Shegos & Associates, 1999; Powers & Jaklitsch, 1992; Rotheram-Borus, 1991): "Tutoring to address academic deficits must be made available to help homeless children keep up with their school work and compensate for the disruptions caused by their loss of housing" (Rafferty, 1991, p. 142). That is, it is routinely suggested that "tutoring services may help homeless students achieve success at school . . . despite gaps in prior learning" (Johnson, 1992, p. 173). In addition, the tutored child "may also benefit socially and emotionally from the experience" (Eddowes & Butcher, 2000, p. 38).

> The extra attention directed to academic needs can make a dramatic difference for some homeless students. The differences between success and failure may be only 15 minutes of one-on-one tutoring twice a week, a little extra time for the teacher to explain a prerequisite concept, or an aide who can listen to a child read for a few minutes each day. (Johnson, 1992, p. 173)

The benefits of providing *homework support*, often discussed in conjunction with academic tutoring, is another theme in the supplemental support chronicle (Hightower et al., 1997; Swick, 1997; Tower & White, 1989). The initial chapter in the narrative is the widely recognized finding that homeless students have weak support systems to sustain homework (e.g., limited space, absence of routines, lack of privacy and quiet time, absence of home libraries and materials; Solarz, 1992; Stronge, 2000; Tierney et al., 2008), "conditions that create difficulties for students in concentrating and studying" (Shane, 1996, p. 36). The middle chapter in the story focuses on the need to provide programs to support the ability of homeless children and youth to complete homework assignments (Gonzalez, 1992; Tower, 1992; Whitman et al., 1990). A nice summary of the story line to this point has been provided by Eddowes (1992):

> Homeless children have great difficulty completing homework. Usually lacking where they live are a place to do it, a table and chair, and privacy or quiet space. Reference materials may not be available, and the parents may be unable to provide any assistance. Teachers should have an understanding of this problem and find ways to provide supplementary materials and/or a supervised place in which children can complete the homework at school. (p. 109)

The final chapter of the homework support story documents the tale of students who no longer fall behind in school and who experience academic success (Johnson, 1992; Tower, 1992).

Two additional types of academic supports are highlighted at times in the homeless education literature. First, some reviewers advocate for programs to provide *job training* for homeless adolescents (Emerson & Lovitt, 2003; Levin et al., 2005).

> Programs are needed to enable homeless young people to complete specialized employment and training programs. Employment, job-readiness training, and other supportive services are needed before youth can secure and maintain employment. High-risk youth are often ill-prepared for work, requiring intensive preparation, including job training and placement. While homeless, these youth have little or no access to such programs. (Robertson, 1990, p. 53)

Relatedly, advocates maintain that well-resourced *college transition programs* to help homeless adolescents move easily into higher education can be helpful (Duffield et al., 2007; Tierney et al., 2008). Reviewers underscore the importance of assisting homeless students in managing the paperwork needed to apply to college as well as providing scholarship aid to allow them to attend once admitted (Moore, 2007; Pires & Silber, 1991).

Nonacademic Supplemental Supports

Non-academic activities, such as sports and clubs, are often critical for engaging youth in school and guiding them toward graduation. (Julianelle, 2007, p. 4)

~◦✧◦~

*Schools realize that much learning occurs outside the confines of the
classroom, and extracurricular and recreational programs promote both
educational and self-esteem development. Linkages between the school,
shelter, and community organizations can facilitate the creation of out-of-
school educational and recreational options that benefit homeless students.*
(Vissing, 2000, p. 55)

～⌒ⁱ⌒～

Scholars suggest that schools can do much to assist homeless children
and youth by creating meaningful opportunities for involvement in a
variety of cocurricular programs. Nunez (1994b) maintains that these
"activities [which] are essential to round out a child's education and social
development . . . are especially important for homeless children who are
often consumed by the anxiety and confusion they feel" (p. 78). He and
other researchers document that homeless student involvement in these
nonacademic support services is quite low (Tierney et al., 2008), thus
revealing the considerable potential for assistance in this area.

Participation in these extracurricular programs, it is asserted, can promote a variety of benefits for homeless minors. For example, Hightower
and associates (1997) report that such programs "provide an emotional
and physical outlet and can foster important relationships among children,
youth, and adults" (p. 21).

> After-school programs can be beneficial in providing these chil-
> dren with a safe and supervised environment where they can play
> as well as have the time and support of other adults. For homeless
> children, such programs represent important developmental
> opportunities to interact with peers, engage in fun activities, and
> have access to school supplies and equipment that otherwise might
> not be available. (Daniels, 1992, p. 109)

Duffield and Lovell (2008) remark that this involvement can help homeless
students "feel comfortable, safe, and wanted" (p. 14). Nunez (1994a), in
turn, argues that these "extracurricular activities not only round out children's education but also help to improve their socialization skills and
self-esteem. [They] encourage children to attend school and to see education as both enjoyable and important. [They] also help children develop
coping mechanisms to deal with the pressures of growing up in a volatile
urban environment" (p. 29).

To make these programs work for homeless students, analysts assert
that participation fees must be waived (Johnson, 1992; Vissing, 2000), "that
homeless youth not [be] denied access to services and activities due to
their financial circumstances" (Julianelle, 2007, p. 29). They call for strong
adult mentors to be part of these cocurricular experiences (Tierney et al.,
2008). They advocate for the elimination of "enrollment and application

deadlines that present barriers to homeless youth's participation in a wide variety of non-academic programs" (Julianelle, 2007, p. 28). Reviewers suggest that homeless youngsters be involved in an assortment of different types of experiences, recreational activities, school clubs, enrichment programs, and so forth (Anooshian, 2000; Wilder et al., 2003). As we see more fully later, they call for coordination in the provision of these programs between school and agency/community groups (Rafferty, 1991). And perhaps most importantly, because "transportation is the most significant barrier to participation in before and after-school programs" (Rafferty, 1991, p. 142), they ask that special transportation be made available for homeless children and youth.

❖ COLLABORATING WITH OTHER AGENCIES AND ORGANIZATIONS

Progress will require coordinated, integrated actions involving a wide spectrum of people directly and indirectly involved. (Williams, 2003, p. 7)

Given the wide variety of concerns related to homelessness, teaming with colleagues across disciplines and agencies is essential in the creation of comprehensive and well-integrated supports for young children and families experiencing homelessness. (Reed-Victor et al., 2003, p. 7)

An effective response to the educational needs of homeless children and youth involves many community agencies working together with schools to address the myriad needs of families and youth. (Duffield & Lovell, 2008, p. 14)

Schools must coordinate and collaborate with shelters and other homeless service providers to help ensure that homeless children and youths have prompt and convenient access to social services. (Medcalf, 2008, p. 108)

Perhaps no element in the portfolio of strategies to assist homeless children and their families (and unaccompanied youth) is highlighted more frequently than the importance of establishing collaboratives among those in a position to help these displaced persons (Bowen et al., 1989; Heflin, 1991; Williams, 2003). Or, as Tucker (1999) amplifies, "one of the strongest messages common to all of the literature on homeless education is the importance of collaboration with the goal of integrated services" (p. 101). It is consistently reported that (1) "serving children and youth in homeless situations is a community issue, not just a school issue" (Moore, 2005a,

p. 7); (2) "a coordinated collaborative approach to education seems to be especially important when dealing with homeless students" (Stronge, 2000, p. 13); and (3) "schools and agencies serving homeless children and their families must work collaboratively to coordinate efforts" (Medcalf, 2008, p. 109). That is, "mechanisms should be established to promote coordination among the service providers in order to optimize the delivery of services to young people and to ensure that no needy youth 'fall between the cracks'" (Rothman, 1991, p. 54)—"that broad, multi-agency coordination on the local level is essential to ensure that homeless youth can enroll in, attend, and succeed in school" (Julianelle, 2007, p. 39). In short, "the effectiveness of education for the homeless hinges on a high level of collaboration among professionals interacting with students and their families" (Korinek et al., 1992, p. 143).

The Case Against the Status Quo

School alone cannot begin to solve the problems of homelessness.
(Stronge & Hudson, 1999, p. 12)

A school that educates the homeless cannot handle the challenge alone.
(Gonzalez, 1992, p. 203)

Analysts arrive at the conclusion of the nonviability of current arrangements from two different directions—critique and a sense of possibility. From the critical analysis side, they affirm that the staggering complexity of the problems associated with homelessness precludes any single agency from resolving matters (Moore, 2005a; Newman & Beck, 1996; Tucker, 1999). According to these reviewers, no single "agency possesses the comprehensive authority" (Bowen et al., 1989, p. 53). Neither does any "single agency [have] all the appropriate information and resources to meet their [homeless persons] multiple needs" (Hightower et al., 1997, p. 40). In particular, analysts correctly observe that "schools were not intended to address the multitude of economic, education, and personal obstacles faced by homeless children" (Moore, 2005a, p. 6), and "the needs of homeless youth are too many and too pressing for schools to address alone" (Lindsey & Williams, 2002, p. 5). That is, "schools cannot do it alone" (Tucker, 1999, p. 104).

These same scholars assert that "successful efforts to address the issues can only stem from a comprehensive approach based on the collaborative efforts of various service providers working together" (Moore, 2005a, p. 5): "The multiple needs of homeless children make collaboration among schools, social service agencies, and the private sector necessary to ensure them a normal quality of life and education" (Yon et al., 1993,

p. 421). Without this interagency collaboration, it is held, the provisions of the laws designed to advantage homeless students are made "meaningless" (Tucker, 1999, p. 91). Relatedly, analysts maintain that "resources are simply too scarce to attempt to deal with problems in isolation" (Helge, 1992, p. 221).

Others in the critical analysis camp lobby for coordination of effort to assist homeless youngsters because they see major problems associated with the fragmentation of services and the isolated nature of service delivery (Dworsky, 2008; Moore, 2005b; Tucker, 1999)—the division of the helping field into separate and nonlinked sections of action or what Bruder (1997) describes as "the fragmentation of multiple service providers" (p. 241) and what Julianelle (2007) refers to as "a fragmented and uncoordinated service delivery system" (p. 40). That is, a core finding of homeless researchers is that "many agencies that work with homeless children [and youth] continue to do so in isolation from others" (Eddowes & Butcher, 2000, p. 40), that the profession is characterized by a "conglomeration of uncoordinated initiatives and programs" (Moore, 2005b, p. 7). They find that oftentimes, "services are highly specialized or piecemeal rather than being comprehensive. . . . They deal with a specific type of problem rather than the needs of the whole person" (Baron, 2003, p. 39): "The service delivery system is composed of independent agencies, institutions and organizations, and each provide[s] a specific service or function, usually in a different location. As a result, each type of service provider has his/her own orientation toward the child who needs a multitude of preventive and remedial services and supports" (Bruder, 1997, p. 239). Not only does this service-delivery approach fail to provide the planful scaffolding of support needed by homeless youngsters, it leads to considerable duplication of services and "waste[s] valuable resources" (Nunez & Collignon, 2000, p. 129). Particularly troubling, critics assert, is the separation of schools and shelters, each from the other (Bowman & Barksdale, 2004; Nunez, 1994a; Wilder et al., 2003), a "disjuncture between the shelter and the school" (Tierney et al., 2008, p. 29).

The Solution

School districts and community agencies must collaborate to serve the needs of homeless students. (Ziesemer & Marcoux, 1992, p. 84)

Homeless children can benefit greatly from centers or schools that coordinate services which are needed by these children and their families.
(Eddowes & Butcher, 2000, p. 42)

Both schools and shelters hold a treasury of institutional expertise and resources necessary to provide effective programs for homeless children. To make the best use of all these resources, schools must work with community-based organizations and shelters to develop their own communities of learning. (Nunez & Collignon, 1997, p. 59)

~◠◡◠~

The proposed solution to the status quo of fragmentation will come as a surprise to no one: greater collaboration among agencies that work with homeless families and accompanied children and/or homeless adolescents (Anooshian, 2000; Bass, 1995; Rouse & Fantuzzo, 2009; Ziesemer et al., 1994). What is needed, it is argued, is an "integrated system" (Yon et al., 1993, p. 422) or a "network of service providers" (Funkhouser et al., 2002, p. 44) to replace the current fragmented system of assistance— "multilevel collaboration" (Williams & Korinek, 2000, p. 185) and "interagency collaboration" (Parrish et al., 2003, p. 2), "a tapestry of programs for homeless children and their families" (Tucker, 1999, p. 92).

Neither will it come as a surprise to learn that analysts and advocates regularly suggest that schools are critical to the success of interagency collaboration (Moore, 2005b). Others go even further, holding that schools should "serve as the hub" (Newman & Beck, 1996, p. 99) of social service delivery for homeless children and youth. For a variety of reasons, these reviewers conclude that "school staff may be best suited to spearhead collaborative efforts" (Moore, 2007, p. 12). Scholars note, for example, that schools have a legal mandate to collaborate and "coordinate with local service agencies or programs providing services to homeless children or youth and their families" (Funkhouser et al., 2002, p. 64).

From the user's side of the window, reviewers also (1) argue that oftentimes "there is less stigma attached to services offered by schools than by governmental agencies" (Gewirtzman & Fodor, 1987, p. 242) and (2) find that the homeless "rely upon the school to be the gatekeeper to community resources" (Vissing, 2000, p. 60). They claim that "since schools are a 'universal institution' and possibly the only stable influence in the life of a homeless child, school staff may be the most logical ones to spearhead collaborative efforts" (Moore, 2005b, p. 6).

Schools are mandated by the 1990 McKinney Amendments to coordinate interagency support for homeless children and youth. As a result, they must play a fundamental role in developing and implementing integrative services. Because schools are a universal part of children's and families' lives, using schools as the hub of the service network can be less stigmatizing than offering services at other institutions. (Ritter & Gottfried, 2002, p. 43)

Shape of Collaboration

Service integration is the realization of a collaboration that involves all services and supports engaged by a family. (Bruder, 1997, p. 238)

There are likely to be two major groups: the education system and the homeless system. (Duffield, 2000, p. 212)

The Form

According to scholars who study the issue, interagency partnerships and "collaborations can take many forms" (Tierney et al., 2008, p. 28). Three of these are most often discussed in the homeless literature: the "full service" school model, the task force collaboration model, and the case management model—keeping in mind that they can be used together. Under the full service design, an array of services (educational, nutritional, medical, social, etc.) are housed at the school building, making one-stop service for homeless families and homeless adolescents possible (Lumsden & Coffey, 2001). There is colocation of services (Bruder, 1997). Coordination of the service providers is generally undertaken by school personnel in a collaborative manner.

"Task force" or advisory committee designs pull as many service providers together in a leadership arrangement where energy and resources are examined for collaborative action on the part of the various agencies (Hightower et al., 1997; Moore, 2005b). This design builds an "interagency network" (Bowen et al., 1989, p. 27) "to facilitate collaborative arrangements" (p. 28).

Case management models, in turn, build collaboration not at the institutional or macrolevel, as is the case with the task force model, but at the microlevel, around each homeless youth or child and her family (James et al., 1991; Quint, 1994). This design does not require colocation of services and supports but rather "the use of one central service coordinator to cross agency functions and boundaries" (Bruder, 1997, p. 239). According to Rew (1996), "case management for holistic care of homeless youth involves coordination of services that provide food and shelter, prevent physical injury and illness, reduce stress, promote psychosocial functioning, and enhance spiritual well-being" (pp. 355–356)—"service delivery fluctuates around a family and child's needs as opposed to artificially imposed program limitations" (Bruder, 1997, p. 241).

Scholars also inform us that in the area of interagency partnerships, "the intensity of collaboration can vary depending on the level of involvement and the integration of goals and resources" (Tucker, 1999, pp. 92–93). On the "collaboration" end of the intensity continuum, "partners help each other meet their respective goals without any substantial changes to basic services or regulations" (Yon et al., 1993, p. 415). On the "cooperative" end of the intensity continuum, "partners establish common goals, pool resources, and plan jointly" (p. 415).

The Players

Advocates for homeless children and youth—and their families—maintain that a collaborative network should "include a wide variety of service providers" (James et al., 1991, p. 306), both public and private. At the same time, they underscore the special role that schools and shelters can play in the network (Funkhouser et al., 2002; Rafferty, 1995; Tower & White, 1989). Key service providers highlighted in the homeless literature include those in the educational, social, and health fields, including the following: medical personnel, mental health agencies, disaster relief organizations, homeless shelters and other housing providers, universities, public schools, public parks and recreation departments, police departments, child welfare agencies, transportation departments, elected officials, social service departments, and food and nutrition programs (Duffield, 2000; Eddowes & Butcher, 2000; Julianelle, 2007; Nunez & Collignon, 2000; Vostanis, Grattan, Cumelia, & Winchester, 1997; Woronoff et al., 2006).

In addition, it is often proposed that community groups be woven into the collaborative tapestry. Here analysts highlight the importance of foundations, businesses, faith-based organizations, and civic groups (Masten et al., 1997; Nunez & Collignon, 1997; Quint, 1994; Stronge & Hudson, 1999). Finally, some reviewers suggest that because "homeless youth are the most experienced and well-informed experts regarding their own strengths, challenges, needs, and goals, they should be active participants in all collaborative and youth-serving efforts" (Julianelle, 2007, p. 5).

Elements of Effective Collaboration

There is no one-size-fits-all model for collaboration, so each collaborative group must examine its own unique situation to develop what works best. Building relationships requires consistency over time. (Moore, 2005a, p. 30)

Strong interagency partnerships are built on effective collaboration and a sharing of resources and information to support common activities that will impact educational services for homeless children and adolescents. (Stronge & Hudson, 1999, p. 12)

There is a considerable body of work on collaborative endeavors between organizations and between service agencies, for example, between universities and school districts. It is beyond our charge to examine that larger corpus of work. At the same time, some, although limited (Moore, 2005a, 2005b), insights about collaboratives in the area of supporting homeless children and youth are available, both about barriers to productive collaboration and procedures to make collaboration effective. We devote a few lines to that literature here. For deeper descriptions of these elements in action, that is, to peer in upon some of these collaboratives, see Hightower and colleagues (1997), James and associates (1991), Julianelle (2007), Pires and Silber (1991), Polakow (2003), National Center for Homeless Education (2006a), Taylor and Brown (1996), and especially Moore (2005a).

Reviewers are apt to begin their analysis by describing some of the barriers to effective collaboration. "Inflexible bureaucratic structure" (Moore, 2005a, p. 10), at the heart of the various agencies, is the most common culprit (Stronge & Hudson, 1999): "Bureaucracies are often slow enough without having to coordinate with other equally slow bureaucracies" (Helm, 1992, p. 40). Lack of understanding and appreciation for the work of other partners can be a derailer (Moore, 2005a; Penuel & Davey, 1998), especially failing to "take the time to become familiar with the roles and requirements of other agencies" (Stronge & Hudson, 1999, p. 12) in the partnership. Absence of genuine commitment and a dearth of leadership have been singled out as problems in the homeless literature as well (Penuel & Davey, 1998). Advocating for a specific agency rather than the common mission can also be a deal breaker for collaborative work, as can failing to develop avenues to effectively share information (Moore, 2005a).

On the other hand, scholars such as Moore (2005a) confirm that the following entries are often recorded on the positive side of the collaboration ledger:

- Taking the time to learn about and understand the other partners in the collaborative: "it is vital to know the other collaborative agencies and their staff members" (Moore, 2005a, p. 30)
- Developing buy-in: "establish the expectation that everyone will contribute" (Moore, 2005a, p. 30)
- Developing clear goals and a "collective vision" (Stronge & Hudson, 1999, p. 13) and "clear expectations for the relationships" (Moore, 2005a, p. 30): "the first step is identifying the common thread that can weave participants together" (Moore, 2005a, p. 8)
- Keeping both eyes on the vision and goals: "begin with client issues and problems" (Moore, 2005a, p. 31) instead of prepackaged solutions, agency agendas, or procedures and remember that "collaborating is not the goal but the means to accomplish the goal" (Moore, 2005a, p. 5)
- Establishing "ground rules" (Moore, 2005a, p. 25) to guide action (Stronge & Hudson, 1999): "establish mutually agreed upon policies and procedures" (Penuel & Davey, 1998, p. 10)

◆ Making sure that "the right people are at the table" (Moore, 2005a, p. 8) and "empower[ing] decision making authority within the collaborative instead of requiring each member to clear decisions through their agency channels" (Moore, 2005a, p. 31)

◆ Beginning with "a small manageable project will build confidence to maintain momentum and undertake larger tasks" (Moore, 2005a, p. 31)

◆ Creating a productive climate for mutual work; remember that trust is at the heart of the matter—"successful collaboratives should plan to spend as much time nurturing relationships as planning and implementing projects" (Moore, 2005a, p. 8)

◆ "Establish[ing] honest and frank communication patterns" (Moore, 2005a, p. 31): "the common thread of communication unites efforts of model programs to make them successful" (Nunez & Collignon, 1997, pp. 58–59)

◆ Pooling resources (Hightower et al., 1997; Stronge & Hudson, 1999)

The Benefits of Collaboration

Findings from the present study underscore the value of integrated municipal systems designed in partnership. (Rouse & Fantuzzo, 2009, p. 11)

We began this section by reporting that analysts come to the realization of the importance of collaboration for schools and other agencies and groups from two directions: critique of the status quo in the area of service delivery and a sense of possibility about more effective provision of services for homeless children and youth. In that introductory section, we unpacked the stream of critical analysis. We complete our work here with a snapshot of the benefit side of the story line.

Analysts often point to gains that accrue to the agencies themselves from collaborative work, including a deeper understanding of issues related to homeless youth (Moore, 2005a) and better articulation with colleagues with similar interests (Eddowes & Hranitz, 1989). They also maintain that this more collaborative attack on the problems of homelessness leads to a better system of service as well as natural redundancy that permits some partners to cover potential service gaps. In addition, as Moore (2005a) has concluded, in these partnerships collaborators often find "that working together makes each person's job easier" (p. 15). According to Bruder (1997), collaborative service delivery models bring the following benefits to the agencies themselves—and indirectly to clients:

Most important is more efficient and effective use of service providers and funding streams across agencies resulting in improved service delivery. These models also result in a reduction in service duplication. Collaborative models enable parents and service providers to efficiently locate and manage the necessary services required by the family. Lastly, collaborative models eliminate the need for formal transitions between programs, as services are integrated, comprehensive and longitudinal. (p. 241)

Duffield (2000), in turn, argues that this collaboration is valuable because "there is strength in numbers, and resources can be quickly deployed by working with other groups" (p. 211). Or, as Tucker (1999) asserts, "by working together, resources can be pooled and leveraged to achieve a more comprehensive response to the presenting problems of the child and the family" (p. 92). Indeed, "partnerships with diverse agencies may be the only way to provide all the resources to meet the various needs of homeless children and their families" (Moore, 2005a, p. 30). The takeaway message from the agency perspective, then, is that "collaborative efforts can increase efficiency and reduce duplication of services, which can translate into an expansion of services . . . they enable agencies to work together to craft more comprehensive strategies to help homeless youth" (Julianelle, 2007, p. 5) and children.

Agency benefits are, of course, only an intermediate step in the quest to offer better services, more effective and comprehensive services (Moore, 2005a), for homeless children and their families and for unaccompanied adolescents. And reviewers regularly report that the needs of homeless youngsters are better met in a collaborative model of service delivery (Bowen et al., 1989; Popp, 2004; Rouse & Fantuzzo, 2009; Swick, 2000): "A coordinated model of service delivery enhance[s] the provision of programs and services to homeless children and their families" (Rafferty, 1995, p. 55). Perhaps most salient here, it is claimed, is that "strategic partnerships with public service providers will improve educational outcomes for children" (Rouse & Fantuzzo, 2009, p. 12).

❖ PROMOTING PARENTAL INVOLVEMENT[2]

Another barrier to school success for homeless children is a lack of home support for education. (Medcalf, 2008, p. 26)

~◠˙◠~

The surest way to support homeless children's education is to support their parents. (Nunez & Collignon, 2000, p. 115)

~◠˙◠~

Another issue that is essential to the educational success of students who are homeless is parental involvement. (Stronge & Hudson, 1999, p. 10)

~◠˙◠~

Research on school improvement over the last 30 years has consistently documented parent involvement as a critical variable in the school effects formula. More specifically, studies confirm the significant role that parents of students placed at risk play in helping their children succeed in school (Murphy, 2010). It should come as no surprise, then, to learn that parent involvement is linked to the academic advancement of homeless children. Neither will it be surprising to discover that advocates for children argue that schools need to be more aggressive in "enlisting parents as partners" (Quint, 1994, p. 94) in the education of homeless students, that educators "need to develop and continually refine an 'engagement, participatory' stance in relation to the involvement of homeless families" (Swick, 2004, p. 119). As Stronge (2000) asserts, "it should be clear that a partnership with parents needs to be forged to assist [homeless] students in . . . succeeding in school" (p. 9).

Setting the Stage

Family dysfunction and stress related to the condition of homelessness act as barriers to healthy child development and to parental participation in the education of their children. (Stronge & Hudson, 1999, p. 11)

The introductory section in the parent involvement volume features three themes: the difficulty of creating meaningful parent involvement in the homeless community, the heightened importance of such connections for the well-being of homeless children, and an acknowledgment that schools can do more than they often have done to remove barriers to engagement and to garner the rewards of involvement. Given the detailed portrait of the impacts of homelessness in Chapter 4, we should expect the finding that homelessness negatively affects the will and ability of parents to be active partners in the education of their children. Indeed "parents of homeless students often compound educational problems" (Shane, 1996, p. 36), and "many homeless parents do not (or seemingly cannot) place an appropriate emphasis on the education of their children" (Stronge & Hudson, 1999, p. 11). As a consequence, "homeless children frequently find themselves lacking a parent's critical educational support" (Nunez & Collignon, 2000, p. 115).

At the broadest level, as Nunez and Collignon (2000) reveal, "parents who are in shelters or moving between doubled-up housing situations are overwhelmed by the conditions of deep poverty and homelessness, and are distracted from their children's education" (p. 115). At a more micro-level, analysts report two roots of the engagement problem. To begin with, the severe stresses of homelessness negatively impact family functioning (Bruder, 1997) and push educational issues into the background (Tower &

White, 1989). As Gargiulo (2006) affirms, the need for survival occupies center stage for many homeless families and "meeting basic survival needs may limit significant [school] involvement and participation" (p. 360). "Homeless parents expend tremendous emotional resources trying to meet basic human needs, often leaving little in reserve to offer support and understanding to their young children at a time when their children need it most" (Kelly et al., 2000, p. 175). In addition, even if they conquer the "terrible stress" (Shane, 1996, p. 36) of homelessness, parents often are not in a position to provide the types of supports that would advantage their children (Biggar, 2001; Lumsden & Coffey, 2001). Many have only very limited education themselves (Nunez, 1994b). Living arrangements generally make support all but impossible (Biggar, 2001). Equally important, many homeless parents "have had limited involvement with positive parental role models" (Swick, 2009, p. 328). Even provided time and resources, they simply may not know what to do.

The importance of parental involvement, no matter how arduous it is to secure, is the second theme in our story (Quint, 1994). Indeed, Markward and Biros (2001) argue that homeless "parent involvement in the educational process is critical" (p. 185). And Stronge (2000) reminds us, precisely because of the place of homelessness as the etiological agent for educational problems, that "parent involvement and support are essential if education is to become and remain a priority for homeless children" (p. 7). Acknowledging that "unless the family environment is supportive other efforts to improve children's education likely will be futile" (Stronge, 1992b, p. 244), those schools that establish partnerships with parents are much better positioned to ensure the academic success of homeless children (Ritter & Gottfried, 2002; Swick & Bailey, 2004; Williams & Korinek, 2000).

Finally, there is a thick line of analysis in the literature asserting that schools can do more to promote healthy parental involvement (Rafferty, 1995). There is a sense in the research that in working with homeless students, schools need to shift the focus to the entire family (Tucker, 1999), that "strong teacher–parent–child relationships can act as the beginning point for other positive steps" (Swick, 1997, p. 33). Or, as Quint (1994) captures it, in addressing the needs of homeless students, schools must "recognize that both children and parents are equally important targets" (p. 93).

Parent Education

Homeless parents themselves are often unaware of their children's rights or their own rights. (Funkhouser et al., 2002, p. 21)

～◠◡◠～

For many homeless families, education is badly needed, not only for the children, but also for their parents. (Nunez, 1994b, p. 95)

～◠◡◠～

A basic tenet of parent education for homeless parents of young children must be to empower them with knowledge on meaningful parenting perspectives and practices. (Swick, 2009, p. 329)

~⌒ᵛ⌒~

Guidance in the homeless literature informs us that to "overcome the obstacles to homeless children's success, educators must pave the way to parent education and . . . involvement" (Nunez & Collignon, 2000, p. 119). In this section, we discuss the first issue, parent education. In the next section, we address parent involvement with the school. Both, advocates hold, rest upon the willingness and skill of educators to reach out to parents and keep open productive lines of communication (Finley, 2003; Iowa Department of Education, 2004a): "Teachers, principals, and other staff must reach out to engage the parents of homeless children" (Dworsky, 2008, p. 49).

In the area of parent education, analysts' insights cluster in well-defined categories. They find, for example, that "few [homeless] parents are knowledgeable about their rights and therefore do not know how to advocate for their children" (Hallett, 2007, p. 1): "Many homeless students and their families do not understand the schools and social programs. They do not know and/or understand their rights under the McKinney-Vento Act, state laws, and local policies" (Medcalf, 2008, p. 23). Scholars maintain, therefore, that schools must be more proactive in educating parents about these rights (Duffield et al., 2007; Funkhouser et al., 2002; Rafferty, 1995): "At a minimum, parents must be fully informed about their children's rights under state and federal law" (Dworsky, 2008, p. 48): "Homeless families are often uninformed regarding the rights of their children and the resources that are available to them. It is important for raising awareness on homeless issues to include families so they can make informed decisions about the education of their children" (Stronge & Hudson, 1999, p. 11).

Relatedly, reviewers maintain that schools should provide training to help homeless parents be advocates for themselves and champions for their children (Dworsky, 2008; Swick, 1997; Taylor & Brown, 1996), both within schools and in the larger service community. Thus, according to reviewers such as Hicks-Coolick and colleagues (2003), in the parent educational domain, schools have a role to play in "training parents on how to advocate for the rights of their children, either for services or education" (p. 207).

Other scholars assert that schools should offer education that teaches homeless parents how they can connect to needed services (Swick, 1997, 2005, 2009). That is, they should "conduct awareness training on availability of family resources and provide parents with skills on how to use these resources" (Swick & Bailey, 2004, p. 212)—to "provide assistance in accessing available school and community resources" (Iowa Department of Education, 2004b, p. 116).

For reasons we have explored in earlier chapters (e.g., limited education, poor role models), many homeless parents do not have a well-stocked toolbox of parenting skills (Nabors et al., 2001; Nunez, 1994b). However, since such skills can help create a "buffer to many stressors that otherwise can impede learning" (Swick, 2004, p. 119), it is routinely held that education "on strategies parents can use to help their children [is] essential" (p. 119). So too is education that allows them to "develop skills for being in family leadership roles" (Swick, 2009, p. 330).

Finally, advocates for homeless children and families maintain that educators can and should do more to assist parents in deepening general skills (Markward & Biros, 2001). Here, they argue, through adult education programs, schools can help parents acquire the academic content they often failed to secure when they were younger, such as basic language and literacy skills (Nunez, 1994b; Nunez & Collignon, 1997). Education to complete high school is often highlighted in the literature as well (Nunez, 1994b).

Scholars also see a role for schools in furthering the growth of social and emotional skills of homeless parents, such as "coping skills and communication" (Rothman, 1991, p. 96). They believe that schools should promote life skills as well, such as "budgeting, health, [and] nutrition" (Stronge, 1992b, p. 244) that strengthen [parents'] capacity to function effectively on their own" (Quint, 1994, p. 93), what Nunez (1994b) labels "independent living skills" (p. 106). In particular, schools are being asked to "provide opportunities for parents to learn skills that will help mediate the stress that they and their children experience on a daily basis while they are homeless" (Bruder, 1997, p. 237) and to master skills to promote "healthy family functioning" (Swick, 1997, p. 33). Last, because "a growing majority of homeless heads-of-household lack the basic qualifications necessary for a job that provides for a family" (Nunez, 1994b, p. 96), reviewers propose that schools provide training on general job-related or job-enhancement skills (Swick, 2004), especially those that address the responsibilities of full-time employment (Nunez, 1994b).

Parent Involvement With the School

A variety of enabling supports are needed. (Swick & Bailey, 2004, p. 213)

Schools that work well for homeless children and their families are places where "parents have the opportunity to become partners in the education of their children" (Stronge & Hudson, 1999, p. 11) and where they are "meaningfully included" (Duffield et al., 2007, p. 33) in the life of the school (Crowley, 2003; Josefowicz-Simbeni & Israel, 2006), while there is what Williams and Korinek (2000) call "authentic family involvement"

(p. 197). According to Quint (1994), when homeless parents are "given the opportunity to work as equal partners with school personnel they develop a sense of being valued not only for who they are but for who they can be" (p. 124). Swick (1997) argues that in such partnerships, parents "advance their children's growth as well as their own" (p. 30). Such involvement has been linked to keeping children enrolled and attending school; that is, parent involvement is helpful in keeping children involved (Pires & Silber, 1991; Williams & Korinek, 2000).

Scholars document that involvement does not come easy to homeless parents. They consistently assert that if the goal of participation is to be realized, schools will need to be more proactive. They also identify three broad action strategies to engage homeless parents. A number of authors suggest that schools establish the role of homeless parent advocate or liaison, a person with the responsibility for seeing to it that homeless parents receive the support they need to become involved in the life of the school (Gargiulo, 2006; James & Lopez, 2003). Second, because "homeless parents often lack a context for sharing and help" (Swick, 2009, p. 328), and because "more than any other parent population homeless parents need a support group" (Kling et al., 1996, p. 5), schools, it is held, should develop support networks for these individuals. Such a network would involve them in communication and shared work with other homeless parents (Swick, 2009).

Third, advocates for the homeless suggest that to gain the benefits of involvement, schools should deepen communication with homeless parents: "A key to empowering families who are homeless is in the planning and use of supportive and nurturing communication" (Swick & Bailey, 2004, p. 211). They hold that educators should meet parents on their own ground, at shelters in particular (Landsman, 2006; Pawlas, 1994). Reviewers argue that a high-touch approach is especially important when homeless families first make contact with the school and its personnel (Popp, 2004), what Quint (1994) calls developing a "sense of welcoming" (p. 101). "Ongoing communication plans" (Swick & Bailey, 2004, p. 212) are also seen as important, especially structured follow-up sessions (Popp, 2004; Quint, 1994). So too are structured forums for homeless parents to provide feedback to school personnel (Duffield et al., 2007; Mawhinney-Rhoads & Stahler, 2006).

In addition to these three broad lines of action, analysts provide a series of more concrete suggestions for enhancing involvement of homeless parents. First on that list is the importance of providing "enabling supports like child care and transportation" (Swick, 2009, p. 328) that open the door to possible involvement (James & Lopez, 2003; Swick, 2005). Second is creating "a family friendly school culture" (Swick & Bailey, 2004, p. 211). Other reviewers suggest that providing opportunities for homeless parents to volunteer at the school is an effective way to build linkages between educators and parents of homeless children (Kling et al., 1996; Swick, 2005).

❖ CONCLUSION

In Chapter 6, we discussed ways to ensure student access to schooling. In this chapter, we explored strategies to help students be successful once they arrive at school. We examined seven broad areas of action: (1) developing awareness about homelessness and homeless children and youth, (2) attending to basic needs, (3) creating an effective instructional program, (4) developing a stable and supportive learning environment, (5) providing additional supports, (6) collaborating with other agencies and organizations, and (7) promoting parental involvement.

❖ NOTES

1. Our focus here is on what schools and districts can do to ensure the success of homeless children and youth, that is, on school manipulable factors. We do not address larger variables beyond the school. However, we would be negligent if we failed to state quite clearly that the funding that flows to the nation's schools to work on this problem is inadequate (Duffield & Lovell, 2008; Rafferty, 1995). Available funds "pale in comparison to the needs of children who are trying to attend and succeed in school" (NCFH, 2009, p. 44). Thus, on the larger front beyond the schoolhouse, "the most appropriate gap to fill . . . is funding" (Duffield & Lovell, 2008, p. 6).

2. We are addressing only homeless children (i.e., accompanied minors) here—not homeless youth (i.e., unaccompanied minors).

References

Alker, J. (1992). Ensuring access to education: The role of advocates for homeless children and youth. In J. H. Stronge (Ed.), *Educating homeless children and adolescents: Evaluating policy and practice* (pp. 179–193). Newbury Park, CA: Sage.

American Academy of Pediatrics. (2005). Providing care for immigrant, homeless, and migrant children. *Pediatrics, 115*(4), 1095–1100.

Anooshian, L. (2000). Moving to educational success: Building positive relationships for homeless children. In J. H. Stronge & E. Reed-Victor (Eds.), *Educating homeless students: Promising practices* (pp. 79–98). Larchmont, NY: Eye on Education, Inc.

Anooshian, L. (2005). Violence and aggression in the lives of homeless children: A review. *Aggression and Violent Behavior, 10*(2), 129–152.

Aron, L., & Fitchen, J. (1996). Rural homelessness: A synopsis. In J. Bauhmol (Ed.), *Homelessness in America* (pp. 81–85). Phoenix, AZ: Oryx Press.

Auerswald, C., & Eyre, S. (2002). Youth homelessness in San Francisco: A life cycle approach. *Social Science & Medicine, 54*(10), 1497–1512.

Aviles, A., & Helfrich, C. (1991). Life skill service needs. *Journal of Adolescence, 33*(4), 331–338.

Backer, T., & Howard, E. (2007). Cognitive impairments and the prevention of homelessness: Research and practice review. *Journal of Primary Prevention, 28*(3–4), 375–388.

Baggerly, J., & Borkowski, T. (2004). Applying the ASCA national model to elementary school students who are homeless: A case study. *Professional School Counseling, 8*(2), 116–123.

Bahr, H. (1973). *Skid row: An introduction to disaffiliation.* New York: Oxford University Press.

Bao, W., Whitbeck, L., & Hoyt, D. (2000). Abuse, support, and depression among homeless and runaway adolescents. *Journal of Health and Social Behavior, 41*(4), 408–420.

Baron, S. (2003). Street youth violence and victimization. *Trauma, Violence, and Abuse, 4*(1), 22–44.

Baron, S., & Hartnagel, T. F. (1998). Street youth and criminal violence. *Journal of Research in Crime and Delinquency, 35*(2), 166–192.

Baron, S., & Kennedy, L. (1998). Deterrence and homeless male street youths. *Canadian Journal of Criminology, 40*(1), 27–60.

Baron, S., Kennedy, L., & Forde, D. (2001). Male street youths' conflict: The role of background, subcultural and situational factors. *Justice Quarterly, 18*(4), 759–789.

Barry, P., Ensign, J., & Lippek, S. (2002). Embracing street culture: Fitting health care into the lives of street youth. *Journal of Transcultural Nursing, 13*(2), 145–152.

Bass, D. (1995). Runaways and homeless youths. In Richard L. Edwards (Ed.), *Encyclopedia of social work, 19th edition* (pp. 2060–2067). Washington, DC: National Association of Social Workers.

Bassuk, E. (1984). The homelessness problem. *Scientific American, 251*(1), 40–45.

Bassuk, E. (1992). Women and children without shelter: The characteristics of homeless families. In M. Robertson & M. Greenblatt (Eds.), *Homelessness: A national perspective* (pp. 257–264). New York: Plenum Press.

Bassuk, E., Rubin, L., & Lauriat, A. (1984). Is homelessness a mental health problem? *American Journal of Psychiatry, 141*(12), 1546–1549.

Bassuk, E., Rubin, L., & Lauriat, A. (1986). Characteristics of sheltered homeless families. *American Journal of Public Health, 76*(9), 1097–1101.

Bassuk, E., Weinreb, L., Buckner, J., Browne, A., Salomon, A., & Bassuk, S. (1996). The characteristics and needs of sheltered homeless and low-income mothers. *Journal of the American Medical Association, 276*(8), 640–646.

Bassuk, E., Weinreb, L., Dawson, R., Perloff, J., & Buckner, J. (1997). Determinants of behavior in homeless and low-income housed preschool children. *Pediatrics, 100*(1), 92–101.

Berliner, B. (2002). *Educating homeless students.* Retrieved from http://www .wested.org/pub/docs/431.

Better Homes Fund. (1999). *Homeless children: America's new outcasts.* Newton, MA: Author.

Biggar, H. (2001). Homeless children and education: An evaluation of the Stewart B. McKinney Homeless Assistance Act. *Children and Youth Services Review, 23*(12), 941–969.

Bishaw, A., & Renwick, T. (2009). *Poverty: 2007 and 2008 American Community Surveys.* Retrieved from the United States Census Bureau: http://www.census .gov/prod/2009pubs/acsbr08–1.pdf.

Boesky, L., Toro, P., & Bukowski, P. (1997). Differences in psychosocial factors among older and younger homeless adolescents found in shelters. In E. Smith & J. Ferrari (Eds.), *Diversity within the homeless population: Implications for intervention* (pp. 19–36). New York: Haworth Press.

Bogue, D. J. (1963). *Skid row in American cities.* Chicago: University of Chicago Press.

Booth, R., Zhang, Y., & Kwiatkowski, C. (1999). The challenge of changing drug and sex risk behaviors of runaway and homeless adolescents. *Child Abuse & Neglect, 23*(12), 1295–1306.

Bowen, J., Purrington, G., Layton, D., & O'Brien, K. (1989, March 27). *Educating children and youth: A policy analysis.* Paper presented at the annual meeting of the American Educational Research Association, San Francisco.

Bowman, D., & Barksdale, K. (2004). *Increasing school stability for students experiencing homelessness: Overcoming challenges to providing transportation to the school of origin.* Greensboro, NC: National Center for Homeless Education at SERVE.

Brennan, T., Huizinga, D., & Elliott, D. (1978). *The social psychology of runaways.* Lexington, MA: Lexington Books.

Brickner, P. (1985). Health issues in the care of the homeless. In P. Brickner, L. Scharer, B. Conanan, A. Elvy, & M. Savarese (Eds.), *Health care of homeless people* (pp. 3–18). New York: Springer.

Bruder, M. (1997). Children who are homeless: A growing challenge for early care and education. *Advances in Early Education and Daycare, 9,* 223–246.

Bruns, R. A. (1980). *Knights of the road: A hobo history.* New York: Methuen.

Bryk, A. S., Sebring, P. B., Allensworth, E., Luppescu, S., & Easton, J. Q. (2010). *Organizing schools for improvement: Lessons from Chicago.* Chicago: University of Chicago Press.

Burt, M. (2001). *What will it take to end homelessness?* Retrieved from http://www .urban.org/UploadedPDF/end_homelessness.pdf.

Burt, M. (2007, June 19). *Understanding homeless youth: Numbers, characteristics, multisystem involvement, and intervention options.* Testimony submitted before the U.S. House Committee on Ways and Means Subcommittee on Income Security and Family Support, Washington, DC.

Burt, M., Aron, L., Lee, E., & Valente, J. (2001). *Helping America's homeless: Emergency shelter or affordable housing?* Washington, DC: The Urban Institute.

Burt, M., Hedderson, J., Zweig, J., Ortiz, M., Aron-Turnham, L., & Johnson, S. (2004). *Strategies for reducing chronic homelessness: Final report prepared for US Department of Housing and Urban Development, Office of Policy Development and Research.* Washington, DC: The Urban Institute, and Sacramento, CA: Walter R. McDonald & Associates, Inc.

Carliner, M. (1987). Homelessness: A housing problem? In R. Bingham, R. Green, & S. White (Eds.), *The homeless in contemporary society* (pp. 119–128). Newbury Park, CA: Sage.

Caton, C. (1986). *The homeless experience in adolescent years.* DOI: 10.1002/yd.23319863008

Cauce, A., Paradise, M., Ginzler, J., Embry, L., Morgan, C., Lohr, Y., & Theofelis, J. (2000). The characteristics and mental health of homeless adolescents: Age and gender differences. *Journal of Emotional and Behavioral Disorders, 8*(4), 230–239.

Center for Law and Social Policy. (2002). *The minor parent living arrangement provision.* Washington, DC: Author.

Cochran, B., Stewart, A., Ginzler, J., & Cauce, M. (2002). Challenges faced by homeless sexual minorities: Comparison of gay, lesbian, bisexual, and transgender homeless adolescents with their heterosexual counterparts. *American Journal of Public Health, 92*(5), 773–777.

Crowley, S. (2003). The affordable housing crisis: Residential mobility of poor families and school mobility of poor children. *Journal of Negro Education, 72*(1), 22–38.

Cunningham, C. (2003). *Trends and issues: Social and economic context.* Washington, DC: Office of Educational Research and Improvement.

Daniels, J. (1992). Empowering homeless children through school counseling. *Elementary School Guidance and Counseling, 27*(2), 104–112.

Daniels, J. (1995). Homeless students: Recommendations to school counselors based on semistructured interviews. *The School Counselor, 42*(5), 346–352.

Daniels, J., D'Andrea, M., Omizo, M., & Pier, P. (1999). Group work with homeless youngsters and their mothers. *Journal for Specialists in Group Work, 24*(2), 164–185.

D'Ercole, A., & Struening, E. (1990). Victimization among homeless women: Implications for service delivery. *Journal of Community Psychology, 18*(2), 141–152.

Dolbeare, C. (1996). Housing policy: A general consideration. In J. Baumohl (Ed.), *Homelessness in America* (pp. 34–45). Phoenix, AZ: Oryx Press.

Douglass, A. (1996). Rethinking the effects of homelessness on children: Resiliency and competency. *Child Welfare, 75*(6), 741–751.

Duffield, B. (2000). Advocating for homeless students. In J. H. Stronge & E. Reed-Victor (Eds.), *Educating homeless students: Promising practices* (pp. 203–224). Larchmont, NY: Eye on Education, Inc.

Duffield, B., Heybach, L., & Julianelle, P. (2007). *Educating children without housing: A primer on legal requirements and implementation strategies for educators, advocates and policymakers.* Washington, DC: American Bar Association Commission on Homelessness and Poverty.

Duffield, B., & Lovell, P. (2008). *The economic crisis hits home: The unfolding increase in child and youth homelessness.* Washington, DC: National Association for the Education of Homeless Children and Youth.

Dworsky, A. (2008). *Educating homeless children in Chicago: A case study of children in the family regeneration program.* Chicago: Chapin Hall at the University of Chicago.

Eddowes, E. A. (1992). Children and homelessness: Early childhood and elementary education. In J. H. Stronge (Ed.), *Educating homeless children and adolescents: Evaluating policy and practice* (pp. 99–114). Newbury Park, CA: Sage.

Eddowes, E. A., & Butcher, T. (2000). Meeting the developmental and educational needs of homeless infants and young children. In J. H. Stronge & E. Reed-Victor (Eds.), *Educating homeless students: Promising practices* (pp. 21–43). Larchmont, NY: Eye on Education, Inc.

Eddowes, E., & Hranitz, J. (1989). Educating children of the homeless. *Childhood Education, 65*(4), 197–200.

Edna McConnell Clark Foundation. (1990). *Families on the move: Breaking the cycle of homelessness.* New York: Author.

Egan, J. (2002, March 24). *To be young and homeless.* Retrieved from http://www.nytimes.com/2002/03/24/magazine/to-be-young-and-homeless.html.

Ely, L. (1987). *Broken lives: Denial of education to homeless children.* Washington, DC: National Coalition for the Homeless.

Emerson, J., & Lovitt, T. (2003). The educational plight of foster children in schools and what can be done about it. *Remedial and Special Education, 24*(4), 199–203.

Ennett, S., Bailey, S., & Federman, E. (1999). Social network characteristics associated with risky behaviors among runaway and homeless youth. *Journal of Health and Social Behavior, 40*(1), 63–78.

Ensign, J., & Bell, M. (2004). Illness experiences of homeless youth. *Qualitative Health Research, 14*(9), 1239–1254.

Farrow, J., Deisher, R., Brown, R., Kulig, J., & Kipke, M. (1992). Health and health needs of homeless and runaway youth. *Journal of Adolescent Health, 13*(8), 717–726.

Feitel, B., Margetson, N., Chamas, J., & Lipman, C. (1992). Psychosocial background and behavioral and emotional disorders of homeless and runaway youth. *Hospital and Community Psychiatry, 43*(2), 155–159.

Ferguson, K., & Xie, B. (2008). Feasibility study of the social enterprise intervention with homeless youth. *Research on Social Work Practice, 18*(1), 5–19.

Finley, S. (2003). The faces of dignity: Rethinking the politics of homelessness and poverty in America. *International Journal of Qualitative Studies in Education, 16*(4), 509–531.

First, P. (1992). The reality: The status of education for homeless children and youth. In J. H. Stronge (Ed.), *Educating homeless children and adolescents: Evaluating policy and practice* (pp. 79–96). Newbury Park, CA: Sage.

Fischer, P. (1992). The criminalization of homelessness. In M. Robertson & M. Greenblatt (Eds.), *Homelessness: A national perspective* (pp. 57–64). New York: Plenum Press.

Flaming, D., & Tepper, P. (2006). *Ten-Year strategy to end homelessness: Comprehensive strategy with 25 actions, accountable agencies, timelines, and performance benchmarks to prevent and end homelessness in Los Angeles County.* Underwritten by the Los Angeles Homeless Services Authority. Retrieved from http://economicrt.org/download/form.html.

Fleisher, M. (1995). *Beggars and thieves: Lives of urban street criminals.* Madison: University of Wisconsin Press.

Flynn, K. (1985). The toll of deinstitutionalization. In P. Brickner, L. Scharer, B. Conanan, A. Elvy, & M. Savarese (Eds.), *Health care of homeless people* (pp. 189–203). New York: Springer.

Foscarinis, M. (1996). The federal response: The Stewart B. McKinney Homeless Assistance Act. In J. Baumohl (Ed.), *Homelessness in America* (pp. 160–171). Phoenix, AZ: Oryx Press.

Fox, A., & Duerr Berrick, J. (2007). A response to No One Ever Asked Us: A review of children's experiences in out-of-home care. *Child and Adolescent Social Work Journal, 24*(1), 23–51.

Fraenkel, P., Hameline, T., & Shannon, M. (2009). Narrative and collaborative practices in work with families that are homeless. *Journal of Marital and Family Therapy, 35*(3), 325–342.

Funkhouser, J., Riley, D., Suh, H. J., & Lennon, J. (2002). *The education for homeless children and youth program: Learning to succeed, Volume II: Educating homeless children and youth: A resource guide to promoting practices.* Washington, DC: United States Department of Education.

Gargiulo, R. M. (2006). Homeless and disabled: Rights, responsibilities, and recommendations for serving young children with special needs. *Early Childhood Education Journal, 33*(5), 357–362.

Gewirtzman, R., & Fodor, I. (1987). The homeless child at school: From welfare hotel to classroom. *Child Welfare, 66*(3), 237–245.

Gibbs, H. (2004). Educating homeless children. *Techniques, 79*(2), 25–29.

Glasser, I. (1994). *Homelessness in global perspective.* New York: G. K. Hall.

Gonzalez, M. L. (1992). Educational climate for the homeless: Cultivating the family and school relationship. In J. H. Stronge (Ed.), *Educating homeless children and adolescents: Evaluating policy and practice* (pp. 194–211). Newbury Park, CA: Sage.

Goodman, L. (1991). The prevalence of abuse among homeless and housed poor mothers: A comparison study. *American Journal of Orthopsychiatry, 61*(4), 489–500.

Gore, A. (1990). Public policy and the homeless. *American Psychologist, 45*(8), 960–962.

Greenberg, M., & Baumohl, J. (1996). Income maintenance: Little help now, less on the way. In J. Baumohl (Ed.), *Homelessness in America* (pp. 63–77). Phoenix, AZ: Oryx Press.

Greenblatt, M. (1992). Deinstitutionalization and reinstitutionalization of the mentally ill. In M. Robertson & M. Greenblatt (Eds.), *Homelessness: A national perspective* (pp. 47–56). New York: Plenum Press.

Greene, J., Ennett, S., & Ringwalt, C. (1999). Prevalance and correlates of survival sex among runaway and homeless youth. *American Journal of Public Health, 89*(9), 1406–1409.

Greene, J., Ringwalt, C., & Iachan, R. (1997). Shelters for runaway and homeless youth: Capacity and occupancy. *Child Welfare, 76*(4), 549–561.

Gwadz, M., Gostnell, K., Smolenski, C., Willis, B., Nish, D., Nolan, T., Tharaken, M., & Ritchie, A. (2009). The initiation of homeless youth into the street economy. *Journal of Adolescence, 32*(2), 357–377.

Hagan, J., & McCarthy, B. (1997). *Mean streets: Youth crime and homelessness.* New York: Cambridge University Press.

Hallett, R. (2007, Fall). Education and homeless youth: Policy implementations. *The Navigator: Directions and Trends in Higher Education Policy, 7*(1), 1–7.

Hammer, H., Finkelhor, D., & Sedlak, A. (2002). *Runaway/thrownaway children: National estimates and characteristics* (NISMART report). Washington, DC: U.S. Department of Justice, Office of Justice Programs, Office of Juvenile Justice and Delinquency Prevention.

Hardin, B. (1996). Why the road off the street is not paved with jobs. In J. Baumohl (Ed.), *Homelessness in America* (pp. 46–62). Phoenix, AZ: Oryx Press.

Harris, D. N., & Herrington, C. D. (2006). Accountability, standards, and the growing achievement gap: Lessons from the past half-century. *American Journal of Education, 112*(2), 209–238.

Hartman, C. (1986). *The housing part of the homelessness problem.* DOI: 10.1002/yd.23319863009

Hart-Shegos & Associates, Inc. (1999, December). *Homelessness and its effects on children.* Retrieved from http://www.fhfund.org/_dnld/reports/Supportive Children.pdf.

Hausman, B., & Hammen, C. (1993). Parenting in homeless families: The double crisis. *American Journal of Orthopsychiatry, 63*(3), 358–369.

Heflin, L. J. (1991). *Developing effective programs for special education students who are homeless* (Report No. EDO–EC–91–9). Reston, VA: Council for Exceptional Children. (ERIC Document Reproduction Service No. ED 340 148)

Helge, D. (1992). Educating the homeless in rural and small school district settings. In J. H. Stronge (Ed.), *Educating homeless children and adolescents: Evaluating policy and practice* (pp. 212–231). Newbury Park, CA: Sage.

Helm, V. (1992). The legal context: From access to success in education for homeless children and youth. In J. H. Stronge (Ed.), *Educating homeless children and adolescents: Evaluating policy and practice* (pp. 26–41). Newbury Park, CA: Sage.

Herrington, D., Kidd-Herrington, K., & Kritsonis, M. A. (2006). Coming to terms with No Child Left Behind: Learning to teach the invisible children. *National Forum of Special Education Journal, 18*(1), 1–7.

Hersch, P. (1988). Coming of age on city streets. *Psychology Today, 22*(1), 28–37.

Hicks-Coolick, A., Burnside-Eaton, P., & Peters, A. (2003). Homeless children: Needs and services. *Child & Youth Care Forum, 32*(4), 197–210.

Hightower, A., Nathanson, S., & Wimberly, G. (1997). *Meeting the educational needs of homeless children and youth: A resource for schools and communities.* Washington, DC: U.S. Department of Education.

Hoch, C. (1987). A brief history of the homeless problem in the United States. In R. Bingham, R. Green, & S. White (Eds.), *The homeless in contemporary society* (pp. 16–32). Newbury Park, CA: Sage.

Hombs, M. E. (2001). *American homelessness.* Santa Barbara, CA: ABC-CLIO.

Hombs, M. E., & Snyder, M. (1982). *Homelessness in America: A forced march to nowhere.* Washington, DC: Community for Creative Non-Violence.

Hope, M., & Young, J. (1986). *Faces of homelessness.* Lanham, MD: Rowman & Littlefield Publishers

Hopper, K. (2003). *Reckoning with homelessness.* Ithaca, NY: Cornell University Press.

Hopper, K., & Baumohl, J. (1996). Redefining the cursed word: A historical interpretation of American homelessness. In J. Baumohl (Ed.), *Homelessness in America* (pp. 3–14). Phoenix, AZ: Oryx Press.

Hopper, K., & Hamberg, J. (1984). *The making of America's homeless: From skid row to new poor.* New York: Community Service Society of New York.

Hopper, K., & Milburn, N. (1996). Homelessness among African Americans: A historical and contemporary perspective. In J. Baumohl (Ed.), *Homelessness in America* (pp. 123–131). Phoenix, AZ: Oryx Press.

Hyde, J. (2005). From home to street: Understanding young people's transitions into homelessness. *Journal of Adolescence, 28*(2), 171–183.

Institute for Children and Poverty. (2003). *Children having children: Teen pregnancy and homelessness in New York City.* New York: Author.

Institute for Children and Poverty. (2005). *Miles to go: The flip side of the McKinney-Vento Homeless Assistance Act.* New York: Author.

Iowa Department of Education. (2004a). *Educating the homeless* (Appendix A, Ch. 33 IA Administrative Code). Des Moines, IA: Author.

Iowa Department of Education. (2004b). *Homelessness local program planning and review guides services for homeless children and youth.* Des Moines, IA: Author.

Jackson, K. (2000). *Family homelessness: More than simply a lack of housing.* New York: Garland Press.

Jackson, T. L. (2004, January). *Homelessness and students with disabilities: Educational rights and challenges.* Alexandria, VA: Project Forum (National Association of State Directors of Special Education).

Jacobs, A. (2004, June 27). *For young gays on the streets, survival comes before pride.* Retrieved from http://query.nytimes.com/gst/fullpage.html?res=9D02EFDB1738F934A15755C0A9629C8B63&pagewanted=1.

Jahiel, R. (1987). The situation of homelessness. In R. Bingham, R. Green, & S. White (Eds.), *The homeless in contemporary society* (pp. 99–118). Newbury Park, CA: Sage.

Jahiel, R. (1992a). Health and health care of homeless people. In M. Robertson & M. Greenblatt (Eds.), *Homelessness: A national perspective* (pp. 133–163). New York: Plenum Press.

Jahiel, R. (1992b). Homeless-making processes and the homeless-makers. In R. Jahiel (Ed.), *Homelessness: A prevention-oriented approach* (pp. 269–296). Baltimore: Johns Hopkins University Press.

Jahiel, R. (1992c). Preventative approaches to homelessness. In R. Jahiel (Ed.), *Homelessness: A prevention-oriented approach* (pp. 11–24). Baltimore: Johns Hopkins University Press.

Jahiel, R. (1992d). The definition and significance of homelessness in the United States. In R. Jahiel (Ed.), *Homelessness: A prevention-oriented approach* (pp. 1–10). Baltimore: Johns Hopkins University Press.

James, B., & Lopez, P. (2003). Transporting homeless students to increase stability: A case study of two Texas districts. *Journal of Negro Education, 72*(1), 126–140.

James, E. A. (2005). Prospects for the future: The use of participatory action research to study educational disadvantage. *Irish Educational Studies, 24*(2–3), 199–206.

James, W., Smith, A., & Mann, R. (1991). Educating homeless children. *Childhood Education, 67*(5), 305–308.

Janus, M., McCormack, A., Burgess, A., & Hartman, C. (1987). *Adolescent runaways: Causes and consequences.* Lexington, MA: Lexington Books.

Jencks, C. (1994). *The homeless.* Cambridge, MA: Harvard University Press.

Johnson, A. (1988). *Homelessness in America: A historical and contemporary assessment.* St. Louis, MO: Washington University.

Johnson, J., Jr. (1992). Educational support services for homeless children and youth. In J. H. Stronge (Ed.), *Educating homeless children and adolescents: Evaluating policy and practice* (pp. 153–176). Newbury Park, CA: Sage.

Jozefowicz-Simbeni, D. M. H., & Israel, N. (2006). Services to homeless students and families: The McKinney-Vento Act and its implications for school social work practice. *Children & Schools, 28*(1), 37–44.

Julianelle, P. F. (2007). *The educational successes of homeless youth in California: Challenges and solutions* (California Research Bureau Report). Retrieved from http://www.library.ca.gov/crb/07/07–012.pdf.

Karabanow, J. (2004). *Being young and homeless: Understanding how youth enter and exit street life.* New York: Peter Lang.

Kelly, J., Buehlman, K., & Caldwell, K. (2000). Training personnel to promote quality parent–child interaction in families who are homeless. *Topics in Early Childhood Special Education, 20*(3), 174–185.

Khanna, M., Singh, N. M., Nemil, M., Best, A., & Ellis, C. R. (1992). Homeless women and their families: Characteristics, life circumstances, and needs. *Journal of Child and Family Studies, 1*(2), 155–165.

Kidd, S., & Scrimenti, K. (2004). Evaluating child and youth homelessness. *Evaluation Review, 28*(4), 325–341.

Kiesler, C. (1991). Homelessness and public policy priorities. *American Psychologist, 46*(11), 1245–1252.

King, K., Ross, L., Bruno, T., & Erickson, P. (2009). Identity work among street-involved youth mothers. *Journal of Youth Studies, 12*(2), 139–149.

Kipke, M., Palmer, R., La France, S., & O'Connor, S. (1997). Homeless youths' descriptions of their parents' child-rearing practices. *Youth & Society, 28*(4), 415–431.

Klein, J., Woods, A., Wilson, K., Prospero, M., Greene, J., & Ringwalt, C. (2000). Homeless and runaway youths' access to health care. *Journal of Adolescent Health, 27*(5), 331–339.

Kling, N., Dunn, L., & Oakley, J. (1996). Homeless families in early childhood programs: What to expect and what to do. *Dimensions of Early Childhood, 24*(1), 3–8.

Koegel, P., Burnam, M. A., & Baumohl, J. (1996). The causes of homelessness. In J. Baumohl (Ed.), *Homelessness in America* (pp. 24–33). Phoenix, AZ: Oryx Press.

Korinek, L., Walther-Thomas, C., & Laycock, V. (1992). Educating special needs homeless children and youth. In J. H. Stronge (Ed.), *Educating homeless children and adolescents: Evaluating policy and practice* (pp. 133–152). Newbury Park, CA: Sage.

Kozol, J. (1988). *Rachel and her children.* New York: Three Rivers Press.

Kruks, G. (1991). Gay and lesbian homeless/street youth: Special issues and concerns. *Journal of Adolescent Health, 12*(7), 515–518.

Kurtz, P., Kurtz, G., & Jarvis, S. (1991). Problems of maltreated and runaway youth. *Adolescence, 26*(103), 543–555.

Kurtz, P., Lindsey, E., Jarvis, S., & Nackerud, L. (2000). How runaway and homeless youth navigate troubled waters: The role of formal and informal helpers. *Child and Adolescent Social Work Journal, 17*(5), 381–402.

Kusmer, K. (2002). *Down and out, on the road: The homeless in American history.* New York: Oxford University Press.

Landsman, J. (2006). Bearers of hope. *Educational Leadership, 63*(5), 26–32.

LaVesser, P., Smith, E. M., & Bradford, S. (1997). Characteristics of homeless women with dependent children: A controlled study. In E. Smith & J. Ferrari (Eds.), *Diversity within the homeless population: Implications for intervention* (pp. 37–52). New York: Haworth Press.

Leavitt, J. (1992). Homelessness and the housing crisis. In M. Robertson & M. Greenblatt (Eds.), *Homelessness: A national perspective* (pp. 19–34). New York: Plenum Press.

Levin, R., Bax, E., McKean, L., & Schoggen, L. (2005). *Wherever I can lay my head: Homeless youth on homelessness.* Chicago: Center for Impact Research.

Levine, R., Metzendorf, D., & VanBoskirk, K. (1986). Runaway and throwaway youth: A case for early intervention with truants. *Social Work in Education, 8*(2), 93–106.

Levinson, B. M. (1963). The homeless man: A psychological enigma. *Mental Hygiene, 47*(4), 590–599.

Lindblom, E. (1996). Preventing homelessness. In J. Baumohl (Ed.), *Homelessness in America* (pp. 187–200). Phoenix, AZ: Oryx Press.

Lindsey, E., & Williams, N. (2002). How runaway and homeless youth survive adversity: Implications for school social workers and educators. *School Social Work Journal, 27*(1), 1–22.

Lindsey, E. W., Kurtz, P. D., Jarvis, S., Williams, N. R., & Nackerud, L. (2000). How runaway and homeless youth navigate troubled waters: Personal strengths and resources. *Child and Adolescent Social Work Journal, 17*(2), 115–140.

Link, B., Phelan, J., Bresnahan, M., Stueve, A., Moore, R., & Susser, E. (1995). Lifetime and five-year prevalence of homelessness in the United States: New evidence on an old debate. *American Journal of Orthopsychiatry, 65*(3), 347–354.

Link, B., Phelan, J., Stueve, A., Moore, R., Bresnahan, M., & Struening, E. (1996). Public attitudes and beliefs about homeless people. In J. Baumohl (Ed.), *Homelessness in America* (pp. 143–148). Phoenix, AZ: Oryx Press.

Lumsden, L., & Coffey, E. (2001). *Social and economic context: Trends and issues.* Washington, DC: Office of Educational Research and Improvement.

MacLean, M., Embry, L., & Cauce, A. (1999). Homeless adolescents' paths to separation from family: Comparison of family characteristics, psychological adjustment, and victimization. *Journal of Community Psychology, 27*(2), 179–187.

Mallett, S., Rosenthal, D., Myers, P., Milburn, N., & Rotheram-Borus, M. (2004). Practising homelessness: A typology approach to young people's daily routines. *Journal of Adolescence, 27*(3), 337–349.

Markward, M., & Biros, E. (2001). McKinney revisited: Implications for school social work. *Children and Schools, 23*(3), 182–187.

Masten, A. (1992). Homeless children in the United States: Mark of a nation at risk. *Current Directions in Psychological Science: A Journal of the American Psychological Society, 1*(2), 41–44.

Masten, A., Sesma, A., Si-Asar, R., Lawrence, C., Miliotis, D., & Dionne, J. A. (1997). Educational risks for students experiencing homelessness. *Journal of School Psychology, 35*(1), 27–46.

Mawhinney-Rhoads, L., & Stahler, G. (2006). Educational policy and reform for homeless students: An overview. *Education and Urban Society, 38*(3), 288–306.

McCaskill, P., Toro, P., & Wolfe, S. (1998). Homeless and matched housed adolescents: A comparative study of psychopathology. *Journal of Clinical Child & Adolescent Psychology, 27*(3), 306–319.

McChesney, K. (1990). Family homelessness: A systemic problem. *Journal of Social Issues, 46*(4), 191–205.

McChesney, K. (1992). Homeless families: Four patterns of poverty. In M. Robertson & M. Greenblatt (Eds.), *Homelessness: A national perspective* (pp. 245–256). New York: Plenum Press.

Medcalf, N. (2008). *Kidwatching in Josie's world.* Lanham, MD: University Press of America.

Menke, E. M. (2000). Comparison of the stressors and coping behavior of homeless, previously homeless, and never homeless children. *Issues in Mental Health Nursing, 21*(7), 691–710.

Menke, E. M., & Wagner, J. D. (1997). A comparative study of homeless, previously homeless, and never homeless school-aged children's health. *Issues in Comprehensive Pediatric Nursing, 20*(3), 153–173.

Merves, E. (1992). Homeless women: Beyond the bag lady myth. In M. Robertson & M. Greenblatt (Eds.), *Homelessness: A national perspective* (pp. 229–244). New York: Plenum Press.

Mihaly, L. K. (1991, January). *Homeless families: Failed policies and young victims.* Washington, DC: Children's Defense Fund.

Milburn, N., Liang, L., Lee, S., Rotheram-Borus, M., Rosenthal, D., Mallett, S., Lightfoot, M., & Lester, P. (2009). Who is doing well? A typology of newly homeless adolescents. *Journal of Community Psychology, 37*(2), 135–147.

Miller, R. (1982). *The demolition of skid row.* Lexington, MA: D.C. Heath and Company.

Molnar, J., Rath, W., & Klein, T. (1990). Constantly compromised: The impact of homelessness on children. *Journal of Social Issues, 46*(4), 109–124.

Moore, J. (2005a). *Collaborations of schools and social service agencies.* Greensboro, NC: National Center for Homeless Education at SERVE.

Moore, J. (2005b). *Unaccompanied and homeless youth: Review of literature (1995–2005).* Greensboro, NC: National Center for Homeless Education at SERVE.

Moore, J. (2007). *A look at child welfare from a homeless education perspective.* Greensboro, NC: National Center for Homeless Education at SERVE.

Morse, G. (1992). Causes of homelessness. In M. Robertson & M. Greenblatt (Eds.), *Homelessness: A national perspective* (pp. 3–17). New York: Plenum Press.

Murphy, J. (2010). *The educators' handbook for understanding and closing achievement gaps.* Thousand Oaks, CA: Corwin.

Myers, M., & Popp, P. (2003). *Unlocking potential! What educators need to know about homelessness and special education.* Retrieved from http://education.wm.edu/centers/hope/publications/infobriefs/documents/personnel_complete.pdf.

Nabors, L., Proescher, E., & DeSilva, M. (2001). School based mental health prevention activities for homeless and at-risk youth. *Child & Youth Care Forum, 30*(1), 3–18.

National Alliance to End Homelessness. (2003). *Getting housed, staying housed: A collaborative plan to end homelessness.* Retrieved from http://www.endhomelessness.org/content/article/detail/1131.

National Alliance to End Homelessness. (2006). *Fundamental issues to prevent and end youth homelessness.* Retrieved from http://www.endhomelessness.org/files/1058_file_youth_brief_one.pdf.

National Alliance to End Homelessness. (2007). *Fact checker: Family homelessness.* Retrieved from http://www.endhomelessness.org/content/article/detail/1525.

National Alliance to End Homelessness. (2009). *Summary of the HEARTH Act.* Retrieved from http://www.endhomelessness.org/files/2098_file_HEARTH_Act_Summary_FINAL_6_8_09.pdf.

National Center for Homeless Education. (2006a). *Housing agency and school district collaborations to serve homeless and highly mobile students.* Greensboro, NC: National Center for Homeless Education at SERVE.

National Center for Homeless Education. (2006b). *Prompt and proper placement: Enrolling students without records.* Greensboro, NC: National Center for Homeless Education at SERVE.

National Center for Homeless Education. (2006c). Title I and homelessness. Greensboro, NC: National Center for Homeless Education at SERVE.

National Center on Family Homelessness. (2008). *The characteristics and needs of families experiencing homelessness.* Retrieved from http://community.family homelessness.org/sites/default/files/NCFH%20Fact%20Sheet%204-08_0.pdf.

National Center on Family Homelessness. (2009). *America's youngest outcasts: State report card on child homelessness.* Newton, MA: Author.

National Coalition for the Homeless. (2008). *Homeless youth, NCH Fact Sheet #13.* Washington, DC: Author.

National Law Center on Homelessness and Poverty. (1990). *Shut out: Denial of education to homeless children.* Washington, DC: Author.

National Law Center on Homelessness and Poverty. (1995). *A foot in the schoolhouse door: Progress and barriers to the education of homeless children.* Washington, DC: Author.

National Law Center on Homelessness and Poverty. (2004a). *Homelessness in the United States and the human right to housing.* Washington, DC: Author.

National Law Center on Homelessness and Poverty. (2004b). *Key data concerning homeless persons in America.* Washington, DC: Author.

National League of Cities. (2004). *The state of America's cities: The Annual Opinion Survey of Municipal Officials.* Washington, DC: Author.

Neiman, L. (1988). A critical review of resiliency literature and its relevance to homeless children. *Children's Environments Quarterly, 5*(1), 1–25.

Newman, R., & Beck, L. (1996). Educating homeless children: One experiment in collaboration. In J. Cibulka & W. Kritek (Eds.), *Coordination among schools, families, and communities: Prospects for educational reform* (pp. 95–133). Albany: SUNY Press.

Nichols, L., & Gault, B. (2003). The implications of welfare reform for housing and school instability. *Journal of Negro Education, 72*(1), 104–116.

Noell, J., Rhode, P., Seeley, J., & Ochs, L. (2001). Childhood sexual abuse, adolescent sexual coercion and sexually transmitted infection acquisition among homeless female adolescents. *Child Abuse & Neglect, 25*(1), 137–148.

Nunez, R. da Costa. (1994a). Access to success: Meeting the educational needs of homeless children and families. *Social Work in Education, 16*(1), 21–30.

Nunez, R. da Costa. (1994b). *Hopes, dreams, and promise.* New York: Institute for Children and Poverty.

Nunez, R. da Costa, & Collignon, K. (1997). Creating a community of learning for homeless children. *Educational Leadership, 55*(2), 56–60.

Nunez, R. da Costa, & Collignon, K. (2000). Supporting family learning: Building a community of learners. In J. H. Stronge & E. Reed-Victor (Eds.), *Educating homeless students: Promising practices* (pp. 115–133). Larchmont, NY: Eye on Education, Inc.

Oakley, D., & Dennis, D. (1996). Responding to the needs of homeless people with alcohol, drug, and/or mental disorders. In J. Baumohl (Ed.), *Homelessness in America* (pp. 179–186). Phoenix, AZ: Oryx Press.

Pardeck, J. T. (2005). An exploration of child maltreatment among homeless families: Implications for family policy. *Early Childhood Development and Care, 175*(4), 335–342.

Park, J., Metraux, S., Broadbar, G., & Culhane, D. (2004). Child welfare involvement among children in homeless families. *Child Welfare, 83*(5), 423–436.

Parrish, T., Graczewski, C., Stewart-Teitlebaum, A., Van Dyke, N., Bolus, S., & Delano, C. (2003). *Policies, procedures, and practices affecting the education of children residing in group homes* (Report to the California Department of Education). Washington, DC: American Institutes for Research.

Pawlas, G. (1994). Homeless students at the school door. *Educational Leadership, 51*(8), 79–82.

Pearce, K. D. (1995). Street kids need us too: Special characteristics of homeless youth. *Parks & Recreation, 30*(12), 16–19.

Pears, J., & Noller, P. (1995). Youth homelessness: Abuse, gender, and life on the streets. *The Australian Journal of Social Issues, 30*(4), 405–424.

Pennbridge, J., Yates, G., David, T., & Mackenzie, R. (1990). Runaway and homeless youth in Los Angeles County, CA. *Journal of Adolescent Health Care, 11*(2), 159–165.

Penuel, W., & Davey, T. (1998, April 13–17). *Meta-analysis of McKinney programs in Tennessee.* Paper presented at the annual meeting of the American Educational Research Association, San Diego, CA.

Penuel, W., & Davey, T. (2000). Meeting the educational needs of homeless youth. In J. H. Stronge & E. Reed-Victor (Eds.), *Educating homeless students: Promising practices* (pp. 63–78). Larchmont, NY: Eye on Education, Inc.

Peroff, K. (1987). Who are the homeless and how many are there? In R. D. Bingham, R. E. Green, & S. B. White (Eds.), *The homeless in contemporary society* (pp. 33–45). Newbury Park, CA: Sage.

Pires, S., & Silber, J. T. (1991). *On their own: Runaway and homeless youth and programs that serve them.* Washington, DC: Children and Youth at Risk Project, CASSP Technical Assistance Center, Georgetown University Child Development Center.

Polakow, V. (2003). Homeless children and their families: The discards of the post-welfare era. In S. Books (Ed.), *Invisible children in the society and its schools* (pp. 89–110). Mahwah, NJ: Lawrence Erlbaum.

Popp, P. A. (2004). *Reading on the go! Students who are highly mobile and reading instruction.* Greensboro, NC: National Center for Homeless Education at SERVE.

Powers, J., & Jaklitsch, B. (1992). Adolescence and homelessness: The unique challenge for secondary educators. In J. H. Stronge (Ed.), *Educating homeless children and adolescents: Evaluating policy and practice* (pp. 115–132). Newbury Park, CA: Sage.

Powers, J., & Jaklitsch, B. (1993). Reaching the hard to reach: Educating homeless adolescents in urban settings. *Education and Urban Society, 24*(4), 394–409.

Quint, S. (1994). *Schooling homeless children: A working model for America's public schools.* New York: Teachers College Press.

Rabideau, J., & Toro, P. (1997). Social and environmental predictors of adjustment in homeless children. In E. Smith & J. Ferrari (Eds.), *Diversity within the homeless population: Implications for intervention* (pp. 1–17). New York: Haworth Press.

Rafferty, Y. (1991). *And miles to go: Barriers to academic achievement and innovative strategies for the delivery of educational services to homeless children.* Long Island City, NY: Advocates for Children of New York, Inc.

Rafferty, Y. (1995). The legal rights and educational problems of homeless children and youth. *Educational Evaluation and Policy Analysis, 17*(1), 39–61.

Rafferty, Y. (1997). Meeting the educational needs of homeless children. *Educational Leadership, 55*(4), 48–52.

Rafferty, Y., & Shinn, M. (1991). The impact of homelessness on children. *American Psychologist, 46*(11), 1170–1179.

Raleigh-DuRoff, C. (2004). Factors that influence homeless adolescents to leave or stay living on the street. *Child and Adolescent Social Work Journal, 21*(6), 561–572.

Reed-Victor, E. (2000). Resilience and homeless students: Supportive adult roles. In J. H. Stronge & E. Reed-Victor (Eds.), *Educating homeless students: Promising practices* (pp. 99–114). Larchmont, NY: Eye on Education, Inc.

Reed-Victor, E., Popp, P., & Myers, M. (2003). *Using the best that we know: Supporting young children experiencing homelessness.* Richmond: Project HOPE–Virginia, Virginia Department of Education.

Reeg, B., Grisham, C., & Shepard, A. (2002). *Families on the edge: Homeless young parents and their welfare experiences.* Washington, DC: Center for Law and Social Policy.

Reganick, K. A. (1997). Prognosis for homeless children and adolescents. *Childhood Education, 73*, 133–135.

Rescorla, L., Parker, R., & Stolley, P. (1991). Ability, achievement, and adjustment in homeless children. *American Journal of Orthopsychiatry, 61*(2), 210–220.

Rew, L. (1996). Health risks of homeless adolescents. *Journal of Holistic Nursing, 14*(4), 348–359.

Rew, L., Taylor-Seehafer, M., Thomas, N., & Yockey, R. (2001). Correlates of resilience in homeless adolescents. *Journal of Nursing Scholarship, 33*(1), 33–40.

Ringwalt, C., Greene, J., & Robertson, M. (1998). Familial backgrounds and risk behaviors of youth with throwaway experiences. *Journal of Adolescence, 21*(3), 241–252.

Ringwalt, C. L., Greene, J. M., Robertson, M., & McPheeters, M. (1998). The prevalence of homelessness among adolescents in the United States. *American Journal of Public Health, 88*(9), 1325–1329.

Ritter, S. H., & Gottfried, S. (2002). *Tomorrow's child: Benefiting from today's family-school-community-business partnerships.* Tallahassee, FL: Southeastern Regional Vision for Education (SERVE).

Robertson, J. (1992). Homeless and runaway youths: A review of the literature. In M. Robertson & M. Greenblatt (Eds.), *Homelessness: A national perspective* (pp. 287–297). New York: Plenum Press.

Robertson, M., & Greenblatt, M. (1992). *Homelessness: A national perspective.* New York: Plenum Press.

Robertson, M. J. (1990). Homeless youth: An overview of recent literature. In J. Kryder-Coe, L. Salamon, & J. Molnar (Eds.), *Homeless children and youth: A new American dilemma* (pp. 33–68). New Brunswick, NJ: Transaction Publishing.

Rog, D., Holupka, C., & McCombs-Thornton, K. (1995). Implementation of the homeless families program: 1. Service models and preliminary outcomes. *American Journal of Orthopsychiatry, 65*(4), 502–513.

Rog, D., Holupka, C. S., McCombs-Thornton, K., Brito, M. C., & Hambrick, R. (1997). Case management in practice: Lessons from the evaluation of the RWJ/HUD homeless families program. In E. Smith & J. Ferrari (Eds.), *Diversity within the homeless population: Implications for intervention* (pp. 67–82). New York: Haworth Press.

Rollinson, P., & Pardeck, J. (2006). *Homeless in rural America: Policy and practice.* New York: Haworth Press.

Ropers, R. (1988). *The invisible homeless: A new urban ecology.* New York: Human Sciences Press.

Roth, D., Toomey, B., & First, R. (1992). Gender, racial and age variations among homeless persons. In M. Robertson & M. Greenblatt (Eds.), *Homelessness: A national perspective* (pp. 199–211). New York: Plenum Press.

Rotheram-Borus, M., Rosario, M., & Koopman, C. (1991). Minority youths at high risk: Gay males and runaways. In S. Gore & M. Colten (Eds.), *Adolescent stress: Causes and consequences* (pp. 181–200). Hawthorne, NY: Aldine.

Rotheram-Borus, M. J. (1991). Serving runaway and homeless youths. *Family and Community Health, 14*(4), 23–32.

Rotheram-Borus, M. J., Mahler, K., Koopman, C., & Langabeer, K. (1996). Sexual abuse history and associated multiple risk behavior in adolescent runaways. *American Journal of Orthopsychiatry, 66*(3), 390–400.

Rotheram-Borus, M. J., Parra, M., Cantwell, C., Gwadz, M., & Murphy, D. (1996). Runaway and homeless youth. In R. J. DiClemente, W. B. Hansen, & L. E. Ponton (Eds.), *Handbook of adolescent health risk behaviors* (pp. 369–391). New York: Plenum Press.

Rothman, J. (1991). *Runaway and homeless youth: Strengthening services to families and children.* White Plains, NY: Longman.

Rouse, H., & Fantuzzo, J. (2009). Multiple risks and educational well-being: A population-based investigation of threats to early school success. *Early Childhood Research Quarterly, 24*(1), 1–14.

Roy, J., Maynard, M., & Weiss, E. (2008). *The hidden costs of the housing crisis.* Washington, DC: Partnership for America's Economic Success.

Rubin, D., Erickson, C., San Agustin, M., Clearly, S., Allen, J., & Cohen, P. (1996). Cognitive and academic functioning of homeless children compared with housed poor children. *Pediatrics, 97*(3), 289–294.

Russell, L. (1998). *Child maltreatment and psychological distress among urban homeless youth.* New York: Garland Press.

Schmitz, C. L., Wagner, J. D., & Menke, E. M. (2001). The interconnection of childhood poverty and homelessness: Negative impact/points of access. *Families in Society, 82*(1), 69–77.

Scolaro, J. D., & Esbach, E. (2002). *Poverty and the power of knowledge* (Opinion Papers). Orlando, FL: Valencia Community College.

Shaffer, D., & Caton, C. (1984). *Runaway and homeless youth in New York City: A report to the Itelson Foundation of New York City.* New York: Itelson Foundation and New York State Office of Mental Health, Division for Research.

Shane, P. (1996). *What about America's homeless children?* Thousand Oaks, CA: Sage.

Shinn, M., & Weitzman, B. (1996). Homeless families are different. In J. Baumohl (Ed.), *Homelessness in America* (pp. 109–122). Phoenix, AZ: Oryx Press.

Shlay, A., & Rossi, P. (1992). Social science research and contemporary studies of homelessness. *Annual Review of Sociology, 18,* 129–160.

Slavin, P. (2001). *Life on the run, life on the streets.* Retrieved from http://www.cwla.org/articles/cv0107life.htm.

Snow, D., & Anderson, L. (1993). *Down on their luck: A study of homeless street people.* Berkeley: University of California Press.

Snow, D., Anderson, L., Quist, T., & Cress, D. (1996). Material survival strategies on the street: Homeless people as *bricoleurs.* In J. Baumohl (Ed.), *Homelessness in America* (pp. 86–96). Phoenix, AZ: Oryx Press.

Solarz, A. (1992). To be young and homeless: Implications of homelessness for children. In M. Robertson & M. Greenblatt (Eds.), *Homelessness: A national perspective* (pp. 275–286). New York: Plenum Press.

Spence, A., Stephens, R., & Parks, R. (2004). Cognitive dysfunction in homeless adults: A systematic review. *Journal of the Royal Society of Medicine, 97,* 375–379.

Stahler, G., Godboldte, C., Shipley, T., Jr., Shandler, I., Ijoy, L., Weinberg, A., Harrison-Horn, N., . . . Koszowski, L. (1997). Preventing relapse among crack-using homeless women with children: Building bridges to the community. In E. Smith & J. Ferrari (Eds.), *Diversity within the homeless population: Implications for intervention* (pp. 53–66). New York: Haworth Press.

Staller, K. (2004). Runaway youth system dynamics: A theoretical framework for analyzing runaway and homeless youth policy. *Families in Society, 85*(3), 379–390.

Stanistreet, P. (2008). "We're like a family." *Adults Learning,* 14–16.

Stefl, M. (1987). The new homeless: A national perspective. In R. Bingham, R. Green, & S. White (Eds.), *The homeless in contemporary society* (pp. 46–63). Newbury Park, CA: Sage.

Stronge, J. (1992a). The background: History and problems of schooling for the homeless. In J. H. Stronge (Ed.), *Educating homeless children and adolescents: Evaluating policy and practice* (pp. 3–25). Newbury Park, CA: Sage.

Stronge, J. (1992b). Programs with promise: Educational service delivery to homeless children and youth. In J. H. Stronge (Ed.), *Educating homeless children and adolescents: Evaluating policy and practice* (pp. 232–246). Newbury Park, CA: Sage.

Stronge, J. (2000). Educating homeless children and youth: An introduction. In J. H. Stronge & E. Reed-Victor (Eds.), *Educating homeless students: Promising practices* (pp. 1–19). Larchmont, NY: Eye on Education, Inc.

Stronge, J., & Hudson, K. (1999). Educating homeless children and youth with dignity and care. *Journal for a Just and Caring Education, 5*(1), 7–18.

Sullivan, P., & Damrosch, S. (1987). Homeless women and children. In R. Bingham, R. Green, & S. White (Eds.), *The homeless in contemporary society* (pp. 82–98). Newbury Park, CA: Sage.

Sullivan, P., & Knutson, J. (2000). The prevalence of disabilities and maltreatment among runaway children. *Child Abuse and Neglect, 24*(10), 1275–1288.

Swick, K. (1997). Strengthening homeless families and their young children. *Dimensions of Early Childhood, 25*(2), 29–34.

Swick, K. (2000). Building effective awareness programs for homeless students among staff, peers, and community members. In J. H. Stronge & E. Reed-Victor (Eds.), *Educating homeless students: Promising practices* (pp. 165–182). Larchmont, NY: Eye on Education, Inc.

Swick, K. (2004). The dynamics of families who are homeless: Implications for early childhood educators. *Childhood Education, 80*(3), 116–121.

Swick, K. (2005). Helping homeless families overcome barriers to successful functioning. *Early Childhood Education Journal, 33*(3), 195–200.

Swick, K. (2009). Strengthening homeless parents with young children through meaningful parent education and support. *Early Childhood Education Journal, 36*(4), 327–332.

Swick, K., & Bailey, L. (2004). Communicating effectively with parents and families who are homeless. *Early Childhood Education Journal, 32*(3), 211–215.

Taylor, D., Lydon, J., Bougie, E., & Johannsen, K. (2004). "Street kids": Toward an understanding of their motivational context. *Canadian Journal of Behavioural Science, 36*(1), 1–16.

Taylor, T., & Brown, M. (1996). *Young children and their families who are homeless: A university-affiliated program's response.* Washington, DC: Georgetown University Child Development Center.

Terrell, N. (1997). Street life: Aggravated and sexual assaults among homeless and runaway adolescents. *Youth and Society, 28*(3), 267–291.

Tierney, W., Gupton, J., & Hallett, R. (2008). *Transitions to adulthood for homeless adolescents: Education and public policy.* Los Angeles: Center for Higher Education Policy Analysis (CHEPA).

Timberlake, E. M. (1994). Children with no place to call home: Survival in the cars and on the streets. *Child and Adolescent Work Journal, 11*(4), 259–278.

Toro, P. (1998). Homelessness. In A. S. Bellack & M. Herson (Eds.), N. Singh (Vol. Ed.), *Comprehensive clinical psychology, Volume 9: Applications in diverse populations* (pp. 119–135). Exeter, UK: Elsevier Science Ltd.

Toro, P., & Wall, D. (1991). Research on homeless persons: Diagnostic comparisons and practice implications. *Professional Psychology: Research and Practice, 22*(6), 479–488.

Tower, C. C. (1992). The psychosocial context: Supporting education for homeless children and youth. In J. H. Stronge (Ed.), *Educating homeless children and adolescents: Evaluating policy and practice* (pp. 42–61). Newbury Park, CA: Sage.

Tower, C. C., & White, D. (1989). *Homeless students.* Washington, DC: National Education Association.

Tucker, P. (1999). Providing educational services to homeless students: A multifaceted response to a complex problem. *Journal for a Just and Caring Education, 5*(1), 88–107.

Tyler, K., & Melander, A. (2009). Bidirectional partner violence among homeless young adults: Risk factors and outcomes. *Journal of Interpersonal Violence, 24*(6), 1014–1035.

Tyler, K. A., & Cauce, A. M. (2002). Perpetrators of early physical and sexual abuse among homeless and runaway adolescents. *Child Abuse & Neglect: The International Journal, 26*(12), 1261–1274.

Tyler, K. A., Whitbeck, L. B., Hoyt, D. R., & Cauce, A. M. (2004). Risk factors for sexual victimization among male and female homeless and runaway youth. *Journal of Interpersonal Violence, 19*(5), 503–520.

United Way of New York City. (2002). *Slicing the apple: Need amidst affluence in New York City.* New York: Author.

Urban Institute. (2000). *A new look at homelessness in America.* Retrieved from http://www.urban.org/url.cfm?ID=900366.

U.S. Conference of Mayors. (2004). *A status report on hunger and homelessness in America's cities.* Washington, DC: Author.

U.S. Conference of Mayors. (2007). *A status report on hunger and homelessness in America's cities.* Washington, DC: Author.

U.S. Conference of Mayors. (2008). *A status report on hunger and homelessness in America's cities.* Washington, DC: Author.

U.S. Department of Education. (2000). *Education for Homeless Children and Youth Program. Title VII, Subtitle B of the McKinney-Vento Homeless Assistance Act report to Congress fiscal year 2000.* Washington, DC: Author.

U.S. Department of Housing and Urban Development, Office of Community Planning and Development. (2009). *The 2008 annual homeless assessment report to Congress.* Retrieved from http://www.hudhre.info/documents/4thHomelessAssessmentReport.pdf.

Van der Ploeg, J. (1989). Homelessness: A multidimensional problem. *Children and Youth Services Review, 11*(1), 45–56.

Van Ry, M. (1992). The context of family: Implications for educating homeless children. In J. H. Stronge (Ed.), *Educating homeless children and adolescents: Evaluating policy and practice* (pp. 62–78). Newbury Park, CA: Sage.

Vissing, Y. (2000). Meeting the educational needs of intermediate and middle school homeless students. In J. H. Stronge & E. Reed-Victor (Eds.), *Educating homeless students: Promising practices* (pp. 45–61). Larchmont, NY: Eye on Education, Inc.

Vissing, Y. (2004). Prepping homeless students for school. *Education Digest: Essential Readings Condensed for Quick Review, 69*(7), 34–38.

Vostanis, P., Grattan, E., Cumelia, S., & Winchester, C. (1997). Psychosocial functioning of homeless children. *Journal of the American Academy of Child and Adolescent Psychiatry, 36*(7), 881–889.

Wallace, S. (1965). *Skid row as a way of life.* Totowa, NJ: The Bedminster Press.

Weinreb, L., & Buckner, J. (1993). Homeless families: Program responses and public policies. *American Journal of Orthopsychiatry, 63*(3), 400–409.

Wells, M., & Sandhu, H. (1986). The juvenile runaway: A historical perspective. *Free Inquiry in Creative Sociology, 14*(2), 143–147.

Whitbeck, L., & Hoyt, D. (1999). *Nowhere to grow: Homeless and runaway adolescents and their families.* Hawthorne, NY: Aldine.

Whitbeck, L., Hoyt, D., & Ackley, K. (1997). Abusive family backgrounds and later victimization among runaway and homeless adolescents. *Journal of Research on Adolescence, 7*(4), 375–391.

Whitman, B., Accardo, P., Boyert, M., & Kendagor, R. (1990). Homelessness and cognitive performance in children: A possible link. *Social Work, 35*(6), 516–519.

Wilder, L., Obiakor, F., & Algozzine, B. (2003). Homeless students in special education: Beyond the myth of social dissonance. *The Journal of At-Risk Issues, 9*(2), 9–16.

Williams, B. T., & Korinek, L. (2000). Designing effective school programs for homeless students. In J. H. Stronge & E. Reed-Victor (Eds.), *Educating homeless students: Promising practices* (pp. 183–201). Larchmont, NY: Eye on Education, Inc.

Williams, L. (2003). *Fragmented: Improving education for mobile students.* Washington, DC: Poverty & Race Research Action Council.

Wood, D., Valdez, B. R., Hayashi, T., & Shen, A. (1990). Health of homeless children and housed poor children. *Pediatrics, 86*(6), 858–866.

Woods, C. J. (1997). Pappas school: A response to homeless students. *Clearing House, 70,* 302–304.

Woods, C. J., & Harrison, D. (1994). A magnet for homeless students: The Thomas J. Pappas Regional Education Center. *Clearing House, 68*(2), 123–126.

Woronoff, R., Estrada, R., & Sommer, S. (2006). *Out of the margins: A report on regional listening forums highlighting the experiences of lesbian, gay, bisexual, transgender, and questioning youth in care.* Arlington, VA: Child Welfare League of America.

Wright, B., Capsi, A., Moffitt, T., & Silva, P. (1998). Factors associated with doubled-up housing—A common precursor to homelessness. *Social Service Review,* 92–111.

Yon, M. (1995). Educating homeless children in the United States. *Equity and Excellence in Education, 28*(1), 58–62.

Yon, M. G., Mickelson, R. A., & Carlton-LaNey, I. (1993). A child's place: Developing interagency collaboration on behalf of homeless children. *Education and Urban Society, 25*(4), 410–423.

Zieman, G. L., & Benson, G. P. (1980). School perceptions of truant adolescent boys. *Behavioral Disorders, Programs, Trends, and Concerns of Children with Behavioral Problems, 5*(4), 212–222.

Ziesemer, C., & Marcoux, L. (1992). Academic and emotional needs of homeless students. *Social Work in Education, 14*(2), 77–85.

Ziesemer, C., Marcoux, L., & Marwell, B. E. (1994). Homeless children: Are they different from other low-income children? *Social Work, 39*(6), 658–668.

Index

CORWIN

A SAGE Company

The Corwin logo—a raven striding across an open book—represents the union of courage and learning. Corwin is committed to improving education for all learners by publishing books and other professional development resources for those serving the field of PreK–12 education. By providing practical, hands-on materials, Corwin continues to carry out the promise of its motto: **"Helping Educators Do Their Work Better."**